The Complete Labrador Handbook

BY

LINDA WHITWAM

ISBN- 13: 978- 1542648233

Copyright

Acknowledgements

My sincere thanks to the dedicated Labrador Retriever breeders, owners and canine experts who have generously contributed their time and expertise to this book. Their knowledge and love of their dogs shines through; without them, this book would not have been possible.

Specialist Article Authors

ROBIN ANDERSON

ANDREW BAKER

AMANDA DEANE

JENNY DOBSON

Contributors

Special thanks to (in alphabetical order): Amanda Deane, Andrew Baker, Anne Johnson, Avril Bartolomy, Caroline Smith, Christine Eynon, Christopher Clarke, Colin Hinkley, Diane Stanford, Elizabeth Halsall, Elizabeth Harrington, Guy Bunce and Chloe Spencer, Hilary and Wayne Hardman, Jenny Dobson, Julie McDonough, Kate Smith, Katrina S. Byrne, Kirsty Jones, Labrador Retriever Rescue Southern England, Liz Vivash, Lynn Aungier, Nadine Lapskas, Nicola Smith, Pat Nugent, Robin Anderson and Gerrie Owren, Sandra Underhill, Sarah Edwards and Guy Stewart, Sarah Nuttall, Sharon Jarvis, Stephen and Jane Armstrong, Teresa Gordy-Brown, Trudy Williams, and Dr Sara Skiwski.

All of the UK breeders involved in this book are 'Kennel Club Assured Breeders'.
All of the US breeders have achieved the 'AKC Breeder of Merit' accolade.

TABLE OF CONTENTS

1. Meet the Labrador

The Labrador Retriever is quite simply the most popular dog on the planet. No other breed has such a unique bond with humans in so many different ways. Not only does the Lab (as he is affectionately known) make an outstanding family pet, he is also a retriever in the field par excellence.

This medium-sized dog with the big heart is the most versatile of dogs. He works in search and rescue, assists the military and police, detects drugs and explosives - even cancer. Labradors also work as Guide Dogs for the Blind, Hearing Dogs for the Deaf, they become certified therapy dogs that 'read' to children at libraries, visit the elderly in nursing homes, and calm crowds at public events. They bring companionship and happiness to autistic children.

They excel in the show ring and at obedience events, and do well at agility and other canine competitions. Above all, they are the most willing and loyal companions to anyone who has ever owned one.

The Labrador is even-tempered, biddable, tolerant, sociable and has a strong desire to please his owners. He is handsome, intelligent, affectionate, good with children and loves a challenge – both physical and mental. Given enough exercise and stimulation, the Labrador is a happy, friendly dog that is easy to train and gets along with everybody and other animals.

His sunny temperament has made him the dog of choice for countless households and his retrieving instincts mean that he is popular with field sport enthusiasts as well.

The Labrador's heritage is as a working dog, bred to pick up game on the shoot. He is in the Gundog Group in the UK and Sporting Group in the USA, and was first recognised by the Kennel Club in the UK in 1903 and by the AKC (American Kennel Club) in 1917. Although the exact origins of the breed are hazy, it is thought that today's Lab is descended from a breed known hundreds of years ago as the Lesser Newfoundland or St. John's Water Dog, from Newfoundland in Canada. Fishermen used these hard working dogs to pull carts, retrieve fallen fish and haul fishing nets through the water – even in icy conditions.

Today's Labrador still has that dense, water-repellent coat and loves a swim. As a sporting dog, the breed needs physical and mental exercise – how much depends on the individual dog, his ancestry and the amount of exercise he gets used to as a young dog. The (UK) Kennel Club recommends "more than two hours per day."

There are three colours of Labrador and, broadly, two types. The colours are black - which was the original colour, yellow and chocolate (or liver). Some 28 UK Kennel Club Assured Labrador Breeders and three AKC Breeders of Merit have given their time to share their vast experience of the breed in this book. We asked them for their thoughts on the different types of Labrador.

The general consensus regarding colour is that, in terms of temperament, there is no real difference between the colours; the main factor is the temperament of the parents. Breeders advise anyone who hasn't got their puppy yet to see the dam (mother) and sire (father) of the puppy - or at least the dam – to get an idea of temperament. If the parents seem unfriendly or disinterested, consider getting a puppy from a different litter; well-bred Labradors are engaged and friendly.

There are more black Labradors retrieving on shoots and taking part in Field Trial competitions, as black is the original working strain. However, yellow Labradors also make good retrievers. In the UK there are fewer chocolate Labs picking up on shoots, as the chocolates (livers) were originally bred for the show ring. The situation is slightly different in the USA, where the ancestry is different; many breeders produce an all-purpose Labrador, and chocolates can be found on hunts or taking part in field competitions.

Some breeders commented that some chocolates can have more of an individual "quirky" or even "scatty" personality, which can make them great fun to own, sometimes a little more challenging to train – but definitely worth the effort for fans of this colour.

There is also a difference between "show" and "working" Labradors, both in appearance and nature. In the USA, the two types are referred to as American (working) and English (show) Labradors – you may also hear the terms "bench" Labrador for a show dog and "field" Labrador for a working dog.

The original working (American) Labrador generally has a lighter, leaner, slightly taller frame and longer leg and neck (proportionally) than a show Lab, and looks more athletic. He has a lighter coat and a narrower head with a longer "snipe-like" nose. The show (English) type has a more "chunky" and powerful appearance, being wider and heavier. He has a thicker coat, thicker "otter-like" tail, shorter muzzle and legs.

As you might expect, a Labrador bred purely from working bloodlines has a high mental and physical drive. Not only does he need a lot of daily exercise, he also thrives on mental challenges, such as training. After all, he has been bred to run all day and use his skill to find game - which may be hidden in the undergrowth or in water. Dogs that take part in field sports can work up to eight or more hours a day; this is a high octane dog. Due to their high drive, pure-bred field dogs are often better suited to a working life, rather than life as a family pet – unless you can devote considerable time and effort to meet their needs.

The show Labrador has been bred to have a calmer disposition. He has to be patient enough to wait for hours until it's his turn to be inspected by the judge, and then to remain composed once inside the show ring. He still has exercise needs and enjoys a mental challenge, such as playing Fetch, but may be more mellow and laid-back in nature, compared to a purely working Labrador. Read **Labrador Types and Exercise** in **Chapter 9** for more detailed information.

In reality, the litters from many modern breeders are often a mixture of show and working bloodlines, unless they have been bred for a specific purpose, such as the show ring or field sports. Several breeders in this book think that a Labrador with a combination of English and American (show and working) lines is an excellent combination. One UK breeder said: "I have mixed the lines deliberately to try and get the best of both worlds – correct construction (so important in a working breed), and sound, biddable temperaments."

It pays to find out as much as you can from the breeder about what the parents and ancestors were bred for. If you already have your Labrador, contact your breeder to find out what type he is to help you better understand and train him.

Downsides to Labradors?

Does the Labrador have any downsides, and with all of these amazing talents, how come some Labradors end up in rescue centres?

Sometimes people enter into dog ownership without considering all of the consequences, and although Labradors have all of the qualities listed, this is also an active breed which needs a fair bit of space inside and outside the home. They love swimming – even in dirty ponds - and running off the lead, through mud, leaves, undergrowth, etc. Ours used to love eating cow dung, and they may drool, so if you are extremely house-proud, a Labrador might not be the best breed for you.

You also need to have the finances for proper veterinary care, regular worming and de-fleaing treatments, pet insurance, food, and so on. Labs are great with children, but a lively young Labrador combined with lively young children can be a recipe for disaster if none is well-trained!

And, like any breed, the Labrador can be a challenge. Often Labs are extremely boisterous and clumsy for the first two or three years of their lives. You and the kids can get bowled over (literally) as your adolescent canine enthusiastically races around and jumps up at people, full of the joys of life and everything and everyone in it. Without proper training and sufficient exercise and play time, this unfocused energy can lead to a lively dog which is too much to handle for some families.

One experienced US breeder described it thus: "One thing to remember about Labradors - and I stress this all the time – is that they are like little four-legged, fur covered five-year-old brats with ADD (Attention Deficit Disorder) for the first two, sometimes three years! Then one day they grow-up mentally (closer to age three, I believe) and you find you have the greatest dog in the world.

"Yes, they are brats and yes, they can be a handful. But once they mature, they are a unique breed like no other. So, if you invest the time into training and socializing them when they are young, you will be rewarded one day soon with the greatest companion you could ever ask for."

Of course, not all Labradors are so extreme, but, if you get a puppy or young Lab, be prepared for a lively chewing machine until he or she settles down. Having been bred to pick things up in their mouths, Labradors can be serious chewers - mobile phones and chargers, batteries, wires, carpets, shoes....all are fair game if left lying around within reach of young dogs. Labradors have been described as "the vacuum cleaners" of the canine world, as they will eat just about anything. This obsession with food is a great motivator when training, but also means that you have to monitor your dog's weight as, when it comes to food, most Labs don't know when they've had enough.

Despite all of this, ask those who really know Labradors and they all say the same: It's no wonder the Labrador is the most popular breed; there is something really special about this dog.

Labrador Characteristics

The (UK) Kennel Club describes the Labrador as: "The most popular of all pedigree breeds and his popularity comes from his versatility as family companion, service dog, guide dog as well as a working gundog."

The AKC describes the breed as "Active, friendly and outgoing, Labs play well with others." It adds a fuller description of the physical appearance and character: "The Labrador Retriever is a strongly built, medium-sized, short-coupled dog possessing a sound, athletic, well-balanced conformation that enables it to function as a retrieving gun dog; the substance and soundness to hunt waterfowl or upland game for long hours under difficult conditions; the character and quality to win in the show ring; and the temperament to be a family companion.

"Physical features and mental characteristics should denote a dog bred to perform as an efficient retriever of game with a stable temperament suitable for a variety of pursuits beyond the hunting environment. The most distinguishing characteristics of the Labrador Retriever are its short, dense, weather resistant coat; an "otter" tail; a clean-cut head with broad back skull and moderate stop; powerful jaws; and its "kind," friendly eyes, expressing character, intelligence and good temperament."

Good breeders not only breed for appearance, but also for temperament and, with working Labradors, how good the dam and sire are at doing a specific job, e.g. retrieving. As you've read, the breed in general has an excellent temperament - but there is another major factor involved in the creation of an adult dog's character - and that is environment, or how you raise and treat your dog; nature AND nurture.

Once he has left the litter, your pup takes his lead from you as he learns to react to the world around him. Up to the age of four months is a critical time for socialisation. It is essential to spend time introducing your puppy to other animals and humans, as well as noises, new places and situations from a few days after you bring him home. Through your guidance and good socialisation, your little Lab learns whom he can trust, whether to be afraid, how much he can get away with, and so on. He also learns not to be selfish and to share you, his food and toys with others. A dog comfortable in his surroundings without fear or anxieties is an easy dog to live with.

To say all dogs of the same breed are alike would be akin to saying that all Americans are optimistic and friendly and all Brits are polite and reserved. It is, of course, a huge generalisation! There are grumpy, unfriendly Americans and rude in-your-face Brits.

However, it is also true to say that being friendly and optimistic are general American traits (just like the Labrador!), as is being polite in Britain.

It's the same with dogs. Each individual has his or her unique character, but there are certain traits which are common within the breed. See **Chapter 8. Canine Behaviour** for more detailed information on typical Labrador traits and temperament.

Breeders on Labradors

We asked 31 breeders what first attracted them to the Labrador and why it is the most popular breed of all. Here are some of their comments:

Sarah Nuttall, Gamblegate Labradors, Lancashire: "I wanted dogs with an excellent temperament, that are trainable and make a good family pet, with a large gene pool. Labradors are so popular as pets as they are loving and trustworthy with people, particularly children. They need little grooming, they are relatively easy to train, not fussy with food and, if bred from health-tested stock, should have a healthy life."

Christopher Clarke, Reedfen Labradors, Cambridgeshire: "They are such a wonderfully faithful, loyal, loving, intelligent, caring companion. They will never be angry or upset with you; they are always pleased to see you and a well-bred show type looks absolutely stunning! The working type can be trained to perform so many different tasks for us humans that they have become indispensable in various roles, such as detection of all manner of objects and devices, to aid people with varying abilities, to bring back our dinner or to work as a therapy dog in schools and residential homes. What more could you possibly ask of a breed? The Labrador is the ultimate multi-purpose breed."

Hilary Hardman, Larwaywest Labradors, Dorset: "They are very easy to love and live with. They are extremely open and trusting and, with the right start as puppies and correctly guided, they make the most superb pets. If brought up with children in the correct manner, they are also wonderful with children."

Lynn Aungier, Alatariel Labradors, Surrey: "We wanted a dog that would fit in with family life, be big enough that they wouldn't be bullied by bigger dogs and also have the right energy level for walks and trips to Cumbria, walking the fells and mountains. We were looking for a breed that was easy to train and gentle, and a Labrador just ticked all the right boxes. They are a perfect breed, providing they are given stimulation, exercise and training – but I guess that is true with all dogs as a basic requirement of the owner. I think they are popular because they are Man's Best Friend."

Nicola Smith, Geowins Labradors, Surrey: "I took a Lab on from my cousin, who was emigrating, and it was true love from then on - I was hooked!"

Andrew Baker, Saffronlyn Gundogs, South Yorkshire: "I was brought up around Labradors so they have always been prevalent in my life. In my opinion, they are one of the most intelligent, loyal and loving breeds of dog that just want to please. I train gundogs for a living and I am a gundog show judge and help to train most breeds, yet I find the Labrador the most willing and eager to learn."

Katrina Byrne, Glenhugo Labradors, South Aberdeenshire, Scotland: "Labradors, as a rule, have good temperaments, they are loyal, trustworthy and relatively easy to train, compared to some other breeds. They have good life spans and, with the correct breeding, relatively few health issues."

Caroline Smith, Flyenpyg Labradors, Lancashire: "Labradors are awesome. I grew up with them and will never be without one; whatever task you ask of them, they'll try. I have workers, agility, rally, show and obedience girls – they can really put their paw to anything!"

Trudy Williams, Yaffleswood Labradors, West Sussex: "Labradors are just so eager to please, easy to train and have fantastic temperaments. They are social and are not aloof like some breeds, not over-independent individuals or too manic. They are basically a good all-rounder, whether as a pet or a working dog."

Amanda Deane, Tanronens Labradors, Lincolnshire: "I wanted a pet for the family and, as I had children and lived in the country, I thought this was the best breed; it is for this reason that I believe Labradors are the most popular - they are very biddable, will fit in most places and love to be loved."

Jenny Dobson, Lakemeadow Labradors, South Yorkshire: "Even back in the 1960s, Labs had the reputation of being the ideal "family dog" and I think my parents particularly wanted a dog that would be trainable. I had been doing voluntary weekend work at the training centre for Guide Dogs for the Blind in Bolton, and Labs just seemed the obvious choice.

"I should add that I do also love their appearance with their lovely, soft, kind expression, their short, easy-care coat and general low maintenance, their size and lack of "exaggeration" of features, etc. - all of which make them ideal for my lifestyle."

Elizabeth Halsall, Lisouletta Labradors, Surrey: "They are loving, kind and wonderful with children. They have soft mouths and big warm hearts."

Julie McDonough, Rangemaster Working Gundogs, Powys, Wales: "I chose the Labrador, as it was a breed that people trust with temperament and a good all-round family pet. It was only after I started to attended gundog training that I realised how enjoyable it was to teach a dog to do what it was bred for; retrieving."

Sarah Edwards, Fernwills Labradors, Colchester, Essex: "Labradors are a good combination of energetic, laid-back, loving, gentle, intelligent and biddable. They are exceptional family dogs and highly tolerant of young children. I had one as a child, so have always been very drawn to the breed. Having run a doggie day-care business for several years, I would now not choose anything else, as no other breed's personality can come close to the Labrador."

Robin Anderson, Grampian Labradors, New England, USA: "Originally, my husband and I wanted a family pet, good with children, and with a coat meant for enjoying our sailboat and beach activities. After lots of research and asking lots of families with dogs what they had and why they liked what they had, I knew a Labrador Retriever would be a good pet for the family.

"After living with the dog for 11+ years and in two countries - where she charmed everyone of all ages - I knew I wanted to do more with and for the breed, and to help more families enjoy what I enjoyed. The breed is #1 in the world because it is an easy-to-live-with breed, compatible with so many lifestyles, and has the ability to provide just about anything a person could think of in terms of work or play."

Sandra Underhill, Labs To Love, California, USA: "The Labrador is an excellent family dog that withstands handling by children!"

Teresa Gordy-Brown, Ashland Labradors, Tennessee, USA: "Temperament; hands down, temperament! The Labrador is a very biddable canine, maybe one of the most versatile breeds on the planet. You can't find many breeds or mixes that blend into so many different lifestyles and environments with absolute ease. The Labrador is a truly remarkable breed that can do anything you train him for: duck hunting, Search and Rescue, therapy, PTSD, Diabetic Alert Dogs, Guide Dogs, show dogs, obedience, agility, flyball, coursing, dock diving, police dogs, drug detection and ..Oh, the absolute most important thing a Labrador is great at; being your companion above all else.

"He loves you, the neighbours, the kids, the grandkids. He loves little Johnny from down the street and even the stray cat that comes around from time to time. The absolute only fault of a well-bred Labrador is that he will never meet a stranger. Your property sign should not say: "Beware of Dog," rather: "Beware, Dog Licks you to Death!""

We also asked the breeders to sum up their Labradors in three or four words. This is what they said:

- 🐾 Intelligent, faithful, loving, companion
- 🐾 Stunning, loyal, athletic
- 🐾 Loyal and intelligent family members
- 🐾 Intelligent, happy, loyal
- 🐾 Addictive, adorable, loving, irresistible
- 🐾 Loyal, biddable, kind, fun
- 🐾 Happy, devoted, water-loving retriever
- 🐾 Biddable, loving, cheeky
- 🐾 Everyone's best friend
- 🐾 Loyal, obedient, intelligent
- 🐾 Loving, biddable, cuddly and smart!
- 🐾 Wonderful, happy dog
- 🐾 Loyal, fun and a joy to have around
- 🐾 The most wonderful companion
- 🐾 Loyal, trustworthy, biddable
- 🐾 The best multi-purpose dog
- 🐾 Loving, beautiful, gentle, faithful
- 🐾 Labradors are all love
- 🐾 Loyal, loving, obedient, honest
- 🐾 The perfect family companion dog
- 🐾 Loving, athletic, biddable, loyal
- 🐾 Loyal, loving and my best friends
- 🐾 Loving, happy and fun
- 🐾 Always very hungry!

....

Read on to find the right puppy. Then learn how to take good care of the newest member of your family for the rest of his or her life, and how to build a unique bond that will become one of the most important things in your life - and certainly in his or hers.

2. History of the Labrador

The St John's Water Dog

The exact origins of the Labrador Retriever are shrouded in the mists of time. But we do know that it lies with the hardy fishermen who worked the freezing waters off the island of Newfoundland, now part of the province of Newfoundland and Labrador, Canada, hundreds of years ago.

The founding breed of the Labrador is thought to be the rugged St John's Water Dog (also called the St. John's Dog or Lesser Newfoundland) that emerged through ad-hoc breedings by early settlers of the island in the 16th century. This dog was black in colour with white "tuxedo" markings on the chest, muzzle and feet – occasionally, these markings can still be seen on some of today's Labrador Retrievers, when the white chest mark is known as a "medallion." They are often more pronounced on Labrador mixes and crossbreeds.

The ancestors of the St. John's Water Dog are not entirely known; it is likely they were a random-bred mix of English, Irish and Portuguese working breeds. The dog is often referred to as a "landrace," i.e. it was not a pedigree; it was bred for a job, rather than for a specific look. The dogs were described as having a short thick coat, rudder-like tail, high endurance and a great love of swimming.

Newfoundland was settled by English fisherman as early as the 1500s and the St. John's Water Dogs developed alongside the fishing industry. The English fisherman working in Newfoundland used the dog to retrieve fish that had fallen off their hooks, as well to help haul nets and long fishing lines through the water back to their boats. These dogs were considered workaholics and enjoyed their retrieving tasks – even in freezing weather and icy water.

They would work long hours in the cold waters and then be brought home to play with the fisherman's children. The breed was very eager to please and its retrieving abilities made an ideal hunting companion and sporting dog; it was known to retrieve ptarmigan and even seal. So, even in these early days, the Labrador's ancestors had a reputation as keen, versatile workers with excellent temperaments.

The St. John's Water Dog was the ancestor of the modern retrievers, including the Flat Coated Retriever, Chesapeake Bay Retriever, Golden Retriever and Labrador Retriever. It was also an ancestor of the larger, gentle Newfoundland dog, probably through breeding with Mastiffs brought to the island by the generations of Portuguese fishermen who had fished offshore since the 15th century.

The breed survived until the early 1980s. Our photo, dating back to the late 1970s, shows the last two St. John's Water Dogs – unfortunately both were male (despite one of them being called Lassie!) and the breed became extinct upon their deaths. The decline was caused by a combination of two factors. In an attempt to encourage sheep raising, heavy restrictions and taxes were placed on any dogs not used in the production of sheep during the 19th century.

Secondly, their main overseas destination - England - imposed rigorous long-term quarantine on imported dogs after a rabies outbreak in 1885 – but not before many Newfoundland fishermen had sold their water dogs to British dog dealers, who then sold them on to people wanting to improve their retriever lines.

In 1807 a ship called Canton from Baltimore carried some St. John's Water Dogs destined for Poole, England, probably as breeding stock for what was to become a British aristocrat's retriever kennel. The Canton shipwrecked, but not before the crew were saved, along with two dogs - a black bitch called Canton and a "dingy red" dog, Sailor. The captain sold them back in the USA for a guinea each and these two are believed to be the foundation stock of the Chesapeake Bay Retriever.

This "dingy red" is what we today refer to as "chocolate" or "liver" in the Labrador. We know from Sailor that this was a natural colour in the original St. John's Water Dog. Along with yellow, the chocolate was a recessive colour which would occasionally appear in litters. During the early breeding programmes, these "off colours" were often culled, until they were finally accepted and registered by the UK and American Kennel Clubs.

In 1822, explorer W.E. Cormack crossed the island of Newfoundland by foot. In his journal he wrote: "*The dogs are admirably trained as retrievers in fowling, and are otherwise useful.....The smooth or short haired dog is preferred because in frosty weather the long haired kind become encumbered with ice on coming out of the water.*"

An early report by a Colonel Hawker described the dog as: "*By far the best for any kind of shooting. He is generally black and no bigger than a Pointer, very fine in legs, with short, smooth hair and does not carry his tail so much curled as the other; is extremely quick, running, swimming and fighting....and their sense of smell is hardly to be credited.*"

The first St. John's dog was said to be brought to England in or around 1820, but the breed's reputation had already spread to England; there is a story that the 2nd Earl of Malmesbury saw a St. John's Water Dog on a fishing boat and immediately made arrangements with traders to have some of these dogs imported to England.

(Pictured is Lassie, aged 13)

In his book "*Excursions In and About Newfoundland During the Years 1839 and 1840*", the geologist Joseph Beete Jukes describes the St. John's Water Dog: "*A thin, short-haired, black dog came off-shore to us to-day. The animal was of a breed very different from what we understand by the term Newfoundland dog in England. He had a thin, tapering snout, a long thin tail, and rather thin, but powerful legs, with a lank body, – the hair short and smooth.*

"*These are the most abundant dogs in the country...They are no means handsome, but are generally more intelligent and useful than the others...I observed he once or twice put his foot in the water and paddled it about. This foot was white, and Harvey said he did it to "toil" or entice the fish. The whole proceeding struck me as remarkable, more especially as they said he had never been taught anything of the kind.*"

Today, in both Newfoundland and the Maritime provinces, there are still large black mixed-breed dogs with many characteristics of the original St. John's Water Dog.

The Aristocratic Connection

The 19th century was a time of great interest in dog breeding in England. Unusually for the time, it was a hobby enjoyed right across the social spectrum, from working men to aristocrats. The working "fanciers" often favoured the smaller breeds, as they were inexpensive to keep and could live in cramped little houses with the family. Those of noble birth were more often associated with larger, sporting dogs.

The first Conformation Dog Show was held from June 28th to 29th, 1859, at Newcastle-upon-Tyne. It was an added attraction to the annual cattle show and only the sporting breeds of setters and pointers were allowed to enter - the prizes were guns! But, despite this limited beginning, the genie was out of the bag and the Conformation Dog Show went on to become hugely popular in Victorian times – and still is. It was followed 14 years later by the formation of The Kennel Club and 11 years after that (1884) by the American Kennel Club.

These organisations began to draw up Breed Standards which stated how a particular breed of dog should look and act. Before that, the same breed of dog could come in varying shapes, sizes and colours. The 19th and early 20th centuries saw much experimentation by fanciers with different dogs from varied backgrounds. New breeds were being created from the bloodlines of several types of dogs and it was often not until the late 19th and turn of the 20th century that the first Breed Standards were drawn up.

Several aristocrats were involved in creating the dog we know today as The Labrador Retriever. James Edward Harris, the 2nd Earl of Malmesbury, imported St John's Water Dogs and bred retrievers from them for duck shooting on his estate at Heron Court on the south coast, particularly because of their acknowledged expertise in water fowling, their "close coat which turns water off like oil" and a tail "like an otter." These early dogs so impressed the Earl with their skill and ability for retrieving anything within the water and on shore, that he devoted his entire kennel to developing and stabilising the breed.

In the 1830s, the 5th Duke of Buccleuch, Walter Francis Montagu Douglas Scott, and his uncle, the 10th Earl of Home, were among the first to import dogs from Newfoundland to their estates in the Scottish Borders for use as gundogs because of their excellent retrieving capabilities.

Pictured in 1856 is Nell, owned by the 11th Earl of Home. This is the first known photograph of a Labrador Retriever.

During the 1880s, the 3rd Earl of Malmesbury, the 6th Duke of Buccleuch and the 12th Earl of Home collaborated to develop and establish the modern Labrador breed. The dogs Buccleuch Avon and Buccleuch Ned - given by Malmesbury to Buccleuch - were mated with bitches carrying blood from those originally imported by the 5th Duke and the 10th Earl of Home. Their offspring are considered to be the ancestors of modern Labradors.

The History Of The Buccleuch Labrador states that eventually a kennel of 30 to 40 couples was maintained with keepers responsible for training the dogs, while the 6th Duke's youngest son, Lord George Scott, managed the breeding programme: *"By the 1920s, the kennel contained 150 dogs. However, the 7th Duke was not active in maintaining the line and no new dogs were imported between 1890 and 1930, due to a Sheep Protection Act in Newfoundland and the introduction of quarantine restrictions."* The Buccleuch Kennels still exist today and still produce top Labradors.

Early Labrador Retrievers

In the *Complete Book of the Dog*, published in 1922, Leighton Robert, gives a description of the early retrievers descended from the Newfoundland dogs and explains why the dogs became so popular: *"It gradually came to be realized that even the Spaniel's capacity for retrieving was limited. A larger and quicker dog was wanted to divide the labour, and to be used solely as a retriever in conjunction with the other gun dogs.*

"The Poodle was tried for retrieving with some success, and he showed considerable aptitude in hounding and fetching wounded wild duck; but he, too, was inclined to maul his birds and deliver them dead. Even the Old English Sheepdog was occasionally engaged in the work, and various crosses with Spaniel or Setter and Collie were attempted in the endeavour to produce a grade breed having the desired qualities of a good nose, a soft mouth, and an understanding brain, together with a coat that would protect its wearer from the ill effects of frequent immersion in water.

"It was when these efforts were most active - namely, about the year 1850 - that new material was discovered in a black-coated dog recently introduced into England from Labrador. He was a natural water-dog, with a constitution impervious to chills, and entirely free from the liability to ear canker, which had always been a drawback to the use of the Spaniel as a retriever of waterfowl. Moreover, he was himself reputed to be a born retriever of game, and remarkably sagacious.

"One very remarkable attribute of the Retriever is that, notwithstanding the known fact that the parent stock was mongrel and that in the early dogs the Setter type largely predominated, the ultimate result has favoured the Labrador cross distinctly and prominently, proving how potent, even when grafted upon a stock admittedly various, is the blood of a pure race, and how powerful its influence for fixing type and character over the other less vital elements with which it is blended.

"It is only comparatively recently that we have realized how excellent an all-round sporting dog the Retriever has become. In many cases, indeed, where grouse and partridge are driven or walked-up a well-broken, soft-mouthed Retriever is unquestionably superior to Pointer, Setter, or Spaniel, and for general work in the field he is the best companion that a shooting man can possess."

Pictured is Buccleuch Avon, one of the main ancestors of the modern Labrador Retriever.

Buccleuch Avon

A Country Life article of 1908 mistakenly ascribed this new colour to a "freak": *"In the same kennels at Hyde may also be seen the rare sight of a breed of pure yellow Labradors. These dogs are owned by Captain C. E. Radclyffe, and, like the above-mentioned white retrievers, they owe their origin to a freak. In one litter sired by a celebrated black Labrador owned by Captain Radclyffe there were two yellow puppies, a dog and a bitch. By breeding from this yellow dog, named Ben, his owner has now collected a splendid kennel of yellow dogs; and, curious to say, unlike the white retriever, Gipsy, quite 75 per cent, of the puppies by this yellow Labrador are true to the colour of their sire, even when he is mated with a black bitch.*

"Their owner has not been experimenting long enough to prove whether or no by interbreeding with the young yellow Labradors he will be able to perpetuate the breed, but he has every confidence that such will prove to be the case. In support of this theory he quotes an instance of where a light—coloured and almost white Labrador bitch, owned by the Hon. Francis Dawnay, was

mated with the yellow dog Ben (pictured), and all the puppies were either yellow or white in colour. It is noteworthy that none of these white or yellow dogs is an albino as regards the colour of its eyes, etc., and, moreover, they are as good workers in the field as were their black ancestors.

"It seems a pity that these dogs cannot be exhibited on the show bench, in order that the sporting public may see how very picturesque and handsome they are in appearance; but it is understood that some rule prohibits judges from awarding prizes to any such dogs unless they are black in colour. It is believed that these two breeds of retrievers are unique, and, needless to remark, their respective owners consider them to be priceless, consequently none of them has ever been sold."

Yellow Labradors - and later the chocolates - were not "freaks." They occurred when both parents carried the recessive gene for these colours. Initially, the yellows could not be shown, but they were later accepted and included in the Breed Standard.

By 1870, the name "Labrador Retriever" had become common in England and the breed went on to be finally recognised by The Kennel Club in 1903. The chocolate Labrador emerged in the 1930s - although two liver spotted pups were documented as being born at the Buccleuch kennels in 1892. Many chocolate labs are said to trace back to a black dog born in England in 1932, FC Banchory Night Light. He came from the line of Dual Ch. Banchory Bolo (1915), who appeared to be a carrier of the chocolate gene from Buccleuch Avon. Banchory Bolo was also known for carrying a trait of white hairs under the feet (Bolo pads).

Labradors in the United States

In the late 19th century, American hunters used Setters and Pointers to cover large areas and heavy cover. Although there was – and still is - a difference between British shoots and American hunts, the Labrador's popularity as a sporting dog increased throughout the 20th century. At the British 'driven' shoots, dogs walked at heel, before 'marking' (being trained to note where the bird has fallen), then retrieving game. However, the size and variations of American terrain, combined with the many different types of cover, made more demands on the working dog.

At that time, American hunters were using Springer Spaniels to find upland game and Chesapeake Bay Retrievers to retrieve birds from water. They began taking an interest in the Labrador when they realised that it was as good as the Springer on the uplands and the Chesapeake in the water – perhaps even better as the short coat repelled water and did not ice up. The Labrador had the added bonus of an excellent and willing temperament.

The American Kennel Club (AKC) accepted the breed in 1917, but a decade later only 23 Labrador Retrievers had been registered. It wasn't until the 1920s - and particularly after an American Kennel Gazette entitled *'Meet the Labrador Retriever'* - that the breed became much more popular.

The Labrador Retriever had the distinction of becoming the first dog to appear on the cover of Life Magazine. It was a was a black Labrador Retriever that was featured in the December 12th, 1938 issue alongside the following text: *"The dog on this week's cover is Blind of Arden, who won the No. 1 U.S. retriever stake of the year on Nov. 21, had his picture taken at Southampton by LIFE photographer George Karger.*

"A stylish black labrador, with a sly arrogance about him, Blind is now 4, has been trained for hunting ever since he could stumble into the field. He lives on the big estate of his owner, W. Averell Harriman, near Tuxedo, N.Y., where he practices on live pheasants for half an hour each day with his handler, Jasper Briggs."

The accompanying report stated: *"Long before the end of the tests, it was evident that W. Averell Harriman's Labrador, Blind of Arden, was the best in the field for 1938. Working without a mistake, this picture retriever capped a great performance with a remarkable blind recovery.*

"For this event, a dead duck, unseen by the dogs, was planted on an island. At signal from his handler, Blind jumped into water and swam to the island. There he scented the bird, looked back only twice to the handler, who with his arm waved him in the right direction. Quickly finding the duck, Blind picked it up with a firm mouth, started swimming back to his handler. Then, after delivering bird, he sat stylishly on his haunches. This, however, was pure showmanship, and the judges were instructed to pay no attention to it.

"A marvelously intelligent, stocky dog, always friendly with children and the favorite of lady spectators at the trial the jet-black Labrador has become popular in the U. S. only in the last ten years. Originally a breed of hunting dogs in Newfoundland they were imported into England by fishermen during the early 19th Century. Because of English ignorance of New World geography, they were called "Labradors," and were brought to the U. S. under that name."

During the latter part of the 20th century, the breed's appeal as a pet, as well as a working dog, rapidly increased. The Labrador Retriever has been the top dog in both the United States and the UK every year since 1990/91.

Sources:

Archive www.archive.org

Chest of Books http://chestofbooks.com

Wikipedia https://en.wikipedia.org

The Complete Book of the Dog, 1922, by Leighton Robert

Country Life, February 29th, 1908

Life Magazine, December 12th, 1938

3. Breed Standard

The **breed standard** is what makes a Labrador a Labrador, a Great Dane a Great Dane and a Chihuahua a Chihuahua. It is a blueprint not only for the appearance of each breed, but also for character and temperament, how the dog moves and what colours are acceptable. In other words, it ensures that the Labrador looks and acts like a Labrador and is "fit for function."

The breed standard is laid down by the breed societies. In the UK it's the Kennel Club, and in the USA it's the AKC (American Kennel Club) that keeps the register of pedigree – purebred - dogs. Dogs entered in conformation shows run under Kennel Club and AKC rules are judged against this ideal list of attributes. Breeders approved (or 'Assured' in the UK) by the Kennel Clubs agree to produce puppies in line with the breed standard and maintain certain welfare conditions.

The Labrador is listed in the Gundog Group in the UK and the Sporting Group in the USA.

Kennel Club Assured Breeders select only the best dogs for reproduction, based on factors such as the health, looks, temperament and the character of the parents and their ancestors. They do not simply take any available male and female and allow them to randomly breed.

The same is true of AKC Breeders of Merit: "AKC Breeders are dedicated to breeding beautiful purebred dogs whose appearance, temperament, and ability are true to their breed. These breeders are the heart of AKC."

They also aim to reduce or eradicate genetic illnesses. In the case of Labs these include joint and eye problems. The Kennel Clubs in the UK, North America and Europe all have lists of breeders. If you have not yet got a puppy, this is a good place to start looking for one. Visit the Kennel Club website in your country for details of approved breeders.

A breed standard is an essential factor in maintaining the look and temperament of any breed. But in the past, breeders of some types of dog have concentrated too closely on the physical appearance of the animal without paying enough attention to soundness and health.

In response, the Kennel Club set up Breed Watch, which serves as an 'early warning system' to identify points of concern for individual breeds. In the UK the Labrador Retriever is listed in Category 2, with Category 1 being the breeds with no major points of concern and Category 3 being: "Breeds where some dogs have visible conditions or exaggerations that can cause pain or discomfort."

Labradors have the following "Points of concern for special attention by judges:"
- Legs too short in proportion to depth of body and to length of back
- Significantly overweight

Labradors are bred from a fairly large gene pool, compared with some other breeds. The average COI (Coefficient of Inbreeding) for Labrador Retrievers is 6.5%, which is right around the ideal of 6.25%.

UFAW (Universities Federation for Animal Welfare) says: "Essentially, COI measures the common ancestors of dam and sire, and indicates the probability of how genetically similar they are. There are consequences to being genetically similar, some good, some bad. The fact that dogs within individual breeds are so genetically similar is what makes them that breed - and why, if you breed any Labrador to any other Labrador, the puppies will look recognisably like Labradors."

It goes on to explain why a high COI can be a problem: "Inbreeding will help cement 'good' traits but there's a danger of it also cementing bad ones. In particular, it can cause the rapid build-up of disease genes in a population. Even if a breed of dog is lucky enough to be free of serious genetic disorders, inbreeding is likely to affect our dogs in more subtle, but no less serious, ways."

Anyone buying a Labrador puppy is advised to ask to see the relevant health certificates for the pup and its parents before committing. Prospective UK owners can also check the COI of their chosen puppy and parents using the Kennel Club's **Mate Select** programme at www.thekennelclub.org.uk/services/public/mateselect

If you are serious about getting a Labrador, then study the breed standard before visiting any puppies, so you know what a well-bred example should look like. There may be some variation in appearance between working and pet or show Labradors, but the main points remain the same. And if you've already bought one, these are features your dog should display:

Kennel Club Breed Standard (UK)

Last updated October 2009.

The Kennel Club says: "A Breed Standard is the guideline which describes the ideal characteristics, temperament and appearance including the correct colour of a breed and ensures that the breed is fit for function. Absolute soundness is essential. Breeders and judges should at all times be careful to avoid obvious conditions or exaggerations which would be detrimental in any way to the health, welfare or soundness of this breed.

"From time to time certain conditions or exaggerations may be considered to have the potential to affect dogs in some breeds adversely, and judges and breeders are requested to refer to the Breed Watch section of the Kennel Club website at www.thekennelclub.org.uk/services/public/breed/watch for details of any such current issues. If a feature or quality is desirable it should only be present in the right measure. However if a dog possesses a feature, characteristic or colour described as undesirable or highly undesirable it is strongly recommended that it should not be rewarded in the show ring."

General Appearance

Strongly built, short-coupled, very active; broad in skull; broad and deep through chest and ribs; broad and strong over loins and hindquarters.

Characteristics - Good-tempered, very agile (which precludes excessive body weight or excessive substance). Excellent nose, soft mouth; keen love of water. Adaptable, devoted companion.

Temperament - Intelligent, keen and biddable, with a strong will to please. Kindly nature, with no trace of aggression or undue shyness.

Head and Skull - Skull broad with defined stop; clean-cut without fleshy cheeks. Jaws of medium length, powerful not snipy. Nose wide, nostrils well developed.

Eyes – Medium size, expressing intelligence and good temper; brown or hazel.

Ears - Not large or heavy, hanging close to head and set rather far back.

Mouth - Jaws and teeth strong with a perfect, regular and complete scissor bite, i.e. upper teeth closely overlapping lower teeth and set square to the jaws.

Neck - Clean, strong, powerful, set into well placed shoulders.

Forequarters - Shoulders long and sloping. Forelegs well boned and straight from elbow to ground when viewed from either front or side.

Body - Chest of good width and depth, with well sprung barrel ribs - this effect not to be produced by carrying excessive weight. Level topline. Loins wide, short-coupled and strong.

Hindquarters - Well developed, not sloping to tail; well-turned stifle. Hocks well let down, cowhocks highly undesirable.

Feet - Round, compact; well arched toes and well developed pads.

Tail - Distinctive feature, very thick towards base, gradually tapering towards tip, medium length, free from feathering, but clothed thickly all round with short, thick, dense coat, thus giving 'rounded' appearance described as 'Otter' tail. May be carried gaily but should not curl over back.

Gait/Movement - Free, covering adequate ground; straight and true in front and rear.

Coat - Distinctive feature, short dense without wave or feathering, giving fairly hard feel to the touch; weather-resistant undercoat.

Colour - Wholly black, yellow or liver/chocolate. Yellows range from light cream to red fox. Small white spot on chest permissible.

Size - Ideal height at withers: dogs: 56-57 cms (22-22½ins); bitches: 55-56 cms (21½-22 ins).

Faults

Any departure from the foregoing points should be considered a fault and the seriousness with which the fault should be regarded should be in exact proportion to its degree and its effect upon the health and welfare of the dog and on the dog's ability to perform its traditional work.

Note: Male animals should have two apparently normal testicles fully descended into the scrotum.

American Kennel Club Breed Standard (USA)

The AKC breed standard for the Labrador runs to several pages and is one of the most detailed of all the breed standards. Although largely the same, one difference between the UK and USA standards is that sometimes Labradors are taller and leggier in the USA, with an allowable height of up to 24½ inches for a male and 23½ inches for a female, compared with 22½ inches and 22 inches in the UK. Here is the American Breed Standard:

General Appearance: The Labrador Retriever is a strongly built, medium-sized, short-coupled, dog possessing a sound, athletic, well-balanced conformation that enables it to function as a retrieving gun dog; the substance and soundness to hunt waterfowl or upland game for long hours under difficult conditions; the character and quality to win in the show ring; and the temperament to be a family companion.

Physical features and mental characteristics should denote a dog bred to perform as an efficient Retriever of game with a stable temperament suitable for a variety of pursuits beyond the hunting environment. The most distinguishing characteristics of the Labrador Retriever are its short, dense, weather resistant coat; an "otter" tail; a clean-cut head with broad back skull and moderate stop; powerful jaws; and its "kind," friendly eyes, expressing character, intelligence and good temperament.

Above all, a Labrador Retriever must be well balanced, enabling it to move in the show ring or work in the field with little or no effort.

The typical Labrador possesses style and quality without over refinement, and substance without lumber or cloddiness. The Labrador is bred primarily as a working gun dog; structure and soundness are of great importance.

Size, Proportion and Substance: Size -The height at the withers for a dog is 22½ to 24½ inches; for a bitch is 21½ to 23½ inches. Any variance greater than ½ inch above or below these heights is a disqualification.

Approximate weight of dogs and bitches in working condition: dogs 65 to 80 pounds; bitches 55 to 70 pounds. The minimum height ranges set forth in the paragraph above shall not apply to dogs or bitches under 12 months of age.

Proportion -Short-coupled; length from the point of the shoulder to the point of the rump is equal to or slightly longer than the distance from the withers to the ground. Distance from the elbow to the ground should be equal to one half of the height at the withers. The brisket should extend to the elbows, but not perceptibly deeper. The body must be of sufficient length to permit a straight, free and efficient stride; but the dog should never appear low and long or tall and leggy in outline.

Substance - Substance and bone proportionate to the overall dog. Light, "weedy" individuals are definitely incorrect; equally objectionable are cloddy lumbering specimens. Labrador Retrievers shall be shown in working condition well-muscled and without excess fat.

Head: Skull-The skull should be wide; well-developed but without exaggeration. The skull and foreface should be on parallel planes and of approximately equal length. There should be a moderate stop-the brow slightly pronounced so that the skull is not absolutely in a straight line with the nose. The brow ridges aid in defining the stop. The head should be clean-cut and free from fleshy cheeks; the bony structure of the skull chiseled beneath the eye with no prominence in the

cheek. The skull may show some median line; the occipital bone is not conspicuous in mature dogs. Lips should not be squared off or pendulous, but fall away in a curve toward the throat. A wedge-shape head, or a head long and narrow in muzzle and back skull is incorrect as are massive, cheeky heads. The jaws are powerful and free from snippiness- the muzzle neither long and narrow nor short and stubby.

Nose -The nose should be wide and the nostrils well-developed. The nose should be black on black or yellow dogs, and brown on chocolates. Nose color fading to a lighter shade is not a fault. A thoroughly pink nose or one lacking in any pigment is a disqualification.

Teeth -The teeth should be strong and regular with a scissors bite; the lower teeth just behind, but touching the inner side of the upper incisors. A level bite is acceptable, but not desirable. Undershot, overshot, or misaligned teeth are serious faults. Full dentition is preferred. Missing molars or pre-molars are serious faults.

Ears -The ears should hang moderately close to the head, set rather far back, and somewhat low on the skull; slightly above eye level. Ears should not be large and heavy, but in proportion with the skull and reach to the inside of the eye when pulled forward.

Eyes -Kind, friendly eyes imparting good temperament, intelligence and alertness are a hallmark of the breed. They should be of medium size, set well apart, and neither protruding nor deep set. Eye color should be brown in black and yellow Labradors, and brown or hazel in chocolates. Black, or yellow eyes give a harsh expression and are undesirable. Small eyes, set close together or round prominent eyes are not typical of the breed. Eye rims are black in black and yellow Labradors; and brown in chocolates. Eye rims without pigmentation is a disqualification.

Neck, Topline and Body: Neck -The neck should be of proper length to allow the dog to retrieve game easily. It should be muscular and free from throatiness. The neck should rise strongly from the shoulders with a moderate arch. A short, thick neck or a "ewe" neck is incorrect.

Topline -The back is strong and the topline is level from the withers to the croup when standing or moving. However, the loin should show evidence of flexibility for athletic endeavor.

Body -The Labrador should be short-coupled, with good spring of ribs tapering to a moderately wide chest. The Labrador should not be narrow-chested; giving the appearance of hollowness between the front legs, nor should it have a wide spreading, bulldog-like front. Correct chest conformation will result in tapering between the front legs that allows unrestricted forelimb movement. Chest breadth that is either too wide or too narrow for efficient movement and stamina is incorrect. Slab-sided individuals are not typical of the breed; equally objectionable are rotund or barrel chested specimens. The underline is almost straight, with little or no tuck-up in mature animals. Loins should be short, wide and strong; extending to well developed, powerful hindquarters. When viewed from the side, the Labrador Retriever shows a well-developed, but not exaggerated forechest.

Tail -The tail is a distinguishing feature of the breed. It should be very thick at the base, gradually tapering toward the tip, of medium length, and extending no longer than to the hock. The tail should be free from feathering and clothed thickly all around with the Labrador's short, dense coat, thus having that peculiar rounded appearance that has been described as the "otter" tail. The tail should follow the topline in repose or when in motion. It may be carried gaily, but should not curl over the back. Extremely short tails or long thin tails are serious faults. The tail completes the balance of the Labrador by giving it a flowing line from the top of the head to the tip of the tail.

Docking or otherwise altering the length or natural carriage of the tail is a disqualification.

Forequarters: Forequarters should be muscular, well-coordinated and balanced with the hindquarters.

Shoulders -The shoulders are well laid-back, long and sloping, forming an angle with the upper arm of approximately 90 degrees that permits the dog to move his forelegs in an easy manner with strong forward reach. Ideally, the length of the shoulder blade should equal the length of the upper arm. Straight shoulder blades, short upper arms or heavily muscled or loaded shoulders, all restricting free movement, are incorrect.

Front Legs -When viewed from the front, the legs should be straight with good strong bone. Too much bone is as undesirable as too little bone, and short legged, heavy boned individuals are not typical of the breed. Viewed from the side, the elbows should be directly under the withers, and the front legs should be perpendicular to the ground and well under the body. The elbows should be close to the ribs without looseness. Tied-in elbows or being "out at the elbows" interfere with free movement and are serious faults. Pasterns should be strong and short and should slope slightly from the perpendicular line of the leg. Feet are strong and compact, with well-arched toes and well-developed pads. Dew claws may be removed. Splayed feet, hare feet, knuckling over, or feet turning in or out are serious faults.

Hindquarters: The Labrador's hindquarters are broad, muscular and well-developed from the hip to the hock with well-turned stifles and strong short hocks. Viewed from the rear, the hind legs are straight and parallel. Viewed from the side, the angulation of the rear legs is in balance with the front. The hind legs are strongly boned, muscled with moderate angulation at the stifle, and powerful, clearly defined thighs.

The stifle is strong and there is no slippage of the patellae while in motion or when standing. The hock joints are strong, well let down and do not slip or hyper-extend while in motion or when standing. Angulation of both stifle and hock joint is such as to achieve the optimal balance of drive and traction. When standing the rear toes are only slightly behind the point of the rump. Over angulation produces a sloping topline not typical of the breed. Feet are strong and compact, with well-arched toes and well-developed pads. Cowhocks, spread hocks, sickle hocks and over-angulation are serious structural defects and are to be faulted.

Coat: The coat is a distinctive feature of the Labrador Retriever. It should be short, straight and very dense, giving a fairly hard feeling to the hand. The Labrador should have a soft, weather-resistant undercoat that provides protection from water, cold and all types of ground cover. A slight wave down the back is permissible. Woolly coats, soft silky coats, and sparse slick coats are not typical of the breed, and should be severely penalized.

Color: The Labrador Retriever coat colors are black, yellow and chocolate. Any other color or a combination of colors is a disqualification. A small white spot on the chest is permissible, but not desirable. White hairs from ageing or scarring are not to be misinterpreted as brindling.

Black -Blacks are all black. A black with brindle markings or a black with tan markings is a disqualification.

Yellow -Yellows may range in color from fox-red to light cream, with variations in shading on the ears, back, and underparts of the dog.

Chocolate -Chocolates can vary in shade from light to dark chocolate. Chocolate with brindle or tan markings is a disqualification.

Movement: Movement of the Labrador Retriever should be free and effortless. When watching a dog move toward oneself, there should be no sign of elbows out. Rather, the elbows should be held neatly to the body with the legs not too close together. Moving straight forward without pacing or weaving, the legs should form straight lines, with all parts moving in the same plane.

Upon viewing the dog from the rear, one should have the impression that the hind legs move as nearly as possible in a parallel line with the front legs. The hocks should do their full share of the work, flexing well, giving the appearance of power and strength. When viewed from the side, the shoulders should move freely and effortlessly, and the foreleg should reach forward close to the ground with extension. A short, choppy movement or high knee action indicates a straight shoulder; paddling indicates long, weak pasterns; and a short, stilted rear gait indicates a straight rear assembly; all are serious faults.

Movement faults interfering with performance including weaving; side-winding; crossing over; high knee action; paddling; and short, choppy movement, should be severely penalized.

Temperament: True Labrador Retriever temperament is as much a hallmark of the breed as the "otter" tail. The ideal disposition is one of a kindly, outgoing, tractable nature; eager to please and non-aggressive towards man or animal. The Labrador has much that appeals to people; his gentle ways, intelligence and adaptability make him an ideal dog. Aggressiveness towards humans or other animals, or any evidence of shyness in an adult should be severely penalized.

Disqualifications: 1. Any deviation from the height prescribed in the Standard. 2. A thoroughly pink nose or one lacking in any pigment. 3. Eye rims without pigment. 4. Docking or otherwise altering the length or natural carriage of the tail. 5. Any other color or a combination of colors other than black, yellow or chocolate as described in the Standard.

Approved February 12, 1994 Effective March 31, 1994

....

Glossary:

Withers - shoulders

Stop - area between a dog's eyes, below the skull

Stifle - knee

Occipital bone - bony bump seen at the top rear of the skull on some breeds

Brindle - a brownish or tawny colour, with streaks of other colour

....

4. Choosing a Labrador Puppy

Once you have decided that the Labrador is the dog for you, the best way to select a puppy is with your head - and not with your heart. With their beautiful big eyes, velvet coats, comical antics and eagerness to please, there are few more endearing things on this Earth than a litter of Labrador puppies. If you go to view a litter, the pups are sure to melt your heart and it is extremely difficult – if not downright impossible - to walk away without choosing one.

So, it's essential to do your research before you visit any litters. Decide if you want a puppy bred from show lines, working lines or a mixture of both and then select **a responsible breeder with health-tested parents** (of the puppy, not the breeder!) and one who knows Labradors inside out. After all, apart from getting married or having a baby, getting a puppy is one of the most important, demanding, expensive and life-enriching decisions you will ever make.

Just like babies, puppies will love you unconditionally - but there is a price to pay. In return for their loyalty and devotion, you have to fulfil your part of the bargain.

In the beginning, you have to be prepared to devote much of your day to your new puppy. You have to feed him several times a day and housetrain him virtually every hour, you have to give him your attention and start to gently introduce the rules of the house as well as take care of his health and welfare. You also have to be prepared to part with hard cash for regular healthcare and pet insurance.

If you are not prepared, or unable, to devote the time and money to a new arrival, if you have a very young family or if you are out at work all day, then now might not be the right time to consider getting a puppy. Labradors, like all breeds with working origins, are happiest when they are mentally and physically stimulated.

If left alone too long or under-exercised, these large, loyal dogs can become bored and even destructive. This is a natural reaction and is not the dog's fault; he is simply responding to the environment, which is failing to meet his needs. Labradors are happiest when involved – either in the midst of family life or when there is a task to do, such as picking up on a shoot, training or service work. Pick a healthy pup and he or she should live for more than a decade, maybe even into the teens if you're lucky, so getting a Lab is definitely a long-term commitment. Before taking the plunge, ask yourself some questions:

Have I Got Enough Time?

In the first days after leaving his - or her - mother and littermates, your puppy will feel very lonely and probably even a little afraid. You and your family have to spend time with your new arrival to make him feel safe and sound. Ideally, for the first few days you will be around all of the time to help him settle and to start bonding with him. If you work, book a couple of weeks off (this may not be possible for some of our American readers who get shorter vacations than their European counterparts), but don't just get a puppy and leave him or her all alone in the house a couple of days later. Housetraining (potty training) starts the moment your pup arrives home. Then, after the first few days and once he's feeling more settled, start to introduce short sessions of a couple of minutes of behaviour training to teach your new pup the rules of the house. Labrador puppies can be very boisterous and early training to stop puppy biting and jumping up are a must.

Begin the socialisation process by taking him out of the home to see buses, trains, noisy traffic, kids, etc. - but make sure you CARRY HIM until the vaccinations have taken effect. Puppies can be very sensitive to all sorts of things and it's important to start the socialisation process as soon as possible. The more he is introduced to at this early stage, the better, and a good breeder will already have started the process.

Once he has had the all-clear following vaccinations, get into the habit of taking him out of the house and garden or yard for a short walk every day – more as he gets older. New surroundings stimulate interest and help to stop puppies becoming bored and developing unwanted behaviour issues. He also needs to get used to different noises. Although Labradors are low maintenance on the grooming front, make time to gently brush your pup and check his ears are clean to get him used to being handled and groomed right from the beginning. Many breeders will recommend that you have your pup checked out by a vet within a few days of taking him home. You'll also need to factor in time to visit the vet's surgery for regular healthcare visits and annual vaccinations.

How Long Can I Leave Him?

This is a question we get asked all of the time and one which causes much debate among new and prospective owners. All dogs are pack animals; their natural state is to be with others. So being alone is not normal for them, although many have to get used to it. The Labrador has not been bred to be a guard dog; he or she wants to be around you or other dogs.

Another issue is the toilet; all Labradors have smaller bladders than humans. Forget the emotional side of it, how would you like to be left for eight hours without being able to visit the bathroom? So how many hours can you leave a dog alone? Well, a useful guide comes from the canine rescue organisations. In the UK, they will not allow anybody to adopt if they are intending to leave the dog alone for more than four or five hours a day.

Dogs left at home alone a lot become bored and, in the case of Labradors and other dogs bred to do a job, they can become depressed and/or destructive. Of course, it depends on the character and temperament of your dog, but a lonely Lab may display signs of unhappiness by chewing, barking, digging, urinating, bad behaviour, or just being plain sad and disengaged.

A puppy or fully-grown dog must NEVER be left shut in a crate all day. It is OK to leave a puppy or adult dog in a crate if he or she is happy there, but all our breeders said the same, the door should never be closed for more than a few hours during the day. A crate is a place where a puppy or adult should feel safe, not a prison. Ask yourself why you want a dog – is it for selfish reasons or can you really offer a good home to a young puppy - and then adult dog - for a decade or longer?

Home Preparation

Labradors are adaptable. They usually live among families in homes across the globe, but some are working dogs that retrieve game in the field and may live in kennels. However, one thing they all have in common is that they need exercise and regular access to the Great Outdoors. Labradors are not lap dogs, they love being outdoors, and some of this exercise time should be spent off the lead. One reason why some Labs end up in rescue centres is that their owners did not realise how much exercise and stimulation these dogs need.

Labradors are highly intelligent, and breeders find them one of the easiest breeds to housetrain – provided you are diligent in the beginning. At a minimum, puppies should go out immediately after waking up, about 20-30 minutes after eating each meal, and right before bed. See **Chapter 6** for more information on how to housetrain your puppy.

Make sure there are no poisonous plants or chemicals in your garden. Common plants toxic to dogs include crocus, daffodil, azalea, wisteria, cyclamen, sweet pea, lily of the valley, tulips, hyacinth and lily. The Kennel Club has a list of poisonous house and garden plants here: http://bit.ly/1nCv1qJ A word of warning: don't leave your puppy unattended in the garden or yard, as dognapping is on the increase.

Labrador puppies are little chewing machines and puppy-proofing your home should involve moving anything sharp, breakable or chewable - including your shoes - out of reach of sharp little teeth. Lift electrical cords, mobile phones and chargers, remote controls, etc. out of reach and block off any off-limits areas of the house - such as upstairs or your bedroom - with a child gate or barrier, especially as he will probably be following you around the house in the first few days. There's more specific advice from breeders on preparing your home later in this chapter.

Family and Children

One of the reasons you have decided on a Labrador may well be because you have children. With their easy-going and loving personalities, Labradors make excellent family pets. Your children will, of course, be delighted about your new arrival. But remember that puppies are small and delicate (as are babies), so you should never leave babies or young children and dogs alone together – no matter how well they get along. Small kids lack co-ordination and a young Labrador may inadvertently get poked in the eye or trodden on if you don't keep an eye on him or her.

Often puppies regard children as playmates (just like a small child regards a puppy as a playmate) and young Labs are both playful and boisterous. They may chase, jump and nip a small child if left together unsupervised. This is not aggression; this is normal play for puppies. Train your pup to be gentle with your children and your children to be gentle with your puppy.

See **Chapter 9. Exercise** on how to deal with puppy biting. Discourage the kids from constantly picking up your gorgeous new puppy. They should learn respect for the dog, which is a living creature with his or her own needs, not a toy.

Make sure your puppy gets enough time to sleep – **which is most of the time in the beginning** - so don't let children (or adults!) constantly pester him. Sleep is very important to puppies, just as it is for babies. Also, allow your Labrador to eat at his or her own pace uninterrupted; letting youngsters play with the dog while eating is a no-no as it may promote gulping of food or food aggression. Another reason some dogs end up in rescue centres is that owners are unable to cope with the demands of small children AND a dog. On the other hand, it is also a fantastic opportunity for you to educate your little darlings (both human and canine) on how to get along with each other and set the pattern for wonderful life-long friendships.

Single People

Many single adults own dogs, but if you live alone, getting a puppy will require a lot of dedication on your part. There will be nobody to share the responsibility, so taking on a dog requires a huge commitment and a lot of your time if the dog is to have a decent life. If you are out of the house all day as well, it is not really fair to get a puppy, or even an adult dog. Left alone all day, they will feel isolated, bored and sad. However, if you work from home or are at home all day and you can spend considerable time with the pup every day, then great; a Labrador will undoubtedly become your best friend.

Older People

If you are older or have elderly relatives living with you, Labradors can be great company. Provided their needs are met, they are affectionate, easy-going and love to be with people. If you are older, make sure you have the energy and patience to deal with a young puppy and then a large dog. All Labs need plenty of daily exercise, so if you are not in the best of health, a small dog that requires less exercise and outdoor time might be a better option – or an older Labrador. A young, boisterous Lab is, in all honesty, probably a step too far for an elderly person or couple.

Dogs can, however, be great for fit, older people. My father is in his mid-80s, but takes his dog out walking for an hour to 90 minutes every day - a morning and an afternoon walk and then a short one last thing at night – even in the rain or snow. He grumbles occasionally, but it's good for him and it's good for the dog, helping to keep both of them fit and socialised! They get fresh air, exercise and the chance to communicate with other dogs and their humans.

Dogs are also great company indoors – you're never alone when you've got a dog. Many older people get a canine companion after losing a loved one (a husband, wife or previous much-loved dog). A pet gives them something to care for and love, as well as a constant companion. However, owning a dog is not cheap, so it's important to be able to afford annual pet insurance, veterinary fees, a quality pet food, etc. The RSPCA in the UK has estimated that owning a dog costs an average of around £1,300 ($1,700) a year.

Other Pets

However friendly your puppy is, if you already have other pets in your household, they may not be too happy at the new arrival. Labradors generally get on well with other animals, but it might not be a good idea to leave your hamster or pet rabbit running loose with your pup; most young Labs have play or prey instincts.

Spend time to introduce them to each other gradually and supervise the sessions in the beginning. Labrador puppies are naturally curious and playful and they will sniff and investigate other pets. Depending on how lively you pup is, you may have to separate them to start off with, or put your boisterous and playful Labrador puppy into a pen or crate initially to allow a cat to investigate without being mauled by a hyperactive pup who thinks the cat is a great playmate.

This will also prevent your puppy from being injured. If the two animals are free and the cat lashes out, he or she could scratch your pup's eyes. Just type 'Labrador puppy and cat' into YouTube to see how the two might interact. A timid cat might need protection from a bold, playful Labrador - or vice versa. A bold cat and a timid young Labrador will probably settle down together quickest! If things seem to be going well with no aggression after one or two supervised sessions, then let them loose together. Take the process slowly, if your cat is stressed and frightened he may decide to leave. Our feline friends are notorious for abandoning home because the food and facilities are better down the road. Until you know that they can get on, don't leave them alone together.

Gender

You have to decide whether you want a male or a female puppy. In terms of gender, much depends on the temperament of the individual dog - the differences WITHIN the sexes are greater than the differences BETWEEN the sexes. One difference, however, is that males are generally larger than females. Another is that females have heat cycles and, unless you have her spayed, you will have to restrict your normal exercise routine when she comes into heat (every six months or so) to stop unwanted attention from other dogs. Your main point of reference in terms of size and temperament is to look at the puppy's parents; see what they are like and discuss with your breeder which puppy would best suit you.

If you already have dogs or are thinking of getting more than one, you do, however, have to consider gender. You cannot expect an un-neutered male to live with an unspayed female without problems. Similarly, two uncastrated males may not always get along; there may simply be too much testosterone and competition. If an existing dog is neutered (male) or spayed (female) and you plan to have your puppy neutered or spayed, then gender should not be an issue. Many breeders will specify that your Labrador pup has to be spayed or neutered within a certain timeframe. This is not because they want to make more money from breeding Labradors; it is to protect the breed from indiscriminate breeding.

Which Colour?

There are three colours of Labrador: **yellow, black** and **chocolate**. Not 'golden'; Golden Retrievers are golden and Labradors are yellow. Yellow can range from fox red to pale cream and these shades are all accepted by the Kennel Clubs. A Labrador puppy does not have to be the same colour as his or her parents; it all depends what genes they inherit.

According to the American Kennel Club (AKC): "The Labrador Retriever coat colors are black, yellow and chocolate. Any other color or a combination of colors is a disqualification. A small white spot on the chest is permissible, but not desirable." The UK Kennel Club states: "Colour - Wholly black, yellow or liver/chocolate. Yellows range from light cream to red fox. Small white spot on chest permissible."

So, despite what you may have heard, there is no such thing as a purebred 'silver Labrador', nor 'charcoal', nor 'champagne'. These Labradors are also known as 'dilutes' in the USA, which more accurately describes the specific 'dd' colour gene they carry, and they are a bone of great contention in the Labrador world. Most established breeders say they are not true Labradors, believing that some Weimaraner blood was introduced by one particular US kennel, probably in the 1950s. They are opposed to silvers as their breeders focus mainly on producing the colour, thereby narrowing (instead of broadening) the gene pool - which in turn leads to hereditary health issues. Research has shown some evidence of hair loss and skin problems with dilute Labradors, see http://research.omicsgroup.org/index.php/Labrador_Retriever_coat_colour_genetics. Nevertheless, a number of American breeders are producing 'silver Labradors', and they have been known in the UK since 2006.

US breeder Teresa Gordy-Brown, administrator of The Federation for the Preservation of the Labrador Retriever (FPLR), explains: "The American Kennel Club Labrador Retriever Stud Book closed in 1917 when the AKC officially recognized the Labrador Retriever as a breed. When a stud book closes, it means that absolutely no cross-breeding (i.e. mixing with other breeds to create a breed or improve upon certain features) can be done.

"Since the very beginning of time, gamekeepers and earlier breeders of the Labrador in England never reported the silver colour. Today, some would like to argue that the silver puppies were culled (killed), which is why they were never seen early on. Although there is absolutely no proof that silver puppies were culled, there IS proof that chocolates (livers) and yellows were culled, even though they appeared early on in the breed's history. But there is never any mention of silver.

"Fast forward to the late 1940s/50s in the United States, when one particular kennel bred both Labradors and Pointers. Back then, record-keeping and separation of dogs by both breed and gender was not mandatory. This particular kennel, known as 'Kellogg' began marketing 'Pointing Labradors'. When you research all the pedigrees of silver or other dilute Labradors, they all trace back to Kellogg...every last one!"

Despite the fact that silver is not a recognised colour, it is possible to get pedigree papers with a silver Lab, as the AKC registers silvers as a shade of chocolate – something that many Labrador breeders are campaigning to change. As one breeder said: "If you want a silver dog, go and buy a Weimaraner!"

We would advise anyone who hasn't chosen their puppy yet to stick to black, yellow (of whatever shade) or chocolate. We also believe that health, temperament and size are at least as important as colour, so chat with the breeder; she knows her puppies well, and discuss which one would best fit in with your household and lifestyle. That beautiful little fox red puppy with the timid disposition may not be the best choice if you have a busy household full of lively kids and pets. According to the breeders involved in this book, breeding and temperament have far more influence than coat colour. The view of Christopher Clarke, of Reedfen Labradors, Cambridgeshire, is typical: "I do believe that by using the correct methods for the individual dog, they can all be trained to a degree. I think it's much more to do with type rather than colour."

An exception to this is if you are specifically looking for a working (field) dog; as yet there are no chocolate field champions (in the UK). You will see more black Labs at field events and shoots in the UK, although there are lots of good yellow Labs at these events too. Black was the original colour for Labradors and, according to the UK's Field magazine: "A telling statistic in The Best of the Best, a history of the IGL (International Gundog League) retriever championship, is that in the period 1909-2011, 1,790 black Labradors qualified to run, compared to just 367 yellows." However, yellows, including fox reds, are becoming more popular in the field. Winners of the 2010, 2012 and 2014 IGL Championship were all yellow. Service dogs, such as Guide Dogs for the Blind, are usually yellow, while chocolate Labs are more often kept as pets or seen in the show ring.

American breeder Robin Anderson added: "Statistically, in competitions in the USA, the black Labrador is the most popular, then the yellows, and then the chocolate Labradors, so it makes sense that there are more black field champions than chocolates. I do know there are many highly titled chocolate field Labradors in our country, and some of our American hunters swear by a nice chocolate dog to hunt with. My co-breeder loves the yellows because you can actually see them in the shadows, compared to the black dogs whose faces vanish when they are far away on a hunt, and another of our co-breeders loves his chocolate Labs.

"Honestly, I don't think it is color that makes the difference; it is the temperament of the dog and how the trainer works with the dog to bring it to full potential. I believe that the liver gene across the breeds causes dogs to think on a different plane. All the chocolate Labradors I have had are much smarter and more amusing, causing me to become a better trainer. Two steps ahead of the chocolate Labrador is a must because they think in such unique ways, compared to the other two colors."

More than One Dog

Well-socialised Labradors have no problem sharing their home with other dogs. Supervised sessions from an early age help everyone to get along and for the other dogs to accept your friendly new puppy. It's usually a good idea to introduce your pup to your other dog(s) for the first time outdoors on neutral ground, rather than in the house or in an area one dog regards as his own. You don't want the established dog to feel he has to protect his territory, nor the puppy to feel he is in an enclosed space and can't get away.

If you are thinking about getting more than one pup, consider waiting until your first Labrador is an adolescent or adult before getting a second, so your older dog is calmer and can help train the younger one. Coping with, training and housetraining one puppy is hard enough, without having to do it with two. On the other hand, some owners prefer to get the messy part over and done with in one go and get two together – but this will require a lot of your time for the first few weeks and months.

Owning two dogs can be twice as nice - or double the trouble, and double the vet's bills. There are a number of factors to consider. This is what one UK rescue organisation has to say: "Think about why you are considering another dog. If, for example, you have a dog that suffers from separation anxiety, then rather than solving the problem, your second dog may learn from your first and you then have two dogs with the problem instead of one. The same applies if you have an unruly adolescent; cure the problem first and only introduce a second dog when your first is balanced."

"A second dog will mean double vet's fees, insurance and food. You may also need a larger car, and holidays will be more problematic. Sit down with a calculator and work out the expected expense – you may be surprised. Two dogs will need training, both separately and together. If the dogs do not receive enough individual attention, they may form a strong bond with each other at the expense of their bond with you. If you are tempted to buy two puppies from the same litter - DON'T! Your chances of creating a good bond with the puppies are very low and behaviour problems with siblings are very common.

"Research your considered breed well, it may be best to buy a completely different breed to add balance. If you have a very active dog, would a quieter one be best to balance his high energy or would you enjoy the challenge of keeping two high energy dogs? You will also need to think of any problems that may occur from keeping dogs of different sizes and ages. If you own an elderly Chihuahua, then an adolescent Labrador may not be a good choice! If you decide to purchase a puppy, you will need to think very carefully about the amount of time and energy that will be involved in caring for two dogs with very different needs. "A young puppy will need to have his exercise restricted until he has finished growing and will also need individual time for training.

"If you decide to keep a dog and bitch together, then you will obviously need to address the neutering issue."

....

Top 10 Tips For Working Labrador Owners

We would certainly not recommend getting a Labrador if you are out at work all day. But if you're determined to get one when you're out for several hours at a time, here are some useful points:

1. Either come home during your lunch break to let your dog out or employ a dog walker (or neighbour) to take him out for a walk in the middle of the day. If you can afford it, leave him at doggie day care where he can socialise with other dogs.

2. If not, do you know anybody you could leave your dog with during the day? Consider leaving your dog with a reliable friend, relative or neighbour who would welcome the companionship of a dog without the full responsibility of ownership.

3. Take him for a walk before you go to work – even if this means getting up at the crack of dawn – and spend time with him as soon as you get home. Exercise generates serotonin in the brain and has a calming effect. A dog that has been exercised will be less anxious and more ready for a good nap.

4. Leave him in a place of his own where he feels comfortable. If you use a crate, leave the door open, otherwise his favourite dog bed or chair. You may need to restrict access to other areas of the house to prevent him coming to harm or chewing things you don't want chewed. If possible, leave him in a room with a view of the outside world; this will be more interesting than staring at four blank walls.

5. Make sure that it does not get too hot during the day and there are no cold draughts in the place where you leave him.

6. Leave toys available to play with to prevent destructive chewing (a popular occupation of bored Labradors). Stuff a Kong toy – pictured - with treats to keep him occupied for a while. Choose the right size of Kong; you can even smear the inside with peanut butter or another favourite to keep him busy for longer.

7. Food and drink: Although most Labradors love their food, it is still generally a good idea to put food down at specific meal times and remove it after 15 or 20 minutes if uneaten to prevent your dog becoming fussy or 'punishing' you for leaving him alone by refusing to eat. **Make sure he has access to water at all times.** Dogs cannot cool down by sweating; they do not have many sweat glands (which is why they pant, but this is much less efficient than perspiring) and can die without sufficient water.

8. Consider getting a companion for your Labrador. This will involve even more of your time and twice the expense, and if you have not got time for one dog, you have hardly time for two. A better idea is to find someone you can leave the dog with during the day.

9. Consider leaving a radio or TV on very softly in the background. The 'white noise' can have a soothing effect on some pets. If you do this, select your channel carefully – try and avoid one with lots of bangs and crashes or heavy metal music!

10. Stick to the same routine before you leave your dog home alone. This will help him to feel secure. Before you go to work, get into a daily habit of getting yourself ready, then feeding and exercising your Labrador. Dogs love routine. But don't make a huge fuss of him when you leave as this can also stress the dog; just leave the house calmly

Similarly, when you come home, your Labrador will feel starved of attention and be pleased to see you. Greet him normally, but try not to go overboard by making too much of a fuss as soon as you walk through the door. Give him a pat and a stroke then take off your coat and do a few other things before turning your attention back to him. Lavishing your Labrador with too much attention the second you walk through the door may encourage needy behaviour or separation anxiety.

Puppy Stages

It is important to understand how a puppy develops into a fully-grown dog. This knowledge will help you to be a good owner. **The first few months and weeks of a puppy's life will have an effect on his behaviour and character for the rest of his life.** This Puppy Schedule will help you to understand the early stages:

Birth to seven weeks	A puppy needs sleep, food & warmth. He needs his mother for security & discipline and littermates for learning & socialisation. The puppy learns to function within a pack & learns the pack order of dominance. He begins to become aware of his environment. During this period, puppies should be left with their mother.
Eight to 12 weeks	A puppy should NOT leave his mother before eight weeks. At this age the brain is fully developed & **he now needs socialising with the outside world.** He needs to change from being part of a canine pack to being part of a human pack. This period is a fear period for the puppy, avoid causing him fright and pain.
13 to 16 weeks	Training & formal obedience should begin. **This is a critical period for socialising with other humans, places & situations.** This period will pass easily if you remember that this is a puppy's change to adolescence. Be firm & fair. His flight instinct may be prominent. Avoid being too strict or too soft with him during this time & praise his good behaviour.

Four to eight months	Another fear period for a puppy is between seven to eight months of age. It passes quickly, but be cautious of fright or pain which may leave the puppy traumatised. The puppy reaches sexual maturity & dominant traits are established. Your Labrador should now understand the following commands: 'sit', 'down', 'come' & 'stay'.

Plan Ahead

Most puppies leave the litter for their new homes when they are around eight weeks old. It is important that they have enough time to develop and learn the rules of the pack from their mothers and litter mates. Some puppies take a little longer to develop physically and mentally, and a puppy that leaves the litter too early often suffers with issues, for example a lack of confidence and problems interacting with other dogs, throughout life. Breeders who allow their pups to leave home before eight weeks are probably more interested in a quick buck than a long-term puppy placement. In the USA, many states specify that a puppy may not be sold before eight (or sometimes seven) weeks of age. And if you want a well-bred Labrador, it certainly pays to plan ahead as most good breeders have waiting lists.

Choosing the right breeder is one of the most important decisions you will make. Like humans, your puppy will be a product of his or her parents and will inherit many of their characteristics. His temperament and how healthy your puppy will be now and throughout his life will largely depend on the genes of his parents. Responsible breeders health test their dogs, they check the health records and temperament of the parents and only breed from suitable stock - and good breeding comes at a price.

Prices vary a great deal for Labrador puppies. As a very broad rule of thumb, for a fully health-tested pet puppy from a Kennel Club or AKC-recognised breeder, expect to pay £600 to £900 in the UK and anything from $1,000 to $2,000 or more in the USA, depending on where you live. If a Labrador pup is being sold for much less, you have to ask why. Dogs with show or working potential often cost more.

A healthy Labrador will be your irreplaceable companion for the next decade or more, so why buy an unseen puppy, or one from a pet shop or general advertisement? Would you buy an old wreck of a car or a house with structural problems just because it was cheap? The answer is probably no, because you know you would be storing up stress and expense in the future.

If a healthy Labrador is important to you, wait until you can afford one. Good breeders do not sell their dogs on general purpose websites or in pet shops. Many reputable Labrador breeders do not have to advertise, such is the demand for their puppies. Many have their own websites; you must learn to spot the good ones from the bad ones, so do your research.

Pictured is Hilary Hardman's delightful puppy Maddox. Photo by Caro Dell of Workingline Images.

We strongly recommend visiting the breeder personally at least once and follow our **Top 12 Tips for Selecting a Good Breeder** to help you make the right decision. Buying a poorly-bred puppy may save you a few hundred pounds or dollars in the short term, but could cost you thousands in extra veterinary bills in the long run - not to mention the terrible heartache of having a sickly dog. Rescue groups know only too well the dangers of buying a poorly-bred dog; years of problems can arise, usually health-related, but there can also be temperament issues, or bad behaviour due to lack of socialisation at the breeder's.

Where NOT to buy a Labrador Puppy

There are no cast iron guarantees that your puppy will be 100% healthy and have a good temperament, but choosing a Labrador breeder who is registered with the Kennel Club in your country or who belongs to a Labrador club increases these chances enormously. There are several Labrador clubs in the UK and USA and most have strict entry guidelines and Code of Ethics; see back of book for details.

If, for whatever reason, you're not able to buy a puppy from a breeder with a proven track record, how do you avoid buying one from a 'backstreet breeder' or puppy mill (puppy farm)? These are people who just breed puppies for profit and sell them to the first person who turns up with the cash. Unhappily, this can end in heartbreak for a family months or years later when their puppy develops problems due to poor breeding.

Price is a good guide, and with Labradors you often do get what you pay for. A cheap puppy usually means that corners have been cut somewhere along the line — and it's often health. If a pup is advertised at a price that seems too good to be true; then it is. You can bet your last dollar that the dam and sire are not superb examples of their breed, that they haven't been fully health tested, and that often the puppies are not being fed premium quality food or even kept in the house with the family where the breeder should start to socialise and housetrain them.

Here's some advice on what to avoid:

The Labrador is the most popular of all the breeds and unscrupulous breeders have sprung up to cash in on the Lab's popularity. While new owners might think they have bagged 'a bargain,' this more often than not turns out to be false economy and an emotionally disastrous decision when the puppy develops health problems due to poor breeding, or behavioural problems due to lack of socialisation during the critical early phase of his or her life.

Buying from a puppy mill or someone breeding for profit means that you are condemning other dogs to a life of misery. If nobody bought these cheap puppies, there would be no puppy mills.

In September 2013, The UK's Kennel Club issued a warning of a puppy welfare crisis, with some truly sickening statistics. As many as one in four puppies bought in the UK may come from puppy farms - and the situation is no better in North America. The Press release stated: "As the popularity of online pups continues to soar:

- Almost one in five pups bought (unseen) on websites or social media die within six months

- One in three buy online, in pet stores and via newspaper adverts - outlets often used by puppy farmers – this is an increase from one in five in the previous year

- The problem is likely to grow as the younger generation favour mail order pups, and breeders of fashionable breeds flout responsible steps."

The Kennel Club said: "We are sleepwalking into a dog welfare and consumer crisis as new research shows that more and more people are buying their pups online or through pet shops, outlets often used by cruel puppy farmers, and are paying the price with their pups requiring long-term veterinary treatment or dying before six months old. The increasing popularity of online pups is a particular concern. Of those who source their puppies online, half are going on to buy 'mail order pups' directly over the internet." The KC research found that:

- One third of people who bought their puppy online, over social media or in pet shops failed to experience 'overall good health'

- Almost one in five puppies bought via social media or the internet die before six months old

- Some 12% of puppies bought online or on social media end up with serious health problems that require expensive on-going veterinary treatment from a young age

Caroline Kisko, Kennel Club Secretary, said: "More and more people are buying puppies from sources such as the internet, which are often used by puppy farmers. Whilst there is nothing wrong with initially finding a puppy online, it is essential to then see the breeder and ensure that they are doing all of the right things. This research clearly shows that too many people are failing to do this, and the consequences can be seen in the shocking number of puppies that are becoming sick or dying. We have an extremely serious consumer protection and puppy welfare crisis on our hands."

The research revealed that the problem was likely to get worse as mail order pups bought over the internet are the second most common way for the younger generation of 18 to 24-year-olds to buy a puppy (31%). Marc Abraham, TV vet and founder of Pup Aid, said: "Sadly, if the 'buy it now' culture persists, then this horrific situation will only get worse. There is nothing wrong with sourcing a puppy online, but people need to be aware of what they should then expect from the breeder.

"For example, you should not buy a car without getting its service history and seeing it at its registered address, so you certainly shouldn't buy a puppy without the correct paperwork and health certificates and without seeing where it was bred. However, too many people are opting to buy directly from third parties such as the internet, pet shops, or from puppy dealers, where you cannot possibly know how or where the puppy was raised.

"Not only are people buying sickly puppies, but many people are being scammed into paying money for puppies that don't exist, as the research showed that 7% of those who buy online were scammed in this way." The Kennel Club has launched an online video and has a Find A Puppy app to show the dos and don'ts of buying a puppy. View the video at www.thekennelclub.org.uk/paw

Caveat Emptor – Buyer Beware

Here are some signs that a puppy may have arrived via a puppy mill, a puppy broker (somebody who makes money from buying and selling puppies) or even an importer. Our strong advice is that if you suspect that this is the case, walk away. You can't buy a Rolls Royce or a Lamborghini for a couple of thousand pounds or dollars - you'd immediately suspect that the 'bargain' on offer wasn't the real thing. No matter how lovely it looked, you'd be right - and the same applies to Labradors. Here are some signs to look out for:

Here are some signs that a puppy may have arrived via a puppy mill, a puppy broker (somebody who makes money from buying and selling puppies) or even an importer. Our strong advice is that if you suspect that this is the case, walk away. You can't buy a Rolls Royce or a Lamborghini for a couple of thousand pounds or dollars - you'd immediately suspect that the 'bargain' on offer wasn't the real thing. No matter how lovely it looked, you'd be right - and the same applies to Labradors. Here are some signs to look out for:

* Websites – buying a puppy from a website does not necessarily mean that the puppy will turn out to have problems. But avoid websites where there are no pictures of the home, environment and owners. If they are only showing close-up photos of cute puppies, click the **X** button

* Don't buy a website puppy with a shopping cart symbol next to his picture

* Don't commit to a website puppy unless you have seen it face-to-face. If this is not possible, at the very least you must speak (on the phone) with the breeder and ask questions; don't deal with an intermediary

* At the breeder's, you hear: "You can't see the parent dogs because......" ALWAYS ask to see the parents and, as a minimum, see the mother and how she looks and behaves

* If the breeder says that the dam and sire are Kennel Club or AKC registered, insist on seeing the registration papers

* Ignore photographs of so-called 'champion' ancestors (unless you are buying from an approved breeder), in all likelihood these are fiction

* The puppies look small for their stated age. A committed Labrador breeder will not let her puppies leave before they are eight weeks old

* The person you are buying the puppy from did not breed the dog themselves

* The place you meet the puppy seller is a car park or place other than the puppies' home

* The seller tells you that the puppy comes from top, caring breeders from your or another country. Not true. There are reputable, caring breeders all over the world, but not one of them sells their puppies through brokers

* Ask to see photos of the puppy from birth to present day. If the seller has none, there is a reason – walk away

* Price – if you are offered a very cheap Labrador, he or she almost certainly comes from dubious stock. Careful breeding, taking good care of mother and puppies and health screening all add up to one big bill for breeders. Anyone selling their puppies at a knock-down price has certainly cut corners

* If you get a rescue Labrador, make sure it is from a recognised rescue group – see **Chapter 15. Labrador Rescue** for details - and not a 'puppy flipper' who may be posing as a do-gooder, but is in fact getting dogs (including stolen ones) from unscrupulous sources

In fact, the whole brokering business is just another version of the puppy mill and should be avoided at all costs. Bear in mind that for every cute Labrador puppy you see from a puppy mill or broker, other puppies have died. Good Labrador breeders will only breed from dogs which have been carefully selected for health, temperament, physical shape and lineage. There are loads of good Labrador breeders out there, spend the time to find one.

Here's some sound advice from Teresa Gordy-Brown, of Ashland Labradors, Tennessee, who has been breeding Labradors for more than 30 years: "THE BAD: Shy away from the 'Puppy For Sale' internet sites that list multiple breed puppy sales, such as Puppyfind.com, Petfinder.com, nextdaypets and breeders.net. You know the sites; you click on a drop down menu to 'Select the breed you are looking for', then up pops 50 different listings of puppies from different kennels or individuals.

"These sites are used frequently by puppy millers, dog brokers and in general poor quality breeders with poor quality animals. It is known fact that they 'bait/switch'. This means that they bait their ads with pictures of lovely puppies and/or dogs that are NOT the animal for sale and, in most cases, not even of an animal they own. Many steal pictures from reputable breeders' sites of darling pups and adults and place those pictures on their ad. Then, when someone makes a purchase, they are sent a dog that is the same breed/color and sex, but clearly NOT the one pictured!

"I have had my dogs and puppies pictures stolen on many occasions. I have even had these people say they have a litter sired by one of our Champion stud dogs with a direct link back to my studs page. They are dishonest, so avoid at all cost.

"THE SHODDY: Now, let's say you type in 'Labrador Breeders in Tennessee' or 'Georgia' or 'Florida'. What frequently pops up (for any state) is a website called Labradorbreeders(insert state here).com or (State)Labradorbreeders.net or Purebredbreeder.com, etc. These are **dog broker sites.**

"A dog broker is someone who finds buyers (acts as a second party) for pups produced from puppy mills and bad breeders. These online sites are jammed packed full of poorly-bred pups, highly over-priced and in most cases they are known to use the same pictures to advertise hundreds of pups of the same color/sex/breed in different states. They mislead you into thinking the puppy is located in your state, only for you to later find out it was shipped in to you from five states away.

"Forget about warranties, forget about dealing with the breeder. By the time you get that puppy, he or she has changed hands several times and is exposed to many different pups that the broker hauls around. Not a good risk to take.

"THE WORST: pet stores, auctions and flea markets. No doubt you have heard "Never purchase from a pet store as they are all puppy mill-bred puppies." IT IS TRUE! By the time they get to the store, they have been transformed from a feces/urine/flea infested rag into the cutest puppy ever. Sickly, raised in cages, filth and more. Flea markets are full of Amish puppy mill pups. They are deplorable.

"Auctions are used for those pups a breeder can't find a home for. Don't fall victim to these people. I know how many of us want to reach out and save these puppies and give them a good home, but when you pay for them, you are just keeping these type of deplorable people in the breeding business and causing their dogs to suffer at the cost of being bred over and over until they die or are killed when they are no longer able to produce puppies.

"Just stay away from newspaper ads, Craigslist, eBay Pets, AKC online advertising. None of these are used by reputable breeders. Even AKC online ads are full of back yard breeders galore. Some terms you will not find on reputable breeder websites include: USDA Inspected - If you see these words run! It means they ARE NOT hobby breeders. They usually are high volume mass producers (puppy mills).

"Another is AKC Approved Breeder - There is no such thing! AKC does NOT approve breeders, they are just a registry body and AKC registration does not denote the quality of the breeder or the quality of the animals that are being produced! You should be looking for 'AKC Breeder of Merit. If you see Silver Labradors, White Labradors, Charcoal Labradors or Champagne Labradors advertised, run!" (**Author's Note**: In the UK, look for 'Kennel Club Assured Breeder.') Here are some signs to help the savvy buyer spot a good breeder:

Top 12 Tips for Choosing a Good Breeder

1. Choose a Labrador breeder whose dogs are health tested with certificates to prove it.

2. Visit the Kennel Club and Labrador clubs' websites in your country to find a good breeder in your area.

3. Good breeders keep the dogs in the home as part of the family - not outside in kennel runs, garages or outbuildings. Check that the area where the puppies are kept is clean and that the puppies themselves look clean.

4. Their Labradors appear happy and healthy. Check that the pup has clean eyes, ears, nose and bum (butt) with no discharge. The pups are alert, excited to meet new people and don't shy away from visitors. Pictured is Wybie, bred by Hilary Hardman, Larwaywest Labradors, Dorset, UK. Photo courtesy of Caro Dell of Workingline Images.

5. A good breeder will encourage you to spend time with the puppy's parents - or at least the mother - when you visit. They want your family to meet the puppy and are happy for you to visit more than once.

6. They are very familiar with Labradors, although some may also have other breed(s).

7. All responsible breeders should provide you with a written contract and health guarantee. They will also show you records of the puppy's visits to the vet, vaccinations, worming medication, etc. and explain what other vaccinations your puppy will need. They will agree to take a puppy back within a certain time frame if it does not work out for you, or if there is a health problem.

8. They feed their adults and puppies high quality dog food and give you some to take home and guidance on feeding and caring for your puppy. They will also be available for advice after you take your puppy home.

9. They don't always have pups available, but keep a list of interested people for the next available litter. They don't over-breed, but do limit the number of litters from their dams. Over-breeding or breeding from older females can be detrimental to the female's health.

10. If you have selected a breeder and checked if/when she has puppies available, go online to the Labrador forums before you visit and ask if anyone already has a dog from this breeder. If you are buying from a good breeder, the chances are someone will know her dogs or at least her reputation. If the feedback is negative, cancel your visit and start looking elsewhere.

11. A good breeder will, if asked, provide references from other people who have bought their puppies; call at least one before you commit. They will also agree to take a puppy back within a certain time frame if it does not work out for you, or if there is a health problem.

12. And finally ... good Labrador breeders want to know their beloved pups are going to good homes and will ask YOU a lot of questions about your suitability as owners. DON'T buy a puppy from a website or advert where a PayPal or credit card deposit secures you a puppy without any questions.

Labrador puppies should not be regarded as must-have accessories. They are not objects; they are warm-blooded, living, breathing creatures. Happy, healthy dogs are what everybody wants. Taking the time now to find a responsible and committed breeder with healthy Labradors is time well spent. It could save you a lot of time, money and heartache in the future and help to ensure that you and your chosen puppy are happy together for many years to come.

Important Questions to Ask a Breeder

Some of these points have already been covered, but here's a reminder and checklist of the questions you should be asking.

Have the parents been health screened? Buy a Labrador pup with health tested parents – hips and eyes at the very minimum, with certificates to prove it. Ask what guarantees the breeder or seller is offering in terms of genetic illnesses, and how long these guarantees last – 12 weeks, a year, a lifetime? It will vary from breeder to breeder, but good ones will definitely give you some form of guarantee, and this should be stated in the puppy contract. They will also want to be informed of any hereditary health problems with your puppy, as they may choose not to breed from the dam or sire (mother or father) again. Some breeders keep a chart documenting the full family health history of the pup – ask if one exists and if you can see it.

Can you put me in touch with someone who already has one of your puppies?

Are you registered with the Kennel Club (UK) or AKC (USA) or a member of a Labrador breed club? Not all good Labrador breeders are members, but this is a good place to start.

How long have you been breeding Labradors? You are looking for someone who has a track record with the breed.

How many litters has the mother had? Females should not have litters until they are two years old and then only have a few litters in their lifetime. The UK Kennel Club will not register puppies from a dam who has had more than four litters. Check the age of the mother, too young or too old is not good for her health.

What happens to the female(s) once she/they have finished breeding? Are they kept as part of the family, rehomed in loving homes or sent to animal shelters?

Do you breed any other types of dog? Buy from a Labrador specialist, preferably one who does not breed lots of other breeds of dog - unless you know they have a good reputation.

What is so special about this litter? You are looking for a breeder who has used good breeding stock and his or her knowledge to produce healthy, handsome dogs with good temperaments, not just cute dogs in fancy colours. All Labrador puppies look cute, don't buy the first one you see – be patient and pick the right one. If you don't get a satisfactory answer, look elsewhere.

What do you feed your adults and puppies? A reputable breeder will feed a top quality dog food and advise that you do the same.

What special care do you recommend? Your Labrador will probably need regular grooming, trimming and ear cleaning.

What is the average lifespan of your dogs? Generally, pups bred from healthy stock tend to live longer.

How socialised and housetrained is the puppy? Good breeders will raise their puppies as part of the household and start the socialisation and potty training process before they leave.

What healthcare have the pups had so far? Ask to see records of flea treatments, wormings and vaccinations.

Has the puppy been microchipped?

Why aren't you asking me any questions? A good breeder will be committed to making a good match between the new owners and their puppies. If the breeder spends more time discussing money than the welfare of the puppy and how you will care for him, you can draw your own conclusions as to what his or her priorities are – and they probably don't include improving the breed. Walk away.

 Take your puppy to a vet to have a thorough check-up within 48 hours of purchase. If your vet is not happy with the health of the dog, no matter how painful it may be, return the pup to the breeder. Keeping an unhealthy puppy will only cause more distress and expense in the long run.

Puppy Contracts

All good Labrador breeders should provide you with an official Puppy Contract. This protects both buyer and seller by providing information on diet, worming, vaccination and veterinary visits from the birth of the puppy until he or she leaves the breeder. You should also have a health guarantee for a specified time period. A Puppy Contract will answer such questions as whether the puppy:

- Is covered by breeder's insurance and can be returned if there is a health issue within a certain period of time
- Was born by Caesarean section
- Has been micro-chipped and/or vaccinated and details of worming treatments
- Has been partially or wholly toilet trained
- Has been socialised and where it was kept
- And what health issues the pup and parents have been screened for
- What the puppy is currently being fed by the breeder and if any food is being supplied
- Details of the dam and sire

(Pictured weighing in is Guy Bunce and Chloe Spencer's Pluto, of Dizzywaltz Labradors, Berkshire, UK).

It's not easy for caring breeders to part with their puppies after they have lovingly bred and raised them to eight weeks of age or older, and so many supply extensive care notes for new owners, which may include details such as:

- ❧ The puppy's daily routine
- ❧ Feeding schedule
- ❧ Vet and vaccination schedule
- ❧ General puppy care
- ❧ Toilet training
- ❧ Socialisation

New owners should do their research before visiting a litter as once there, the cute Labrador puppies will undoubtedly be irresistible and you will buy with your heart rather than your head. If you have any doubts at all about the breeder, seller or the puppy, WALK AWAY. Spend time beforehand to research a good Labrador breeder with a proven track record and reduce the chances of health and behaviour problems later on.

In the UK, The Royal Society for the Prevention of Cruelty to Animals (RSPCA) has a downloadable puppy contract endorsed by vets and animal welfare organisations .You can see a copy here and should be looking for something similar from the breeder or seller of the puppy: http://puppycontract.rspca.org.uk/webContent/staticImages/Microsites/PuppyContract/Downloads/PuppyContractDownload.pdf

....

Top 12 Tips for Choosing a Healthy Labrador

Once you've selected your breeder and a litter is available, you then have to decide WHICH puppy to pick. A good breeder will ask questions about you, your family and lifestyle in order to try and match you with a puppy to fit in with your schedule. Here are some signs to look for when selecting a puppy:

1. Your chosen puppy should have a well-fed appearance. He or she should not, however, have a distended abdomen (pot belly) as this can be a sign of worms - or other illnesses (such as Cushing's disease in adults). The ideal puppy should not be too thin either, you should not be able to see his ribs.

2. His or her nose should be cool, damp and clean with no discharge.

3. The pup's eyes should be bright and clear with no discharge or tear stain. Steer clear of a puppy which blinks a lot, this could be the sign of a problem.

4. His gums should be clean and pink.

5. The pup's ears should be clean with no sign of discharge, soreness or redness and no unpleasant smell.

6. Check the puppy's rear end to make sure it is clean and there are no signs of diarrhoea.

(This healthy litter was bred by Jenny Dobson, Lakemeadow Labradors, South Yorkshire).

7. The pup's coat should look clean, feel soft, not matted - and puppies should smell good! The coat should have no signs of ticks or fleas. Red or irritated skin or bald spots could be a sign of infestation or a skin condition. Also, check between the toes of the paws for signs of redness or swelling.

8. Choose a puppy that moves freely without any sign of injury or lameness. It should be a fluid movement, not jerky or stiff, which could be a sign of joint problems.

9. When the puppy is distracted, clap or make a noise behind him - not so loud as to frighten him - to make sure he is not deaf.

10. Finally, ask to see veterinary records to confirm your puppy has been wormed and had his first injections.

If you are unlucky enough to have a health problem with your pup within the first few months, a reputable breeder will allow you to return the pup. Also, if you get the Labrador puppy home and things don't work out for whatever reason, good breeders should also take the puppy back. Make sure this is the case before you commit.

Breeders' Advice on Breeders

Teresa Gordy-Brown has these tips on how to spot a good breeder: "Reputable breeders are hobby breeders who do not have to advertise in any of the venues mentioned previously. They frequently have individual websites, referrals from previous purchasers, other breeders, veterinarians or Labrador club websites. They breed only one breed...sometimes two, but never multiple breeds of dogs. They never advertise the words 'rare, mini, massive' or other similar selling points.

"They will be a member of one or more of a breed specific clubs, either their breed parent club or a regional Specialty Club. They health test their dogs. They frequently are involved with rescue for their breed or contribute financially to rescue or other organizations dedicated to their breed. They raise and train their dogs in a clean, healthy environment. They LOVE their dogs. They participate in some sort of venue (dog shows, performance events, etc.). To find a quality breeder, ask for referrals and if you're searching the internet, start with breed clubs.

"Good breeders raise pups to be proud of. You become part of their extended family when you take home one of their pups. Expect them to be picky. Some may appear rude, but please be persistent!

After all, they are not looking to make a sale, rather to find the best possible match for each puppy they produce. If you're patient and look for the right breeder first, then the right puppy will come along. There is so much more to a quality breeder, but these are the basics. Just do your homework. Word of mouth from previous puppy owners is worth its weight in gold!"

Pictured is Teresa's beautiful chocolate Stormy C's Sweet Serenade At Ashland ('Siren'), and here's a list of her health certificates: Hips OFA Good. Elbows OFA Normal. CERF: Clear. Heart Clear/Cardiologist PRA Carrier. EIC Clear. CNM Clear. CN Clear. HNPK Clear. Long Coat Clear. D-Locus Clear. Color Genotype: bbEEDD

"And one last thing, recently it was brought to my attention from a puppy inquiry that someone was advertising show quality Labrador puppies in the city where I live and they sent me the website link. After three seconds on their site, it was obvious it was a backyard breeder; no pedigrees, NO health clearances - and they have never stepped foot inside of a show ring. How can they possibly have show quality puppies for sale? They DON'T.

"Final point: no breeder worth a grain of salt advertises with the words 'Show Quality'. The proper term is 'Show Prospect,' as you can never guarantee a puppy will make a future show dog; there are too many variables. Next, if your dogs don't even have a pedigree, they have never been shown nor put a paw inside the ring, so you have no way of knowing if the puppies from those dogs would be show prospects!"

Here's what other breeders said, starting with Hilary Hardman: "I have heard of breeders claiming their dog or bitch is "fully health tested," when they may only have had their hips done, and one using a dog as a sire and not declaring that he is a carrier for SD2. These are just a couple of examples; there are many more."

Guy Bunce, Dizzywaltz Labradors, Berkshire: "Lots of the prospective owners who found their way to us told us horror stories. We went the extra mile with all our dogs, with a robust Puppy Plan socialisation programme www.thepuppyplan.com, all medical checks, micro chipping, and one of us is always at home during the eight weeks we have the puppies to play with, monitor and train them.

"We obtained KC Assured Breeder status in order to make sure we were doing things correctly. We even created a very detailed website with pages for all the puppies detailing how they are getting on, their emerging characters, growth and weight. When a new owner puts a deposit down, we also give them access to our puppy webcam so that they can learn more about their puppy and also so we feel accountable to them."

Christine Eynon, Baileylane Labradors, Herefordshire: "The KC and AKC do a wonderful job for selective purchasers who understand the requirements of getting a quality puppy and where to look, but there are still people breeding under the radar with no paperwork and puppies being sold for £150 or£200 down the local (pub). This is where things need tightening but how I am not sure. The import of puppies from abroad is appalling and also needs sorting."

Lynn Aungier, Alatariel Labradors, Surrey, has some cautionary tales: "A friend rescued a puppy that was in our local pet shop behind closed doors. The pup was about five months old, had been at the pet shop since she was eight weeks and had had no socialisation, etc. The pet shop said she was a pedigree, but quite clearly she was from a puppy farm. She is a lovely little dog now, but it has taken a lot of care and hard work to overcome her bad start.

"Another friend bought a crossbreed for a significant amount of money - a lot more than people pay for pedigree dogs, which amazes me. She arranged to go and visit the dogs and the breeder was surprised when she wasn't taking the puppy that day."

(Pictured is Lynn's Raven enjoying a hydrotherapy session).

"My friend was asked no questions, was shown an adult dog that had no interest in the puppies, so quite clearly was not the mother (she also did not appear to have had a recent litter). When she went back the following day to collect the puppy, the breeder wasn't even at the house; a neighbour let her in and said to just leave the money on the side. It amazes me that she bought the dog from this breeder, but she felt she was rescuing the puppy.

"A different friend bought a dog from a couple who had been walking their small Staffordshire Bull Terrier puppy during her first season when a male Labrador came along and the inevitable happened; she had a litter before she was even one-year-old herself. The owners did not take her to the vet for any check-ups. The bitch nearly died during whelping as the puppies were too big for her to deliver, and of the 10 puppies, five died during whelping. The couple didn't worm the puppies and weaned them on scrambled egg and leftovers; they lost another two puppies before eight weeks. My friend was emotionally attached to the plight of the litter and bought a puppy.

"There are so many stories like this, breeding a litter of puppies takes commitment and a level of care and understanding about the health of the sire and dam etc. that are fundamental to raising a healthy, happy litter of dogs. We had 10 in our first litter and worked very hard to keep all 10 healthy. It makes me so cross that there is no control over who breeds and how they do it."

Caroline Smith, Flyenpyg Labradors, Lancashire, added: "There are plenty of breeders who pass off litters from fake mums and dads and there are lots who will register an extra pup so they have spare papers hanging around. I believe if we were all made to DNA profile our dogs, it would go a long way in stopping these unnecessary practices for greed."

Diane Stanford, Tragenheath Labradors, Warwickshire: "When I first started my journey looking into buying my chocolate Lab, I found it to be a bit of a nightmare, you are trying to read so many books about what to look for, what questions to ask. We looked at some lovely Labradors. The parents were beautiful, everything about them looked perfect, but the one thing that held me back was they were not KC-registered, which didn't at the time bother me too much, but they had had no health tests done.

"The breeder said that all the puppies before had been fine and they were all healthy as her Labs were healthy so why wouldn't the pups be fine? She said she didn't believe in the need for health testing. Hence I had to walk away from them."

(Pictured are Diane's healthy duo, Freya and Bea).

Kate Smith, Ardenbrook Labradors, Warwickshire: "I am a Moderator on the popular Facebook group 'Lab Forums', and there are constant stories from those joining with puppies with problems, as well as from rescue groups. As a family, we also encountered a puppy farmer during the search for our first Lab, back in 1997."

Another UK breeder added: "I've not necessarily had experience of unscrupulous breeders, but an uneducated one. Someone I know from a shoot recently rang me and said that they wanted puppies from their bitch and did I know of any nice fox red dogs? I said I did, but that they would only breed with bitches who had the relevant health tests. They then asked what these were and I told them. They said their dog did not have these, but then asked if my friend was around today as their bitch was ready now - and they could get the hips scored some time in the following week and get an eye test later as well!"

Another breeder of working dogs, Julie McDonough, of Rangemaster Working Labradors, Powys, said: "I've heard of false pedigrees, bogus siblings and pups with bad health. My advice is always do your homework and background checks, research the breeder, how many litters have they bred, (but just because they breed a lot of pedigree Labradors doesn't make them a good breeder) how often, how many different breeds do they breed or own?

"Always see the dam (mother) with the litter and does she interact with the pups, does she look like she has had the litter, does the colour match with the mating of dam and sire, i.e. Yellow X Yellow will only produce Yellow; Chocolate x Chocolate will only produce Chocolate or/and Yellow. If the breeder phones and offers you another pup instead of the pup you have chosen, walk away and leave well alone."

Liz Vivash, Wightfyre Labradors, Isle of Wight: "I met a woman in the vet's last week who had been sold a Chihuahua puppy for £1,200 (c$1,560). She was told it would come with the same things we would offer, but when she went to collect it - and therefore fell in love with it - she was not given everything. The puppy was only six weeks old, it was not vaccinated, flead or wormed. It had no five-generation pedigree, and was not KC-registered - although it was by the time I spoke to her – she was also told to microchip the puppy herself! She had bought the puppy off the internet and had not gone through the KC, or any other reputable site. I will agree it is difficult to tell who is good or not, though. The vets told me that she was the third case they had seen that day, but not all the same breed or breeder."

Sarah Edwards, Fernwills Labradors, Essex: "I have never met or dealt with an unscrupulous breeder, but they are definitely out there – especially as one can purchase a Labrador for only £300 or so. These will be puppy-farmed and very unhealthy Labradors, no doubt. If you want a good Labrador, look at the more expensive ones - but still scrutinise the health tests as some people charge a lot for pups that don't necessarily have strong pedigrees either!"

The problem is as bad, if not worse, in the USA. Robin Anderson, Grampian Labradors, New England told us: "There are many unscrupulous so-called 'breeders' in our region and locally to me. One in particular makes it seem terrific that they breed for 'rare' colors. They take the unsuspecting pet buyer's money and, when things go wrong, they don't stand by the 'product' They do the very basic health checks on breeding stock, present their puppies in an idyllic setting, and then cash the check.

"I've had to evaluate their 'product' for our local breed rescue on a number of occasions because it was the owners' only resort when the breeder refused to help out and take the dogs back. Reputable breeders always stand by their dogs, no matter how old or what the problem is, and help the owner in distress deal with the dog."

Sandra Underhill, Labs To Love, California: "I have heard of breeders that don't health test because they think their stock is healthy, only to have that puppy come down with something that could have been avoided if the adult had been health tested and removed from the breeding pool."

Picking the Right Temperament

You've picked a Labrador, presumably, because you like the way they look and you love this breed's unique bond with humans, its willingness to please, biddable temperament and friendly get-along-with-everybody, nature. However, while Labradors may share many common characteristics and temperament traits, each puppy also has his own individual character, just like humans.

The friendly, pleasant nature of the Labrador suits most people. Visit the breeder to see how your chosen pup interacts and get an idea of his character in comparison to his littermates. Some puppies will run up to greet you, pull at your shoelaces and playfully bite your fingers. Others will be more content to stay in the basket sleeping. Watch their behaviour and energy levels. Are you an active person who enjoys lots of daily exercise or would a less hyper puppy be more suitable? Choose the puppy which will best fit in with your family and lifestyle.

A submissive dog will by nature be more passive, less energetic and also possibly easier to train. A dominant dog will usually be more energetic and lively. He or she may also be more stubborn and need a firmer hand when training or socialising with other dogs. If you already have a dominant dog at home, you have to be careful about introducing a new dog into the household; two dominant dogs may not live together comfortably.

There is no good or bad, it's a question of which type of character will best suit you and your lifestyle. Here are a couple of quick tests to try and gauge your puppy's temperament; they should be carried out by the breeder in familiar surroundings so the puppy is relaxed. It should be pointed out that there is some controversy over temperament testing, as a dog's personality is formed by a combination of factors, which include inherited temperament, socialisation, training and environment (or how you treat your dog):

- The breeder puts the pup on his or her back on her lap and gently rests her hand on the pup's chest, or

- She puts her hands under the pup's tummy and gently lifts the pup off the floor for a few seconds, keeping the pup horizontal. A puppy that struggles to get free is less patient than one which makes little effort to get away. A placid, patient dog is likely to fare better in a home with young children than an impatient one. Here are some other useful signs to look out for –

- Watch how he interacts with other puppies in the litter. Does he try and dominate them, does he walk away from them or is he happy to play with his littermates? This may give you an idea of how easy it will be to socialise him with other dogs

- After contact, does the pup want to follow you or walk away from you? Not following may mean he has a more independent nature

- If you throw something for the puppy is he happy to retrieve it for you or does he ignore it? This may measure their willingness to work with humans

- If you drop a bunch of keys behind the Labrador puppy, does he act normally or does he flinch and jump away? The latter may be an indication of a timid or nervous disposition. Not reacting could also be a sign of deafness

Decide which temperament would fit in with you and your family and the rest is up to you. Whatever hereditary temperament your Labrador has, it is true to say that dogs that have constant positive interactions with people and other animals during the first four months of life will generally be happier and more stable. In contrast, a puppy plucked from its family too early and/or isolated for long periods will be less happy, less socialised, more needy, and may well display behaviour problems later on.

Puppies are like children. Being properly raised contributes to their confidence, sociability, stability and intellectual development. The bottom line is that a pup raised in a warm, loving environment with people is likely to be more tolerant and accepting, and less likely to develop behaviour problems.

For those of you who prefer a scientific approach to choosing the right puppy, we are including the full Volhard Puppy Aptitude Test (PAT). This test has been developed by the highly-respected Wendy and Jack Volhard who have built up an international reputation over the last 30 years for their invaluable contribution to dog training, health and nutrition. Their philosophy is: "We believe that one of life's great joys is living in harmony with your dog."

They have written several books and the Volhard PAT is regarded as an excellent method for evaluating the nature of young puppies. Jack and Wendy have also written the Dog Training for Dummies book. Visit their website at www.volhard.com for details of their upcoming dog training camps, as well as their training and nutrition groups.

The Volhard Puppy Aptitude Test

Here are the ground rules for performing the test: The testing is done in a location unfamiliar to the puppies. This does not mean they have to be taken away from home. A 10-foot square area is perfectly adequate, such as a room in the house where the puppies have not been.

✓ The puppies are tested one at a time. There are no other dogs or people, except the scorer and the tester, in the testing area

✓ The puppies do not know the tester

✓ The scorer is a disinterested third party and not the person interested in selling you a puppy

✓ The scorer is unobtrusive and positions himself so he can observe the puppies' responses without having to move

The puppies are tested before they are fed. The puppies are tested when they are at their liveliest. Do not try to test a puppy that is not feeling well.

Puppies should not be tested the day of or the day after being vaccinated. Only the first response counts! Tip: During the test, watch the puppy's tail. It will make a difference in the scoring whether the tail is up or down. The tests are simple to perform and anyone with some common sense can do them. You can, however, elicit the help of someone who has tested puppies before and knows what they are doing.

Social attraction - the owner or caretaker of the puppies places it in the test area about four feet from the tester and then leaves the test area. The tester kneels down and coaxes the puppy to come to him or her by encouragingly and gently clapping hands and calling. The tester must coax the puppy in the opposite direction from where it entered the test area. Hint: Lean backward, sitting on your heels instead of leaning forward toward the puppy. Keep your hands close to your body encouraging the puppy to come to you instead of trying to reach for the puppy.

Following - the tester stands up and slowly walks away encouraging the puppy to follow. Hint: Make sure the puppy sees you walk away and get the puppy to focus on you by lightly clapping your hands and using verbal encouragement to get the puppy to follow you. Do not lean over the puppy.

Restraint - the tester crouches down and gently rolls the puppy on its back for 30 seconds. Hint: Hold the puppy down without applying too much pressure. The object is not to keep it on its back but to test its response to being placed in that position.

Social Dominance - let the puppy stand up or sit and gently stroke it from the head to the back while you crouch beside it. See if it will lick your face, an indication of a forgiving nature. Continue stroking until you see a behaviour you can score. Hint: When you crouch next to the puppy avoid leaning or hovering over it. Have the puppy at your side, both of you facing in the same direction.

During testing maintain a positive, upbeat and friendly attitude toward the puppies. Try to get each puppy to interact with you to bring out the best in him or her. Make the test a pleasant experience for the puppy.

Elevation Dominance - the tester cradles the puppy with both hands, supporting the puppy under its chest and gently lifts it two feet off the ground and holds it there for 30 seconds.

Retrieving - the tester crouches beside the puppy and attracts its attention with a crumpled up piece of paper. When the puppy shows some interest, the tester throws the paper no more than four feet in front of the puppy encouraging it to retrieve the paper.

Touch Sensitivity - the tester locates the webbing of one the puppy's front paws and presses it lightly between his index finger and thumb. The tester gradually increases pressure while counting to ten and stops when the puppy pulls away or shows signs of discomfort.

Sound Sensitivity - the puppy is placed in the center of the testing area and an assistant stationed at the perimeter makes a sharp noise, such as banging a metal spoon on the bottom of a metal pan.

Sight Sensitivity - the puppy is placed in the center of the testing area. The tester ties a string around a bath towel and jerks it across the floor, two feet away from the puppy.

Stability - an umbrella is opened about five feet from the puppy and gently placed on the ground. During the testing, make a note of the heart rate of the pup, this is an indication of how it deals with stress, as well as its energy level. Puppies come with high, medium or low energy levels. You have to decide for yourself, which suits your life style.

Dogs with high energy levels need a great deal of exercise, and will get into mischief if this energy is not channeled into the right direction.

Finally, look at the overall structure of the puppy. You see what you get at 49 days age (seven weeks). If the pup has strong and straight front and back legs, with all four feet pointing in the same direction, it will grow up that way, provided you give it the proper diet and environment. If you notice something out of the ordinary at this age, it will stay with puppy for the rest of its life. He will not grow out of it.

Scoring the Results

Following are the responses you will see and the score assigned to each particular response. You will see some variations and will have to make a judgment on what score to give them –

TEST	RESPONSE	SCORE
SOCIAL ATTRACTION	Came readily, tail up, jumped, bit at hands	1
	Came readily, tail up, pawed, licked at hands	2
	Came readily, tail up	3
	Came readily, tail down	4
	Came hesitantly, tail down	5

	Didn't come at all	6
FOLLOWING	Followed readily, tail up, got underfoot, bit at feet	1
	Followed readily, tail up, got underfoot	2
	Followed readily, tail up	3
	Followed readily, tail down	4
	Followed hesitantly, tail down	5
	Did not follow or went away	6
RESTRAINT	Struggled fiercely, flailed, bit	1
	Struggled fiercely, flailed	2
	Settled, struggled, settled with some eye contact	3
	Struggled, then settled	4
	No struggle	5
	No struggle, strained to avoid eye contact	6
SOCIAL DOMINANCE	Jumped, pawed, bit, growled	1
	Jumped, pawed	2
	Cuddled up to tester and tried to lick face	3
	Squirmed, licked at hands	4
	Rolled over, licked at hands	5
	Went away and stayed away	6
ELEVATION DOMINANCE	Struggled fiercely, tried to bite	1
	Struggled fiercely	2
	Struggled, settled, struggled, settled	3
	No struggle, relaxed	4
	No struggle, body stiff	5
	No struggle, froze	6
RETRIEVING	Chased object, picked it up and ran away	1
	Chased object, stood over it and did not return	2
	Chased object, picked it up and returned with it to tester	3
	Chased object and returned without it to tester	4
	Started to chase object, lost interest	5
	Does not chase object	6
TOUCH SENSITIVITY	8-10 count before response	1

	6-8 count before response	2
	5-6 count before response	3
	3-5 count before response	4
	2-3 count before response	5
	1-2 count before response	6
SOUND SENSITIVITY	Listened, located sound and ran toward it barking	1
	Listened, located sound and walked slowly toward it	2
	Listened, located sound and showed curiosity	3
	Listened and located sound	4
	Cringed, backed off and hid behind tester 5	5
	Ignored sound and showed no curiosity	6
SIGHT SENSITIVITY	Looked, attacked and bit object	1
	Looked and put feet on object and put mouth on it	2
	Looked with curiosity and attempted to investigate, tail up	3
	Looked with curiosity, tail down	4
	Ran away or hid behind tester	5
	Hid behind tester	6
STABILITY	Looked and ran to the umbrella, mouthing or biting it	1
	Looked and walked to the umbrella, smelling it cautiously	2
	Looked and went to investigate	3
	Sat and looked, but did not move toward the umbrella	4
	Showed little or no interest	5
	Ran away from the umbrella	6

The scores are interpreted as follows:

Mostly 1s - Strong desire to be pack leader and is not shy about bucking for a promotion.
Has a predisposition to be aggressive to people and other dogs and will bite.
Should only be placed into a very experienced home where the dog will be trained and worked on a regular basis.

Tip: Stay away from the puppy with a lot of 1's or 2's. It has lots of leadership aspirations and may be difficult to manage. This puppy needs an experienced home. Not good with children.

Mostly 2s - Also has leadership aspirations. May be hard to manage and has the capacity to bite. Has lots of self-confidence. Should not be placed into an inexperienced home. Too unruly to be good with children and elderly people, or other animals. Needs strict schedule, loads of exercise and lots of training. Has the potential to be a great show dog with someone who understands dog behaviour.

Mostly 3s - Can be a high-energy dog and may need lots of exercise. Good with people and other animals. Can be a bit of a handful to live with. Needs training, does very well at it and learns quickly. Great dog for second-time owner.

Mostly 4s - The kind of dog that makes the perfect pet. Best choice for the first time owner.
Rarely will buck for a promotion in the family. Easy to train, and rather quiet.
Good with elderly people, children, although may need protection from the children.
Choose this pup, take it to obedience classes, and you'll be the star, without having to do too much work!

Tip: The puppy with mostly 3's and 4's can be quite a handful, but should be good with children and does well with training. Energy needs to be dispersed with plenty of exercise.

Mostly 5s - Fearful, shy and needs special handling. Will run away at the slightest stress in its life. Strange people, strange places, different floor or surfaces may upset it. Often afraid of loud noises and terrified of thunderstorms. When you greet it upon your return, may submissively urinate. Needs a very special home where the environment doesn't change too much and where there are no children. Best for a quiet, elderly couple. If cornered and cannot get away, has a tendency to bite.

Mostly 6s – So independent that he doesn't need you or other people. Doesn't care if he is trained or not - he is his own person. Unlikely to bond to you, since he doesn't need you. A great guard dog for gas stations! Do not take this puppy and think you can change him into a lovable bundle - you can't, so leave well enough alone.

Tip: Avoid the puppy with several 6's. It is so independent it doesn't need you or anyone. He is his own person and unlikely to bond to you.

The Scores

Few puppies will test with all 2s or all 3s, there'll be a mixture of scores. For that first time, wonderfully easy to train, potential star, look for a puppy that scores with mostly 4s and 3s. Don't worry about the score on Touch Sensitivity - you can compensate for that with the right training equipment.

It's hard not to become emotional when picking a puppy - they are all so cute, soft and cuddly. Remind yourself that this dog is going to be with you for eight to 16 years. Don't hesitate to step back a little to contemplate your decision. Sleep on it and review it in the light of day. Avoid the puppy with a score of 1 on the Restraint and Elevation tests. This puppy will be too much for the first-time owner. It's a lot more fun to have a good dog, one that is easy to train, one you can live with and one you can be proud of, than one that is a constant struggle.

Getting a Dog From a Shelter - Don't overlook an animal shelter as a source for a good dog. Not all dogs wind up in a shelter because they are bad. After that cute puppy stage, when the dog grows up, it may become too much for its owner. Or, there has been a change in the owner's circumstances forcing him or her into having to give up the dog.

Most of the time these dogs are housetrained and already have some training. If the dog has been properly socialised to people, it will be able to adapt to a new environment. Bonding may take a little longer, but once accomplished, results in a devoted companion.

So you see, it's not all about the colour or the cutest face! When getting a puppy, your thought process should run something like this:

1. Decide to get a Labrador
2. Decide if you want one from show or working stock (English or American) or a mixture of both
3. Find a good breeder whose dogs are health tested
4. Find one with a litter available when you are ready for a puppy – or wait
5. Decide on a male or female
6. Pick one with a suitable temperament to fit in with your family

Some people pick a puppy based on how the dog looks. If coat colour, for example, is very important to you, make sure the other boxes are ticked as well.

5. Bringing Your Puppy Home

Getting a new puppy is so exciting. You can't wait to bring your fluffy little bundle of joy home. Before that happens you probably dream of all the things you and your little soul mate are going to do together; snuggling down by the fire, going for walks in the countryside, playing games together, setting off on holiday, maybe even taking part in competitions, shoots or shows.

Your pup has, of course, no idea of your big plans, and the reality when he or she arrives can be a big shock for some owners. Puppies are wilful little critters with minds of their own and sharp teeth. They leak at both ends, constantly demand your attention, bite the kids or anything else to hand, cry a lot for the first few days and don't pay a blind bit of notice to your commands. There is a lot of work ahead before the two of you develop a unique bond. Your pup has to learn what is required of him or her before he or she can start to meet some of your expectations, and you have to understand what your pup needs from you.

Once your new arrival lands in your home, your time won't be your own, but you can get off to a good start by preparing things before the big day. Here's a list of things to think about getting beforehand (your breeder may supply some of these):

Puppy Checklist

- ✓ A dog bed or basket
- ✓ Bedding – old towels or a blanket which can easily be washed (avoid strong detergents)
- ✓ If possible, a towel or piece of cloth which has been rubbed on the puppy's mother to put in the bed
- ✓ A collar or harness and lead (leash)
- ✓ An identification tag for the collar or harness
- ✓ Food and water bowls, preferably stainless steel
- ✓ Puppy food – find out what the breeder is feeding and stick with it initially
- ✓ Puppy treats (preferably healthy ones, not rawhide)
- ✓ Lots of newspapers for housetraining
- ✓ Poo(p) bags
- ✓ Toys and chews suitable for puppies
- ✓ A puppy coat if you live in a cool climate
- ✓ A crate if you decide to use one
- ✓ Old towels for cleaning your puppy and covering the crate

AND PLENTY OF TIME!

Later on you'll also need grooming brushes (possibly a Furminator – see **Chapter 13. Grooming**), dog shampoo, flea and worming products (which you can buy from your vet) and maybe a travel crate. Below is a list of some of the items provided by one Kennel Club Assured Breeder and sent home with each puppy:

- ✓ A personalised blanket that smells of home
- ✓ A soft toy (that your puppy has grown up with)
- ✓ A soft fleece ring tug toy
- ✓ A Beco bone chew toy
- ✓ A Beco tug rope
- ✓ A large textured ball
- ✓ Toilet bags
- ✓ Puppy pads
- ✓ Puppy harness
- ✓ Puppy lead
- ✓ Puppy collar
- ✓ Engraved collar ID tag
- ✓ A puppy bowl
- ✓ A bag of Royal Canin puppy food

Puppy Proofing Your Home

Before your puppy arrives, you may have to make a few adjustments to make your home safe and suitable. Puppies are small bundles of instinct and energy (when they are awake), with little common sense and even less self-control. Young Labradors love to play and have a great sense of fun. They often have bursts of energy before they run out of steam and spend much of the rest of the day sleeping. All young Labs are curious and most of them are boisterous - especially when they grow into adolescents and start throwing their weight around – literally. So, don't leave Grandma alone with a lively 'teenage' Lab if she's just had a hip operation – she's in danger of getting accidentally bowled over in all the excitement!

Puppies are like babies and it's up to you to look after them and set the boundaries – both physically and in terms of behaviour – but gently and one step at a time. Create an area where the puppy is allowed to go, perhaps one or two rooms, preferably with a hard floor which is easy to clean, and keep the rest of the house off-limits, at least until housetraining (potty training) is complete. The room(s) should be near a door to the garden or yard for housetraining. Restricting the area also helps the puppy settle in. At the breeder's he was probably had a den and an area to

run around in. Suddenly having the freedom of the whole house can be quite daunting - not to mention messy.

You can buy a barrier specifically made for dogs or use a baby gate, which may be cheaper. Although designed for infants, they work perfectly well with dogs; you might even find a second-hand one on eBay. Choose one with narrow vertical gaps or mesh and check that your puppy can't get his head stuck between the bars, or put a covering or mesh over the bottom of the gate initially. You can also make your own barrier, but bear in mind that cardboard and other soft materials are likely to get chewed.

Gates can be used to keep the puppy enclosed in a single room or specific area or put at the bottom of the stairs. A puppy's bones are soft, and recent studies have shown that if very young pups are allowed to climb or descend stairs regularly, they can develop joint problems later in life. This is worth bearing in mind, especially as Labs can be prone to hip or elbow problems.

The puppy's designated area or room should not be too hot, cold or damp and it must be free from draughts. Little puppies can be sensitive to temperature fluctuations and don't do well in very hot or very cold conditions. If you live in a hot climate, your new pup may need air conditioning in the summertime.

Tip Don't underestimate your puppy! Young Labs are agile and determined; they can jump and climb, so choose a barrier higher than you think necessary.

Just as you need a home, so your puppy needs a den. This den is a haven where your pup feels safe, particularly in the beginning after the traumatic experience of leaving his or her mother and littermates. Young puppies sleep for 18 hours or longer a day at the beginning; this is normal. You have a couple of options with the den; you can get a dog bed or basket, or you can use a crate. Crates have long been popular in North America and are becoming increasingly used in the UK, particularly as it can be quicker to housetrain a puppy using a crate.

It may surprise some American readers to learn that normal practice in the UK has often been to initially contain the puppy in the kitchen or utility room, and later to let the dog roam around the house. Some owners do not allow their dogs upstairs, but many do. The idea of keeping a dog in a cage like a rabbit or hamster is abhorrent to some animal-loving Brits.

However, a crate can be a useful aid if used properly. Using one as a prison to contain a dog for hours on end certainly is cruel, but the crate has its place as a sanctuary for your dog. It is the dog's own safe space and they know no harm will come to them in there. **See Chapter 6. Crate Training and Housetraining** for getting your Labrador used to - and even to enjoy - being in a crate.

Most puppies' natural instinct is not to soil the area where they sleep. Put plenty of newspapers down in the area next to the den and your pup should choose to go to the toilet here if you are not quick enough to get outside. Of course, he or she may also decide to trash their designated area by chewing their blankets and shredding the newspaper – patience is the key!

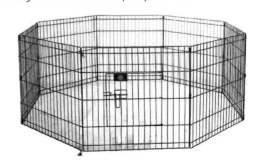

Rather than using a crate, some owners prefer to create a safe penned area for their pup. You can make your own barriers or buy a manufactured playpen. Playpens come in two types, mesh or fabric. A fabric pen is easy to put up and take down, but can be chewed so may not last long. A metal mesh pen (pictured below) is a better bet; it can be expanded and will last longer, but is not quite as easy to put up or take down.

One breeder said: "A play pen can be used in much the same way as a crate and has an advantage of being very versatile in separating eating, sleeping and- in the early days - toileting. They are ideal for the busy Mum or Dad who has other things on their mind and can't possibly watch the puppy, children and try and tidy the house or prepare dinner. Again, it is peace of mind for the owner, knowing the pup is safe and not chewing anything it shouldn't."

With initial effort on your part and a willing pupil, housetraining a Labrador should not take long. One of the biggest factors influencing the success and speed of housetraining is your commitment - another reason for taking time off work, if at all possible, when your puppy arrives. You may also want to remove your Oriental rugs and other treasured possessions to other rooms until your little darling is fully housetrained and has stopped chewing everything in sight.

If you have young children, the time they spend with the puppy should be limited to a few short sessions a day. Plenty of sleep is **essential** for the normal development of a young dog. You wouldn't wake a baby every hour or so to play and the same goes for puppies. Wait a day or two - preferably longer – before inviting friends round to see your gorgeous little puppy. However excited you are, your new arrival needs a few days to get over the stress of leaving mother and siblings and to start bonding with you.

If you have a garden or yard that you intend letting your puppy roam in, make sure that every little gap has been plugged. You'd be amazed at the tiny holes puppies can escape through. Don't leave your puppy unattended in the beginning, as they can come to harm. Also, dogs are increasingly being targeted by thieves, who are even stealing from gardens. Make sure there are no poisonous plants which your pup might chew and check there are no low plants with sharp leaves or thorns which could cause eye or other injuries.

There are literally dozens of plants which can harm a puppy if ingested, including azalea, daffodil bulbs, lily, foxglove, hyacinth, hydrangea, lupin, rhododendron, sweet pea, tulip and yew. The Kennel Club has a list of some of the most common ones here: http://bit.ly/1nCv1qJ and the ASPCA has an extensive list for the USA at: http://bit.ly/19xkhoG

For puppies to grow into well-adjusted dogs, they have to feel comfortable and relaxed in their new surroundings and need a great deal of sleep. They are leaving the warmth and protection of their mother and littermates and for the first few days at least, most puppies may feel very sad. It is important to make the transition from the birth home to your home as easy as possible. Your pup's life is in your hands. How you react and interact with him in the first few days and weeks will shape your relationship and his character for the years ahead.

....

Chewing and Chew Toys

Like babies, most puppies are organic chewing machines and so remove anything breakable and/or chewable within the puppy's reach – including wooden furniture. Obviously you cannot remove your kitchen cupboards, doors, sofas and fixtures and fittings, so don't leave your new arrival unattended for any length of time where he can chew something which is hard to replace.

Young Labs are enthusiastic chewers, so chew toys are a must. Don't give old socks, shoes or slippers or your pup will regard your footwear as fair game, and avoid rawhide chews as they can get stuck in the dog's throat. A safe alternative to real bones or plastic chew bones are natural reindeer antler chew toys (pictured), which have the added advantage of calcium.

Other good choices include Kong toys, which are pretty indestructible, and you can put treats (frozen or fresh) or smear peanut butter inside to keep your dog occupied while you are out. Dental bones are great for cleaning your dog's teeth, but many don't last for very long with an intensive chewer; one that can is the Nylabone Dura Chew Wishbone, which is made of a type of plastic infused with flavours appealing to dogs. Get the large size and throw it away if it starts to splinter after a few weeks. The Zogoflex Hurley and the Goughnut are both strong and float, so good for swimmers - you'll get your money back on both if your Lab destroys them. For safety, the Goughnut has a green exterior and red interior, so you can tell if your dog has penetrated the surface - as long as the green is showing, you can let your dog "goughnuts."

A natural hemp or cotton tug rope is another option, as the cotton rope acts like dental floss and helps with teeth cleaning. It is versatile and can be used for fetch games as well as chewing.

The First Few Days

Before you collect your puppy, let the breeder know what time you will arrive and ask him or her not to feed the pup for three or four hours beforehand - unless you have a very long journey, in which case the puppy will need to eat something. He will be less likely to be car sick and should be hungry when he lands in his new home. (The same applies to an adult dog moving to a new home).

When you arrive, ask for an old towel or toy which has been with the pup's mother — you can leave one on an earlier visit to collect with the pup. Or take one with you and rub the mother with it to collect her scent and put this with the puppy for the first few days. It may help him to settle in. In the US, some Labradors may be shipped to your home. You can still ask for a toy or towel.

Make sure you get copies of any health certificates relating to the parents. A good breeder will also have a Contract of Sale or Puppy Contract which outlines everyone's rights and responsibilities— see **Chapter 4. Choosing a Labrador Puppy**. It should also state that you can return the puppy if there are health issues within a certain time frame — although if you have picked your breeder carefully, it will hopefully not come to this. The breeder will give you details of worming and any vaccinations. Most good breeders supply information sheets and a puppy pack for new owners.

Find out exactly what the breeder is feeding and how much. You cannot suddenly switch a dog's diet; their digestive systems cannot cope with a sudden change. In the beginning, stick to whatever the puppy is used to. Again, good breeders will send some food home with the puppy.

The Journey Home

Bringing a new puppy home in a car can be a traumatic experience. Your puppy will be devastated at leaving his or her mother, brothers and sisters and a familiar environment. Everything will be strange and frightening and he or she may well whimper and whine - or even bark - on the way home. If you can, take somebody with you on that first journey. Under no circumstances have the puppy on your lap while driving. It is simply too dangerous - a Labrador puppy is cute, lively and far too distracting.

The best and safest way to transport the pup is in a crate — either a purpose-made travel crate or a wire crate which he will use at home. Put a comfortable blanket in the bottom - preferably rubbed with the scent of the mother. Ask your travel companion to sit next to the crate and talk softly to the frightened little bundle of nerves. If you don't have a crate, your passenger may wish to hold the puppy. If so, have an old towel between the person and the pup as he may quite possibly urinate (the puppy, not the passenger!)

If you have a journey of more than a couple of hours,

make sure that you take water and offer the puppy a drink en route. He may need to eliminate or have diarrhoea (hopefully, only due to nerves), but don't let him outside on to the ground in a strange place as he is not yet fully vaccinated. If you have a long journey, cover the bottom of the crate with a waterproof material and put newspapers in half of it, so the pup can eliminate without staining the car seats.

Arriving Home

As soon as you arrive home, let your puppy into the garden or yard and when he 'performs,' praise him for his efforts. These first few days are critical in getting your puppy to feel safe and confident in his new surroundings. Spend time with your new arrival, talk to him often in a reassuring manner. Introduce him to his den and toys, slowly allow him to explore and show him around the house – once you have puppy-proofed it.

Lab puppies are extremely curious - and amusing, you might be surprised at his reactions to everyday objects (in the UK you only have to think of the hugely popular Andrex advert to know this is true). Puppies explore by sniffing and using their mouths, so don't scold for chewing. Instead, put objects you don't want chewed out of reach and replace them with chew toys.

If you have other animals, introduce them slowly and in supervised sessions on neutral territory or outdoors where there is space so neither feels threatened - preferably once the pup has got used to his new surroundings, not as soon as you walk through the door. Gentleness and patience are the keys to these first few days, so don't over-face him. Have a special, gentle puppy voice and use his name often in a pleasant, encouraging manner. Never use his name to scold or he will associate it with bad things. The sound of his name should **always** make him want to pay attention to you as something good is going to happen - praise, food, playtime, and so on.

Resist the urge to pick the puppy up all the time – not matter how irresistible he is! Let him explore on his own legs, encouraging a little independence. One of the most important things at this stage is to ensure that your puppy has enough sleep – which is nearly all of the time - no matter how much you want to play with him or watch his antics when awake.

If you haven't decided what to call your new puppy yet, 'Shadow' might be a good suggestion, as he or she will follow you everywhere! Many puppies from different breeds do this, but Labradors like to stick close to their owners – both as puppies and adults. Our website receives many emails from worried new owners. Here are some of the most common concerns:

- My puppy won't stop crying or whining
- My puppy is shivering
- My puppy won't eat
- My puppy is very timid
- My puppy follows me everywhere, she won't let me out of her sight
- My puppy sleeps all the time, is this normal?

These behaviours are quite common at the beginning. They are just a young pup's reaction to leaving his mother and littermates and entering into a strange new world. It is normal for puppies to sleep most of the time, just like babies. It is also normal for some puppies to whine a lot during the first couple of days. A few puppies might not whine at all. If they are confident and have been very well socialised and partly housetrained by the breeder, settling in will be much easier.

Make your new pup as comfortable as possible, ensuring he has a warm (but not too hot), quiet den away from drafts, where he is not pestered by children or other pets. Handle him gently, while giving him plenty of time to sleep. During the first couple of nights try your best to ignore the pitiful cries, but you should still get up in the middle of the night to take him into the garden or yard. However, if you pick up or play with your pup every time he cries, he will learn that this behaviour gives him the reward of your attention.

A puppy will think of you as the new mother and it is quite normal for them to want to follow you everywhere, but after a few days start to leave your pup for short periods of a few minutes, gradually building up the time. A puppy unused to being left alone for short periods can grow up to have separation anxiety - see **Chapter 8. Canine Behaviour** for more information.

If your routine means you are normally out of the house for a few hours during the day, get your puppy on a Friday or Saturday so he has at least a couple of days to adjust to his new surroundings. A far better idea is to book time off work to help your puppy settle in, if you can and, if you don't work, leave your diary free for the first couple of weeks. Helping a new pup to settle in is virtually a full-time job.

This can be a frightening time for some puppies. Is your puppy shivering with cold or is it nerves? Avoid placing your pup under stress by making too many demands. Don't allow the kids to pester the pup and, until they have learned how to handle a dog, don't allow them to pick him up unsupervised, as they could inadvertently damage his delicate little body.

If your pup won't eat, spend time gently coaxing. If he leaves his food, take it away and try it later. Don't leave it down all of the time or he may get used to turning his nose up at it. The next time you put something down for him, he is more likely to be hungry. If your puppy is crying, it is probably for one of the following reasons:

- 🐾 He is lonely
- 🐾 He is hungry
- 🐾 He wants attention from you
- 🐾 He needs to go to the toilet

If it is none of these, then physically check him over to make sure he hasn't picked up an injury. Try not to fuss over him. If he whimpers, just reassure him with a quiet word. If he cries loudly and tries to get out of his allotted area, he probably needs to go to the toilet. Even if it is the middle of the night, get up (yes, sorry, this is best) and take him outside. Praise him if he goes to the toilet.

The strongest bonding period for a puppy is between eight and 12 weeks of age. The most important factors in bonding with your puppy are TIME spent with him and PATIENCE, even when he or she makes a mess in the house or chews something he shouldn't. Remember, your Lab pup is just a baby (dog) and it takes time to learn not to do these things. Spend time with your pup and you will have a loyal friend for life. Labradors are very focused on their humans and that emotional attachment may grow to become one of the most important aspects of your life – and certainly his.

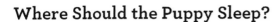

Where Should the Puppy Sleep?

Where do you want your new puppy to sleep? You cannot simply allow him or her to wander freely around the house – at least not in the beginning. Ideally, he will be in a contained area, such as a pen or crate, at night. While it is not acceptable to shut a dog in a cage all day, you can keep your puppy in a crate at night until he or she is housetrained. Even then, some adult dogs still prefer to sleep in a crate.

You also have to consider whether you want the pup to permanently sleep in your bedroom or elsewhere. If it's the bedroom, do not allow him to jump on and off beds and/or couches or race up and down stairs until he has stopped growing, as this can cause joint damage.

 Most breeders now recommend putting the puppy in a crate (or similar) on the floor next to your bed for the first two or three nights before moving him to the permanent sleeping place. Knowing you are close and being able to smell you will help overcome initial fears. He will probably still cry when you move him out of your bedroom, but that should soon stop, as he will have had those few days to get used to his new surroundings and feeling safe with you.

NOTE: Very few eight-week-old puppies can go through the night without needing to wee (and sometimes poo); their bladders and self-control simply aren't up to it. To speed up housetraining, consider getting up half way through the night from Day One for the first week or so to let your pup outside for a wee. Just pick him up, take him outside with the minimum of fuss, praise the wee and put him back into the crate. After that, he should be able to last for around six hours, so set your alarm for an early morning call, and by the age of three months, a seven-hour stretch without accidents is realistic, if you've been vigilant with the daily housetraining.

We don't recommend letting your new pup sleep on the bed. He will not be housetrained and also a puppy needs to learn his place in the household and have his own den. It's up to you whether you decide to let him on the bed when he's older – although do you really want to share your bed with a fully-grown 50-odd pound Labrador that may well have collected mud, grass, burrs, insects, etc. while on his daily walks?

If you do allow your dog to sleep in the bedroom but not on the bed, be aware that Labradors -like most other dogs - snuffle, snore, fart and, if not in a crate, pad around the bedroom in the middle of the night and come up to the bed to check you are still there! None of this is conducive to a good night's sleep.

While it is not good to leave a dog alone all day, it is also not healthy to spend 24 hours a day together. He becomes too reliant on you and this increases the chances of separation anxiety when you do have to leave him. A Labrador puppy used to being on his own every night is less likely to develop attachment issues, so consider this when deciding where he should sleep. Our dog sleeps in his own bed in our bedroom and also has separation anxiety. Any future dogs we have will sleep in a separate room from us after the first couple of nights – no matter how hard that is in the beginning when the puppy whimpers.

If you decide you definitely do want your pup to sleep in the bedroom from Day One, put him in a crate or similar with a soft blanket covering part of the crate initially. Put newspapers inside or set your alarm clock as very few pups are able to last the night without urinating.

Advice from the Breeders

We asked a number of breeders what essential advice they would give to new owners of Labrador puppies, and if any surprises were in store for new owners. They had lots of tips and advice about puppy proofing the home and garden or yard.

Hilary and Wayne Hardman, of Larwaywest Labradors, Dorset: "Be prepared! Do your homework, and don't be afraid to ask questions of the breeder, who should have already supplied plenty of information about what to expect and do when you first take your puppy home. There is a lot to do before bringing your puppy home. I could, and indeed have, written a booklet on it which I give my puppy buyers several weeks before they collect their puppy. There are many dangers, including poisonous substances to be aware of, never drop your puppy, over-exercising...the list goes on and on.

"Some people, if ill-prepared, do not realise that Labradors are not born trained, not even half-trained! They have the raw materials to BE trained and learn self-discipline, but the owner must put in the work and training if they wish to have a well-adjusted, obedient and trustworthy member of the family."

Stephen and Jane Armstrong, of Carnamaddy Labradors, County Antrim, Northern Ireland: "Give the puppy time to explore its new surroundings do not over-feed. Make sure that there are no electric leads and curtain cords within reach or anything that could be hazardous. Puppies use their mouths to explore."

Colin Hinkley, Sanglier Labradors, East Sussex: "Watch out for exposed cables and small children's toys that puppies could swallow. Don't let them jump up and off from furniture to protect hips and elbows, be aware of plants (indoor and outdoor) that could be poisonous, and make sure larger dogs don't harm them. Housetraining should not take very long, as long as you are consistent and don't ask too much of them as babies. Don't ask them to do anything they are not capable of doing."

Sharon Jarvis, of Paulsharo Labradors, Lincolnshire: "Don't let the pup jump on and off of furniture, in and out of the car or up and down stairs, as these things will damage their hips and elbows causing problems in later life – and don't over-exercise. Get the pup out even before inoculations (carried only); this is the start of being socialised. Be consistent."

(Photo courtesy of Sharon Jarvis).

"Keep electrical wires away from pups and don't leave them unattended for a minute when not in the crate. If you leave them and they get into mischief, you only have yourself to blame, not the puppy. Teething - pups need to chew, and hopefully not your expensive shoes! I wet an old tea towel (dish towel) and tie a knot in the middle, so you have a sausage shape with a knot. I then freeze it and give it to puppy - it relieves sore gums and the need to chew. I also give them raw carrots from the fridge. Bongela (used for teething babies) also helps, just smear it on their gums.

"My puppies are all trained to a recall whistle before they leave me. It's the most important lesson learned and the owners will never have a problem with a pup not coming back."

Christine Eynon, of Baileylane Labradors, Herefordshire, has a number of tips: "Always see Mum and siblings in the home environment to see what you are getting and what size the pup will be. Make sure you can afford puppy food and vet bills and that you have the time to train and devote to puppy, who will be with you 12 plus years, hopefully. Never bring a puppy into a very young family and never leave a pup or dog with young children unless supervised. Realise how much time a puppy needs and deserves and how much they grow."

(Photo courtesy of Christine Eynon).

"Give puppy a space of its own, make puppy secure with blanket, hot water bottle, clock or music and do not take puppy to bed with you, but let it sleep near if necessary until it feels secure, and then move it further away.

"Always be consistent. Be aware of poisonous plants and dangerous substances around, as Lab puppies will eat anything. Put shoes, keys, glasses, mobiles, etc. up high. I have lost one mobile, a pair of glasses and a set of keys to my puppy - expensive!"

Kirsty Jones, of Serengoch Labradors, Mid Wales, agrees: "If it is in their reach, it is fair game! Remove anything that you do not want the puppy to get at, puppies explore with their mouths – they do not mean to chew those £300 glasses, they are curious! Set the puppy up to succeed, not fail. Also, new owners shouldn't be afraid to ask questions of the breeder.

"One of the things which surprises new owners is just how much a puppy sleeps! We always advise owners to let the pup sleep as much as is needed and to give the puppy somewhere quiet where they won't be disturbed. Puppies need to sleep to help them develop."

Nadine Lapskas, of Trencrom Kennels, Bournemouth, bred her first litter last year: "Our pups left at eight weeks nearly housetrained and the new owners all stated within a couple of weeks they were fully trained in their new homes. One tip is to be consistent, look for signs they need to go toilet to support their training. Also, ensure the puppy has company the first couple of days to help settle. Like a child, you need to proof your home as puppies will chew and pick up anything."

Caroline Smith, of Flyenpyg Labradors, Lancashire jokes: "Make sure all electrical wires are hidden away, not just covered up. A puppy has a special built-in sensor in its muzzle that finds and destroys cables, especially phone chargers. It's a skill they have! Things about Labradors pups that surprise their owners are the amount of poop they produce, the noise a puppy emits on its first night and the razor sharp teeth."

Nicola Smith, of Geowins Labradors, who has bred Labs for 18 years: "I always do an advisory sheet outlying many aspects, in short: teach them early their boundaries within the home and teach them early the front door rule, i.e. not to run out watching what they eat whilst out and about as labs can be greedy as we know. If the puppy is lethargic and not eating, be cautious. Although mine always have their first injection before they leave, you never know."

Andrew Baker of Saffronlyn Gundogs, South Yorkshire: "Labradors are notorious chewers and will check everything out with their mouths. Keep out of their reach anything that could be poisonous or dangerous to their health. Make sure that the garden is puppy-proof and that they can't get out or crawl under anything. That pair of designer shoes that cost a fortune, keep them out of the way unless you want them chewed up. Provide plenty of toys, plenty of chews and a bed to call its own. The puppy will soon get to know what it can and can't do.

"By their very nature, Labrador puppies are inquisitive and have lots of energy. They are quick learners and I think that is one of the things that new owners are amazed about. My little 10-week-old bitch will sit and stay until I tell her to go to her food. They are gorgeous."

Guy Bunce, of Dizzywaltz Labradors, Berkshire: "My top tip is that time is your best friend. Think along the lines that bringing a puppy home is the same as bringing a new-born baby home. This formative time is crucial for both training and relationship building. We would not consider a new owner who was not prepared to take time off work or who could not provide constant company and supervision for the first two weeks."

Also, to assure a smooth transition for the puppy between breeder and new owner, the new owner should provide a 'smelly' item of clothing to the breeder. We recommended that the new owner

wears a T-shirt in bed for a few nights and then gives it to us and we then let the puppy sleep on it. The T-shirt goes home with the puppy.

"This not only gets the pup used to the smell of their new owner and home, but also provides a sense of security when the pup gets home as, if he or she is allowed to sleep on the T-shirt, it also smells of their littermates and Mum." Guy added: "However much we warn new owners, they are always surprised by the energy the new addition to their house has."

Photo of Tinkerbelle courtesy of Guy Bunce and Chloe Spencer.

Katrina Byrne, of Glenhugo Labradors, South Aberdeenshire: "You should try to remember that the puppies have been taken away from their Mum and siblings, so will be confused and a little lost. We always give the new owners a blanket that smells of Mum and litter to make the transition a little easier."

New breeder Lynn Aungier, of Alatariel Labradors, Surrey: "A tired puppy is a happy puppy; stimulation from toys, play and sensible exercise is essential. Socialisation to sights, sounds and experiences is one of the most important things a new owner needs to be thinking about to make sure they have a well-adjusted, confident dog. Don't allow behaviour that may be cute and funny in a small puppy that you would not like in an adult dog, it is far harder to untrain an unwanted behaviour than to stop it in the first place.

"One of the things which surprise new owners about Labrador pups is how much time they need in the early days and weeks; they need to be taught to settle and be still. Initially, we found how 'bitey' Pip was a real challenge, so teaching her 'off' and bite inhibition were the first things we did."

Trudy Williams, of Yaffleswood Labradors, West Sussex: "Spend time with the pup, start socialisation before all of their jabs (carrying outside near traffic, into shops, past schools, etc.). and don't over-exercise, especially with children and other dogs.

"I recently had a text from a first-time dog owning friend who had picked up an eight- week-old pup. After a week they said that they were frightened of the pup because it kept biting their trouser legs. I told them to tuck them in their socks. People don't realise about the nipping and biting or how much effort is required in lead training. Another thing that is underestimated is the level of destruction a Labrador can wreak with its chewing, which can continue up to 18 months or two years of age."

Elizabeth Halsall, of Lisouletta Labradors, Surrey: "My owners are supplied with an extensive puppy pack that lists what to beware of in the first week or so. As puppies grow up, they like to chew especially, so I do try to warn people to put their precious items away. The amount of work a puppy creates can be overwhelming, especially if you have a very young family and I sometimes don't think people appreciate that. I was very keen to understand my owners' lifestyles and if they had owned a dog before and knew the pitfalls. My contract stated that if anyone was unable to cope for any reason to contact me and I would take the puppy and rehome for them."

Jenny Dobson, of Lakemeadow Labradors, South Yorkshire shares her 50 years' experience of Labrador puppies: "Remember this puppy is only a baby, and do not expect too much too soon. It will need you to provide food, water, care, somewhere to sleep, firm guidelines as to what behaviour is acceptable to you and what is not! It is totally dependent on you to provide a caring and stable environment in which it can grow and develop.

"Be aware that, at least initially, this tiny creature is going to disrupt your routine totally and make lots of demands on you. However, as you develop a bond with your puppy its demands will not feel as onerous. Maintain a relationship with your breeder, and if in doubt about anything, contact them.

"Be vigilant to dangers, e.g. children picking puppies up and trying to carry them, electric cables that can get chewed, leaving doors or gates open, leaving items - particularly valuable items, mobiles, glasses, etc. - lying around that curious puppies will pick up, leaving pups unsupervised in gardens (dog thefts appear to be on the increase), etc. Use your common sense!

"Be prepared for (at least a few) disturbed nights. If your puppy is unhappy, he will let you know vocally - generally very loudly and at four in the morning. I include advice and tips on how to train your puppy to settle at night in my Puppy Pack. Puppies, from about six or seven weeks old until they get their second teeth, turn into piranhas! I always give puppy purchasers advice on how to handle puppy play biting, which can be very challenging, particularly to families with small children."

Sarah Edwards, of Fernwills Labradors, Essex: "Labradors are huge chewers and just want to put everything and anything in their mouths. The most important thing to make sure is all the electronic wires are out of reach or safely tucked away in specialised covers etc. Wires are so inviting! Make sure anything else precious is raised up at least a metre. Watch out for wagging tails of destruction when hot cups of tea are on the coffee table. Don't leave shoes, bags, food within reach of a Labrador puppy (or an adult for that matter). Slippers are a classic favourite!"

Julie McDonough, of Rangemaster Working Gundogs, Powys: "Your puppy should be fit and healthy when you bring it home, preferably seen by the breeder's vet prior to leaving the breeders: no mucky eyes or badly upset tummies. All puppies can get stressed when leaving their breeder and slight runny stools can be experienced, but not heavy diarrhoea - and certainly no blood in the stools. New owners should get their puppy vet-checked promptly by their own vet to ensure the pup is free from any defects or illness. Most good breeders sell their pups with insurance which covers the pup for a few weeks, and also a Contract of Sale; any major defects and the breeder should be contacted without delay.

"Every puppy should get used to a collar of some type, but please remove it if the puppy is left unattended, as collars can be caught up on all sorts, such as paws - and in one particular instance, a radiator thermostat. One of my puppy owners came home to a flooded kitchen after the pup got caught up and pulled the radiator off the wall!"

"I think most puppy owners are surprised on how much puppies sleep through the first couple of weeks. They are also surprised by how sharp their young teeth are until they lose their puppy teeth."

Kate Smith, of Ardenbrook Labradors, Warwickshire: "As an Assured Breeder, all puppies' owners have extensive guidance provided in their Puppy Pack, and there is good advice on the Kennel Club website. Joining The Puppy Plan provides lots of useful advice and guidance: www.thepuppyplan.com

"A lot of people think they need to 'wear out' a Labrador puppy with lots of exercise in order to get it to settle and sleep. In fact, this is the worst thing they can do – the Labrador is an active breed, so the more exercise you give your puppy the more it will want. This is a breed that is built for stamina and as an adult will run all day without effort. Giving a puppy too much exercise can result in permanent joint damage, so following the five-minute rule is important (five minutes of exercise per month of age, up to twice a day). In fact, mental stimulation will tire out a puppy far more than exercise, so little training games and activity toys are far more effective with this intelligent breed.

"Regarding surprises for new owners: first of all (and I'm sure this applies to any puppy), they don't follow the rules! Yes, do lots of reading, but don't expect things to go by the book. Your puppy will have its own ideas. A good breeder will be there to help you through the early weeks – I have a secret Facebook group for just this purpose, so someone will always be there with help and advice."

Liz Vivash, of Wightfyre Labradors, Isle of Wight: "We give a whole pack of information to the new forever parents, and give them lots of advice re cables, toys, steps, stairs, couches, food, etc. But we know that it is easier for them to read it all at home, as they will not remember all that we tell them. I did have one family, though, who videoed me telling them stuff!"

Avril Bartolomy, of Prestonfield Labradors, East Sussex, adds: "Give the puppy a bed which he or she will treat as their 'safe area'. One thing which surprises some new owners is how much attention their new puppy needs."

USA breeder Robin Anderson, of Grampian Labradors, New England, says: "The first item I always insist on new puppy owners having in duplicate is a crate the dog can grow into. One is for the house and one is for the car. They are taking an infant home, so not only should the infant be properly restrained in the car, it also needs a safe place for the home. The second bit of advice is to put the house crate next to the side of the adult's bed who is the lightest sleeper. If they can prevent the 'wind up' at night, and soothe the new baby back to sleep, housetraining at night will be quiet and smooth. There will be no 2am trips outside in any weather with an eight to nine-week old puppy because the humans haven't let the puppy train them to spring him from puppy prison!

"In a house there are dangers lurking in every corner, including electrical cords, house plants, socks, and LEGO bricks. I recommend a new puppy owner crawl on hands and knees to look at the home from the perspective of the puppy and puppy proof it before they take their precious cargo into the house. Once people are on board with Grampian, there aren't too many surprises when they get the puppy home. I send weekly homework to the clients for eight weeks before the puppy goes home with them. Maybe the biggest surprise, especially if this is a first-time dog family, is how much love is felt over the new addition. Until you have your first dog, you simply can't imagine how hard you fall in love."

Teresa Gordy-Brown, of Ashland Labradors, Tennessee, has bred Labradors since 1984 and says: "Keep the puppy isolated away from strange dogs or places where dogs frequent, such as dog parks, pet stores and so forth. Follow your breeder's advice on timing to start puppy training classes (I prefer 12 to 16 weeks).

"The first place you should ever take your puppy to besides home is the vet's office for a complete health exam. Please do not delay this! Why take a puppy home for a week, become attached and then only find out later you have a health issue? Keep puppy OFF the floor at the vet's office and do not allow other pet owners there to touch your puppy. It is possible that they just brought in a sick dog with a contagious virus. Better safe than sorry.

"Once you are home with puppy, please make sure the puppy has no access to electrical cords and that you restrict his area to either an exercise pen or laundry room. Remember puppies CHEW. They pee, poop, yelp and bark. Anything you do not want destroyed is totally dependent upon the human supervising that puppy.

"A puppy needs to be a part of your human pack for optimum socialization and training. I personally prefer the puppy close by in an adjoining room from my bedroom in the evening so I can hear him and he can hear me. I don't feel it is necessary for me to always be in the same room as the puppy. He needs to learn it is okay to be alone and that I will always return.

"One thing which surprises some owners is how quickly they adjust. Most fear the puppy will be sad and miss his mother and littermates. Some do take a day to adjust, but it never ceases to amaze me that the number one thing everyone reports back to me is just how quickly the puppies settle into the new environment and routine."

Sandra Underhill, of Labs To Love, California, makes an excellent point that highlights one further reason why it is worth choosing a good breeder: "The well-socialized puppy is so much easier to integrate into your family than a puppy pulled out of an outdoor kennel and taken home."

She adds: "Too much food or any change in diet can cause loose stools, so feed less than what the food bag recommends."

Vaccinations and Worming

It is **always** a good idea to have your Labrador checked out by a vet within a few days of picking him up. Some Puppy Contracts even stipulate that the dog should be examined by a vet within a certain time frame – often 48 hours. This is to everyone's benefit and, all being well, you are safe in the knowledge that - at least at the time of purchase - your puppy is healthy.

Keep your pup away from other dogs in the waiting room as he will not be fully protected against canine diseases until the vaccination schedule is complete. All puppies need these injections; very occasionally a pup has a reaction, but this is very rare and the advantages of immunisation far outweigh the disadvantages.

Vaccinations

An unimmunised puppy is at risk every time he meets other dogs as he has no protection against potentially fatal diseases – another point is that it is unlikely a pet insurer will cover an unvaccinated dog. It should be stressed that vaccinations are generally quite safe and side effects are uncommon. If your Labrador is unlucky enough to be one of the **very few** that suffers an adverse reaction, here are the signs to look out for; a pup may exhibit one or more of these:

MILD REACTION - Sleepiness, irritability and not wanting to be touched. Sore or a small lump at the place where he was injected. Nasal discharge or sneezing. Puffy face and ears.

SEVERE REACTION - Anaphylactic shock. A sudden and quick reaction, usually before leaving the vet's, which causes breathing difficulties. Vomiting, diarrhoea, staggering and seizures.

A severe reaction is rare. There is a far greater risk of your Labrador either being ill and/or spreading disease if he does not have the injections.

The usual schedule is for the pup to have his first vaccination at six to eight weeks of age. This will protect him from a number of diseases in one shot. In the UK these are Distemper, Canine Parvovirus (Parvo), Infectious Canine Hepatitis (Adenovirus) and Kennel Cough (Bordetella). In the US this is known as DHPP. Puppies in the US also need vaccinating separately against Rabies. There are optional vaccinations for Coronavirus and - depending on where you live and if your dog is regularly around woods or forests - Lyme Disease.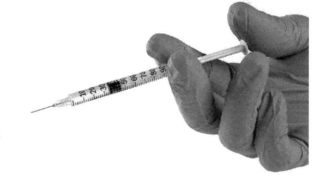

The puppy requires a second vaccination at 10 to 12 and the third and last is done at 14 to 16 weeks (USA). In the UK, the first vaccination is usually at six weeks of age (or eight) and the second one four weeks later.

Diseases such as Parvo and Kennel Cough are highly contagious and you should not let your new arrival mix with other dogs - unless they are your own and have already been vaccinated - until a week after his last vaccination, otherwise he will not be fully immunised. Parvovirus can also be transmitted by fox faeces.

You shouldn't take your new puppy to places where unvaccinated dogs might have been, like the local park. This does not mean that your puppy should be isolated - far from it. This is an important time for socialisation. It is OK for the puppy to mix with another dog which you 100% know has been vaccinated and is up to date with its annual boosters. Perhaps invite a friend's dog round to play in your yard/garden to begin the socialisation process.

Once your puppy is fully immunised, you have a window of a few weeks when it's the best time to introduce him to as many new experiences - dogs, people, traffic, noises, other animals, etc. This critical period before the age of four and a half or five months is when he is at his most receptive. Socialisation should not stop at that age, but continue for the rest of your dog's life; but it is particularly important to socialise young puppies.

Currently, in the UK, your dog will currently need a booster injection every year of his life. The vet should give you a record card or send you a reminder, but it's also a good idea to keep a note of the date in your diary. Tests have shown that the Parvovirus vaccination gives most animals at least seven years of immunity, while the Distemper jab provides immunity for at least five to seven years and it is now believed that vaccinating every year can stress a dog's immune system. In the US, many vets now recommend that you take your dog for a 'titer' test once he has had his initial puppy vaccinations and one-year booster.

Titers

These are now being used by some breeders and owners, mainly in the US. The thinking behind them is to avoid a dog having to have annual vaccinations. It's fair to say that the verdict is still out in the UK. One English vet commented that a titer is only good for the day on which it is carried out, and that antibody levels may naturally drop off shortly afterwards, possibly leaving the animal at risk. He added that the dog would still need vaccinating against Leptospirosis.

To 'titer or 'titering' is to take a blood sample from a dog (or cat) to determine whether he or she has enough antibodies to guarantee immunity against a particular disease, usually Parvovirus, Distemper and Adenovirus (Canine Hepatitis). If so, then an annual injection is not needed. Titering is not recommended for Leptospirosis, Bordetella or Lyme Disease, as these vaccines provide only short-term protection, and many states still require proof of a Rabies vaccination.

The vet can test the blood at his or her clinic without sending off the sample, thereby keeping costs down for the owner. A titer for Parvovirus and Distemper currently costs around $100 or less. Titer levels are given as ratios and show how many times blood can be diluted before no antibodies are detected. So, if blood can be diluted 1,000 times and still show antibodies, the ratio would be 1:1000, which is a 'strong titer,' while a titer of 1:2 would be 'weak.' A strong (high) titer means that your dog has enough antibodies to fight off that specific disease and is immune from infection. A weak titer means that you and your vet should discuss revaccination - even then your dog might have some reserve forces known as 'memory cells' which will provide antibodies when needed.

(If you are going on holiday and taking your dog to kennels, check whether the kennel accepts titer records; many don't).

Worming

All puppies need worming (technically, deworming). A good breeder will give the puppies their first dose of worming medication at around two weeks old, then probably again at five and eight weeks before they leave the litter – or even more often. Get the details and inform your vet exactly what treatment, if any, your pup has already had.

The main worms affecting puppies are roundworm and tapeworm. In certain areas of the US, the dreaded heartworm can also pose a risk. Roundworm can be transmitted from a puppy to humans – most often children - and can in severe cases cause blindness, or miscarriage in women, so it's important to keep up to date with worming.

Worms in puppies are quite common; they are often picked up through their mother's milk. If you have children, get them into the habit of washing their hands after they have been in contact with the puppy – lack of hygiene is the reason why children are most susceptible. Most vets recommend worming a puppy once a month until he is six months old, and then around every two to three months.

In the US, dogs are given a monthly heartworm pill. It should be given every month when there is no heavy frost (as frost kills mosquitos that carry the disease); giving it all year round gives the best protection. The heartworm pill is by prescription only and deworms the dog monthly for heart worm, round, hook, and whip worm.

If your Labrador is regularly out and about running through woods and fields, it is important to stick to a regular worming schedule, as he is more likely to pick up worms than one which spends less time in the Great Outdoors.

Fleas can pass on tapeworms to dogs, but a puppy would not normally be treated unless it is known for certain he has fleas - and then only with caution. You need to know the weight of your Lab and then speak to your vet about the safest treatment to rid your puppy of the parasites.

It is not usually worth buying a cheap worming or flea treatment from a supermarket, as they are usually far less effective than more expensive vet-recommended preparations, such as **Drontal**.

Many people living in the US have contacted our website claiming the parasite treatment **Trifexis** has caused severe side effects, and even death, to their dogs. Although this evidence is only anecdotal, you might want consider avoiding Trifexis to be on the safe side - even if your vet recommends it.

6. Crate Training and Housetraining

If you are unfamiliar with them, crates may seem like a cruel punishment for a lovable Labrador puppy. They are, however, becoming increasingly popular to help with housetraining (potty training), to give you and the puppy short breaks from each other and to keep the dog safe at night or when you are not there. Breeders, trainers, behaviourists and people who show dogs all use them and, as you will read, many Labrador breeders believe they are also a valuable aid in helping to housetrain your dog.

Getting Your Dog Used to a Crate

If you decide to use a crate, then remember that it is not a prison to restrain the dog. It should only be used in a humane manner and time should be spent to make the puppy or adult dog feel like the crate is his own safe little haven. If the door is closed on the crate, your puppy must ALWAYS have access to water while inside. If used correctly and if time is spent getting the puppy used to the crate, it can be a godsend.

Crates may not be suitable for every dog. Labradors are not like hamsters or pet mice which can adapt to life in a cage; they thrive on being involved and living with others. Being caged all day is a miserable existence, and a crate should never be used as a means of confinement because you are out of the house all day.

If you do decide to use one - perhaps to put your dog in for short periods while you leave the house, or at night - the best place for it is in the corner of a room away from cold draughts or too much heat. And because Labradors like to be near their family, which is you and/or the other dogs, don't put the crate in a utility room or garage away from everybody else or the dog will feel lonely and isolated.

Dogs with thick coats like the Labrador can overheat indoors. When you buy a crate, get a wire one (like the one pictured) which is robust and allows air to pass through, not a plastic one which may get very hot. If you cover the crate, don't cover it 100% or you will restrict the flow of air.

The crate should be large enough to allow your dog to stretch out flat on his side without being cramped, and he should be able to turn round easily and to sit up without hitting his head on the top. A fully-grown Labrador will require a 42" crate (a 36" crate may be large enough for a small Lab), whereas a puppy can start off in a 24" crate. If you only intend buying one, get one of the larger sizes and divide it until your puppy grows into the full-sized crate.

Here is Midwest Pet Products sizing guide for crates, based on the anticipated adult weight of your dog: www.midwestpetproducts.com/midwestdogcrates/dog-crate-sizes.

You have a number of options when it comes to deciding where to put the crate. Perhaps consider leaving it in the kitchen or another room (preferably one with an easy-to-clean surface) where there are people during the day. If you have noisy children, you have to strike the balance between putting the crate somewhere where he won't feel isolated, yet is able to get some peace and quiet from the kids. You could then bring it into your bedroom for the first few nights until the puppy settles; this is now increasingly recommended by many breeders. Many advise putting the crate right next to the bed for the first couple of nights or so – even raised up next to the bed, so the puppy doesn't feel alone. A couple of nights with broken sleep is worth it if it helps the young pup to settle in, as he or she will often then sleep thought the night quicker. After that, you could put the crate in a nearby place where the dog can hear or smell you at night-time - such as the landing - or you could leave it in the same place, e.g. the kitchen, 100% of the time.

It is only natural for any dog to whine in the beginning. He is not crying because he is in a cage. He would cry if he had the freedom of the room and he was alone - he is crying because he is separated from you. However, with patience and the right training, he will get used to it and some come to regard the crate as a favourite place. Some owners make the crate their dog's only bed, so he feels comfortable and safe in there. Crates aren't for every owner or every Labrador, but used correctly, they can:

- 🐾 Create a canine den
- 🐾 Be a useful housetraining tool
- 🐾 Give you and the dog a bit of a break from each other
- 🐾 Limit access to the rest of the house while your dog learns the household rules
- 🐾 Be a safe way to transport your dog in a car

If you use a crate right from Day One, initially cover half of it with a blanket to help your puppy regard it as a den. He also needs bedding and it's a good idea to put a chew in as well. A large crate may allow your dog to eliminate at one end and sleep at the other, but this may slow down his housetraining. So, if you are buying a crate which will last for a fully grown Labrador, get adjustable crate dividers – or make them yourself (or put a box inside) - to block part of it off while he is small so that he feels safe and secure, which he won't do in a very big crate.

You can order a purpose-made crate mat or a 'vet bed' to cover the bottom of the crate and then put some bedding on top. Vet beds are widely used by vets to make dogs feel warm, secure and cosy when receiving treatment, but they're just as good for using in the home. They are made from double-strength polyester with high fibre density to retain extra heat and allow air to permeate. They also have drainage properties, so if your pup has an accident, he or she will stay dry, and they are a good choice for older dogs as the added heat is soothing for ageing muscles and joints, and for any dogs recovering from surgery or treatment. Another added advantage of a vet bed is that you can wash it often and it shouldn't deteriorate.

Bear in mind that a bored or lively Labrador puppy is a little chew machine so, at this stage, don't spend a lot of money on a fluffy floor covering for the crate as it is likely to get destroyed. Many breeders recommend **not** putting newspapers in one part of the crate, as this encourages the pup to soil the crate. If you have bought your puppy from a reputable breeder, she will probably already have started the housetraining process, and an eight-week-old pup should be able to last several hours without needing the toilet. It's then a case of setting your alarm clock to get up after five or six hours to let the pup out to do his or her business for the first week or so. You might not like it, but this will certainly speed up housetraining.

Once you've got your crate, you'll need to learn how to use it properly so that it becomes a safe, comfortable den for your dog and not a prison. Here's a tried-and-tested method of getting your dog firstly to accept a crate, and then to actually want to spend time in there.

Initially a pup might not be too happy about going inside, but he will be a lot easier to crate train than an adult dog which has got used to having the run of your house. These are the first steps:

1. Drop a few tasty puppy treats around and then inside the crate.

2. Put your puppy's favourite bedding or toy in there.

3. Keep the door open.

4. Feed your puppy's meals inside the crate. Again, keep the door open.

Place a chew or treat INSIDE the crate and close the door while your puppy is OUTSIDE the crate. He will be desperate to get in there! Open the door, let him in and praise him for going in. Fasten a long-lasting chew inside the crate and leave the door open. Let your puppy go inside to spend some time eating the chew.

IMPORTANT: Always remove your dog's collar before leaving him unattended in a crate. A collar can get caught in the wire mesh.

After a while, close the crate door and feed him some treats through the mesh while he is in there. At first just do it for a few seconds at a time, then gradually increase the time. If you do it too fast, he will become distressed. Slowly build up the amount of time he is in the crate. For the first few days, stay in the room, then gradually leave for a short time, first one minute, then three, then 10, 30 and so on.

Next Steps

5. Put your dog in his crate at regular intervals during the day - maximum two hours.

6. Don't crate only when you are leaving the house. Place the dog in the crate while you are home as well. Use it as a 'safe' zone.

7. By using the crate both when you are home and while you are gone, your dog becomes comfortable there and not worried that you won't come back, or that you are leaving him alone. This helps to prevent separation anxiety later in life.

8. Give him a chew and remove his collar, tags and anything else which could become caught in an opening or between the bars.

9. Make it very clear to any children that the crate is NOT a playhouse for them, but a 'special room' for the dog.

10. Although the crate is your dog's haven and safe place, it must not be off-limits to humans. You should be able to reach inside at any time.

The next point is important:

11. Do not let your dog immediately out of the crate if he barks or whines, or he will think that this is the key to opening the door. Wait until the barking or whining has stopped for at least 10 seconds before letting him out.

A puppy should not be left in a crate for long periods except at night time, and even then he has to get used to it first. Whether or not you decide to use a crate, the important thing to remember is that those first few days and weeks are a critical time for your puppy. Try and make him feel as safe and comfortable as you can. Bond with him, while at the same time gently and gradually introducing him to new experiences and other animals and humans.

A crate is a good way of transporting your Labrador in the car. Put the crate on the shady side of the interior and make sure it can't move around; put the seatbelt around it if necessary. If it's very sunny and the top of the crate is wire mesh, cover part of it so your dog has some shade and put the windows up and the air conditioning on.

Never leave your Labrador unattended in a vehicle; he can quickly overheat - or be targeted by thieves.

Allowing your dog to roam freely inside the car is not a safe option, particularly if you - like me – are a bit of a 'lead foot' on the brake and accelerator! Don't let him put his head out of the window either, he can slip and hurt himself and the wind pressure can cause an ear infection or bits of dust, insects, etc. to fly into his eyes. Special travel crates are useful for the car, or for taking your dog to the vet's or a show. Try and pick one with holes or mesh in the side to allow free movement of air (pictured), rather than a solid plastic one, in which your Labrador can soon get hot.

Labrador Breeders on Crates

Traditionally crates have been more popular in America than in the UK and the rest of Europe, but opinion is slowly changing and more owners are starting to use crates on both sides of the Atlantic. This is perhaps because people's perception of a crate is shifting from regarding it as a cage to thinking of it as a safe haven as well as a useful tool to help with housetraining and transportation, when used correctly.

Without exception, the breeders in this book believe that a crate should not be used for punishment or to imprison a dog all day while you are away from the house. This is cruel for any dog, but particularly a Labrador, who loves to be with his humans. As you will read, opinions vary as to how long a puppy should be left in a crate. The keys to successful crate training are firstly to spend time enticing the dog into the crate so that he or she starts to enjoy spending time in there. Remember that most puppies will not initially like being in a crate and patience, along with the right techniques, are required. Secondly, never leave your Labrador in there if he or she is distressed by it.

Here's what the breeders say, starting with Teresa Gordy-Brown, Ashland Labradors, Tennessee, USA: "Crate training is a wonderful aide to help housetrain puppies, but should only be used as a special place with a treat and toys when you are too busy to watch after the puppy, or at bedtime. Also, when acclimated to a crate at an early age, you are giving your Labrador a place of his own when he needs to get away and nap or when company is over. Crate training also helps to eliminate separation anxiety.

"The use of a crate should be limited to only short periods of time that you cannot watch your Labrador - especially younger Labradors that have not earned the trust to be loose in the house unattended. We also use the crate at night for puppies during the housetraining routine. This way they are confined and cannot possible wander around to pee or poop in another room. Most crate-trained Labradors love their crate. The door can be removed or left open and the Lab will go right in on his own for nap time."

Robin Anderson, Grampian Labradors, New England, USA: "We always recommend using a crate for sleeping and unsupervised time as well as car rides. Most of our eight-week-old puppies can last from about 11pm until 5am or 6 am in the crate overnight, and they need around two-hour intervals when they are napping to be crated for their own safety, as well as peace during naptime. Healthy growing pups will sleep for around 16 hours out of every 24 hours, so plan wakeful times out of the crate and sleep times in the crate."

Sarah Edwards, Fernwills Labradors, Essex, is one of the three UK breeders involved in this book who does not use a crate: "We have never used crates ourselves, however, we do recommend them, as we know they can work exceptionally well. Labradors grow fast so larger crates are recommended. This can be a problem when they are tiny pups as the space is so big that they feel happy to do their business at one end if left in there long enough."

Pictured is Sarah's Carpenny Leonada at Gamblegate JW, aged 12 months, bred by Mrs Penny Carpanini. Photo by Photocall.

"We always recommend owners halve the size of the crate using a cardboard wall in the early days, thereby encouraging the pup to cry out if they are requiring the toilet....don't give them too much space! Crates can also work very well if there are young children in the house, as it can be easy to define the space that the pup has to 'get away' from the children. The rule is to leave the pup alone when they are in the crate, as they want some peace and quiet. Many adult dogs still enjoy the peace and quiet of their crate in a rowdy family environment and use it just like a bed and a safe place. It is often humans who have problems with crates as they see them as 'cages'. I would never leave a pup in a crate for longer than a couple of hours alone unless it is overnight. Labradors need a lot of company and should not be left alone in general for longer than four hours."

Nicola Smith, Geowins Labradors, Surrey: "I do not use a crate, but I support any new owner that likes to and I always get the puppies used to a crate with me for practice before they go if I know the new owner wants to use one. I always say to put the puppy in there for their rest periods in the day, so they are used to being in there, even if they don't have to be."

Guy Bunce and Chloe Spencer, of Dizzywaltz Labradors, Berkshire: "All our dogs were crate trained initially for the purpose of housetraining. As soon as the dog is housetrained, the crates are no longer used and the dog is allowed free rein of the house when we are out or at night. The dog should never be left during the day in the crate longer than two hours and you should build up to this time."

Sarah Nuttall, Gamblegate Labradors, Lancashire, agrees with the two-hour rule: "All my dogs are crate trained and sleep in them through choice; I recommend initially feeding puppy in there to get him used to it. The maximum time a puppy should be left in a crate is two hours, except overnight."

Stephen Armstrong, Carnamaddy Labradors, County Antrim, Northern Ireland: "I only use a crate with attached pen for a pup when I'm going out and there's no one at home - even then it would only be for a maximum of two hours. With regard to crate training, leave the crate open for the pup to explore, toilet the pup before crating it and give it some toys to play with. Begin by leaving the pup for 10 minutes and build the time up."

Colin Hinkley, Sanglier Labradors, East Sussex: "I do use crates for up to one and a half hours at a time for puppies. After that, they need to come out to use the toilet. A crate is not to be used for punishment."

Amanda Deane, Tanronens Labradors, Lincolnshire: "I do use a crate occasionally, but mainly for safety reasons, i.e. for not chewing things they shouldn't and also, if it is with an older dog, to protect the puppy from being knocked around during play. A puppy should only be left in a crate as little time as possible. My tip for new owners would be to spend the time in getting the puppy used to a crate a bit at a time using a few titbits and always praising the puppy; the Labrador puppy will, in time, then go in willingly with the door left open."

Jenny Dobson, of Lakemeadow Labradors, South Yorkshire, has been breeding Labs since 1968: "I always recommend crate training to puppy purchasers. I only started using a crate myself about five years ago, and have found it has made puppy rearing so much less stressful. It is important to make going into the crate a positive experience and NOT a punishment, and puppies appear to appreciate having a secure den that they can retire to.

"Crates can also help facilitate housetraining, as pups are generally reluctant to soil the area in which they sleep. Crates can give peace of mind when the pups are at the 'chewing phase'. Some puppies never steal items or destroy things, but many do, and having somewhere to safely contain the puppy can be very helpful - especially if you have to go out and leave the puppy unsupervised for a time. I would suggest using a crate overnight initially and for short periods during the day, but not for periods of more than a few hours at a time."

Kate Smith, Ardenbrook Labradors, Warwickshire: "I absolutely encourage new owners to use a crate, and provide a crate training help sheet in their puppy packs. A puppy should not be left crated for more than four hours during the day (night time is different), and this should be built up gradually."

Katrina Byrne, Glenhugo Labradors, South Aberdeenshire: "We do use a crate, it is introduced into our puppy area at around four weeks and we put a blanket over the top, back and sides and it becomes a 'safe haven' for the puppies and dogs. Often, if our dogs are very tired, they will go into their crates. It's important that this is their space – you should avoid allowing children to get into the crate with them.

"Our crate door is always open for the dogs to come and go as they please, if you are shutting your dog in the crate, its essential the crate is the correct size and the dog should really only be in there for a few hours." Pictured feeling on top of the world, courtesy of Katrina, are Glenhugo Pensing Sativa Mollis (Tilly) on the left, aged four, and her daughter, Glenhugo Black Beauty (Tippy), aged two.

Trudy Williams, Yaffleswood Labradors, West Sussex: "I really advocate crate training, especially having recently worked with two eight-month-old Spaniels that were given the run of the kitchen/garden during the summer. Once winter hit they did not know the difference between inside and out, so were soiling everywhere.

"Puppy should be in the crate overnight to start; a crate also acts as security for pup. Using a crate is a way to prevent things going wrong. If I am popping out I will put pup in the crate so it is safe while I am out, and the pup is not chewing or soiling. I do the same if we are eating dinner or I am doing any jobs where I cannot supervise the pup. A crate is also a refuge from small children. During the day, a pup will only be in there for a maximum of a couple of hours at a time. Familiarity with a crate is invaluable as recently my one-year-old sliced through a tendon and has had to be restricted, so she was happy to go in the crate away from boisterous play with the other dogs.

"All pups should be made familiar with a crate in a positive way by being fed in there, having treats in there, etc. It should not be put in a crate as a means of punishment. Also avoid only putting the pup in a crate when you are going out or leaving. Make sure the pup is happy in the crate when you are around, as it will associate the crate with being left alone otherwise."

Caroline Smith, Flyenpygs Labradors, Lancashire, is another fan: "I love crates; all my puppies are happy to be in one – it's perfect for later on in life too, for convalescence or for time away from children/new puppy, etc. A crate is also brilliant for leaving a pup when you need a bath, cooking tea or sorting out the kids, and for toilet training overnight. A pup can easily do six hours at eight weeks, providing it is toileted beforehand by the breeder.

"Make the crate a happy place – feed in it, leave it open with her bed in it and she'll trot off to it when she's tired. If she's quite a sociable dog, have the crate nearer to you; if you live in a busy household, try putting it more out of the way, so she has somewhere to go for some peace."

Andrew Baker, of Saffronlyn Gundogs, South Yorkshire, has working dogs, but still uses a crate some of the time: "Yes, I do crate my Labradors, but not all the time. My older dogs aren't crated, but my two younger dogs are crated at night-time. The length of time depends on how old the dog is. My younger dogs are kennelled during the summer months and spend a good deal of their time outside." Photo of Andrew's Murphy by Caroline Bridges Photography.

Lynn Aungier, of Alatariel Labradors, Surrey, is a new breeder; her black working Labrador, Pip, has had one litter. Lynn says: "We used a crate for Pip and now for her puppies (they have individual crates). Pip used a crate at night and while we were out up to the age of about 18 months; she used to sleep in it when the door was open as well. The maximum time Pip and the puppies have ever been left alone is four hours. Up until they were all eight months I didn't like to leave them for more than two hours at a time, as I didn't like the thought of them needing the toilet. I have slowly increased this now and as the two we kept, Luna and Raven, are nearly a year old and they are OK to be left for four hours maximum.

"Crates are really good for puppies, they have their own den that they can go to and feel safe. We put blankets over three sides of our crates and they are much happier like this. Crates are good for us humans too – puppies get up to mischief if they aren't being watched, and a crate gives us somewhere that is safe while we are cooking dinner, doing the hoovering, having a shower, etc. It also gives us 'brain rest' and helps to prevent unwanted behaviour. I have found them useful when the puppy has gotten wound up and excited – in the crate with a Kong toy and they soon calm down.

"We used the crate with Pip right from day one; puppies are used to being contained in one area at a breeder's – no one would allow a whole litter the run of the house, it would be utter carnage! Make the crate their space, feed them dinner there, and reward them with a biscuit for 'going to bed.' Making the crate into a game initially and letting the puppy know that is their space pays off."

Sharon Jarvis, Paulsharo Labradors, Lincolnshire: "I have a 15-month-old dog that loves his crate and a 13-week-old bitch that loves her crate. I feed all my puppies in their crate. To start, just throw a treat in the crate giving the command "Kennel Labradors love their food! If a puppy is crying in the crate, and they are just crying to come out, only open the door when they are quiet. Use the command "Quiet" or you will be training the pup to cry to be let out. Always let the pup outside in the garden when they have just woken up or after their dinner."

Kirsty Jones, Serengoch Labradors, Mid Wales: "We use crates for all our dogs – it is a fantastic tool, especially for travelling and when the household is busy. They are fine to be left in the crate overnight, but during the day, it really should be limited to just the necessary time, e.g. if you are out of the house or if the dog would not be safe loose."

Hilary Hardman, Larwaywest Labradors, Dorset: "All our puppies are crate trained. The crate should be used as a safe house and place of rest for the puppy and used for as long as the puppy needs to be contained to avoid destructive behaviours developing when left alone. It should never be used as a place for punishment, other than for very short periods of 'time out' (no more than a couple of minutes) to help the puppy understand an undesirable behaviour is unwanted or the puppy is over-tired and fractious. Our dogs love crates; they make a bee-line for it and happily go in and lie down!"

Top 12 Housetraining Tips

How easy are Labradors to housetrain?

Well, the good news is that, according to our breeders, compared with many other breeds, the Labrador is easy to housetrain. But the catch is that the dog is only as good as his or her owners. In other words, the speed and success of housetraining often depends largely on one factor: the time and effort you are prepared to put in - especially during the first couple of weeks. The more vigilant you are during the early days, the quicker your dog will be housetrained. It's as simple as that. Taking the advice in this chapter and being consistent with your routines and repetitions is the quickest way to toilet train (potty train) your Labrador pup.

You have four big factors in your favour when it comes to housetraining:

1. Labradors are highly intelligent.
2. They are very eager to please their owners and love being praised.
3. Most would sell their own mothers for a treat.
4. A puppy's instinct is not to soil his or her own den.

From about the age of three weeks, a pup will leave his sleeping area to go to the toilet. Most good breeders will already have started the housebreaking process with their puppies, so when you pick up your little bundle of joy, all you have to do is ensure that you carry on the good work. (Photo of this handsome pup courtesy of Katrina Byrne, Glenhugo Labradors).

If you're starting from scratch when you bring

your pup home, your new arrival thinks that the whole house is his den and may not realise that this is not the place to eliminate. Therefore you need to gently and persistently teach him that it is unacceptable to make a mess inside the home. Labradors, like all dogs, are creatures of routine - not only do they like the same things happening at the same times every day, but establishing a regular routine with your dog also helps to speed up obedience and toilet training.

Dogs are also very tactile creatures, so they will pick a toilet area which feels good under their paws. Many dogs like to go on grass - but this will do nothing to improve your lawn, so you should think carefully about what area to encourage your Labrador to use. You may want to consider a small patch of gravel crushed into tiny pieces in your garden, or a corner of the garden or yard away from any attractive flower beds.

Some breeders advise against using puppy pads for any length of time as puppies like the softness of the pads, which can encourage them to eliminate on other soft areas - such as your carpets or bed. Although puppy pads are often more commonly used by people living in apartments, several breeders and owners do use puppy pads, alongside regularly taking the puppy outside to eliminate, and gradually reduce the area covered by the pads.

Follow these tips to speed up housetraining:

1. **Constant supervision** is essential for the first week or two if you are to housetrain your puppy quickly. This is why it is important to book the week or so off work when you bring him home. Make sure you are there to take him outside regularly. If nobody is there, he will learn to urinate or poo(p) inside the house.

2. **Take your pup outside at the following times:**

   🐾 As soon as he wakes – every time

   🐾 Shortly after each feed

   🐾 After a drink

   🐾 When he gets excited

   🐾 After exercise or play

   🐾 Last thing at night

   🐾 Initially every hour - whether or not he looks like he wants to go

You may think that the above list is an exaggeration, but it isn't. Housetraining a pup is almost a full-time job for the first few days. If you are serious about toilet training your puppy quickly, then clear your diary for a few days and keep your eyes firmly glued on your pup...learn to spot that expression or circling motion just before he makes a puddle - or worse – on your floor.

3. Take your Labrador to **the same place** every time, you may need to use a lead in the beginning - or tempt him there with a treat. Some say it is better to only pick him up and dump him there in an emergency, as it is better if he learns to take himself to the chosen toilet spot. Dogs naturally develop a preference for going in the same place or on the same surface. Take or lead him to the same patch every time so he learns this is his toilet area. **No pressure – be patient.** You must allow your distracted little darling time to wander around and have a good sniff before performing his duties – but do not leave him, stay around a short distance away. Sadly, puppies are not known for their powers of concentration; it may take a while for them to select the perfect bathroom!

4. **Housetraining is reward-based.** Praise him or give him a treat immediately after he has performed his duties in the chosen spot. Labradors love praise and learn quickly, and reward-based training is the most successful method for quick results.

5. **Share the responsibility.** It doesn't have to be the same person who takes the dog outside all the time. In fact it's easier if there are a couple of you, as housetraining is a very time-consuming business. Just make sure you stick to the same principles, command and patch of ground.

6. **Stick to the same routine.** Dogs understand and like routine. Sticking to the same one for mealtimes, short exercise sessions, play time, sleeping and toilet breaks will help to not only housetrain him quicker, but help him settle into his new home.

7. **Use the same word** or command when telling your puppy to go to the toilet – or while he is in the act. He will gradually associate this phrase or word with toileting and you will even be able to get him to eliminate on command after some weeks.

8. **Use your voice if you catch him in the act indoors.** A short sharp negative sound is best - NO! ACK! EH! - it doesn't matter, as long as it is loud enough to make him stop. Then start running enthusiastically towards your door, calling him into the garden and the chosen place and patiently wait until he has finished what he started indoors. It is no good scolding your dog if you find a puddle or unwanted gift in the house but don't see him do it; he won't know why you are cross with him. Only use the negative sound if you actually catch him in the act.

9. **No punishment.** Accidents will happen at the beginning, do not punish your Labrador for them. He is a baby with a tiny bladder and bowels, and housetraining takes time - it is perfectly natural to have accidents early on. Remain calm and clean up the mess with a good strong-smelling cleaner to remove the odour, so he won't be tempted to use that spot again. Dogs have a very strong sense of smell; use a special spray from your vet or a hot solution of washing powder to completely eliminate the odour. Smacking or rubbing his nose in it can have the opposite effect - he will become afraid to do his business in your presence and may start going behind the couch or under the bed, rather than outside.

10. **Look for the signs.** These may be whining, sniffing the floor in

a determined manner, circling and looking for a place to go, or walking uncomfortably - particularly at the rear end! Take him outside straight away, and try not to pick him up all the time. He has to learn to walk to the door himself when he needs to go outside.

11. **If you use puppy pads, only do so for a short time** or your puppy will get used to them.

12. **Use a crate at night-time** and for the first couple of weeks, set your alarm clock. An eight-week-old pup should be able to last five or six hours if the breeder has already started the process. Get up five hours after you go to bed and take the pup outside to eliminate. After a couple of days, gradually increase the time by 15 minutes. By the age of four or five months a Labrador pup should be able to last eight hours without needing the toilet – provided you let him out last thing at night and first thing in the morning. Before then, you will have a lot of early mornings!

If using a crate, remember that during the day the door should not be closed until your Labrador is happy with being inside. At night-time it is acceptable to close the door, but we would recommend keeping the pup close to you for the first two or three nights. He needs to believe that the crate is a safe place and not a trap or prison. If you don't want to use a crate, then section off an area inside one room or use a puppy pen to confine your pup at night.

One British breeder added this piece of advice: "If you are getting a puppy, invest in a good dressing gown and an umbrella!"

Breeders on Housetraining

Christopher Clarke, Reedfen Labradors, Cambridgeshire: "I would say it takes less than a month to housetrain a Labrador, probably less than two weeks if the new owner is on the ball! My best advice is always take the puppy outside after sleeping, feeding etc. then give lots of praise once they have been to the toilet. Put paper or vet bed down near to the back door to encourage the puppy to at least walk towards the door and, most importantly, WATCH your puppy and OPEN the door for him or her. This seems to me to be where a lot of new owners fall down."

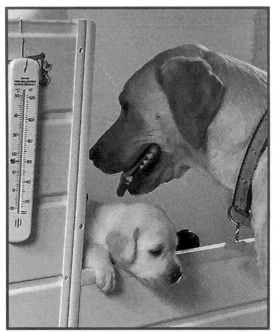

Guy Bunce: "Disney (the mum) was housetrained in two weeks, and Elsa (one of Disney's pups that we kept) took about the same amount of time. The one tip I would suggest is planning to have plenty of time on your hands the first few weeks of your new dog coming home to ensure the dog never toilets inside; constant vigilance. You need to be able to prevent the dog going to the toilet in the house - even once - at all costs.

"Our routine was simple: I took a week off work and took the puppy outside every 45 minutes in the day and the puppy slept in its crate at night. I would take it outside at night at the first instance of it whining." Photo of Disney and pup courtesy of Guy and Chloe Spencer, Dizzywaltz Labradors.

Hilary Hardman: "Housetraining takes one to two weeks if done with care. There will always be accidents during the first few months - these should NEVER be punished.

Punishment will simply cause the puppy to hide from the punisher in order not to be discovered - and never ever rub a puppy's nose in an accident.

"The puppy should be observed almost continuously, signs are clear when a puppy needs to spend a penny and when the signs are observed, the puppy should be encouraged outside to the area designated. Each wee should be accompanied with the same word and, when finished, the puppy should be lavished with praise and rewarded, if appropriate. If the same word is used every time the puppy goes for a wee, then eventually this word will make the puppy or dog wee on command, which is very useful. Remember, the puppy will want to wee upon waking, after eating, after playing and in between! The first few weeks are critical to develop good habits. I do not use training pads indoors, nor do I encourage my puppy buyers, as I think it is important to train the puppy to go outside from the start."

Stephen Armstrong: "On average it takes three to four weeks. The advice I give is to take the puppy outside after sleep, play and feeding, as these are the times that the pup will need the toilet - and **be patient!"**

Sharon Jarvis: "It takes from eight weeks to around 12 weeks of age. Be patient and watch for signs that they need to go. Give a command when the pup is having a wee or poo and make it worth the pup's efforts by giving a biscuit from their dog food diet as confirmation they have done well, along with praise. NEVER scold a puppy if it wees inside, just pick it up and put straight outside - but you need to watch so you're ready to praise." Photo of this litter courtesy of Sharon.

Pat Nugent, Marumrose Labradors, Lincolnshire: "The time it takes is dependent on the amount of effort from the owners. I suggest feeding near an open door to the outside so puppy can get out immediately after a meal."

Lynn Aungier: "Our litter was paper trained before they left us at eight weeks; most of them were

going in the garden too. My number one tip would be to use a crate, as pups don't like to toilet in their bed. Set a timer initially and take them outside every 20 to 30 minutes, after they wake, when they have been playing and after they eat. Pups only have little bladders and don't have much time between the urge and the event, so accidents happen - be patient. (One of the puppies had no indoor accidents, one who didn't use a crate took a long time to be housetrained and developed a poo-eating habit, as he ate it during the night."

Nicola Smith: "Mine are virtually there with toilet training by the time they leave at nine weeks onwards."

Andrew Baker: "I have a 10-week-old puppy at the moment. She has been with me two weeks and she is very good, barring the odd accident indoors, at going outside to relieve herself. The one tip I would give to new owners is to be consistent with the training. I find that they pick it up very easily and on average a new Labrador puppy should be fully housetrained in two to three weeks."

Caroline Smith: "My pups leave at eight weeks trained to go on paper. All the new owners have to do is place paper at the back door and within a week the pup will be going outside. She wakes, she pees – even if you think she can't possibly need another wee, she will!"

Katrina Byrne: "Our puppies are largely housetrained when they leave at eight weeks old. It is important that they go straight outside as soon as they wake up and after they eat until they fully understand what's being asked of them."

Trudy Williams: "All puppies that leave me at eight weeks are virtually housetrained and the owners of the last two litters have said that they only have had the odd wee accident and no poos. The key to this was vigilance, regularly taking the pups out after waking up or after meals in weeks four to eight. Thereafter, in a home, crate training has worked 100%."

Jenny Dobson: "It's impossible to generalise. I've had pups clean within days, and others take a couple of months. The most important things to remember are 'don't despair......it will happen', and use plenty of positive reinforcement, consistency and patience."

New breeder Nadine Lapskas, Trencrom Kennels, Dorset: "Our pups left at eight weeks nearly trained and the new owners all stated that within a couple of weeks, they were fully trained in their new homes. One tip: be consistent and look for signs they need to go toilet to support their training." Photo 'Walkies in the Rain' courtesy of Nadine.

Julie McDonough, Rangemaster Working Gundogs, Powys: "Every puppy is different; some pups are very clean from Day One, there is no set rule apart from as soon as pup wakes up from a sleep, or after they have eaten, let them outside. I always go out with them as young pups get distracted running around the garden and forget what they went out for, and then they come in the house and do it! Praise them when they go to the toilet outside, say a command whilst they are emptying themselves, be consistent use the same word or praise every time. I don't expect a young pup to be clean all night long. Dogs don't normally dirty their sleeping bed if they can help it. If your pup is consistently dirtying its crate or bed, I would change the times you feed your pup, and that includes reducing treats prior to bed time."

Kate Smith: "If the breeder has done the groundwork correctly, a pup can be housetrained within a couple of weeks. My advice would be to quiz a breeder about their rearing practices – puppies are naturally clean and will not want to foul their sleeping area. This is easily encouraged and cultivated by giving pups the opportunity to empty in a specific area from an early age."

Liz Vivash, Wightfyre Labradors, Isle of Wight: "We start their training as soon as they have real food – so at four weeks. This means that by the time they leave us at eight weeks, they are pretty much there. The new parents have found that as soon as they are in their forever homes, the puppies know that outside – or on the puppy pad - is where they should be going to the toilet. We recommend a treat after every correct toileting for the first few weeks to help. They should be clean by 16 weeks."

Sarah Edwards: "Housetraining timings depend on two points:
A. It depends on the breeder and how the pups have been raised in the whelping environment. If the pups have been bred outside in kennels on sawdust etc. they may take longer. We breed indoors in our kitchen, so we find that it can be more closely monitored. There is definitely a natural cleanliness we have found in Labradors that even at around three weeks of age the pups move away from the vet bedding in the whelping box to the edges which

contain disposable training pads and newspaper. As they get older, we move these pads to the playpen outside the whelping box and again they gravitate toward the training pads. It is not a perfect solution as they will still toilet randomly in the play area, but recent feedback from our owners has indicated that housetraining has been extremely quick and easy following our change in tactics.

B. It also depends on the new owners and how often they make the effort to take the pup outside and how long the pup is left alone. We always give them some of the same disposable pads to put by the door as soon as the pup comes home with them. The idea is that they don't let the pup eliminate on the pad, but as the pup gravitates towards the pad they take them outside immediately. We recommend taking pups outside every hour and after waking and feeding. This very quickly reinforces where toileting should take place. Keen owners even get up in the middle of the night to avoid crate accidents etc."

Kirsty Jones: "If the breeder has started housetraining, I would estimate it takes about a month, but it requires constant training. If the puppy makes a mistake, ask yourself if you were paying attention! Each pup is different and will show a need to go out in different ways. Pay attention, get to know your pup and develop a routine."

This handsome Labrador is Kirsty's show-bred Roboshalee Way To Tipperary for Serengoch (Gem) aged at 18 months.

Christine Eynon, Baileylane Labradors, Herefordshire. "My pups are pretty well housetrained when they are homed. I use half paper and half vet bed and they soon

learn. They then learn to go in the courtyard and not in our living accommodation, so they are well on their way. Consistency is the answer."

Robin Anderson: "On average, I believe a Labrador's brain and body comes into sync by the time they are five months old. Until then, the human family becomes well trained in taking the puppy outside to potty on a regular basis that is in line with its needs. I tell puppy buyers that they can learn to set their watch by the pup's potty schedule, which at first is every 15 minutes for a tinkle and every 45 minutes for a poo when the puppy is awake and playing. Keep boots by the door because you want to jump into them before an accident happens."

Sandra Underhill, Labs to Love, California adds: "Put a collar on the pup, and have a leash handy to guide puppy outdoors to go potty."

Bear in mind that all of the KC Assured Breeders and AKC Breeders of Merit featured in this book have already put in the time and effort to start housetraining their pups, thereby speeding up the process once you bring your pup home. A puppy which has not been part-housetrained by the breeder or one which has been reared outside of the home will obviously take longer to learn what is expected of him or her.

US breeder Teresa Gordy-Brown says: "Housebreaking Labradors is generally easy and can be done in as little as four weeks if you follow a few basic principles, which are:

1. Always, supervise the puppy when he is out of his crate the first few weeks. Never turn your attention away for a second.

2. Never allow the puppy to have free roam of your house - this comes when they are older and can be trusted. You must restrict his area. A puppy has no idea that inside potty is not the same as outside potty. A puppy not supervised and left in a large room will be happy to go across to the rug and empty his bladder....your fault, not his! He has no clue where his potty place is. This is something you the human must teach.

3. Set up a very strict schedule for the first two weeks and stick to it like glue.

4. Take puppy out to the same spot in the yard to potty.

5. Use a command such as "Go" "Potty" or "Hurry", something he can associate with his actions.

6. Never play with the puppy outside until his 'business' is done. To do otherwise makes him forget what he came outside for. Labrador pups are very easily distracted so it is best to just stand in one spot, making as little fuss as possible, repeat your command of "potty" while the puppy sniffs the ground. After the deed is done, praise and then bring the puppy to a different area of the yard for play time or back in the house.

7. Always remember: a puppy must urinate pretty much after waking from a nap, after drinking and eating and after any period of excitement, such as playtime. Pups have small bladders and learn control as they get older; there will be a few accidents along the way.

8. Depending on the diet and how much you feed, your puppy may have several stools per day. Three on average is a good number for a healthy puppy eating a good kibble. Expect a potty break (poop) at least five to 15 minutes after each meal."

"How can you tell the dogs need to go out?"

GENERAL HOUSETRAINING TIP: As you have read, a trigger can be very effective to encourage your dog to perform his duties. Some people use a clicker or a bell - we used a word; well, two actually. Within a week or so I trained our puppy to urinate on the command of "Wee wee!" Think very carefully before choosing the word or phrase, as I often feel an idiot wandering around our garden last thing at night shouting "Max, WEE WEE!!" in an encouraging manner. (Although I'm not sure that the American expression "GO POTTY!!" sounds much better!

7. Feeding a Labrador

One breeder described Labradors as 'the waste disposal units of the dog world!' And it's true that most of them will eat anything and everything that is put in front of them – as well as a lot that isn't.

But to keep your dog's biological machine in good working order, it's important to supply the right fuel. Feeding the correct diet is an essential part of keeping your Lab fit and healthy. The topic of feeding can be something of a minefield; owners are bombarded with endless choices as well as countless adverts from dog food companies, all claiming that theirs is best.

There is not one food that will give every single dog the shiniest coat, the brightest eyes, the most energy, the best digestion, the least gas, the longest life and stop him from scratching or having skin problems. Dogs are individuals, just like people, which means that you could feed a quality food to a group of dogs and find that most of them thrive on it, some do not so well, while a few might get an upset stomach or even an allergic reaction. The question is: "Which food is best for **my** Labrador?"

If you have been given a recommended food from a breeder, rescue centre or previous owner, stick to this as long as your dog is doing well on it. A good breeder knows which food her dogs thrive on. If you do decide - for whatever reason - to change diet, then this must be done gradually. There are several things to be aware of when it comes to feeding:

1. Most Labradors are highly food motivated. Add to this their eagerness to please and you have a powerful training tool. You can use feeding time to reinforce a simple command on a daily basis.

2. However, their food obsession and voracious appetites mean that most have no self-control when it comes to food, so it is up to you to control your dog's intake and keep the weight in check.

3. Some dogs have food sensitivities or allergies - more on this topic later.

4. Excess gas is not uncommon with Labradors, and one of the main reasons for flatulence is the wrong diet.

5. Many Labradors do not do well on diets with a high grain content.

6. There is anecdotal evidence from breeders that some Labradors do well on a home-made or raw diet - if you have the time and money to stick to it.

7. Often, you get what you pay for with dog food, so a more expensive food is usually – but not always - more likely to provide better nutrition in terms of minerals, nutrients and high quality meats. Cheap foods often contain a lot of grain; read the list of ingredients to find out. Dried foods (called 'kibble' in the US) tend to be less expensive than some other foods. They have improved a lot over the last few years and some of the best ones are now a good

choice for a healthy, complete diet. Dried foods also contain the least fat and most preservatives. Foods such as Life's Abundance dry formulas do not contain any preservatives.

8. Sometimes elderly dogs may just get bored with their diet and go off their food. This does not necessarily mean that they are ill, simply that they have lost interest and a new food should be gradually introduced.

Our dog Max, who has inhalant allergies, is on a quality dried food which the manufacturers claim is 'hypoallergenic,' i.e. good for dogs with allergies. Max seems to do well on it, but not all dogs thrive on dried food. We tried several other foods first; it is a question of owners finding the best food for their dog. If you got your dog from a good breeder, they should be able to advise you.

Beware foods described as 'premium' or 'natural' or both, these terms are meaningless. Many manufacturers blithely use these words, but there are no official guidelines as to what they mean. However **"Complete and balanced"** IS a legal term and has to meet standards laid down by AAFCO (Association of American Feed Control Officials) in the USA.

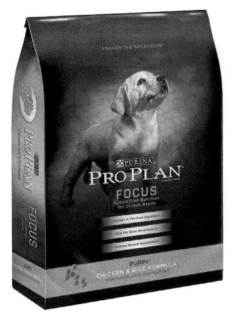

Always check the ingredients on any food sack, packet or tin to see what is listed first; this is the main ingredient and it should be meat or poultry, not grain. If you are in the USA, look for a dog food endorsed by AAFCO. In general, tinned foods are 60-70% water and often semi-moist foods contain a lot of artificial substances and sugar. Choosing the right food for your Labrador is important; it will influence his health, coat and sometimes even temperament.

There are three stages of your dog's life to consider when feeding: Puppy, Adult and Senior (also called Veteran). Some manufacturers also produce a Junior feed for adolescent dogs. Each represents a different physical stage of life and you need to choose the right food during each particular phase. (This does not necessarily mean that you have to feed Puppy, then Junior, then Adult then Senior food, some breeders switch their young dogs to Adult formulas fairly soon). Also, a pregnant female will require a special diet to cope with the extra demands on her body; this is especially important as she nears the latter stages of pregnancy.

Many owners feed their Labs twice a day; this helps to stop a hungry dog gulping food down in a mad feeding frenzy, and reduces the risk of Bloat (see **Chapter 11. Health** for more details). Some owners of fussy eaters or older dogs who have gone off their food give two different meals each day to provide variety. One meal could be dried kibble, while the other might be home-made, with fresh meat, poultry and vegetables, or a tinned food. If you do this, make sure the two separate meals provide a balanced diet and that they are not too rich in protein – especially with young dogs.

We will not recommend one brand of dog food over another, but do have some general tips to help you choose what to feed. There is also some advice for owners of dogs with food allergies and intolerance; there is anecdotal evidence that some Labs have an intolerance or sensitivity to grain and that many suffer from excess gas.

Food allergies are a growing problem in the canine world generally. Sufferers may itch, lick or chew their paws and/or legs, or rub their face. They may also get frequent ear infections as well as redness and swelling on their face. Switching to a grain-free diet can help to alleviate the symptoms, as your dog's digestive system does not have to work as hard. In the wild, a dog or wolf's staple diet would be meat with some vegetable matter from the stomach and intestines of the herbivores (plant-eating animals) he ate – but no grains. Dogs do not digest corn or wheat (which are often staples of cheap commercial dog food) very efficiently. Grain-free diets still provide carbohydrates through fruits and vegetables, so a dog still gets all the necessary nutrients.

15 Top Tips for Feeding your Lab

1. If you choose a manufactured food, don't pick one where meat or poultry content is NOT the first item listed on the bag or tin. Foods with lots of cheap cereals or sugar are not the best choice.

2. Some dogs suffer from sensitive skin, 'hot spots' or allergies. A cheap food, often bulked up with grain, will only make this worse. If this is the case, bite the bullet and choose a high quality – usually more expensive – food, or consider a raw diet. You'll probably save money in vets' bills in the long run and your dog will be happier. A food described as 'hypoallergenic' on the sack means 'less likely to cause allergies.'

3. Consider feeding your Lab twice a day, rather than once. Smaller feeds are easier to digest, and reduce flatulence (gas) as well as the risk of **Bloat**. Puppies need to be fed more often; discuss exactly how often with your breeder.

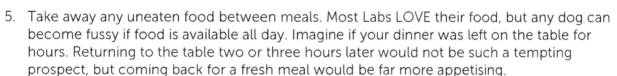

4. Establish a feeding regime and stick to it. Dogs like routine. If you are feeding twice a day, feed once in the morning and then again at tea-time. Stick to the same times of day. Do not give the last feed too late, or your dog's body will not have chance to process or burn off the food before sleeping. He will also need a walk or letting out in the garden or yard after his second feed to allow him to empty his bowels. Feeding at the same times each day helps your dog establish a toilet regime.

5. Take away any uneaten food between meals. Most Labs LOVE their food, but any dog can become fussy if food is available all day. Imagine if your dinner was left on the table for hours. Returning to the table two or three hours later would not be such a tempting prospect, but coming back for a fresh meal would be far more appetising.

   Also, when food is left all day, some dogs take the food for granted and lose their appetite. They start leaving food and you are at your wits' end trying to find something they will actually eat. Put the food bowl down twice a day and take it up after 20 minutes – even if there is some left. If he is healthy and hungry, he'll look forward to his next meal and soon stop leaving food. If a Labrador does not eat anything for a couple of days, it could well be a sign that he is unwell.

6. Do not feed too many titbits (tidbits) and treats between meals. Extra weight will place extra strain on your Lab's joints and organs, have a detrimental effect on health and even lifespan. It also throws a balanced diet out of the window. Try to avoid feeding your dog from the table or your plate, as this encourages attention-seeking behaviour, begging and drooling.

7. Never give your dog cooked bones, as these can splinter and cause choking or intestinal problems. If your Lab is a gulper, avoid giving rawhide, as dogs who rush their food have a tendency to chew and swallow rawhide without first nibbling it down into smaller pieces.

8. If you switch to a new food, do the transition gradually. Unlike humans, dogs' digestive systems cannot handle sudden changes. Begin by gradually mixing some of the new food in with the old and increase the proportion so that after seven to eight days, all the food is the new one. The following ratios are recommended by Doctors Foster & Smith Inc: Days 1-3 add 25% of the new food, Days 4-6 add 50%, Days 7-9 add 75%, Day 10 feed 100% of the new food. By the way, if you stick to the identical brand, you can change flavours in one go.

9. NEVER feed the following items to your dog: grapes, raisins, chocolate, onions, Macadamia nuts, any fruits with seeds or stones, tomatoes, avocadoes, rhubarb, tea, coffee or alcohol. All of these are poisonous to dogs.

10. Check your dog's faeces (aka stools, poo or poop!). If his diet is suitable, the food should be easily digested and produce dark brown, firm stools. If your dog produces soft or light stools, or has a lot of gas or diarrhoea, then the diet may not suit him, so consult your vet or breeder for advice.

11. Feed your dog in stainless steel or ceramic dishes. Plastic bowls don't last as long and can also trigger an allergic reaction around the muzzle in some sensitive dogs. Ceramic bowls are best for keeping water cold.

12. If you have more than one dog, consider feeding them separately. Labradors usually get on fine with other pets, especially if introduced at an early age. But feeding dogs together can sometimes lead to dog food aggression from a dog either protecting his own food or trying to eat the food designated for another.

13. If you do feed leftovers, feed them INSTEAD of a balanced meal, not as well as - unless you are feeding a raw diet. High quality dog foods already provide all the nutrients, vitamins, minerals and calories that your dog needs. Feeding titbits or leftovers may be too rich for your Lab in addition to his regular diet and cause gas, scratching or other problems, such as obesity. You can feed your dog vegetables as a healthy low-calorie treat.

 Get your puppy used to eating raw carrots, pieces of apple, etc. as a treat and he will continue to enjoy them as an adult. If you wait until he's fully grown before introducing them, he may well turn his nose up.

14. Keep your dog's weight in check. Obesity can lead to the development of serious health issues, such as diabetes, high blood pressure and heart disease. Although weight varies from dog to dog, a good rule of thumb is that your Labrador's tummy should be higher than or, at worst, level with his rib cage. If his belly hangs down below it, he is overweight.

15. And finally, always make sure that your dog has access to clean, fresh water. Change the water and clean the bowl regularly – it gets slimy!

Many breeders feed their adult Labradors twice a day, others feed just once, and yet others feed some dogs once a day and some dogs twice a day. As one US breeder put it: "They are not all made from the same cookie cutter." Start your dog on twice-daily feeds from four to six months old and, if he or she seems to be thriving on this regime, stick to it.

Types of Dog Food

We are what we eat. The right food is a very important part of a healthy lifestyle for dogs as well as humans. Here are the main options explained:

Dry dog food - also called kibble, is a popular and relatively inexpensive way of providing a balanced diet. It comes in a variety of flavours and with differing ingredients to suit the different stages of a dog's life. Cheap foods are often false economy, particularly if your Lab does not tolerate grain/cereal very well. You may also have to feed larger quantities to ensure he gets sufficient nutrients.

Canned food - another popular choice – and it's often very popular with dogs too. They love the taste and it generally comes in a variety of flavours. Canned food is often mixed with dry kibble, and a small amount may be added to a dog that is on a dry food diet if he has lost interest in food. It tends to be more expensive than dried food and many owners don't like the mess.

These days there are hundreds of options, some are very high quality and made from natural, organic ingredients and contain herbs and other beneficial ingredients. A part-opened tin can sometimes smell when you open the fridge door. As with dry food, read the label closely. Generally, you get what you pay for and the origins of cheap canned dog food are often somewhat dubious. Some Labs can suffer from diarrhoea or soft stools and/or gas with too much tinned or soft food.

Semi-Moist - These are commercial dog foods shaped like pork chops, salamis, bacon (pictured), burgers or other meaty foods and they are the least nutritional of all dog foods. They are full of sugars, artificial flavourings and colourings to help make them visually appealing.

Labs don't care two hoots what their food looks like, they only care how it smells and tastes; the shapes are designed to appeal to humans. While you may give your dog one as an occasional treat, they are not a diet in themselves and do NOT provide the nutrition your dog needs. Steer clear of them for regular feeding.

Freeze-Dried – (pictured) This is made by frozen food manufacturers for owners who like the convenience – this type of food keeps for six months to a year - or for those going on a trip with their dog. It says 'freeze-dried' on the packet and is highly palatable, but the freeze-drying process bumps up the cost.

Freeze dried is one option if you are considering feeding a raw diet.

Home-Cooked - Some owners want the ability to be in complete control of their dog's diet, know exactly what their dog is eating and to be absolutely sure that his nutritional needs are being met. Feeding your dog a home-cooked diet is time consuming and expensive, and the difficult thing – as with the raw diet - is sticking to it once you have started out with the best of intentions. But many owners think the extra effort is worth the peace of mind.

If you decide to go ahead, you should spend the time to become proficient and learn about canine nutrition to ensure your dog gets all the vital nutrients.

What the Breeders Feed

We asked 30 Labrador breeders what they feed their dogs. We are not recommending one brand over another, but the breeders' answers give an insight to what issues are important when considering food and why a particular brand has been chosen, starting in the UK. (Breeders who feed a raw diet are featured in the next section):

Christopher Clarke, Reedfen Labradors, Cambridgeshire: "I feed a dry kibbled food called Pro Plan made by Purina. It ticks all the boxes for nutrition, it's easy to store, doesn't attract flies or other insects in the summer months and keeps my dogs in great condition. Oh, and most importantly, their stools are always firm and easy to pick up!"

Stephen and Jane Armstrong, Carnamaddy Labradors, Northern Ireland: "We feed Arden Grange to all our dogs – two Labs, two Pugs and a German Shepherd. It's a good food and reasonably priced and we have never had any problems with this food. We also feed raw food mixed with kibble to any of the bitches that are feeding pups, and we start pups off on raw before weaning onto dry."

Anne Johnson, Teazledown Labradors, Lancashire: "I feed Arden Grange complete. I have tried a raw diet, but only the complete, frozen one. With several dogs I found it more bulky for storage, and you must remember to defrost it. I saw no health benefits, so returned to using complete."

Sharon Jarvis, Paulsharo Labradors, Lincolnshire: "I feed my bitches on Royal Canin Mother and Baby Dog whilst pregnant and feed the pups from three to four weeks of age on the same. At eight weeks old the puppies and my other dogs are all fed on CSJ Kibble. If I continued to feed the pups on Royal Canin then they would be like small children on blue Smarties (out of control!) I think Royal Canin also makes dogs gain weight." (Photo of this healthy litter courtesy of Sharon).

Guy Bunce, Dizzywaltz Labradors, Berkshire: "Dog food choice is a minefield. At all costs avoid cheap or supermarket brands. We have tried a raw diet, but found it made the stools runny. We use the Skinners Working line foods. Always research a food and look at the ingredients, avoid brands like Bakers or Pedigree."

Lynn Aungier, Alatariel Labradors, Surrey: "We feed our dogs Orijen, it is a whole prey kibble diet, www.orijenpetfoods.co.uk, they are now on the Six Fish variety. There are no cereals etc. We did a lot of research and Orijen came highly recommended as one of the leading foods on the market. I haven't tried raw feeding – I don't think it would be good with children in the house. "

Nicola Smith, Geowins Labradors, Surrey: "I feed my dog a complete biscuit. I like to know they are getting the correct amount of protein, oils, fibres etc. and they all seem to thrive on it. I have never tried raw meet as I personally don't like dealing with raw meat."

Caroline Smith, Flyenpyg Labradors, Lancaster: "I feed the pups a mix of raw and biscuit. Raw is fabulous for solid poops and the pups love it, but for me, it's too time-consuming and expensive to do it correctly, and I'm of the opinion that since the pet food companies have been doing it for years, they can't all be that bad. I feed kibble with occasional sprats, tripe and raw bones as a treat."

New breeder Diane Stanford, Tragenheath Labradors, Leamington Spa: "I have always fed my dogs on James Wellbeloved. It's a fantastic food, hypoallergenic, they both thrive on it, their coats are glossy and they look fantastic on it. I wouldn't change to anything else as it suits my girls. "

Jenny Dobson, of Lakemeadow Labradors, South Yorkshire, has bred Labs for 50 years: "I would certainly feed raw if I only had one or two dogs, but with several dogs, the storage and preparation makes raw feeding impractical. (I have incidentally used raw feeding in cats and experienced great benefits in terms of health, general condition, reduced volume of excreta, and all my cats- with the exception of one - lived well into their 20s).

"I currently feed a good quality dry, complete, grain-free kibble. This is convenient to buy in bulk online and get delivered; it's clean and easy to store, and easy to feed. As a breeder I am able to obtain a 'breeder club discount' on purchases, which makes this method of feeding relatively inexpensive and it is the most convenient if you have several dogs."

Kate Smith, Ardenbrook Labradors, Warwick: "I feed Autarky, and have done so for many years now. I find it an excellent alternative to the raw diet. I do appreciate the benefits of the raw diet, and would certainly recommend it in certain circumstances, but this food works for me. My dogs work hard during winter months, but keep condition on even so. I do also add raw tripe (more in the winter), and also vegetable trimmings etc. go into their diet, so I suppose it could be described as a mixed diet."

Liz Vivash, Wightfyre Labradors, Isle of Wight: "The puppies get fed four times a day until they are 12 weeks. For lunch and dinner we use Tesco's puppy food, and Eucanuba puppy. We can get both of these easily, and Eucanuba let us have puppy pack for the new owners (so do many others too). We also feed wheat biscuits and milk for two meals a day, breakfast and supper to start with. The adult dogs get Winalot tinned food, and a mix of Tesco's meal and Eucanuba. We find this is not too rich, and we can keep their weight in the right area. They get a bowlful, as we only feed them once a day. They get a Bonio for breakfast."

Katrina Byrne, of Glenhugo Labradors, Scotland, has provided some useful information for feeding puppies. She said: "Our dogs are fed on Hills Puppy Food and owners are always supplied with puppy packs or a small bag of this food and given instructions as to how to wean them off if they have a particular brand they prefer or currently give to their other dogs. I include this table in their Puppy Packs:

Age of Puppy	Number of Meals (per day)	Type of Food	Quantity (per meal)
2months	3	Puppy food	1 cup (100g)
3months	3	Puppy food	1 ¼ cups (125g)
4months	3	Puppy food	1 ½ (cups 150g)
After 4 months	2*	Puppy food	2-2 ½ cups (200-250g)
12 months	2	Adult large breed**	Dependent on weight—consult brand / vet

Slowly increase food each week to reach the required new levels
* You can make the move to two feeds a days – slowly over a seven-day period, slowly reducing the lunch time food and increasing the morning and afternoon food each day
** Make the transition to the adult food over a seven-day period
Days 1-2: ¼ adult and ¾ puppy at each meal
Days 3-4: ½ adult and ½ puppy at each meal

Days 5-6: ¾ Adult and ¼ puppy at each meal
Days 7: adult food

Nadine Lapskas, of Trencrom Kennels, Bournemouth, feeds Hills Science Plan, Pat Nugent, of Marumrose Labradors, Lincolnshire, feeds Royal Canin, as does Julie McDonough, of Rangemaster Working Gundogs, Powys, as well as Amada Deane, of Tanronens Labradors, Lincoln, who adds: "As a treat I do give them a fresh marrow bone for their teeth." Christine Eynon, Baileylane Labradors, Hertfordshire, feeds: "A good quality dried food plus veg, and I cook them some meat."

(Photo of Zak courtesy of Julie McDonough).

In the USA, Sandra Underhill, of Labs To Love, California, says: "Raw is difficult for the layman to feed a nutritious diet, so I recommend kibble from a company with a staff of veterinarians on board; Royal Canin."

Robin Anderson, of Grampian Labradors, New England: "With large numbers of dogs in the house, I feed the highest quality kibble I can, and most of my dogs eat the same brand and type. Pregnant and lactating bitches and hard-working dogs get the highest protein kibble. Pregnant bitches are also given plenty of other 'human' foods that contain protein for at least the first two weeks, which helps milk production.

"Puppies are fed the same brand of food the mother eats, but in the Puppy growth formula. Seniors are fed a Senior diet of the same brand as the dogs on a management formula. I supplement some dogs with freeze dried raw food, but it isn't the main source of food for their meals."

Teresa Gordy-Brown, of Ashland Labradors, Tennessee: "I prefer a quality 'all life stage' kibble, 30% protein to a 20% fat ration for our Labradors. I have most certainly fed raw and still do on a rotation schedule. I used to feed raw meaty bones, such as chicken backs, but now tend to feed more of a meat mixture with omegas 3, 6 as well as enzymes added. The raw diet excels the kibble, but I have found that I cannot achieve the 'bloom' in coat and condition for the show ring if I just feed raw alone. Our Labradors tend to drop coat in handfuls if not fed the 30/20 ration."

The Raw Diet

There is a quiet revolution going on in the world of dog food. After years of feeding dry or tinned dog food, increasing numbers of dog owners - and many breeders - are now feeding a raw diet to their beloved pets. However, the subject is not without controversy and, as you have read, opinions are divided. There is anecdotal evidence that some dogs thrive on it, although scientific proof is lagging behind. Claims made by fans of the raw diet include:

- Reduced symptoms of - or less likelihood of - allergies, and less scratching
- Better skin and coats
- Easier weight management
- Improved digestion

- Less doggie odour and flatulence
- Fresher breath and improved dental health
- Helps fussy eaters
- Drier and less smelly stools, more like pellets
- Reduced risk of bloat
- Overall improvement in general health and less disease
- Higher energy levels
- Most dogs love a raw diet

If your dog is not doing well on a commercially-prepared dog food, you might consider a raw diet. It emulates the way dogs ate before the existence of commercial dog foods, which may contain artificial preservatives and excessive protein and fillers – causing a reaction in some Labradors. Dry, canned and other styles of processed food were mainly created as a means of convenience, but unfortunately this convenience sometimes can affect a dog's health.

Some nutritionists believe that dogs fed raw whole foods tend to be healthier than those on other diets. They say there are inherent beneficial enzymes, vitamins, minerals and other qualities in meats, fruits, vegetables and grains in their natural forms that are denatured or destroyed when cooked. Many also believe dogs are less likely to have allergic reactions to the ingredients on this diet.

Frozen food can be a valuable aid to the raw diet. The food is highly palatable, made from high quality ingredients and dogs usually wolf it down. The downsides are that not all pet food stores stock it, it can be expensive and you have to remember to defrost it.

Critics of a raw diet say that the risks of nutritional imbalance, intestinal problems and food-borne illnesses caused by handling and feeding raw meat outweigh any benefits.

It is true that owners must pay strict attention to hygiene when preparing a raw diet and it may not be a suitable option if there are children in the household. The dog may also be more likely to ingest bacteria or parasites such as Salmonella, E. Coli and Ecchinococcus.

Here are some comments from Labrador breeders who are currently feeding their dogs a raw diet:

Sarah Edwards, Fernwills Labradors, Essex: "We feed a fully biologically appropriate raw diet. We have extremely fit, healthy, shiny-coated dogs with perfect teeth. Even our older Labradors have pearly white teeth due to their regular raw meaty bone eating habits! We only visit the vets for boosters/health checks annually and the odd lameness from too much running about.

"I can't get over how humanising people have been for dogs over the years. The fact that vets sell dog toothbrushes and toothpaste is nonsensical - all required because the 'standard' is feeding dried kibbles which coat the teeth in tartar. A raw meaty bone would solve that one in a heartbeat. This is a subject I am extremely passionate about, so could go on for a while...!"

Trudy Williams, Yaffleswood Labradors, Sussex: "I generally feed raw, but it is always handy to feed dry as well as it is easier if you go away and the dogs go to kennels. Raw is natural and as a dog should eat. I have noticed the dogs' coats are far better and we have not had one runny tummy since switching to raw food."

Gundog trainer Andrew Baker, of Saffronlyn Gundogs, South Yorkshire: "I have always fed my dogs a raw diet from puppies through to adulthood and they thrive on it. I have six dogs -five Labradors and an Irish Setter. Their main meal consists of mince and they also have wings, carcasses, feet and bones. I find that this is the main contribution to them being healthy dogs. The food is delivered frozen and then thawed accordingly.

"I have never had any issues with any of them. I find that their diet contributes immensely to their overall health. Their coats are gleaming, they always look forward to mealtime and their stools are well-formed. There are no issues with gastro-intestinal problems. Their main meal is at tea-time, however if I am out training with them, I will take some treats with me and they have a bone two or three times a week in the morning."

Kirsty Jones, of Serengoch Labradors, Mid Wales: "I feed a raw diet and have found there is much less poop and it smells a lot less. The coats are much shinier and they have a lot less health issues —we had lots of ear infections while feeding kibble."

Colin Hinkley, Sanglier Labradors, East Sussex: "I feed only raw diet to adults, the puppies are brought up on Skinners Puppy for the convenience of new owners. My dogs appear very healthy and happy on raw food." Avril Bartolomy, Prestonfield Labradors, East Sussex adds: "I am converted to raw. It is very natural and full of all the right things, and most of the brands include vegetables, so it is easy to store."

New breeder, Elizabeth Halsall, Surrey: "I feed my dogs a raw diet of meat and biscuits — tripe, beef, cooked chicken — they have leftover vegetables and some raw carrots and veg.

Some dogs enjoy blackberries and apples and lettuce. Mine are not that keen, they will eat pasta - but I stick to the raw diet mainly. Labradors will generally eat anything that they can get their paws on!" (Photo of this mother and litter courtesy of Elizabeth).

There are two main types of raw diet, one involves feeding raw, meaty bones and the other is known as the BARF diet (*Biologically Appropriate Raw Food* or *Bones And Raw Food*), created by Dr Ian Billinghurst.

Raw Meaty Bones

This diet is:

- ❧ Raw meaty bones or carcasses, if available, should form the bulk of the diet
- ❧ Table scraps both cooked and raw, such as vegetables, can be fed
- ❧ As with any diet, fresh water should be constantly available. **NOTE: Do NOT feed cooked bones, they can splinter**

Australian veterinarian Dr Tom Lonsdale is a leading proponent of the raw meaty bones diet. He believes the following foods are suitable:

- Chicken and turkey carcasses, after the meat has been removed for human consumption
- Poultry by-products, including heads, feet, necks and wings
- Whole fish and fish heads
- Sheep, calf, goat, and deer carcasses sawn into large pieces of meat and bone
- Other by-products, e.g. pigs' trotters, pigs' heads, sheep heads, brisket, tail and rib bones
- A certain amount of offal can be included in the diet, e.g. liver, lungs, trachea, hearts, tripe

He says that low-fat game animals, fish and poultry provide the best source of food for pet carnivores. If you feed meat from farm animals (cattle, sheep and pigs), avoid excessive fat and bones that are too large to be eaten.

Some of it will depend on what's available locally and how expensive it is. If you shop around you should be able to source a regular supply of suitable raw meaty bones at a reasonable price. Start with your local butcher or farm shop. When deciding what type of bones to feed your Labrador, one point to bear in mind is that dogs are more likely to break their teeth when eating large knuckle bones and bones sawn lengthwise than when eating meat and bone together.

You'll also need to think about WHERE you are going to feed your dog. A dog takes some time to eat a raw bone and will push it around the floor, so the kitchen may not be the most suitable or hygienic place. Outside is one option, but what do you do when it's raining?

Establishing the right quantity to feed your Labrador is a matter of trial and error. You will reach a decision based on your dog's activity levels, appetite and body condition. High activity and a big appetite show a need for increased food, and vice versa. A very approximate guide, based on raw meaty bones, for the average dog is 15%-20% of body weight per week, or 2%-3% a day. So, if your Lab weighs 30lb (just under 13.6kg), he or she will require 4.5lb-6lb (2-2.7kg) of carcasses or raw meaty bones weekly. Table scraps should be fed as an extra component of the diet. **These figures are only a rough guide** and relate to adult pets in a domestic environment.

Pregnant or lactating females and growing puppies may need much more food than adult animals of similar body weight. Dr Lonsdale says: "Wherever possible, feed the meat and bone ration in one large piece requiring much ripping, tearing and gnawing. This makes for contented pets with clean teeth. Wild carnivores feed at irregular intervals, in a domestic setting regularity works best and accordingly I suggest that you feed adult dogs and cats once daily. If you live in a hot climate I recommend that you feed pets in the evening to avoid attracting flies.

"I suggest that on one or two days each week your dog may be fasted - just like animals in the wild. On occasions you may run out of natural food. Don't be tempted to buy artificial food, fast your dog and stock up with natural food the next day. Puppies...sick or underweight dogs should not be fasted (unless on veterinary advice)."

Table scraps and some fruit and vegetable peelings can also be fed, but should not make up more than one-third of the diet. Liquidising cooked and uncooked scraps in a food mixer can make them easier to digest. **Things to Avoid:**

- Excessive meat off the bone - not balanced

- Excessive vegetables - not balanced
- Small pieces of bone - can be swallowed whole and get stuck
- Cooked bones - get stuck
- Mineral and vitamin additives - create imbalance
- Processed food - leads to dental and other diseases
- Excessive starchy food - associated with bloat
- Onions, garlic, chocolate, grapes, raisins, sultanas, currants - toxic to pets
- Fruit stones (pips) and corn cobs - get stuck
- Milk - associated with diarrhoea. Animals drink it whether thirsty or not and can get fat

Points of Concern

- Old dogs used to processed food may experience initial difficulty when changed on to a natural diet. Discuss the change with your vet first and then, if he or she agrees, switch your dog's diet over a period of a week to 10 days
- Raw meaty bones are not suitable for dogs with dental or jaw problems
- This diet may not be suitable if your dog gulps his food, as the bones can become lodged inside him, larger bones may prevent gulping
- The diet should be varied, any nutrients fed to excess can be harmful
- Liver is an excellent foodstuff, but should not be fed more than once weekly
- Other offal, e.g. ox stomachs, should not make up more than half of the diet
- Whole fish are an excellent source of food, but avoid feeding one species of fish constantly. Some species, e.g. carp, contain an enzyme which destroys thiamine (vitamin B1)
- If you have more than one dog, do not allow them to fight over the food, feed them separately if necessary
- Be prepared to monitor your dog while he eats the bones, especially in the beginning, and do not feed bones with sharp points. Take the bone off your dog before it becomes small enough to swallow
- Make sure that children do not disturb the dog when feeding or try to take the bone away
- Hygiene: Make sure the raw meaty bones are kept separate from human food and clean thoroughly any surface the uncooked meat or bones have touched. This is especially important if you have children. Feeding bowls are unnecessary, your dog will drag the bones across the floor, so feed them outside if you can, or on a floor that is easy to clean
- Puppies can and do eat diets of raw meaty bones, but you should consult the breeder or a vet before embarking on this diet with a young dog

You will need a regular supply of meaty bones - either locally or online - and you should buy in bulk to ensure a consistency of supply. For this you will need a large freezer. You can then parcel up the bones into daily portions. You can also feed frozen bones; some dogs will gnaw them straight away, others will wait for them to thaw.

More information is available from the website www.rawmeatybones.com and I would strongly recommend discussing the matter with your breeder or vet first before switching to raw meaty bones.

The BARF diet

A variation of the raw meaty bones diet is the BARF created by Dr Ian Billinghurst, who owns the registered trademark 'Barf Diet'. A typical BARF diet is made up of 60%-75% of raw meaty bones (bones with about 50% meat, such as chicken neck, back and wings) and 25%-40% of fruit and vegetables, offal, meat, eggs or dairy foods. Bones must not be cooked or they can splinter inside the dog. There is a great deal of information on the BARF diet on the internet.

UK breeder Sarah Nuttall, of Gamblegate Labradors, Lancashire, has bred Labs for 17 years and feeds the BARF diet. She said: "I have been totally raw feeding for about eight years, prior to that I fed complete dry food, but added eggs, yoghurt, cooked meat and fish, fruit and vegetables on an ad hoc basis. In relation to weaning puppies, the commercial food had a horrible smell when water was added to make a paste for puppies and it was difficult to encourage them to eat it. They immediately started to have watery, smelly poo, which didn't seem natural to me. I also noticed that the adults had stinking, sloppy poo which made cleaning the yard a horrible job! They also ate poo and grass which made me suspect that there was a nutritional deficiency in their diet.

"I began to read about the BARF feeding method and decided to try it. The basis of the diet is raw meaty bones, chicken wings, necks, carcass to make about 60% of the diet, plus fruit and vegetables. I buy my chicken from my butcher, who feeds his dogs this way, he gives me larger bones just for chewing and playing. I also buy some frozen meat, offal, tripe etc.

"My adults have a 'smoothie' made from root veg - carrot, raw beetroot etc. - and greens - kale, spinach, stalks from cauliflower - as well as apples, banana (whatever I have really), plus egg, yoghurt, cottage cheese occasionally, over biscuit meal with occasional cod liver oil, brewer's yeast, and a multivitamin added in the morning. Evening is usually two chicken carcass, but sometimes offal or tripe. My dogs never eat poo now and their poo is firm and easy to clean up. All appear to be very healthy, lovely shiny coats, white teeth, fresh breath and no strong doggie smell. I have to wean my puppies from their ground chicken to commercial food and it does upset me to see how reluctant they are to eat it and how upset their tummies become."

You might also consider feeding two different daily meals to your dog - one dry kibble and one raw diet or home-cooked food, for example. If you do, then research the subject, and consult your veterinarian to make sure that the two combined meals provide a balanced diet.

NOTE: Only start a raw diet if you have done your research and are sure you have the time and money to keep it going. There are numerous websites and canine forums with information on switching to a raw diet and everything it involves.

....

Food Allergies

Dog food allergies affect about one in 10 dogs. They are the third most common canine allergy for dogs after atopy (inhaled or contact allergies) and flea bite allergies. While there's no scientific evidence of links between specific breeds and food allergies, there is anecdotal evidence from owners that some Labradors can suffer from food intolerances, particularly grains.

Food allergies affect males and females in equal measure as well as neutered and intact pets. They can start when your dog is five months or 12 years old - although the vast majority start when the dog is between two and six years old. It is not uncommon for dogs with food allergies to also have other types of allergies.

If your Labrador is not well, how do you know if the problem lies with his food or not? Here are some common symptoms to look out for:

- Itchy skin (this is the most common). Your dog may lick or chew his paws or legs and rub his face with his paws or on the furniture, carpet, etc.
- Excessive scratching
- Ear infections
- Hot patches of skin
- Hair loss
- Redness and inflammation on the chin and face
- Recurring skin infections
- Increased bowel movements (maybe twice as often as usual)
- Skin infections that clear up with antibiotics but recur when the antibiotics run out

Allergies or Intolerance?

There's a difference between dog food *allergies* and dog food *intolerance*:

Typical reactions to allergies are skin problems and/or itching

Typical reactions to intolerance are diarrhoea and/or vomiting

Dog food intolerance can be compared to people who get diarrhoea or an upset stomach from eating spicy food. Both can be cured by a change to a diet specifically suited to the individual, although a food allergy may be harder to get to the root cause of. As they say in the canine world: "One dog's meat is another dog's poison." With dogs, certain ingredients are more likely to cause allergies than others. In order of the most common triggers across the canine world in general they are: **Beef, dairy products, chicken, wheat, eggs, corn, and soy.** There is also evidence that some Labradors are sensitive to wheat or grain.

Unfortunately, these most common offenders are also the most common ingredients in dog foods! By the way, don't think if you put your dog on a rice and lamb kibble diet that it will automatically cure the problem. It might, but then again there's a fair chance it won't. The reason lamb and rice were thought to be less likely to cause allergies is simply because they were not traditionally included in dog food recipes - therefore fewer dogs had reactions to them.

It is also worth noting that a dog is allergic or sensitive to an **ingredient**, not to a particular brand of dog food, so it is very important to read the label on the sack or tin. If your Labrador has a reaction to beef, for example, he will react to any food containing beef, regardless of how expensive it is or how well it has been prepared.

Symptoms of food allergies are well documented. Unfortunately, the problem is that these conditions may also be symptoms of other issues such as environmental or flea bite allergies, intestinal problems, mange and yeast or bacterial infections. You can have a blood test on your dog for food allergies, but many veterinarians now believe that this is not accurate enough.

The only way to completely cure a food allergy or intolerance is complete avoidance. This is not as easy as it sounds. First you have to be sure that your dog does have a food allergy, and then you have to discover which food is causing the reaction. Blood tests are not thought to be reliable and, as far as I am aware, the only true way to determine exactly what your dog is allergic to, is to start a food trial. If you don't or can't do this for the whole 12 weeks, then you could try a more amateurish approach, which is eliminating ingredients from your dog's diet one at a time by switching diets – remember to do this over a period of a week to 10 days.

A food trial is usually the option of last resort, due to the amount of time and attention that it requires. It is also called 'an exclusion diet' and is the only truly accurate way of finding out if your dog has a food allergy and what is causing it. Before embarking on one, try switching dog food. A hypoallergenic dog food, either commercial or home-made, is a good place to start. There are a number of these on the market and they all have the word 'hypoallergenic' in the name.

Although usually more expensive, hypoallergenic dog food ingredients do not include common allergens such as wheat protein or soya, thereby minimising the risk of an allergic reaction. Many may have less common ingredients, such as venison, duck or types of fish. Here are some things to look for in a high quality food: meat or poultry as the first ingredient, vegetables, natural herbs such as rosemary or parsley, oils such as rapeseed (canola) or salmon.

There is evidence from some owners that a raw diet can solve the problem, but only start raw feeding if you have the time and commitment to stick to it.

Here's what to avoid if your dog is showing signs of a food intolerance: corn, corn meal, corn gluten meal, meat or poultry by-products (as you don't know exactly what these are or how they have been handled), artificial preservatives (including BHA, BHT, Propyl Gallate, Ethoxyquin, Sodium Nitrite/Nitrate and TBHQBHA), artificial colours, sugars and sweeteners like corn syrup, sucrose and ammoniated glycyrrhizin, powdered cellulose, propylene glycol. If you can rule out all of these and you've tried switching diet without much success, then a food trial may be your only option.

....

Food Trials

Before you embark on one of these, you need to know that they are a real pain-in-the-you-know-what to monitor. You have to be incredibly vigilant and determined, so only start one if you 100% know you can see it through to the end, or you are wasting your time. It is important to keep a diary during a food trial to record any changes in your dog's symptoms, behaviour or habits.

A food trial involves feeding one specific food for 12 weeks, something the dog has never eaten before, such as rabbit and rice or venison and potato. Surprisingly, dogs are typically NOT allergic to foods they have never eaten before. The food should contain no added colouring, preservatives or flavourings.

There are a number of these commercial diets on the market, as well as specialised diets that have proteins and carbohydrates broken down into such small molecular sizes that they no longer trigger an allergic reaction. These are called 'limited antigen' or 'hydrolysed protein' diets.

Home-made diets are another option as you can strictly control the ingredients. The difficult thing is that this must be the **only thing** the dog eats during the trial. Any treats or snacks make the whole thing a waste of time. During the trial, you shouldn't allow your dog to roam freely, as you cannot control what he is eating or drinking when he is out of sight outdoors. Only the recommended diet must be fed. Do NOT give:

- Treats
- Rawhide (not recommended for fast gulping Labs, anyway)
- Pigs' ears
- Cows' hooves
- Flavoured medications (including heartworm treatments) or supplements
- Flavoured toothpastes
- Flavoured plastic toys

If you want to give a treat, use the recommended diet. (Tinned diets can be frozen in chunks or baked and then used as treats). If you have other dogs, either feed them all on the trial diet or feed the others in an entirely different location. If you have a cat, don't let the dog near the cat litter tray. And keep your dog out of the room when you are eating – not easy with a hungry Lab! But even small amounts of food dropped on the floor or licked off of a plate can ruin a food trial, meaning you'll have to start all over again.

Labradors and Grain

Although beef is the food most likely to cause allergies in the general dog population, there is plenty of anecdotal evidence to suggest that the ingredient most likely to cause a problem in some Labradors is grain – just visit any internet forum to see some of the problems owners are experiencing with their Labs. 'Grain' is wheat or any other cultivated cereal crop. Some dogs also react to starch, which is found in grains and potatoes (also bread, pasta rice, etc.).

Labradors as well as many other breeds, especially the Bully breeds, e.g. Bulldogs, Boxers, Bull Terriers and French Bulldogs, **can be prone to a build-up of yeast in the digestive system.** Foods that are high in grains and sugar can cause an increase in unhealthy bacteria and yeast in the stomach. This crowds out the good bacteria in the stomach and can cause toxins to occur that affect the immune system.

When the immune system is not functioning properly the itchiness related to food allergies can cause secondary bacterial and yeast infections, which, in Labradors, often show as ear infections. Other symptoms are skin disorders, hot spots, bladder infections and reddish or dark brown tear stains. Symptoms of a yeast infection also include:

- Itchiness
- A musty smell

🐾 Skin lesions or redness on the underside of the neck, the belly or paws

Although drugs such as antihistamines and steroids will temporarily help, they do not address the root cause. Switching to a grain-free diet may help your dog get rid of the yeast and toxins. Some owners also feed their Labs a daily spoonful of natural or live yoghurt, as this contains healthy bacteria and helps to balance the bacteria in your dog's digestive system - by the way, it works for humans too! Others have switched their dogs to a raw diet.

Switching to a grain-free diet may help to get rid of yeast and bad bacteria in the digestive system. Introduce the new food over a week to 10 days and be patient, it may take two to three months for symptoms to subside – but you will definitely know if it has worked after 12 weeks. Wheat products are also known to produce flatulence in some Labradors, while corn products and feed fillers may cause skin rashes or irritations.

It is also worth noting that some of the symptoms of food allergies - particularly the scratching, licking, chewing and redness - can also be a sign of inhalant or contact (environmental) allergies, which are caused by a reaction to such triggers as pollen, grass or dust. Some dogs are also allergic to flea bites. See **Chapter 12. Skin and Allergies** for more details.

If you suspect your dog has a food allergy, the first port of call should be to the vet to discuss the best course of action. However, many vets' practices promote specific brands of dog food, which may or may not be the best for your dog. Don't buy anything without first checking every ingredient on the label. The website www.dogfoodadvisor.com provides useful information with star ratings for grain-free and hypoallergenic dogs' foods, or www.allaboutdogfood.co.uk if you are in the UK, or www.veterinarypartner.com/Content.plx?P=A&S=0&C=0&A=2499 for more details about canine food trials. We have no vested interest in these sites, but have found them to be good sources of unbiased information.

How Much Food?

This is another question I am often asked. The answer is ... there is no easy answer! The correct amount of food for a dog depends on a number of factors:

🐾 Breed

🐾 Gender

🐾 Age

🐾 Natural energy levels

🐾 Amount of daily exercise

🐾 Health

🐾 Environment

🐾 Number of dogs in the house or kennel

🐾 Quality of the food

🐾 Whether your dog is working, competing, performing a service or simply a pet

Some breeds have a higher metabolic rate than others and energy levels vary tremendously from one dog to the next. Some Labs are

very energetic, while others veer towards the couch potato in personality.

Generally, smaller dogs have faster metabolisms so require a higher amount of food per pound of body weight. Dogs that have been spayed may be more likely to put on weight. Growing puppies and young dogs need more food than senior dogs with a slower lifestyle.

Every dog is different; you can have two Labradors with different energy levels, body shapes and capacity for work or exercise. The energetic dog will burn off more calories. Maintaining a healthy body weight for dogs – and humans – is all about balancing what you take in with how much you burn off. If your dog is exercised a couple of times a day, is retrieving on shoots or competing in field trials or agility, or has regular play sessions with humans or other dogs, he will need more calories than the couch potato Labrador.

And certain health conditions such as an underactive thyroid, diabetes, arthritis or heart disease can lead to dogs putting on weight, so their food has to be adjusted accordingly. Just like us, a dog kept in a very cold environment will need more calories to keep warm than a dog in a warm climate, as they burn extra calories to keep themselves warm. Here's an interesting fact: a dog kept on his own is more likely to be overweight than a dog kept with other dogs, as he receives all of the food-based attention.

Manufacturers of cheaper foods usually recommend feeding more to your dog, as much of the food is made up of cereals, which are not doing much except bulking up the weight of the food – and possibly triggering allergies in your Labrador. The daily recommended amount listed on the

dog food sacks or tins is generally too high – after all, the more your dog eats, the more they sell!

Because there are so many factors involved, there is no simple answer. However, below we have listed a broad guideline of the average number of **calories** a Labrador with medium energy and activity levels needs. (These charts are not suitable for working dogs, as they require specialised high calorie diets during the season).

Pictured retrieving is Julie McDonough's Zak. Photo by Della Bellamy Photography.

We feed our dog a dried hypoallergenic dog food made by James Wellbeloved in England. Here we list their recommended feeding amounts for dogs, listed in kilograms and grams. (28.3 grams=1 ounce, 1kg=2.2lb). The number on the left is the dog's **adult weight** in kilograms.

The numbers on the right are the amount of daily food that an average dog with average energy levels requires, measured in grams (divide this by 28.3 to get the amount in ounces). For example, a three-month-old Lab puppy which will grow into a 5kg (11lb) adult would require around 110 grams of food per day (3.9 ounces).

NOTE: The following Canine Feeding Chart gives only very general guidelines; your dog may need more or less than this. Use the chart as a guideline only and if your dog loses or gains weight, adjust meals accordingly.

PUPPY

Size type	Expected adult body weight	Daily serving in grams and ounces					
		2 mths	3 mths	4 mths	5 mths	6 mths	> 6 mths
LARGE	25kg 55lb	270g 9.5oz	350g 12.3oz	375g 13.2oz	375g 13.2oz	370g 13oz	Change to Large Breed Junior
	32kg 70.5lb	300g 10.6oz	400g 14.1oz	445g 15.7oz	450g 15.9oz	450g 15.9oz	
	40kg 88lb	355g 12.5oz	475g 16.75oz	525g 18.5oz	530g 18.7oz	530g 18.7oz	

JUNIOR

Size type	Expected adult body weight	Daily serving in grams and ounces						16 mths
		6 mths	7 mths	8 mths	10 mths	12 mths	14 mths	
LARGE	25kg 55lb	390g 13.75oz	380g 13.4oz	365g 12.9oz	330g 11.6oz	320g 11.3oz		Change to Large Breed Junior
	32kg 70.5lb	445g 15.7oz	435g 15.3oz	415g 14.6oz	380g 13.4oz	365g 12.9oz		
	40kg 88lb	555g 12.5oz	545g 16.75oz	530g 18.5oz	500g 18.7oz	460g 18.7oz	460g 18.7oz	

ADULT

Size type	Adult body weight	Daily serving in grams and ounces		
		High activity	Normal activity	Low activity
LARGE	25-40kg 55-88lb	380-535g 13.4-18.9oz	330-475g 11.6-16.75oz	285-410g 10-14.5oz

SENIOR

Size type	Adult body weight	Active	Normal
LARGE	25-40kg 55-88lb	345-495g 12.2-17.5oz	300-425g 10.6-15oz

Canine Bloat (GDV, Gastric Dilation-Volvulvus)

One reason that some owners feed their Labs twice a day is to reduce the risk of canine bloat, particularly if their dogs are greedy gulpers. Canine bloat is a serious medical condition which requires urgent medical attention. Without it, the dog can die. In fact, it is one of the leading killers of dogs after cancer.

Bloat is known by several different names: twisted stomach, gastric torsion or Gastric Dilatation-Volvulus (GDV. It occurs mainly in larger breeds, particularly those with deep chests like Great Danes, Doberman Pinschers, Giant Schnauzers and Setters; however, the Labrador can also be affected. Basically, bloat occurs when there is too much gas in the stomach; it is more common in males than in females and dogs over seven years of age.

The causes are not fully understood, but there are some well-known risk factors. One is the dog taking in a lot of air while eating - either because he is greedy and gulping the food too fast, or stressed, e.g. in kennels where there might be food competition. A dog which is fed once daily and gorges himself could be at higher risk, and exercising straight after eating or after a big drink increases the risk (like colic in horses). Another potential cause is diet. Fermentable foodstuffs that produce a lot of gas can cause problems for the stomach if the gas is not burped or passed into the intestines. Bloat can occur with or without the stomach twisting (volvulus).

As the stomach swells with gas, it can rotate 90° to 360°. The twisting stomach traps air, food and water inside and the bloated organ stops blood flowing properly to veins in the abdomen, leading to low blood pressure, shock and even damage to internal organs.

Symptoms - Bloat is extremely painful and the dog will show signs of distress. He may stand uncomfortably or seem anxious for no apparent reason. A dog with bloat will often attempt to vomit every five to 30 minutes, but nothing is fetched up, except perhaps foam. Other signs include swelling of the abdomen (this will usually feel firm like a drum) – general weakness, difficulty breathing or rapid panting, drooling or excessive drinking. His behavior will change and he may do some of the following: whine, pace up and down, look for a hiding place or lick the air.

Tips to Avoid Canine Bloat:

- ❧ Some owners buy a frame for food bowls so they are at chest height for the dog, other experts believe dogs should be fed from the floor – do whichever slows your Lab down

- ❧ Buy a bowl with nobbles in (pictured) and moisten your dog's food – both of these will slow him down

- ❧ Feed twice a day rather than once

- ❧ Diet - avoid dog food with high fats or which use citric acid as a preservative, also avoid tiny pieces of kibble

- ❧ Don't let your dog drink too much water just before, during or after eating. Remove the water bowl just before mealtimes, but be sure to return it soon after

- ❧ Stress can possibly be a possible trigger, with nervous and aggressive dogs being more susceptible; maintain a peaceful environment for your dog, particularly around mealtimes

- ❧ IMPORTANT: Avoid vigorous exercise before or after eating, allow one hour either side of mealtimes before strenuous exercise

Bloat can kill a dog in less than one hour. If you suspect your Labrador has bloat, get him into the car and off to the vet IMMEDIATELY. Even with treatment, mortality rates range from 10% to 60%. With surgery, this drops to 15% to 33%.

Overweight Dogs

It is far easier to regulate your Labrador's weight and keep it at a healthy level than to try and slim down a voraciously hungry Labrador when he becomes overweight. Labradors are often food obsessed and prone to putting on weight and, sadly, overweight and obese dogs are susceptible to a range of illnesses. According to James Howie, Veterinary Advisor to Lintbells, some of the main ones are:

Joint disease – excessive body weight may increase joint stress, which is a risk factor in joint degeneration (arthrosis), as is cruciate disease (knee ligament rupture). Joint disease tends to lead to a reduction in exercise that then increases the likelihood of weight gain which reduces exercise further. A vicious cycle is created. Overfeeding growing Labradors can lead to various problems, including the worsening of hip dysplasia. Weight management may be the only measure required to control clinical signs in some cases.

Heart and lung problems – fatty deposits within the chest cavity and excessive circulating fat play important roles in the development of cardio-respiratory and cardiovascular disease.

Diabetes – resistance to insulin has been shown to occur in overweight dogs, leading to a greater risk of diabetes mellitus.

Tumours – obesity increases the risk of mammary tumours in female dogs.

Liver disease – fat degeneration may result in liver insufficiency.

Reduced Lifespan - one of the most serious proven findings in obesity studies is that obesity in both humans and dogs reduces lifespan.

Exercise intolerance – this is also a common finding with overweight dogs, which can compound an obesity problem as fewer calories are burned off and are therefore stored, leading to further weight gain. Obesity also puts greater strain on the delicate respiratory system of Labradors, making breathing even more difficult for them. Most Labradors are extremely loyal companions and very attached to their humans. However, beware of going too far in regarding your dog as a member of the family. It has been shown that dogs regarded as 'family members' (i.e. anthropomorphosis) by the owner are at greater risk of becoming overweight. This is because attention given to the dog often results in food being given as well.

The important thing to remember is that many of the problems associated with being overweight are reversible. Increasing exercise increases the calories burned, which in turn reduces weight. If you do put your dog on a diet, the reduced amount of food will also mean reduced nutrients, so he may need a supplement during this time.

Feeding Puppies

Feeding your Labrador puppy the right diet is important to help his young body and bones grow strong and healthy. Puppyhood is a time of rapid growth and development, and puppies require different levels of nutrients to adult dogs.

For the first six weeks, puppies need milk about five to seven times a day, which they take from their mother. Generally they make some sound if they want to feed. The frequency is reduced when the pup reaches six to eight weeks old. Labrador puppies should stay with their mothers and littermates until **at least** eight weeks old.

(Photo courtesy of Christine Eynon, of Baileylane Labradors, Ross on Wye, Herefordshire).

During this time, the mother is still teaching her offspring some important rules about life. For the first few days or weeks after that, it's a good idea to continue feeding the same puppy food and at the same times as the breeder. Dogs do not adapt to changes in their diet or feeding habits as easily as humans.

If you live far away from the breeder, you might also want to consider taking a large container to fill with water at the breeder's house and mixing this water with your own tap water back home. Different types of water, e.g. moving from a soft water area to a hard water area or vice versa, can upset a sensitive pup's stomach.

At home you can then slowly change his food based on information from the breeder and your vet —although some owners prefer to stick with the same food, as recommended by the breeder. This should be done very gradually by mixing in a little more of the new food each day over a period of seven to 10 days. If at any time your puppy starts being sick, has loose stools or is constipated, slow the rate at which you are switching him over. If he continues vomiting, seek veterinary advice as he may have a problem with the food you have chosen. Puppies who are vomiting or who have diarrhoea quickly dehydrate.

Because of their special nutritional needs, you should only give your puppy a food that is approved either just for puppies or for all life stages. If a feed is recommended for adult dogs only, it won't have enough protein, and the balance of calcium and other nutrients will not be right for a pup. Puppy food is very high in calories and nutritional supplements, so you want to switch to a junior or adult food once he leaves puppyhood, which is at about six months old. Feeding puppy food too long can result in obesity and orthopaedic problems.

Getting the amount and type of food right for your pup is important. Feeding too much will cause him to put on excess pounds, and overweight puppies are more likely to grow into overweight adults. As a very broad guideline, Labradors normally mature into fully developed adults at around two years old.

DON'T:

* Feed table scraps from the table. Your Labrador will get used to begging for food, it will also affect a puppy's carefully balanced diet

* Feed food or uncooked meat that has gone off. Puppies have sensitive stomachs

DO:

* Regularly check the weight of your growing puppy to make sure he is within normal limits for his age. There are charts available on numerous websites, just type "puppy weight chart" into Google – you'll need to know the exact age and current weight of your puppy

* Take your puppy to the vet if he has diarrhoea or is vomiting for two days or more

🐾 Remove his food after it has been down for 15 to 20 minutes. Food available 24/7 encourages fussy eaters

How Often?

Labrador puppies have small stomachs but big appetites, so feed them small amounts on a frequent basis. Establishing a regular feeding routine with your puppy is a good idea, as this will also help to toilet train him. Get him used to regular mealtimes and then let him outside to do his business straight away when he has finished. Puppies have fast metabolisms, so the results may be pretty quick! Don't leave food out for the puppy so that he can eat it whenever he wants, as you need to be there for the feeds because you want him and his body on a set schedule. Smaller meals are easier for him to digest and energy levels don't peak and fall so much with frequent feeds. There is some variation between recommendations, but as a general rule of thumb:

🐾 Up to the age of three or four months, feed your puppy three or four times a day

🐾 Then three times a day until he is four to six months old

🐾 Twice a day until he is one year old

🐾 Then once or twice a day for the rest of his life

Labradors are known for their healthy appetites and will eat most things put in front of them, it's up to you to control their intake and manage their diet. Stick to the correct amount; you're doing your pup no favours by overfeeding him. Unless your puppy is particularly thin (which is unlikely if he has been well bred), don't give in - no matter how much your cute pup pleads with his big, soulful eyes. You must be firm and resist the temptation to give him extra food or treats.

A very broad rule of thumb is to feed puppy food for a year, but some owners start earlier on adult food, while others delay switching until their Labrador is 18 months or even two years old. If you are not sure, consult your breeder or your vet.

 Labs are very loving companions. If your dog is not responding well to a particular family member, a useful tactic is to get that person to feed the dog every day. The way to a Labrador's heart is often through his or her stomach!

Feeding Seniors

Once your adolescent dog has switched to an adult diet he will be on this for several years. However, as a dog moves towards old age, his body has different requirements to those of a young dog. This is the time to consider switching to a senior diet.

++Dogs are living longer than they did 30 years ago. There are many factors contributing to this, including better immunisation and veterinary care, but one of the most important factors is better nutrition. Generally a dog is considered to be 'older' or senior if he is in the last third of his normal life expectancy.

Some owners of large breeds, such as Great Danes (with an average lifespan of nine years) switch their dogs from an adult to a senior diet when they are only six or seven years old. A Labrador's lifespan is around 11 to 14 years and when and if you switch depends on your individual dog, his or her energy levels and general health. Look for signs of your dog slowing down or having joint problems. If you wish to discuss it with your vet, you can describe any changes at your dog's annual vaccination appointment, rather than having the expense of a separate consultation.

As a dog ages his metabolism slows, his joints stiffen, his energy levels decrease and he needs less exercise, just as with humans. You may notice in middle or old age that your dog starts to put weight on. An adult diet may be too rich and have too many calories, so it may be the time to move to a senior diet. Having said that, some dogs stay on a normal adult diet all of their lives – although the amount is usually decreased and supplements added, e.g. for joints.

Even though he is older, keep his weight in check, as obesity in old age only puts more strain on his body - especially joints and organs - and makes any health problems even worse. Because of lower activity levels, many older dogs will gain weight and getting an older dog to slim down can be very difficult. It is much better not to let your Lab get too chunky than to put him on a diet. But if he is overweight, put in the effort to shed the extra pounds. This is one of the single most important things you can do to increase your Labrador's quality AND length of life.

Other changes in canines are again similar to those in older humans and as well as stiff joints or arthritis, they may move more slowly and sleep more. Hearing and vision may not be so sharp and organs don't all work as efficiently as they used to; teeth may have become worn down. When this starts to happen, it is time to consider feeding your old friend a senior diet, which will take these changes into account. Specially formulated senior diets are lower in protein and calories but help to create a feeling of fullness.

Older dogs are more prone to develop constipation, so senior diets are often higher in fibre - at around 3% to 5%. Wheat bran can also be added to regular dog food to increase the amount of fibre - but do not try this if your Lab has a low tolerance or intolerance to grain. If your dog has poor kidney function, then a low phosphorus diet will help to lower the workload for the kidneys.

Ageing dogs have special dietary needs, some of which can be provided in the form of supplements, such as glucosamine and chondroitin, which help joints. Two popular joint supplements in the UK are GWF Joint Aid for dogs, used by several breeders, and Lintbell's Yumove. If your dog is not eating a complete balanced diet, then a vitamin/mineral supplement is recommended to prevent any deficiencies. Some owners also feed extra antioxidants to an older dog – ask your vet's advice on your next visit. Antioxidants are also found naturally in fruit and vegetables.

While some older Labs suffer from obesity, others have the opposite problem – they lose weight and are disinterested in food. If your old dog is getting thinner and not eating well, firstly get him checked out by the vet to rule out any possible diseases. If he gets the all-clear, your next challenge is to tempt him to eat. He may be having trouble with his teeth, so if he's on a dry food, try smaller kibble or moistening it with water or gravy.

Our dog loved his twice daily feeds until he recently got to the age of 10 when he suddenly lost interest in his food, which is a hypoallergenic kibble. We tried switching flavours within the same brand, but that didn't work. After a short while we mixed his daily feeds with a little gravy and a spoonful of tinned dog food – Bingo! He's wolfing it down again and lively as ever.

Some dogs can tolerate a small amount of milk or eggs added to their food, and home-made diets of boiled rice, potatoes, vegetables and chicken or meat with the right vitamin and mineral supplements can also work well.

See **Chapter 16. Caring for Older Dogs** for more information on looking after a senior Labrador.

Reading Dog Food Labels

A NASA scientist would have a hard job understanding some manufacturers' labels, so it's no easy task for us lowly dog owners. Here are some things to look out for on the manufacturers' labels:

🐾 The ingredients are listed by weight and the top one should always be the main content, such as chicken or lamb. Don't pick one where grain is the first ingredient; it is a poor quality feed. Some Labradors can develop grain intolerances or allergies, and often it is specifically wheat they have a reaction to

🐾 High on the list should be meat or poultry by-products, these are clean parts of slaughtered animals, not including meat. They include organs, blood and bone, but not hair, horns, teeth or hooves

🐾 Chicken meal (dehydrated chicken) has more protein than fresh chicken, which is 80% water. The same goes for beef, fish and lamb. So, if any of these meals are number one on the ingredient list, the food should contain enough protein

🐾 A certain amount of flavourings can make a food more appetising for your dog. Choose a food with a specific flavouring, like *'beef flavouring'* rather than a general *'meat flavouring'*, where the origins are not so clear

Ingredients: Chicken, Chicken By-Product Meal, Corn Meal, Ground Whole Grain Sorghum, Brewers Rice, Ground Whole Grain Barley, Dried Beet Pulp, Chicken Fat (preserved with mixed Tocopherols, a source of Vitamin E), Chicken Flavor, Dried Egg Product, Fish Oil (preserved with mixed Tocopherols, a source of Vitamin E), Potassium Chloride, Salt, Flax Meal, Sodium Hexametaphosphate, Fructooligosaccharides, Choline Chloride, Minerals (Ferrous Sulfate, Zinc Oxide, Manganese Sulfate, Copper Sulfate, Manganous Oxide, Potassium Iodide, Cobalt Carbonate), DL-Methionine, Vitamins (Ascorbic Acid, Vitamin A Acetate, Calcium Pantothenate, Biotin, Thiamine Mononitrate (source of vitamin B1), Vitamin B12 Supplement, Niacin, Riboflavin Supplement (source of vitamin B2), Inositol, Pyridoxine Hydrochloride (source of vitamin B6), Vitamin D3 Supplement, Folic Acid), Calcium Carbonate, Vitamin E Supplement, Brewers Dried Yeast, Beta-Carotene, Rosemary Extract.

🐾 Guaranteed Analysis – This guarantees that your dog's food contains the labelled percentages of crude protein, fat, fibre and moisture. Keep in mind that wet and dry dog foods use different standards. (It does not list the digestibility of protein and fat and this can vary widely depending on their sources).

While the Guaranteed Analysis is a start in understanding the food quality, be wary about relying on it too much. One pet food manufacturer made a mock product with a guaranteed analysis of 10% protein, 6.5% fat, 2.4% fibre, and 68% moisture (similar to what's on many canned pet food labels) – the ingredients were old leather boots, used motor oil, crushed coal and water!

🐾 Find a food that fits your dog's age, breed and size. Talk to your breeder, vet or visit an online Labrador forum and ask other owners what they are feeding their dogs

🐾 If your Lab has a food allergy or intolerance to wheat, check whether the food is gluten free; all wheat contains gluten

🐾 Natural is best. Food labelled *'natural'* means that the ingredients have not been chemically altered, according to the FDA in the USA. However, there are no such guidelines governing foods labelled *'holistic'* – so check the ingredients and how it has been prepared

🐾 In the USA, dog food that meets minimum nutrition requirements has a label that confirms this. It states: ***"[food name] is formulated to meet the nutritional***

Crude Protein (min)	32.25%
Lysine (min)	0.43%
Methionine (min)	0.49%
Crude Fat (min)	10.67%
Crude Fiber (max)	7.3%
Calcium (min)	0.50%
Calcium (max)	1.00%
Phosphorus (min)	0.44%
Salt (min)	0.01%
Salt (max)	0.51%

levels established by the AAFCO Dog Food Nutrient Profiles for [life stage(s)]"

Even better, look for a food that meets the minimum nutritional requirements *'as fed'* to real pets in an AAFCO-defined feeding trial, then you know the food really delivers the nutrients that it is *'formulated'* to AAFCO feeding trials on real dogs are the gold standard. Brands that do costly feeding trials (including Nestlé and Hill's) indicate so on the package.

NOTE: Dog food labelled *'supplemental'* isn't complete and balanced. Unless you have a specific, vet-approved need for it, it's not something you want to feed your dog for an extended period of time. Check with your vet if in doubt.

If it all still looks a bit baffling, you might find the following websites, mentioned earlier, very useful. The first is www.dogfoodadvisor.com run by Mike Sagman. He has a medical background and analyses and rates hundreds of brands of dog food based on the listed ingredients and meat content. You might be surprised at some of his findings. The second is www.allaboutdogfood.co.uk run by UK canine nutritionist David Jackson.

To recap: no one food is right for every dog; you must decide on the best for yours. If you have a puppy, initially stick to the same food that the breeder has been feeding the litter, and only change diet later and gradually. Once you have decided on a food, monitor your puppy or adult. The best test of a food is how well your dog is doing on it.

If your Labrador is happy and healthy, interested in life, has enough energy, is not too fat and not too thin, doesn't scratch a lot and has healthy-looking stools, then...

Congratulations, you've got it right!

8. Canine Behaviour

Just as with humans, a dog's personality is made up of a combination of temperament and character.

Temperament is the nature – or inherited characteristics - a dog is born with; a predisposition to act or react in a certain way. This is why getting your puppy from a good breeder is so important. Not only will he or she produce puppies from physically healthy dams and sires, but they will also look at the temperament of the dogs and only breed from those with good traits. You should also think carefully about what type of Labrador you want: from working or show (American or English) stock or a mixture of both.

Character is what develops through the dog's life and is formed by a combination of temperament and environment. How you treat your dog will have a huge effect on his or her personality and behaviour. Starting off on the right foot with good routines for your puppy is very important; so treat your dog well, spend time with him and make time for plenty of socialisation and exercise. All dogs need different environments, scents and experiences to keep them stimulated and well-balanced. Labradors enjoy swimming and time spent off the lead (leash) running free.

Praise good behaviour, use positive methods and keep training short and fun. At the same time, all dogs should understand the "No" (or similar) command. Just as with children, a dog has to learn boundaries to adapt successfully and be content with his or her environment. Be consistent so your dog learns the guidelines quickly. All of these measures will help your dog grow into a happy, well-adjusted and well-behaved adult dog who is a delight to be with.

If you adopt a Labrador from a rescue centre, you may need a little extra patience. These eager-to-please people-loving dogs may also arrive with some baggage. They have been abandoned by their previous owners for a variety of reasons - or perhaps forced to produce puppies in a puppy mill - and may very well still carry the scars of that trauma. They may feel nervous and insecure, they may be needy or aloof, and they may not know how to properly interact with a loving owner. Your time and patience is needed to teach these poor animals to trust again and to become happy in their new forever homes.

Understanding Canine Emotions

As pet lovers, we are all too keen to ascribe human characteristics to our dogs; this is called *anthropomorphism* – "the attribution of human characteristics to anything other than a human being." Most of us dog lovers are guilty of that, as we come to regard our pets as members of the family - and Labradors certainly regard themselves as members of the family. An example of anthropomorphism might be that the owner of a male dog might not want to have him neutered because he will "miss sex," as a human might if he or she were no longer able to have sex. This is simply not true. A male dog's impulse to mate is entirely governed by his hormones, not emotions. If he gets the scent of a bitch on heat, his hormones (which are just chemicals) tell him he has to mate with her. He does not stop to consider how attractive she is or whether she is 'the one' to produce his puppies. No, his reaction is entirely physical, he just wants to dive in there and get on with it!

It's the same with females. When they are on heat, a chemical impulse is triggered in their brain making them want to mate – with any male, they aren't at all fussy. So don't expect your little princess to be all coy when she is on heat, she is not waiting for Prince Charming to come along - the tramp down the road or any other scruffy pooch will do! It is entirely physical, not emotional.

Food is another issue – especially for Labradors. A dog will not stop to count the calories of that lovely treat (you have to do that). No, he or she is driven by food and just thinks about getting the treat. Most non-fussy eaters will eat far too much, given the opportunity.

Labradors are very loving, incredibly loyal and extremely eager to please you, and if yours doesn't make you laugh from time to time, you must have had a humour by-pass. All of this adds up to one thing: an extremely endearing and loving family member that it's all too easy to reward - or spoil. Treating a Labrador like a child is a habit to be avoided.

If your dog is kept indoors, it's fine to treat him like a member of the family - as long as you keep in mind that he is a canine and not a human. Understand his mind, patiently train him to learn his place in the household and that there are household rules he needs to learn – like not jumping on the couch when he's covered in mud - and you will be rewarded with a companion who is second to none and fits in beautifully with your family and lifestyle.

Dr Stanley Coren is a psychologist well known for his work on canine psychology and behaviour. He and other researchers believe that in many ways a dog's emotional development is equivalent to that of a young child. Dr Coren says: "Researchers have now come to believe that the mind of a dog is roughly equivalent to that of a human who is two to two-and-a-half years old. This conclusion holds for most mental abilities as well as emotions.

"Thus, we can look to human research to see what we might expect of our dogs. Just like a two-year-old child, our dogs clearly have emotions, but many fewer kinds of emotions than found in adult humans. At birth, a human infant only has an emotion that we might call excitement. This indicates how excited he is, ranging from very calm up to a state of frenzy. Within the first weeks of life the excitement state comes to take on a varying positive or a negative flavour, so we can now detect the general emotions of contentment and distress.

"In the next couple of months, disgust, fear, and anger become detectable in the infant. Joy often does not appear until the infant is nearly six months of age and it is followed by the emergence of shyness or suspicion. True affection, the sort that it makes sense to use the label "love" for, does not fully emerge until nine or ten months of age."

So, our Labradors can truly love us – but we knew that already!

According to Dr Coren, dogs can't feel shame, so if you are housetraining your puppy, don't expect him to be ashamed if he makes a mess in the house, he can't; he simply isn't capable of feeling shame. But he will not like it when you ignore him when he's behaving badly, and he will love it when you praise him for eliminating outdoors. He is simply responding to your reaction with his simplified range of emotions.

However, this story from one UK breeder gives us food for thought. She told us told us that when her Labrador has done something naughty, she is sent to the bathroom for a couple of minutes: "Our breeding chocolate 'punishes' herself. If there is something she thinks she has done that will get her told off, she goes and sits in the bathroom – and you then have to hunt round the house to see if you can find what she thinks she has done!"

Dr Coren also believes that dogs cannot experience guilt, contempt or pride. I'm no psychology expert, but I'm not sure I agree. Take a Labrador to a local dog show or obedience class, watch him perform and then maybe win a rosette - is the dog's delight something akin to pride? And Labradors can certainly experience joy. They love your attention and praise at home, and just watch a working Labrador out in the field if you want to see a happy dog. When they run through the dense undergrowth or dive into a pond and return with a present for you in the form of a deceased bird or small mammal - isn't there a hint of pride there?

Labradors can certainly show empathy - "the ability to understand and share the feelings of another" - and this is one reason why they make such excellent therapy and service dogs. Like many intelligent breeds, they can pick up on the mood and emotions of the owner.

One emotion that all dogs can experience is jealousy. It may display itself by possessive or aggressive behaviour over food or a toy, for example. An interesting article was published in the PLOS (Public Library of Science) Journal in 2014 following an experiment into whether dogs get jealous. Building on research that shows that six-month old infants display jealousy, the scientists studied 36 dogs in their homes and video recorded their actions when their owners displayed affection to a realistic-looking stuffed canine (pictured).

Over three-quarters of the dogs were likely to push or touch the owner when they interacted with the decoy. The envious mutts were more than three times as likely to do this for interactions with the stuffed dog compared to when their owners gave their attention to other objects, including a book. Around a third tried to get between the owner and the plush toy, while a quarter of the put-upon pooches snapped at the dummy dog!

"Our study suggests not only that dogs do engage in what appear to be jealous behaviours, but also that they were seeking to break up the connection between the owner and a seeming rival," said Professor Christine Harris from University of California in San Diego.

The researchers believe that the dogs understood that the stuffed dog was real. The authors cite the fact that 86% of the dogs sniffed the toy's rear end during and after the experiment!

"We can't really speak of the dogs' subjective experiences, of course, but it looks as though they were motivated to protect an important social relationship. Many people have assumed that jealousy is a social construction of human beings - or that it's an emotion specifically tied to sexual and romantic relationships," said Professor Harris. "Our results challenge these ideas, showing that animals besides ourselves display strong distress whenever a rival usurps a loved one's affection."

Typical Labrador Traits

Every dog is different, of course. But within the breeds, there are some similarities. Here are some typical Labrador characteristics - some of them also apply to other breeds of dog, but put them all together and you have a blueprint for the Labrador.

1. Perhaps more than any other dog, the Labrador has developed a unique bond with humans, and is able to fulfil more roles to assist us than any other breed. Labradors excel as working retrievers and in obedience competitions; they are search and rescue dogs as well as service and therapy dogs, helping a wide range of people, including those with visual or hearing difficulties, adults with epilepsy or diabetes, and autistic children; they assist the military, they can be trained to detect drugs, explosives and even cancer and, above all, they are loyal companions.

2. The Labrador was originally bred as a working gundog to retrieve game; many are still used for this purpose. Dogs bred from working lines often have a greater need for mental stimulation and higher exercise demands than other types of dog, such as those bred purely for companionship. Even if your Labrador is a pet, he or she still has those natural instincts to some extent. (Pictured is gundog trainer Andrew Baker, of Saffronlyn Gundogs, South Yorkshire, with his dog, Murphy. Photo by Caroline Bridges Photography).

3. They also have very soft mouths for retrieving - and can carry things very gently in their mouths.

4. Labradors have a naturally kind, friendly and easy-going temperament; the American Kennel Club describes them as "gentle, intelligent and family-friendly."

5. Labradors are generally tolerant and non-aggressive (provided they have been properly socialised). They are known for getting along well with children - although young children and dogs should always be supervised — as well as other dogs and other pets.

6. Young Labradors can be extremely boisterous, jumping up and knocking things over, and some owners wonder what they have let themselves in for. They usually settle down by around two years of age.

7. They are the most popular dog on the planet, and make wonderful companions and family dogs - as long as they get enough physical and mental stimulation.

8. Labradors are highly intelligent dogs that enjoy being involved. They love to play both indoor and outdoor games and enjoy activities that challenge them, such as obedience events, field trials or retrieving on a shoot.

9. They do not make good guard dogs; they are too friendly. Many Labs do not bark a lot.

10. Labradors are known for being extremely greedy. On the plus side, this is a great training aid; on the downside, you have to constantly monitor their diet and weight.

11. Labradors are very eager to please their owners; they are intelligent and love treats. All of this adds up to them being one of the easiest of all the breeds to train – provided you put the time in. They respond well to praise and treats, but do not like rough handling or heavy-handed training. Labs can be trained to a very high level in a number of different fields.

12. The same goes for housetraining; a Labrador can get the hang of it in a week or two, provided you are extremely vigilant in the beginning.

13. Exercise varies from one Lab to another. Much depends on what bloodlines they come from and what they get used to as a puppy. They are, however, large dogs and the UK Kennel Club recommends two or more hours of exercise per day.

14. They love water and are good swimmers. They have a hardy, double coat and most cope well with cold water and snow.

15. Most Labs are happy to chill out and snuggle up with their owners after a good exercise session.

16. An under-exercised, under-stimulated Labrador will display poor behaviour, as any dog will.

17. Labradors are honest, loyal dogs that become very attached to their owners. They will steal your heart - OK, that's not very scientific, but ask anyone who owns one!

....

Cause and Effect

As you've read, treated well, socialised and trained, well-bred Labradors make devoted canine companions and excellent working and competitive dogs. They are affectionate and sociable, they love being around people or other dogs. Once you've had one, no other dog seems quite the same.

But sometimes Labradors, just like other breeds, can develop behaviour problems. There are numerous reasons for this; every dog is an individual with his or her own temperament and environment, both of which influence the way he or she interacts with you and the world. Poor behaviour may result from a number of factors, including:

- Poor breeding
- Boredom, due to lack of exercise or mental challenges
- Being left alone too long
- Lack of socialisation
- Lack of training
- Being badly treated
- A change in living conditions
- Anxiety or insecurity
- Fear
- Being spoiled

Bad behaviour may show itself in a number of different ways, such as:

- Constantly demanding attention
- Chewing or destructive behaviour
- Jumping up

- ✤ Excessive barking
- ✤ Biting or nipping
- ✤ Growling
- ✤ Soiling or urinating inside the house
- ✤ Aggression towards other dogs

This chapter looks at some familiar behaviour problems and is geared towards dogs kept in the house as pets (rather than working dogs kennelled outside). Although every dog is different, some common causes of unwanted behaviour are covered, along with tips to help improve the situation. The best way to avoid poor behaviour is to put in the time early on to socialise and train your dog, and nip any potential problems in the bud. If you are rehoming a dog, you'll need extra time and patience to help your new arrival unlearn some bad habits.

....

10 Ways to Avoid Bad Behaviour

Different dogs have different reasons for exhibiting bad behaviour. There is no simple cure for everything. Your best chance of ensuring your dog does not become badly behaved is to start out on the right foot and follow these simple guidelines:

1. **Buy from a good breeder.** They use their expertise to match suitable breeding pairs, taking into account factors such as good temperament, health and being "fit for function."
2. **Start socialisation right away.** We now realise the vital role that early socialisation plays in developing a well-rounded adult dog. It is essential to expose your dog to other people, places, animals and experiences as soon as possible. Give him a few days to settle in and then start – even if this means carrying him places until his vaccination schedule is complete. Lack of socialisation is one of the major causes of unwanted behaviour. Exposing your puppy to as many different things as possible goes a long way in helping a dog become a more stable, happy and trustworthy companion.

IMPORTANT: Socialisation does not end at puppyhood. Labradors are social creatures that thrive on sniffing, seeing, hearing and even licking. While the foundation for good behaviour is laid down

during the first few months, good owners will reinforce social skills and training throughout a dog's life. Labradors love to be at the centre of the action and it is important that they learn when young that they are not also the centre of the universe. Socialisation helps them to learn their place in that universe and to become comfortable with it.

3. **Start training early** - you can't start too soon. Like babies, Labrador puppies have incredibly enquiring minds that can quickly absorb a lot of new information. You can start teaching your puppy to learn his own name as well as some

simple commands a couple of days after you bring him home.

4. **Basic training should cover several areas**: housetraining, chew prevention, puppy biting, simple commands like 'sit', 'come', 'stay' and familiarising him with a collar or harness and lead. Adopt a gentle approach and keep training sessions short. Labradors are sensitive to you and your mood and do not respond well to harsh words or treatment. Start with five or 10 minutes a day and build up. Often the way a dog responds to his or her environment is a result of owner training and management – or lack of it. Puppy classes or adult dog obedience classes are a great way to start, but make sure you do your homework afterwards. Spend a few minutes each day reinforcing what you have both learned in class - owners need training as well as dogs!

5. **Reward your dog for good behaviour.** All behaviour training should be based on positive reinforcement; so praise and reward your dog when he does something good. Generally, Labradors live to please their owners, and this trait speeds up the training process. The main aim of training is to build a good understanding between you and your dog.

6. **Ignore bad behaviour**, no matter how hard this may be. If, for example, your dog is chewing his way through your shoes, the couch or toilet rolls or eating things he shouldn't, remove him from the situation and then ignore him. For some dogs even negative attention is some attention. Or if he is constantly demanding your attention, ignore him. Remove yourself from the room so he learns that you give attention when you want to give it, **not** when he demands it. The more time you spend praising and rewarding good behaviour, while ignoring bad behaviour, the more likely he is to respond to you. If your pup is a chewer – and most are - make sure he has plenty of durable toys to keep him occupied. Labradors can chew their way through flimsy toys in no time.

7. **Take the time to learn what sort of temperament your dog has.** Is she by nature a nervous or confident girl? What was she like as a puppy, did she rush forward or hang back? Does she fight to get upright when on her back or is she happy to lie there? Is she a couch potato or a ball of fire? Your puppy's temperament will affect her behaviour and how she responds to the world around her. A timid Labrador will certainly not respond well to a loud approach on your part, whereas an energetic, strong-willed one will require more patience and exercise.

8. **Exercise and stimulation.** A lack of either is another major reason for dogs behaving badly. Regular daily exercise, indoor or outdoor games and toys are all ways of stopping your dog from becoming bored or frustrated.

9. **Learn to leave your dog.** Just as leaving your dog alone for too long can lead to problems, so can being with him 100% of the time. The dog becomes over-reliant on you and then gets stressed when you leave; this is called *separation anxiety*. When your dog first arrives at your house, start by leaving him for a few minutes every day and gradually build it up so that after a few weeks you can leave him for up to four hours.

10. **Love your Labrador – but don't spoil him,** however difficult that might be. You don't do your dog any favours by giving him too many treats, constantly responding to his demands for attention or allowing him to behave as he wants inside the house.

Separation Anxiety

It's not just dogs that experience separation anxiety - people do too. About 7% of adults and 4% of children suffer from this disorder. Typical symptoms for humans are:

❧ Distress at being separated from a loved one

❧ Fear of being left alone

Our canine companions aren't much different to us. When a dog leaves the litter, his owners become his new family or pack. It's estimated that as many as 10% to 15% of dogs suffer from separation anxiety. It is an exaggerated fear response caused by separation from their owner. Labradors are not particularly susceptible to separation anxiety, but some can suffer from it if they have not spent time away from their owners when young.

Separation anxiety is on the increase and recognised by behaviourists as the most common form of stress for dogs. Millions of dogs suffer from separation anxiety.

It can be equally distressing for the owner - I know because our dog, Max, suffers from this. He howls whenever we leave home without him. Fortunately his problem is only a mild one. If we return after only a short while, he's usually quiet. Although if we silently sneak back home and peek in through the letterbox, he's never asleep. Instead he's waiting by the door looking and listening for our return. It can be embarrassing. Whenever I go to the Post Office, I tie him up outside and even though he can see me through the glass door, he still barks his head off - so loud that the people inside can't make themselves heard. Luckily the lady behind the counter is a dog lover and, despite the large **'GUIDE DOGS ONLY'** sign outside, she lets Max in. He promptly dashes through the door and sits down beside me, quiet as a mouse!

Tell-Tale Signs

Does your Labrador do any of the following?

❧ Follow you from room to room – even the toilet - whenever you're home?

❧ Get anxious or stressed when you're getting ready to leave the house?

❧ Howl, whine or bark when you leave?

❧ Tear up paper or chew cushions, couches or other objects?

❧ Dig, chew, or scratch at the carpet, doors or windows trying to join you?

❧ Soil or urinate inside the house, even though he is housetrained? (This **only** occurs when left alone)

❧ Exhibit restlessness - such as licking his coat excessively, pacing or circling?

- Greet you ecstatically every time you come home – even if you've only been out to empty the bins?

- Wait by the window or door until you return?

- Dislike spending time alone in the garden or yard?

- Refuses to eat or drink if you leave him?

- Howl or whine when one family member leaves - even though others are still in the room or car?

If so, he or she may suffer from separation anxiety. Fortunately, in many cases this can be cured.

Causes

Dogs are pack animals and being alone is not a natural state for them. Puppies should be patiently taught to get used to short periods of isolation slowly and in a structured way if they are to be comfortable with it. A puppy will emotionally latch on to his new owner, who has taken the place of his mother and siblings.

He will want to follow you everywhere initially and, although you want to shower him with love and attention, it's important to leave your new puppy alone for short periods in the beginning to avoid him becoming totally dependent on you. In our case, I was working from home when we got Max. With hindsight, we should have regularly left him alone for short periods more often in the critical first few weeks and months.

Adopted dogs may be particularly susceptible to separation anxiety. They may have been abandoned once already and fear it happening again.

There are several causes, one or more of which can trigger separation anxiety. These include:

- Not being left alone for short periods when young

- Poor socialisation with other dogs and people resulting in too much focus and dependence on you, his owner

- Boredom, Labradors are intelligent dogs and need physical and mental exercise

- Being left for too long by owners who are out of the house for much of the day

- Leaving a dog too long in a crate or confined space

- Being over-indulgent with your dog; giving him too much attention

- Making too much of a fuss when you leave and return to the house

- Mistreatment in the past, a dog from a rescue centre may have insecurities and feel anxious when left alone

- Wilful behaviour due to a lack of training

Symptoms are not commonly seen in middle-aged dogs, although dogs that develop symptoms when young may be at risk later on. Separation anxiety is, however, common in elderly dogs. Pets age and - like humans - their senses, such as hearing and sight, deteriorate. They become more dependent on their owners and may then become more anxious when they are separated from them - or even out of view.

It may be very flattering and cute that your dog wants to be with you all the time, but insecurity and separation anxiety are forms of panic, which is distressing for your Labrador. If he shows any signs, help him to become more self-reliant and confident; he will be a happier dog.

So what can you do if your dog is showing signs of canine separation anxiety? Every dog is different, but here are some tried and tested techniques that have proved effective for some dogs.

12 Tips to Combat Separation Anxiety

1. After the first two or three days, practise leaving your new puppy or adult dog for short periods, starting with a minute or two and gradually lengthening the time you are out of sight.

2. Tire your Labrador out before you leave him alone. Take him for a walk or play a game before leaving and, if you can, leave him with a view of the outside world, e.g. in a room with a patio door or low window.

3. Keep arrivals and departures low key and don't make a big fuss. For example, when I come home, Max is hysterically happy and runs round whimpering with a toy in his mouth. I make him sit and stay and then let him out into the garden without patting or acknowledging him. I pat him several minutes later.

4. Leave your dog a 'security blanket,' such as an old piece of clothing you have recently worn that still has your scent on it, or leave a radio on - not too loud - in the room with the dog. Avoid a heavy rock station! If it will be dark when you return, leave a lamp on a timer.

5. Associate your departure with something good. As you leave, give your dog a rubber toy, like a Kong, filled with a tasty treat, or a frozen treat. This may take his mind off of your departure. (Some dogs may refuse to touch the treat until you return home).

6. If your dog is used to a crate, try crating him when you go out. Many dogs feel safe there, and being in a crate can also help to reduce destructiveness. Always take the collar off first. Pretend to leave the house, but listen for a few minutes. NEVER leave a dog in a crate with the door closed all day; two or three hours are long enough during the day.

Warning: if your dog starts to show major signs of distress, remove him from the crate immediately as he may injure himself.

7. Structure and routine can help to reduce anxiety in your dog. Carry out regular activities, such as feeding and exercising, at the same time every day.

8. Dogs read body language very well, many Labradors are intuitive. They may start to fret when they think you are going to leave them. One technique is to mimic your departure routine when you have no intention of leaving. So put your coat on, grab your car keys, go out of the door and return a few seconds later. Do this randomly and regularly and it may help to reduce your dog's stress levels when you do it for real.

9. Some dogs show anxiety in new places, get him better socialised and used to different environments, dogs and people.

10. However lovable your Labrador is, if he is showing early signs of anxiety when separating from you, do not shower him with attention all the time when you are there. He will become too dependent on you.

11. If you have to leave the house for a few hours at a time, ask a neighbour or friend to call in - or drop the dog off with them.

12. Getting another dog to keep the first one company can help, but first ask yourself whether you have the time and money for two or more dogs. Can you afford double the vet's and food bills?

....

Sit-Stay-Down

Another technique for helping to reduce separation anxiety is to practise the common "sit-stay" or "down-stay" exercises using positive reinforcement. The goal is to be able to move briefly out of your dog's sight while he is in the "stay" position. Through this your dog learns that he can remain calmly and happily in one place while you go about your normal daily life. You have to progress slowly with this. Get your dog to sit and stay and then walk away from him for five seconds, then 10, 20, a minute and so on. Reward your dog with a treat every time he stays calm.

Then move out of sight or out of the room for a few seconds, return and give him the treat if he is calm, gradually lengthen the time you are out of sight. If you're watching TV with your Labrador snuggled up at your side and you get up for a snack, say "stay" and leave the room. When you come back, give him a treat or praise him quietly. It is a good idea to practise these techniques after exercise or when your dog is a little sleepy (but not exhausted), as he is likely to be more relaxed.

Canine separation anxiety is NOT the result of disobedience or lack of training. It's a psychological condition; your dog feels anxious and insecure.

NEVER punish your dog for showing signs of separation anxiety – even if he has chewed your best shoes. This will only make him worse.

NEVER leave your dog unattended in a crate for long periods or if he is frantic to get out, it can cause physical or mental harm. If you're thinking of leaving an animal all day in a crate while you are out of the house, get a rabbit or a hamster - not a dog.

Excessive Barking

Dogs, especially youngsters and adolescents, sometimes behave in ways you might not want them to, until they learn that this type of unwanted behaviour doesn't earn any rewards. Labradors are not usually excessive barkers – in fact, most of them don't bark very much - but any dog can bark a lot, until he learns not to.

Some puppies start off by being noisy from the outset, while others hardly bark at all until they reach adolescence or adulthood. On our website we get emails from dog owners worried that their young dogs are not barking enough. However, we get many more from owners whose dogs are barking too much! Some Labradors will bark if someone comes to the door – and then welcome them like best friends - while others remain quiet. However, they do not make good guard dogs, as they are friendly with everyone.

There can be a number of reasons a Labrador barks too much. He may be lonely, bored or demanding your attention. He may be possessive and over-protective and so barks (or howls) his head off when others are near you. Excessive, habitual barking is a problem that should be corrected early on before it gets out of hand and drives you and your neighbours nuts.

The problem often develops during adolescence or early adulthood as your dog becomes more confident. If your barking dog is an adolescent, he is probably still teething, so get him a good selection of hardy chews, and stuff a Kong toy with a treat or peanut butter to keep him occupied and gnawing. But give him these when he is quiet, not when he is barking.

Your behaviour can also encourage excessive barking. If your dog barks non-stop for several seconds or minutes and then you give him a treat to quieten him, he associates his barking with getting a nice treat. A better way to deal with it is to say in a firm voice: "Quiet" after he has made a few barks. When he stops, praise him and he will get the idea that what you want him to do is stop. The trick is to nip the bad behaviour in the bud before it becomes ingrained.

If he's barking to get your attention, ignore him. If that doesn't work, leave the room and don't allow him to follow you, so you deprive him of your attention. Do this as well if his barking and attention-seeking turns to nipping. Tell him to "Stop" in a firm voice - not shouting - remove your hand or leg and, if necessary, leave the room.

As humans, we can use our voice in many different ways: to express happiness or anger, to scold, to shout a warning, and so on. Dogs are the same; different barks and noises give out different messages. **Listen** to your dog and try and get an understanding of Labrador language. Learn to recognise the difference between an alert bark, an excited bark, a demanding bark, a nervous, high pitched bark, an aggressive bark or a plain "I'm barking 'coz I can bark" bark!

If your dog is barking at other dogs, arm yourselves with lots of treats and spend time calming your dog down. When he or she starts to bark wildly at another dog - usually this happens when your dog is on a lead – distract your dog by letting them sniff a treat in your hand. Make your dog sit down and give a treat. Talk in a gentle manner and keep showing and giving your dog a treat for remaining calm and not barking. There are several videos on YouTube that show how to deal with this problem in the manner described here.

....

Speak and Shush!

Generally, Labradors are not good guard dogs, most of them couldn't care less if somebody breaks in and walks off with the family silver – they are more likely to approach the burglar for a treat or a pat. But if you do have a problem with excessive barking when somebody visits your home, the Speak and Shush technique is one way of getting a dog to quieten down.

If your Labrador doesn't bark and you want him to, a slight variation of this method can also be used to get him to bark as a way of alerting you that someone is at the door.

When your dog barks at an arrival at your house, gently praise him after the first few barks. If he persists, gently tell him that that is enough. Like humans, some dogs can get carried away with the sound of their own voice, so try and discourage too much barking from the outset. The Speak and Shush technique teaches your dog or puppy to bark and be quiet on command. Get a friend to stand outside your front door and say "Speak" - or "Woof" or "Alert." This is the cue for your accomplice to knock or ring the bell – don't worry if you both feel like idiots, it will be worth the embarrassment!

When your dog barks, praise him profusely. You can even bark yourself in encouragement! After a few good barks, say "Shush" and then dangle a tasty treat in front of his nose. He will stop barking as soon as he sniffs the treat, because it is physically impossible for a dog to sniff and woof at the same time.

Praise your dog again as he sniffs quietly and then give him the treat. Repeat this routine a few times a day and your Labrador will quickly learn to bark whenever the doorbell rings and you ask him to speak. Eventually your dog will bark after your request but BEFORE the doorbell rings, meaning he has learned to bark on command. Even better, he will learn to anticipate the likelihood of getting a treat following your "Shush" request and will also be quiet on command.

With Speak and Shush training, progressively increase the length of required shush time before offering a treat - at first just a couple of seconds, then three, five, 10, 20, and so on. By alternating instructions to speak and shush, the dog is praised and rewarded for barking on request and also for stopping barking on request.

You need to have some treats at the ready, waiting for that rare bark. Wait until he barks - for whatever reason - then say "Speak" or whatever word you want to use, praise him and give him a treat. At this stage, he won't know why he is receiving the treat. Keep praising him every time he barks and give him a treat. After you've done this for several days, hold a treat in your hand in front

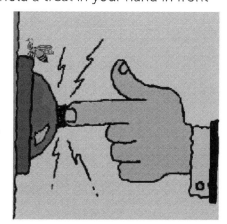

of his face and say "Speak." Your dog will probably still not know what to do, but will eventually get so frustrated at not getting the treat that he will bark. At which point, praise him and give him the treat. We trained our Labrador to do this in a week or so and now he barks his head off when anybody comes to the door or whenever we give him the command: "Speak."

Always use your 'encouraging teacher voice' when training; speak softly when instructing your dog to Shush, and reinforce the Shush with whisper-praise. The more softly you speak, the more your dog will be likely to pay attention. Labradors respond very well to training when it is fun, short and reward-based.

Dealing with Aggression

Some breeds are more prone to aggression than others. Fortunately, this is a problem not often seen in Labradors. However, given certain situations, any dog can growl, bark or even bite.

Our dog almost died after being attacked by five Labradors a couple of years ago (fortunately he eventually made a complete recovery, although he is now more wary of other dogs). He had been happily trotting up a field when suddenly we heard him squealing, and looked round to see a pack of Labradors had set upon him and were "ragging" him like a rabbit. It was the young stud dog which had started the affray. The breeder, who had been exercising the Labs, said that it was the first time anything like this had happened, and that her dogs were not aggressive, (she did pay all of the vet's bills). The vet said that it was the pack mentality which had kicked in and that it could happen with any breed.

The point is not that the Labrador is an aggressive breed; **it isn't**. But ANY dog can be aggressive, given a certain set of circumstances. We don't blame the Labradors; the young male was asserting his superiority and the others just did what was natural – and piled in. Actually, we blame the breeder; firstly, for not properly socialising the male and secondly, for having five dogs off the lead in an area where there are lots of other dogs.

Sometimes a Lab learns unwanted behaviour from another dog or dogs, but more often it is because the dog either feels insecure, or has become too territorial or protective of his food, owner or toys. Puppy biting is not aggression; all puppies bite; they explore the world with their noses and mouths. But it is important to train your cute little pup not to bite, as he may cause injury if he continues as an adult.

Any dog can bite when under stress and, however unlikely it may seem, there are images on the internet of people who have been bitten by Labradors. There is an example of a Labrador with food aggression (that gives Cesar Milan a nasty bite) at: www.youtube.com/watch?v=RO1LoZTmLOY

Here are some different types of aggressive behaviour:

- Growling at you or other people
- Snarling or lunging at other dogs
- Growling or biting if you or another animal goes near his food
- Being possessive with toys
- Growling if you pet or show attention to another animal
- Marking territory by urinating inside the house
- Growling and chasing other small animals
- Growling and chasing cars, joggers or strangers
- Standing in your way, blocking your path
- Pulling and growling on the lead

Aggression is often due to the fact that the dog has not been properly socialised, and so feels threatened or challenged. Rather than being comfortable with new situations, other dogs or intrusions, he responds using "the best form of defence is attack" philosophy and displays aggressive behaviour to anything or anyone he perceives as a threat.

As well as snarling, lunging, barking or biting, you should also look out for other physical signs, such as: raised hackles, top lip curled back to bare teeth, ears up and tail raised.

Labradors love your attention, but they can also become possessive of you, their food or toys, which in itself can lead to bullying behaviour. Aggression may be caused by a lack of socialisation, an adolescent dog trying to see how far he can push the boundaries, nervousness, being spoiled by the owner, jealousy or even fear. This fear may come from a bad experience the dog has suffered or from lack of proper socialisation. Another form of fear-aggression is when a dog becomes over-protective/possessive of his owner, which can lead to barking and lunging at other dogs or humans.

An owner's treatment of a dog can be a further reason. If the owner has been too harsh with the dog, such as shouting, using physical violence or reprimanding the dog too often, this in turn causes poor behaviour. Aggression breeds aggression. Dogs can also become aggressive if they are consistently left alone, cooped up, under-fed or under-exercised. A bad experience with another dog or dogs can also be a cause.

Many dogs are more combative on the lead. This is because once on a lead, they cannot run away. Fight or flight. They know they can't escape, so they make themselves as frightening as possible and bark or growl to warn off the other dog or person. Train your Labrador from an early age to be comfortable walking on the lead. And socialisation is, of course vital – the first four to five months of a puppy's life is the critical time.

If your dog **suddenly** shows a change of behaviour and becomes aggressive, have him checked out by a vet to rule out any underlying medical reason for the crankiness, such as earache or toothache.

Raging hormones can be another reason for aggression. Consider having your Lab spayed or neutered if the vet thinks this may be the cause. A levelling-off of hormones can lead to a more laid-back dog.

Another reason for dogs to display aggression is because they have been spoiled by their owners and have come to believe that the world revolves around them. Not spoiling your dog and teaching him what is acceptable behaviour in the first place is the best preventative measure. Early training, especially during puppyhood and adolescence - before he or she develops unwanted habits - can save a lot of trouble in the future.

Professional dog trainers employ a variety of techniques with a dog that has become aggressive. Firstly they will look at the causes and then they almost always use reward-based methods to try and cure aggressive or fearful dogs. *Counter conditioning* is a positive training technique used by many professional trainers to help change a dog's aggressive behaviour towards other dogs. A typical example would be a dog that snarls, barks and lunges at other dogs while on the lead. It is the presence of other dogs that is triggering the dog to act in a fearful or anxious manner.

Every time the dog sees another dog, he or she is given a tasty treat to counter the aggression. With enough steady repetition, the dog starts to associate the presence of other dogs with a tasty treat. Properly and patiently done, the final result is a dog that calmly looks to the owner for the treat whenever he or she sees another dog while on the lead. Whenever you encounter a potentially aggressive situation, divert your Labrador's attention by turning his head away from the other dog and towards you, so that he cannot make eye contact with the other dog.

Aggression Towards People

Desensitisation is the most common method of treating aggression. It starts by breaking down the triggers for the behaviour one small step at a time. The aim is to get the dog to associate pleasant things with the trigger, i.e. people or a specific person whom he previously feared or regarded as a threat. This is done through using positive reinforcement, such as praise or treats. Successful desensitisation takes time, patience and knowledge. If your dog is starting to growl at people, there are a couple of techniques you can try to break him of this bad habit before it develops into full-blown biting.

One method is to arrange for some friends to come round, one at a time. When they arrive at your house, get them to scatter kibble on the floor in front of them so that your dog associates the arrival of people with tasty treats. As they move into the house, and your dog eats the kibble, praise your dog for being a good boy or girl. Manage your dog's environment. Don't over-face him.

Most Labradors love children, but if yours is at all anxious around them, separate them or carefully supervise their time together in the beginning. Children typically react enthusiastically to dogs and some dogs may regard this as frightening or an invasion of their space.

Some dogs, particularly spoiled ones, may show aggression towards people other than the owner. Several people have written to our website on this topic and it usually involves a partner or husband. Often the dog is jealous of the attention the owner is giving to the other person, or it could be that the dog feels threatened by him. This is, however, more common with Toy breeds.

If it should arise with your Labrador, the key is for the partner to gradually gain the trust of the dog. He or she should show that they are not a threat by speaking gently to the dog and giving treats for good behaviour. Avoid eye contact, as the dog may see this as a challenge. If the subject of the aggression lives in the house, then try letting this person give the dog his daily feeds. The way to a Labrador's heart is often through his stomach.

A crate is also a useful tool for removing an aggressive dog from the situation for short periods of time, allowing him out gradually and praising good behaviour. As with any form of aggression, the key is to take steps to deal with it immediately.

In extreme cases, when a dog exhibits persistent bad behaviour that the owner is unable to correct, a canine professional may be the answer. However, this is not an inexpensive option. Far better to spend time training and socialising your dog as soon as you get him or her.

Coprophagia (Eating Faeces)

It is hard for us to understand why a dog would want to eat his or any other animal's faeces (stools, poop or poo, call it what you will), but it does happen. There is plenty of anecdotal evidence that some dogs love the stuff. Nobody fully understands why dogs do this, it may simply be an unpleasant behaviour trait or there could be an underlying reason.

It is also thought that the inhumane and useless housetraining technique of "sticking the dog's nose in it" when he has eliminated inside the house can also encourage coprophagia.

If your dog eats faeces from the cat litter tray - a problem several owners have contacted us about - the first thing to do is to place the litter tray somewhere where your dog can't get to it – but the cat can. Perhaps on a shelf or put a guard around it, small enough for the cat to get through, but not your Labrador.

Our dog sometimes eats cow or horse manure when out in the countryside. He usually stops when we tell him to and he hasn't suffered any after effects – so far. But again, this is a very unpleasant habit as the offending material sticks to the fur around his mouth and has to be cleaned off.

Sometimes he rolls in the stuff and then has to be washed down. You may find that your Labrador will roll in fox poo to cover the fox's scent. Try and avoid areas you know are frequented by foxes if you can, as their faeces can transmit several diseases, including Canine Parvovirus or lungworm – neither of these should pose a serious health risk if your dog is up to date with vaccinations and worming medication.

Vets have found that canine diets with low levels of fibre and high levels of starch increase the likelihood of coprophagia. If your dog is exhibiting this behaviour, first check that the diet you are feeding is nutritionally complete. Look at the first ingredient on the dog food packet or tin – is it corn or meat? Does he look underweight? Check that you are feeding the right amount. If there is no underlying medical reason, you will have to try and modify your dog's behaviour. Remove cat litter trays, clean up after your dog and do not allow him to eat his own faeces. If it's not there, he can't eat it.

One breeder told us of a Labrador which developed the habit after being allowed to soil his crate as a pup, caused by the owners not being vigilant in their housetraining. The puppy got used to eating his own faeces and then continued to do it as an adult, when it became quite a problem.

Don't reprimand the dog for eating faeces. A better technique is to cause a distraction while he is in the act and then remove the offending material.

Coprophagia is sometimes seen in pups aged between six months to a year and often disappears after this age.

....

Important: This chapter provides just a general overview of canine behaviour. If your Labrador exhibits persistent behavioural problems, particularly if he or she is aggressive towards people or other dogs, you should consider seeking help from a reputable canine behaviourist, such as those listed the Association of Professional Dog Trainers at http://www.apdt.co.uk (UK) or https://apdt.com (USA)

9. Exercise

One thing all dogs have in common – including every Labrador ever born - is that they need daily exercise, and the best way to give them this is through regular walks or by using them for what they were originally bred for: retrieving. Activities such as agility and flyball also allow the Labrador to burn off steam and fulfil its natural instinct for a challenge. Start regular exercise patterns early so your dog gets used to his normal routine; dogs love routine. Daily exercise helps to keep your dog content, healthy and free from disease. It:

- Strengthens respiratory and circulatory systems
- Helps get oxygen to tissue cells
- Wards off obesity
- Keeps muscles toned and joints flexible
- Aids digestion
- Releases endorphins which trigger positive feelings
- Helps to keep dogs mentally stimulated and socialised

How Much Exercise?

Labradors are generally regarded as having medium to high exercise requirements, but there is no one-rule-fits-all solution. The UK Kennel Club recommends "more than two hours per day" and the AKC classes them in the highest category for exercise. However, the amount of exercise that each individual dog needs varies tremendously. It depends on a number of issues, including temperament, natural energy levels, your living conditions, whether your dog is kept with other dogs and, importantly, what he gets used to.

Another factor is whether your dog is bred from show or working stock. There are, of course, big variations from one individual dog to another, but often working (American) Labradors are happiest with more exercise and mental challenges than show Labradors. After all, it makes sense. A Labrador whose parent was bred to run all day and be on the lookout for game is likely to have higher mental and physical energy demands than one bred to have a calmer nature for the show ring. Working dogs are not usually couch potatoes. That's not so say Labradors don't love snuggling up on the couch with you; they most certainly do - they just need their exercise as well.

It is true to say that whatever colour or type you choose, ALL of them require a decent amount of daily exercise. Labradors are not small and they were not bred as companion dogs; they were bred as working dogs - and all working dogs need daily physical and mental stimulation.

When we talk about "exercising" a Labrador, most people think this means taking the dog out for a walk two or three times a day - and it does for most pet owners. However, there are other forms of exercise. Owners of working Labs or those that take part in competitions often train and exercise their dogs in short, high energy sessions.

Owning more than one dog - or having friends with dogs - is a great way for your dog to get lots of exercise. A couple of dogs running round together will get far more exercise than a dog on his own.

Labradors are natural retrievers, i.e. they love fetching things back to you – and you can train your Lab to do this, whether or not you compete or shoot with him. As well as throwing a toy or ball for him to fetch, you can make it more interesting by hiding the object and training your dog to retrieve it - your Lab will love the challenge.

Playing in the garden or yard with toys or balls is also a great way to burn off steam (for both of you!) If you play Frisbee, don't overdo it - especially with young, growing dogs, as this can lead to joint damage. A fenced garden or yard is definitely an advantage, but should not be seen as a replacement for daily exercise away from the home, where a dog can experience new places, scents, other people and dogs. Your dog will enjoy going for walks on the lead (leash), but will enjoy it far more when he is allowed to run free. A Labrador is never happier than when running around chasing an old stick or ball or following a scent.

Pictured above is Caroline Smith's Flyenpyg Snout Like It ('Squeal') competing in an agility class and below: the same dog dummy training. Photos courtesy of Yellow Dog Photography. Leaner Labradors bred from working lines are often very well suited to agility and other athletic canine competitions. (Caroline's Flyenpyg Labradors have both working and show stock in their bloodlines).

If your Lab is happy just to trot along besides you, then you need to devise some games to raise his heartbeat, build muscle and get him fit. As well as throwing a ball or stick, you could arrange walks with other dogs, or invent some games which involve running. If you decide to go jogging with your Labrador, build up the distance gradually. He WILL want to keep up with you, regardless of how fit he is, and you don't want him to have a heart attack

Ideally, you should devote a **minimum** of an hour a day to exercising you dog - longer is preferable – spread over at least two sessions a day. You can hike or shoot with a fit Labrador all day long and still not tire him out. If you don't think you have the time or energy levels for one to two hours of exercise a day, then consider getting a smaller companion breed with a lower drive.

Make sure it is safe to let your dog off the lead, away from traffic and other hazards - and don't let your puppy run free until he has learned the recall. There is also growing concern in both the UK and North America about dog attacks in public parks and dog parks. If you are at all worried about this, avoid popular dog walking areas and find woodlands, fields, beaches or open countryside where your dog can exercise safely.

Establish a Routine

Establish an exercise regime early in your dog's life. If possible, get him used to walks at the same time every day, at a time that fits in with your daily routine. For example, take your dog out after his morning feed, then perhaps again in the afternoon or when you come home from work, and a short toilet trip last thing at night. Labradors were bred to swim and this is a great way for dogs to exercise; many veterinary practices now use water tanks, not only for remedial therapy, but also for canine recreation.

Labradors will dash in and out of the water all day long if you'll let them, but remember that

swimming is a lot more strenuous for a dog than walking or even running. Don't constantly throw that stick or ball into the water - your Labrador will fetch it back until he drops; the same is true if he is following you on your cycle. Overstretching him could place a strain on his heart. He should exercise within his limits. We advise gently drying under your Lab's ear flaps after swimming to reduce the risk of ear infections.

Whatever routine you decide on, stick to it. If you begin by taking your dog out three times a day and then suddenly stop, he will become restless, attention-seeking and possibly destructive because he has been used to more exercise. Conversely, don't expect a dog used to very little exercise to suddenly go on day-long hikes; he will struggle. Labradors make suitable hiking or jogging companions, but they need to work up to longer sessions - and such strenuous activity is not suitable for puppies.

To those owners who say their dog is happy and getting enough exercise playing in the yard or garden, just show him his lead and see how he reacts. Do you think he is excited at the prospect of leaving the home and going for a walk? Of course he is. Nothing can compensate for interesting new scents, meeting other dogs, playing games, frolicking in the snow or going swimming.

Owning a Labrador requires a big commitment from owners – you are looking at daily exercise for 10 or more years. Don't think that as your dog gets older he won't need exercising. Older dogs need exercise to keep their body, joints and systems functioning properly. They need a less strenuous regime – they are usually happier with several short walks (of perhaps 10 minutes or so) a day but still enough to keep them physically and mentally active. Again, every dog is different, some are happy to run right until the end.

Regular exercise can add months or even years to a dog's life. The exception is if your old or sick dog is struggling – he will show you that he doesn't feel well enough to walk far by stopping and looking at you or sitting down and refusing to move.

Most Labradors love snow, but it can sometimes present problems with clumps of snow and ice building up on paws, ears, legs and tummy. Salt or de-icing products on roads and pathways can also cause irritation – particularly if he or she tries to lick it off - as they can contain chemicals that are poisonous to dogs. If your dog gets iced up, you can bathe paws and anywhere else affected in lukewarm (NOT HOT) water. If your dog spends a lot of time in snow, you might even invest in a pair of canine snow boots. These are highly effective in preventing snow and ice balls forming on paws – provided you can get the boots to stay on!

Mental Stimulation

Labradors are very intelligent. This is good news when it comes to training as they generally learn quickly. But the downside is that this intelligence needs to be fed. Without mental challenges, a dog can become bored, unresponsive, destructive, attention-seeking and/or needy. You should factor in play time with your Labrador – even gentle play time for old dogs.

If your Labrador's behaviour deteriorates or he suddenly starts chewing things he's not supposed to or barking a lot, the first question you should ask yourself is: "Is he getting enough exercise?" Boredom through lack of exercise or mental stimulation - such being alone and staring at four walls a lot - leads to bad behaviour and it's why some Labs end up in rescue centres, through no fault of their own.

On the other hand, a Labrador at the heart of the family getting plenty of daily exercise and stimulation is a happy dog and a companion second to none.

Exercising Puppies

There are strict guidelines to stick to with puppies, as it is important not to over-exercise young pups. Their bones and joints are developing and cannot tolerate a great deal of stress, so playing Fetch or Frisbee for hours on end with your young Labrador is not a good option. You'll end up with an injured dog and a pile of vet's bills.

We are often asked how much to exercise a pup. Just like babies, Labrador puppies have different temperaments and some will be livelier and need more exercise than others. The golden rule is to start slowly and build it up. The worst danger is a combination of over exercise and overweight when the puppy is growing. Do not take him out of the yard or garden until he has completed his vaccinations and it is safe to do so – unless you carry him around to start the socialisation process. Then start with short walks on the lead every day. Puppies have enquiring minds. Get yours used to being outside the home environment and experiencing new situations as soon as possible. The general guideline is:

Five minutes of on-lead exercise per month of age

until the puppy is fully grown. That means a total of 15 minutes when he is three months (13 weeks old), 30 minutes when six months (26 weeks) old, and so on. Slowly increase the time as he gets used to being exercised and this will gradually build up his muscles and stamina. This may not sound like much exercise, but too much exercise early on places stress on young joints.

It is, however, OK for your young pup have free run of your garden or yard (once you have plugged any gaps in the fence), provided it has a soft surface such as grass, not concrete. He will take things at his own pace and stop to sniff or rest. If you have other dogs, restrict the time the pup is allowed to play with them, as he won't know when he's had enough. Once he is older, your dog can go out for much longer walks. And when your little pup has grown into a beautiful adult Labrador with a skeleton capable of carrying him through a long and healthy life, it will have been worth all the effort.

A long, healthy life is best started slowly

Recap: Your Labrador will get used to an exercise routine. If you over-stimulate and constantly exercise him as a puppy, he will think this is the norm. This is fine with your playful little pup, but may not be such an attractive prospect when your fully-grown Labrador constantly needs and demands your attention a year or two later, or your work patterns change and you have not so much time to devote to him. The key is to start a routine that you can stick to.

....

Exercise Tips

- Labradors are intelligent and love a challenge. They like to use their brains, particularly working Labs. Make time to play indoor and outdoor games - such as Fetch or Hide-The-Toy - regularly with your dog; even elderly Labradors like to play

- Don't strenuously exercise your dog straight after or within an hour of a meal as this can cause bloat, particularly in larger dogs. Canine bloat causes gases to build up quickly in the stomach, blowing it up like a balloon, which cuts off normal blood circulation to and from the heart. The dog can go into shock and then cardiac arrest within hours. If you suspect this is happening, get the dog to a vet immediately

- If you want your dog to fetch a ball, don't fetch it back yourself or he will never learn to retrieve! Train him when he's young by giving him praise or a treat when he brings the ball or toy back to your feet

- Do not throw a ball or toy repeatedly for a dog if he shows signs of over-exertion. Your dog will fetch to please you and because it's great fun. Stop the activity after a while - no matter how much he begs you to throw it again.

- The same goes for swimming, which is an exhausting exercise for a dog. Ensure he exercises within his limits; repeatedly retrieving from water may cause him to overstretch and get into difficulties. Gentle swimming is a good low-impact activity for older Labradors.

- Exercise older dogs more gently - especially in cold weather when it is harder to get their bodies moving. Have a cool-down period at the end of the exercise to reduce stiffness and soreness; it helps to remove lactic acids from the dog's body, and our 12-year-old loves a body massage

- Some dogs, particularly adolescent ones, may try to push the boundaries when out walking on the lead. If your Labrador stops dead and stares at you or tries to pull you in another direction, ignore him. Do not return his stare, just continue along the way you want to go, not his way.

- Vary your exercise route – it will be more interesting for both of you

- If exercising off-lead at night, buy a battery-operated flashing collar for your dog

- Make sure your dog has constant access to fresh water. Dogs can't sweat much, they need to drink water to cool down

Admittedly, when it is pouring down with rain, freezing cold (or scorching hot), the last thing you want to do is to venture outdoors with your dog. But the lows are more than compensated for by the highs. Exercise helps you: bond with your dog, keep fit, see different places and meet new companions - both canine and human. In short, it enhances both your lives.

....

Socialisation

Your adult dog's character will depend largely on two things. The first is his temperament, which he is born with, and presumably one of the reasons you have chosen a Labrador. (The importance of picking a good breeder who selects breeding stock based on temperament, physical characteristics and health cannot be over-emphasised). The second factor is environment – or how you bring him up and treat him. In other words, it's a combination of **nature and nurture**. And one absolutely essential aspect of nurture is socialisation.

Scientists have come to realise the importance that socialisation plays in a dog's life. We also now know that there is a fairly small window which is the optimum time for socialisation - and this is up to the age of up to around four months.

Most young animals, including dogs, are naturally able to get used to their everyday environment until they reach a certain age. When they reach this age, they become much more suspicious of things they haven't yet experienced. This is why it often takes longer to train an older dog.

The age-specific natural development allows a puppy to get comfortable with the normal sights, sounds, people and animals that will be a part of his life. It ensures that he doesn't spend his life jumping in fright or growling at every blowing leaf or bird in song. The suspicion that dogs develop in later puppyhood – after the critical window - also ensures that they do react with a healthy dose of caution to new things that could really be dangerous - Mother Nature is clever!

Socialisation means 'learning to be part of society', or 'integration'. When we talk about socialising puppies, it means helping them learn to be comfortable within a human society that includes many different types of people, environments, buildings, traffic, sights, noises, smells, animals, other dogs, etc. Your Labrador may already have a wonderful temperament, but he still needs socialising to avoid him thinking that the world is tiny and it revolves around him - which in turn leads to unwanted adult behaviour traits. Some young Labradors have a natural tendency to be very boisterous and good socialisation helps them to learn their place in society and become more relaxed adults.

The ultimate goal of socialisation is to have a happy, well-adjusted dog that you can take anywhere. Socialisation will give your dog confidence and teach him not to be afraid of new experiences. Ever seen a therapy or service Labrador or a Guide Dog in action and noticed how incredibly well-adjusted to life they are? This is no coincidence. These dogs have been extensively socialised and are ready and able to deal in a calm manner with whatever situation they encounter. They are relaxed and comfortable in their own skin - just like you want your dog to be.

You have to start socialising your puppy as soon as you bring him home. Start by socialising him around the house and garden and, if it is safe, carry him out of the home environment (but do not put him on the floor or allow him to sniff other dogs until he's got the all-clear after his vaccinations). Regular socialisation should continue until your dog is around 18 months of age. After that, don't just forget about it. Socialisation isn't only for puppies, it should continue throughout your dog's life. As with any skill, if it is not practised, your dog will become less proficient at interacting with other people, animals, and environments.

Developing the Well-Rounded Adult Dog

Well-socialised puppies usually develop into safer, more relaxed and enjoyable adult dogs. This is because they're more comfortable in a wider variety of situations than poorly socialised canines. Dogs which have not been properly integrated are much more likely to react with fear or aggression to unfamiliar people, dogs and experiences.

Labradors who are relaxed about other dogs, honking horns, cats, farm animals, cyclists, veterinary examinations, crowds and noise are easier to live with than dogs who find these situations challenging or frightening. And if you are planning on showing your dog or taking part in canine competitions, get him used to the buzz of these events early on.

Well-socialised dogs also live more relaxed, peaceful and happy lives than dogs which are constantly stressed by their environment. Socialisation isn't an "all or nothing" project. You can socialise a puppy a bit, a lot, or a whole lot. The wider the range of experiences you expose him to when young, the better his chances are of becoming a more relaxed adult.

Don't over-face your little puppy. Socialisation should never be forced, but approached systematically and in a manner that builds confidence and curious interaction. If your pup finds a new experience frightening, take a step back, introduce him to the scary situation much more gradually, and make a big effort to do something he loves during the situation or right afterwards.

For example, if your puppy seems to be frightened by noise and vehicles at a busy road, a good method would be to go to quiet road, sit with dog away from - but within sight of - the traffic. Every time he looks towards the traffic say "YES" and reward him with a treat. If he is still stressed, you need to move further away. When your dog takes the food in a calm manner, he is becoming more relaxed and getting used to traffic sounds, so you can edge a bit nearer - but still just for short periods until he becomes totally relaxed. Keep each session short and positive.

Meeting Other Dogs

When you take your gorgeous and vulnerable little pup out with other dogs for the first few times, you are bound to be a little nervous. To start with, introduce your puppy to just one other dog — one which you know to be friendly, rather than taking him straight to the park where there are lots of dogs of all sizes racing around, which might frighten the life out of your timid little darling. Always make the initial introductions on neutral ground, so as not to trigger territorial behaviour. You want your Labrador to approach other dogs with confidence, not fear.

From the first meeting, help both dogs experience good things when they're in each other's presence. Let them sniff each other briefly, which is normal canine greeting behaviour. As they do, talk to them in a happy, friendly tone of voice; never use a threatening tone. Don't allow them to sniff each other for too long as this may escalate to an aggressive response. After a short time, get the attention of both dogs and give each a treat in return for obeying a simple command, such as "Sit" or "Stay." Continue with the "happy talk," food rewards and simple commands.

Of course, if you have more than one dog or a number of working Labradors, your puppy will learn to socialise within the pack. However, you should still spend time introducing him to new sights, sounds and animals. Here are some signs of fear to look out for when your dog interacts with other canines:

- Running away
- Freezing on the spot
- Frantic/nervous behaviour, such as excessive sniffing, drinking or playing with a toy frenetically
- A lowered body stance or crouching
- Lying on his back with his paws in the air – this is a submissive gesture
- Lowering of the head, or turning the head away
- Lips pulled back baring teeth and/or growling
- Hair raised on his back (hackles)
- Tail lifted in the air
- Ears high on the head

Some of these responses are normal. A pup may well crouch on the ground or roll on to his back to show other dogs he is not a threat. Try not to be over-protective, your puppy has to learn how to interact with other dogs, but if the situation looks like escalating into something more aggressive, calmly distract the dogs or remove your puppy – don't shout or shriek. The dogs will pick up on your fear and this in itself could trigger an unpleasant situation.

Another sign to look out for is eyeballing. In the canine world, staring a dog in the eyes is a challenge and may trigger an aggressive response. This is more relevant to adult dogs, as a young pup will soon be put in his place by bigger or older dogs; it is how they learn. The rule of thumb with puppy socialisation is to keep a close eye on your pup's reaction to whatever you expose him to so that you can tone things down if he seems at all frightened. Always follow up a socialisation experience with praise, petting, a fun game or a special treat.

One positive sign from a dog is the play bow (pictured), when he goes down on to his front elbows but keeps his backside up in the air. This is a sign that he is feeling friendly towards the other dog and wants to play.

Although Labradors are not naturally aggressive dogs, aggression is often grounded in fear, and a dog which mixes easily is less likely to be aggressive. Similarly, without frequent and new experiences, some Labradors can become timid and nervous when introduced to new experiences. Take your new dog everywhere you can. You want him to feel relaxed and calm in any situation, even noisy and crowded ones. Take treats with you and praise him when he reacts calmly to new situations. Once he has settled into your home, introduce him to your friends and teach him not to jump up. If you have young children, it is not only the dog that needs socialising! Youngsters also need training on how to act around dogs, so both parties learn to respect the other.

 An excellent way of getting your new puppy to meet other dogs in a safe environment is at a puppy class. Ask around locally if any classes are being run. Some vets and dog trainers run puppy classes for very junior pups who have had all their vaccinations. These help pups get used to other dogs of a similar age.

Labrador Types and Exercise

We asked the breeders involved in this book how long they exercise their dogs for and whether the fact that a Labrador was from show or working (American or English) lines made a difference. This is what they said, starting with Kate Smith, of Ardenbrook Labradors, Warwickshire, who is a committee member of The Labrador Club and The Yellow Labrador Club with two decades' experience of the breed: "My dogs are predominately used for the purpose for which the breed was originally developed, that is, working in the field. They also compete in Field Trials and Working Tests, if up to standard. However, my dogs are from a mixture of show and working lines.

"I have found that many of the Field Trial lines are too finely built, particularly the bitches, and are too racy for my taste. I prefer to keep something more akin to the 'old fashioned' Labrador type of the 1950s and 60s. Likewise, I find the 'show type' is too excessive and overdone, and too far removed from the original, 'middleweight hunter' type of dog. I have mixed the lines deliberately to try and get the best of both worlds – correct construction (so important in a working breed), and sound, biddable temperaments.

"Through my involvement of the two Labrador Breed Club committees that I sit on, I have had much experience of the two sides of the breed. There are differences in temperaments, but this is often down to the breeding it's based on, rather than the fact that it's from either 'show' or 'working' stock. This is why it is so important to meet the dam of any prospective litter well in advance, preferably before there are pups on the scene. I know of 'hyper' lines from both sides, and by the same token there are calm, sensible dogs from both sides."

Stephen Armstrong, Carnamaddy Labradors, County Antrim, Northern Ireland, has a yellow bitch from working stock and a chocolate bitch from show stock: "The reason I chose chocolate is that I was told they were more of a challenge to train than the other colours. The only difference I have found is that she is more easily distracted than my yellow bitch when field training; otherwise, housetraining and obedience training is just the same.

"My chocolate has the appearance of a field dog, although her temperament is more easy going. The two dogs get the same tasks and can both retrieve, although the yellow is better at this; more easily biddable and eager to please, but she was bred for this purpose. We exercise them for two to three hours a day."

Nadine Lapskas, Trencrom Kennels, Bournemouth (working): "It varies. We run with them, which means a further 30 minutes a day. Sometimes only one of us runs, sometimes we just walk them, but they have a minimum 30 minutes set exercise - though they play continually outside, and they also come to the horse field and run around. The problem we have is the more exercise they get, the more they need; you can never tire them!"

Colin Hinkley, Sanglier Labradors, East Sussex, has bred all three colours for 30 years: "As long as the parents have a suitable temperament and good confirmation, I have found no difference between the colours in trainability or suitability for any task. My dogs are from show stock - if they are well bred and come from parents with good temperaments, there shouldn't be a difference. Both types (show and working) should get the same amount of exercise, although show dogs will never retrieve as fast in competition. I exercise my dogs for two hours a day."

Sarah Edwards and Guy Stewart, Fernwills Labradors, Essex, run a doggie day care business as well as breeding Labs: "Our own dogs are from a mix of working and show stock, but mainly working stock. In our experience, looking after pure show stock and pure working stock (for our day-care business), there is a difference in personality.

"The heavier show dogs can be more clumsy, playful and initiate more play fights — whereas the working stock lines are more independent and wish to hunt or track scent on a walk, rather than play with each other." Pictured is Sarah and Guy's Poppy at four years old.

Christopher Clarke, Reedfen Labradors, Cambridgeshire: "We exercise them for one hour in the morning and 45 minutes in the evening. We have owned and bred both types. Firstly, the show type looks like the Labrador most people would recognise. They are happy to plod around the home and garden with an hour's play and a little training in the park two or three times a week, but they generally look good whatever they are doing!

"The working type is a much more athletic dog, generally with longer legs, a thinner (snipe-like) face and a leaner body. They will enjoy an hour's training, then an hour's walk and come home eager to do the same again! Both types can be trained to perform tasks; just one may do it a little slower than the other and probably require a break in between tasks. Temperaments can be similar, as in they are all generally eager to please, very faithful, loving and relatively easy to train."

"The working dog strains also appear to be more focused on doing a task. When you get a mix of the two stocks, as with our own dogs, it can be a toning down of the headstrong, independent working side. The working stock, due to their lithe bodies, can really run and run and keep going for some time. Our own dogs are out for 30 to 45 minutes per walk, once or twice a day. However, our older Labradors tend to only have one walk a day - we leave it up to them to let us know if they want a stroll."

Hilary and Wayne Hardman, Larwaywest Labradors, Dorset: "Our dogs are pets first and also trained as gundogs. They work through the shooting season and are occasionally entered into working tests, except one who is a show-type chocolate bitch who is incredibly funny and entertains everyone with her antics and gorgeous personality! Generally, we exercise out dogs for between one and two hours a day. During the summer months there may well be several more hours which are taken up with gundog training, and during the shooting season the working dogs will be out all day two or three times a week."

Christine Eynon, Baileylane Labradors, Herefordshire, has been breeding Labs since 2005: "My dogs are show/breeding dogs, but as I live in country, they do flush out pheasants and are adept at chasing squirrels and rabbits. One of my girls used to fish trout out of the river!

"My girls have two plus hours a day running free, but I curtail pup's exercise as her legs and hips are forming. My rule for pups is five minutes' exercise for every month. It is hard as she is energetic, but you can do a lot of damage exercising too much too soon. As breeders, we do all we can with health checks and this good work can be wiped out with too much exercise early on or the wrong food."

Kirsty Jones, Serengoch Labradors, Mid Wales, has five chocolate Labs and one black one; she has been breeding since 2011 and showing since 2013: "I have one dog that is of working stock; the ones from working stock do often require a bit more stimulation – this does not have to mean exercise, but could mean 'brain games'." Photo of the chocolate Adoraden Milky Way At Serengoch ('Chunk'), courtesy of Kirsty. Chunk is from show stock.

"I feel that there is limited difference in ability, although dogs from proven working stock may have better working abilities than those that are not. I do not feel temperament differs between the two strains. Both need to have good temperaments and this is a big consideration for breeders. I exercise for around an hour a day, both on and off lead."

Sharon Jarvis, Paulsharo Labradors, Lincolnshire (working): "Exercise depends on age - for pups, five minutes for every month of its life. After 12 months of age, they will normally take whatever exercise you can give them. Mine are exercised for about two hours a day, but not all at once. Mental and physical exercise is required. A well-exercised dog will not wreck your home or bark a lot."

Sarah Nuttall, Gamblegate Labradors, Lancashire, has bred mainly chocolate Labs, with some blacks, for 17 years: "My dogs are all from show lines, they tend to be bigger, with more bone than working lines and have a more placid temperament. In my opinion, dogs from show lines can be trained to the gun and used successfully in the field. My dogs have a large play area, but also have approximately 60 minutes' exercise off the lead every day."

Pat Nugent, of Marumrose Labradors, Lincolnshire, has bred chocolates for 10 years: "My dogs are show type or dual purpose; I find that working dogs are more driven. The adults get a minimum of 45-minutes of lead walks or four 10mins interactive off-lead play daily."

Nicola Smith, of Geowins Labradors, Thorpe, Surrey, has bred Labs for 18 years: "I have bred black, yellow and fox red, and I find all their temperaments the same. My dogs are from working stock, I prefer the size and shape of the head and their agility.

"Having met a few show Labs, I like their nature, but not their build; but that is just personal preference. I take ours for their main walk in the morning for around one hour and then the rest of the day they are free to roam and play in our very large garden at home, which is approximately three acres." Photo of this cute pair courtesy of Nicola.

Gundog trainer Andrew Baker, of Saffronlyn Labradors, South Yorkshire, has been involved with Labs for many years, but has just bred one litter -with a second on the way! He says: "I put my working Labrador dog to a bitch I bought and she is three-quarter show lines and one quarter working. They produced strong healthy pups with good bone and size; the type I like. I kept a dog and a bitch from the litter and they have both proven themselves in the field, regularly competing in gundog working tests and picking up on my local shoot throughout the season. My older Labrador, Murphy, was used at stud from around three years old and has produced some lovely pups. He is now 10 and still competes at working tests and picks up on the shoot.

"My dogs are exercised twice daily. My older dogs have an hour each session. As a rule of thumb, I would say for each month of their young life give them five minutes of exercise per day, so that by the time they have reached 12 months of age, they should be able to cope with an hour per day."

Guy Bunce and Chloe Spencer, have been breeding Dizzywaltz Labradors since 2014 in Berkshire: "All our dogs are from working stock and, yes, there is a big difference between the two types in our opinion. Working dogs require a lot more exercise and mental stimulation in order to keep them in check. Without sufficient exercise and stimulation, they can easily develop unwanted behaviours, such as chewing furniture. When selecting new owners for our last litter, we were very careful to make them aware of this and were guided in our decision-making over prospective owners by their working schedule and time available to spend with their dogs. We give ours a one-hour daily walk during the week, plus playtimes with us and/or training, and they get much longer at weekends."

New breeder Lynn Aungier, of Alatariel Labradors, Surrey, said: "We have only had the one litter last year from our first Labrador, Pip, who is now four; she is a black working line Labrador with a good pedigree of field trial champions.

"To protect the puppies' joints and bones, exercise was gradually increased over their first year. The general guideline is five minutes per day of structured exercise, per month of age, where the puppy will be distracted and might not stop when they are tired (like they would at home, for example). If one day this was a bit longer, I didn't obsess. If the pups were bouncy and energetic later in the day,

I did some training to tire the mind, gave them a Kong to chew and lick or another toy to entertain them." Pictured is Pip, left, with her son, Raven, and daughter, Luna.

"After a year I didn't restrict the amount of exercise Pip had. She now has a minimum of a one-hour walk per day, and it will be the same for the puppies once they are a year old. The longest Pip has walked was across the Helvellyn range in the Lake District, which was about 12 miles. She probably started to slow down at about the 10-mile point, but given that the first 2 miles was climbing up, I would imagine she would go a lot further than that if she was on flat ground."

Diane Stanford, of Tragenheath Labradors, Warwickshire, is another new breeder, having produced just one litter of chocolate Labs so far: "My three-year-old Freya is from show stock, her daughter Bea, who is 10 months old, is part show and part working. I have found that Bea is more laid-back in temperament and willing to please. Freya, on the other hand, is a strong-minded Lab that knows her own mind and will lead Bea astray - Freya is usually the ringleader in getting into mischief!

"Being a show dog, Freya hasn't got the stamina of a working dog. She can perform tasks with ease and remember them well; she only needs to be shown something a few times before picking it up. Freya, for instance, will fetch a ball, but won't necessarily bring it back or give it to me. Bea is more on the gundog side; completely ball-orientated, fetching and bringing it back to me and dropping without ever been shown or told to do that. I take my Labs out twice a day for a minimum of 40 minutes off-lead, running for a ball, etc. They need that to burn up all the energy they have."

Caroline Smith, Flyenpyg Labradors, Lancashire: "My dogs have both in their lines – the working dogs are ready to go all the time, whereas the show dogs are more lazy and laid-back. I think the working ones are faster to learn something and more willing to try. My girls have at least two hours' exercise a day normally, but can quite happily have the occasional duvet day on the sofa. They equally love a four-hour beach run or a trip up a Yorkshire Peak!"

Pictured is Caroline's nine-year-old Rhodenash Doughnut The Flyenpyg ('Pig') at The Scottish Kennel Club Championship Show. Photo by Yellow Dog Photography.

Trudy Williams, Yaffleswood Labradors, West Sussex: "My dogs are working bred. There appears to be quite a difference. The working bred dogs seem to be mentally sharper, but also mentally more demanding, which can be physically and mentally challenging - especially for an inexperienced owner. Although all of my three Labs will very happily lounge around the house, if I have been a bit lazy for a few days and they have only been exercised round our garden (of one and a half acres) they tend to get restless and create their own amusement by collecting shoes, throwing them in the air and pouncing on them, or they get pushy by nudging at me. Normally I exercise them for

40 minutes twice a day, plus some ball playing in the garden.

"I train dogs and the show bred ones tend not to be as keen or interested, but they also don't tend to be as naughty. However, I have found where a show-bred dog has, say, a grandparent from working lines in the pedigree, this little bit of spark can shine through and compliments the calmness."

Pictured are Trudy's "girls."

Katrina Byrne, of Glenhugo Labradors, South Aberdeenshire, has bred for more than five years from chocolate and black bitches and black and yellow/fox red dogs – although litters have always been all black: "Our puppies go to show, working and pet homes. All our pups are

energetic and keen to have a job – however I think they are happy whether they are field trialling, in the show ring or having children to play with. Their breeding gives them the ability to perform any task and we try to assist new owners where we can to ensure they are successful in whichever discipline they choose." Katrina has a Puppy Exercise Chart which she includes with her puppy packs. She follows the Five Minute Rule for puppies, and then advises an hour's exercise twice a day once the dog is more than one year old.

Show judge Amanda Deane, Tanronens Labradors, Lincolnshire, has more than 30 years' experience of Labradors: "My dogs are all show stock. Unfortunately, I believe there is a difference in the working and show stock; not so much in their temperament, but in their ability for staying power and agility. I am not saying, though, that the show Labrador does not have the ability to work – he does.

"Regarding exercise, from the age of 12 months, Labradors can do however much you would like to do with them; they love to be included in all family exercise. It's very different if it is a Labrador puppy; it should be introduced slowly to exercise and not taken more than a few yards at first."

One of the few people with an even longer track record with Labradors, is Jenny Dobson, of Lakemeadow Labradors, South Yorkshire, who began breeding Labs in the 1960s: "My own Labs are from show lines. There is definitely a difference in the two types, both in appearance and in temperament. I have never personally owned a Lab from working lines, though I have many friends who do work their dogs, and I have attended shoots and seen Labs working.

"The qualities that a working Lab needs are not those that I, or someone just wanting a family companion dog, would particularly value, e.g. a good hunting sense, speed and agility, boldness and plenty of drive! My gut feeling is that these traits, which have been carefully and deliberately bred into the dog to enable it to retrieve game, do not make it the easiest of companion dogs, that will be 'happy just to hang out around your kitchen'...but that is not based on experience, and I am well aware that there are many Labs from working lines that make excellent family pets.

"My adults have about 50 minutes to an hour a day, which in my case is mainly free-running, as this is easier when you have several dogs at a time to walk. Lead walking is beneficial in terms of both discipline and exercise, and I'm afraid I'm a bit lax with my own dogs in that regard.

"It is a common misconception that Labs need a huge amount of exercise. As with any creature, lack of exercise can lead to obesity, health issues, boredom etc., but Labs really do not need to go for miles every day. In fact, as young puppies, it can actually be damaging to over-exercise, and can exacerbate problems like hip and elbow dysplasia."

Julie McDonough, Rangemaster Working Gundogs, Powys: "All my dogs are from working stock, so I find they are born natural retrievers and are perfect for training; I find they enjoy the mental stimulation of training. Exercise comes into training, as training simple tasks can tire any dog out more than simply going for a walk in the park. I cannot comment on show temperament.

"On a shooting day, our dogs are out for six hours a day, but on a non-shooting day, they are out for two hours. In between they have 20 minutes of training for the adults aged two years or over, and the youngsters aged six months to two years have five to 10 minutes of training, plus short periods of exercise of up to an hour throughout the day."

Liz Vivash, Wightfyre Labradors, Isle of Wight: "Our yellow was from working stock, and she is much taller and skinnier, and the chocolates are from show stock, and are heavier, more stocky and shorter, but they get the same exercise, and are all as good as each other with the tasks they can do. Again, the personality of the dog and their intelligence make the difference. We walk once a day, and they have access to a garden when they want if we are in. Puppies only need a maximum of five minutes a day per month of age, and our 12 year old also needs very little."

Anne Johnson, of Teazledown Labradors and Canine Therapies, Lancashire, has bred Labs for 35 years: "Ours are from show stock. Some Labradors from working lines have a higher level of drive, so may become very frustrated in a pet home without enough mental stimulation. All Labradors should have sound temperaments." Photo courtesy of Anne.

"Show dogs can be trained to retrieve and pick up, providing they are of correct weight, but with heavier bone they may not be able to clear fences easily, and shouldn't be asked to. Our dogs are exercised six times a day for 10 minutes, and twice for longer - up to 40 minutes."

The American breeders involved in this book favour an all-purpose Labrador bred from a mixture of working and show (bench) lines, as Teresa Gordy-Brown, of Ashland Labradors, Tennessee, explains: "In the early 1980s, our first Labradors were from American Field Trial lines. They were more refined in body type, meaning they had a smaller frame (males around 55 to 60 pounds and females around 45 to 50 pounds); they all had slick, single coats, and very narrow and long muzzles. Many had crossed-eyes and harsh expressions, hare (rabbit)-like feet and skinny whip-like tails. Temperament was absolutely that of a 'high-strung meat dog'. They were bred to be fast and nothing more; not a pleasant dog to be a companion, that is for sure.

"Two years of these field Labradors was all I could manage. We then crossed over to what we call 'bench and working lines,' bred directly from English imports or those we imported ourselves. Temperament is the first major difference – this is a dog you can hunt with one day or take into the show ring the next day; a lovely, well-mannered and easily-trained fellow that you are proud to share your home with.

"Aside from temperament, the other big difference is how they look. The bench Labrador is a sturdy, well-muscled dog with medium bone and his coat is very much different from any field

Labrador you will see; a double coat which repels water (needed here for our cold icy waters during duck season). Another feature of the correct Labrador coat is the tail. If the coat is correct, you will have an 'otter-like' tail, thick at the base, gradually tapering to the tip and hair appears to wrap around the tail. Overall the bench Lab is a heavier dog than the field Labrador; generally 20lb heavier for both males and females.

"He is not fat as many people insist ALL bench Labradors are! Rather, if they have the correct coat and bone structure, it does a great job in hiding his overall body condition. The bench Labrador may not be as fast as the smaller, more refined field Labrador, however, the one thing he does have is HEART and determination to please and finish the job you asked of him.

"There is a common misconception to this day that the color of a Labrador's coat affects his temperament and trainability. What it really boils down to is how the dog is bred and raised.

"Our Labradors are out running all day on several fenced acres, so they set the amount of activity they wish to partake in. Anyone not having ample yard space (fenced is a must) should set aside a couple of hours total for walking, playing, fetch and other activities. A bored Labrador neglected of proper exercise becomes destructive and develops many other issues." All three photos below of Ashland Labradors, courtesy of Teresa.

Robin Anderson, of Grampian Labradors, New England: "We breed to The Labrador Club, Inc. Breed Standard. A Labrador is a Labrador and should be a clean, well-muscled, moderate dog that has the instinct to bring game back to the handler or hunter. I can't say every dog we've bred wants to retrieve game, but it is something we strive for in every litter we produce.

"Exercise varies from Labrador to Labrador, depending on the needs and age. They are not bred to be long distance runners, rather they are sprinters and resters. So, if you play hard in the yard for 20-minute intervals, then rest for an hour or two, usually it's enough for the typical pet Labrador. Working Labradors gradually build more stamina so can 'work' longer and harder, but also appreciate being lazy after a hard morning of training. I think the cues need to come from the individual Labrador, rather than make a hard and fast rule about how much and how long."

10. Training a Labrador

Training a young dog is like bringing up a child. Put in the effort early on to teach them the guidelines and you will be rewarded with a well-adjusted, sociable individual who will be a joy to live with. Labradors are intelligent, extremely eager to please and love being with their humans. All of this adds up to one of the easiest breeds of all to train - but only if you put in the time too. Labradors make wonderful companions for us humans, but let yours behave exactly how he wants and you may well finish up with a wilful, attention-seeking adult; it is all too easy to treat a Lab puppy like a human and spoil him.

The secret of good training can be summed up quite simply:

Patience, Consistency, Praise and Reward

Labradors have many excellent qualities, but one of their less desirable traits is greed – most of them will chew or eat anything. However, their love of eating can be used to your advantage if you employ the technique of reward-based training with lots of treats.

 If you can, get your pup used to a small piece of carrot or apple as a healthy, low-calorie alternative to traditional dog treats.

Many owners would say that this breed has empathy (the ability to understand the feelings of others); they respond well to your encouragement and a positive atmosphere. They do not respond well to heavy-handed training methods; Labradors are known for their intelligence and they are most certainly 'biddable', i.e. it is easy to teach them commands, provided you make it clear exactly what you want them to do; don't give conflicting signals.

The Labrador is extremely versatile and can be trained to a very high level in a number of different fields.

Psychologist and canine expert Dr Stanley Coren has written a book called "The Intelligence of Dogs" in which he ranks the breeds. He surveyed dog trainers to compile the list and used "Understanding of New Commands" and "Obey First Command" as his standards of intelligence. He says there are three types of dog intelligence:

- Adaptive Intelligence (learning and problem-solving ability). This is specific to the individual animal and is measured by canine IQ tests

- Instinctive Intelligence. This is specific to the individual animal and is measured by canine IQ tests

- Working/Obedience Intelligence. This is breed-dependant

The brainboxes of the canine world are the 10 breeds ranked in the 'Brightest Dogs' section of his list. All dogs in this class:

- Understand New Commands with Fewer than Five Repetitions

- Obey a First Command 95% of the Time or Better

It will come as no surprise to anyone who has ever owned a Labrador Retriever to know that the breed is in the top group, at Number Seven. (The top six are, in order: Border Collie, Poodle, German Shepherd Dog, Golden Retriever, Doberman Pinscher and Shetland Sheepdog).

By the author's own admission, the drawback of this rating scale is that it is heavily weighted towards obedience-related behavioural traits, which are often found in working dogs (like the Labrador), rather than understanding or creativity (found in hunting dogs). As a result, some breeds, such as the Bully breeds (Bulldogs, French Bulldogs, Mastiffs, Bull Terriers, Pugs, Rottweilers, etc.). are ranked quite low on the list, due to their stubborn or independent nature.

 But as far as Labradors are concerned, it's true to say that you are starting out with a puppy that not only has the intelligence to pick up new commands very quickly, but who also really wants to learn and please you. Three golden rules when training a Labrador are:

1. Training must be reward-based, not punishment based
2. Keep sessions short or your dog will get bored
3. Keep sessions fun, give your Labrador a challenge and a chance to shine

Labradors can push the boundaries when they get to around one year old. If you decide to enlist the help of a professional trainer, choose one registered with the Association of Professional Dog Trainers (APDT); you can find details at the back of the book. Make sure your chosen one uses positive reward-based training methods, as the old alpha-dominance theories have largely been discredited. When you train your dog, it should never be a battle of wills between you and him; it should be a positive learning experience for you both. Bawling at the top of your voice or smacking should play no part in training.

If you have a high spirited, high energy Labrador, you have to use your brain to think of ways that will make training challenging and to persuade your dog that what you want him to do is actually what he wants to do. He will come to realise that when he does something you ask of him, something good is going to happen – treats, verbal praise, pats, play time, etc. With a strong-willed or boisterous dog you need to be firm, but all training should still be carried out using positive techniques.

Establishing the natural order of things is not something forced on a dog through shouting or violence; it is brought about by mutual consent and good training. Like most dogs, Labradors are happiest and behave best when they know and are comfortable with their place in the household. If you have adopted an older dog, you can still train him, but it will take a little longer to get rid of bad habits and instil good manners. Patience and persistence are the keys here.

Socialisation is a very important aspect of training. Your puppy's breeder should have already begun this process with the litter and then it's up to you to keep it going when the pup arrives home. Up to around 16 weeks' old pups can absorb a great deal of information, but they are also vulnerable to bad experiences. Pups who are not properly exposed to different people, other animals and situations can find them very frightening when they do finally encounter them later. They may react by cowering, urinating, barking, growling or biting.

Food possession can also become an issue with some Labradors. But if they have positive experiences with people and animals before they turn 16 weeks of age, they are less likely to be afraid or to try to establish dominance later.

Don't just leave your dog at home in the early days, take him out and about with you, get him used to new people, places and noises. Dogs that miss out on being socialised can pay the price later.

One issue with many young Labradors can be chewing. If you are not careful, some young Labs will chew through anything – including wires, phone chargers, remote controls, bedding, etc. And Labs are not infrequent visitors to veterinary clinics to have 'foreign objects' removed from their stomachs. Train your young Lab only to chew the things you give him – so don't give him your old slippers, an old piece of carpet or anything that resembles something you don't want him to chew. Buy purpose-made long-lasting chew toys.

Jumping up is another common issue. Labradors love everybody and are so enthusiastic about life, so it's often a natural reaction when they see somebody. You don't, however, want your fully-grown dog to jump up on grandma when he has just come back from a romp through the muddy woods and a swim in a dirty pond. Teach him while he is still small not to jump up!

....

12 Training Tips

1. Start training and socialising early. Like babies, puppies learn quickly and it's this learned behaviour that stays with them through adult life. Puppy training should start with a few minutes a day a few days after he has arrived home, even if he's only a few weeks old.

2. Your voice is a very important training tool. Your dog has to learn to understand your language and you have to understand him. Commands should be issued in a calm, authoritative voice - not shouted. Praise should be given in a happy, encouraging voice, accompanied by stroking or patting. If your dog has done something wrong, use a stern voice, not a harsh shriek. This applies even if your Labrador is unresponsive at the beginning.

3. Avoid giving your dog commands you know you can't enforce. Every time you give a command that you don't enforce, he learns that commands are optional. One command equals one response. Give your dog only one command - twice maximum - then gently enforce it. Repeating commands or nagging will make your Labrador tune out. They also teach him that the first few commands are a bluff. Telling your dog to "SIT, SIT, SIT, SIT!!!" is neither efficient nor effective. Give your dog a single "SIT" command, gently place him in the sitting position and then praise him.

4. Train your dog gently and humanely. Labradors do not respond well to being shouted at or hit. Keep training sessions short and upbeat so the whole experience is enjoyable for you and him. If obedience training is a bit of a bore, pep things up a bit by 'play training' by using constructive, non-adversarial games.

5. Begin your training around the house and garden or yard. How well your

dog responds to you at home affects his behaviour away from the home as well. If he doesn't respond well at home, he certainly won't respond any better when he's out and about where there are 101 distractions, such as food scraps, other dogs, people, cats, interesting scents, etc.

6. Mealtimes are a great time to start training your Lab. Teach him to sit and stay at breakfast and dinnertime, rather than just putting the dish down and letting him dash over immediately. In the beginning, he won't know what you mean, so gently place him into the sit position while you say "Sit." Place a hand on his chest during the "Stay" command - gradually letting go – and then give him the command to eat his dinner, followed by encouraging praise - he'll soon get the idea.

7. Use your dog's name often and in a positive manner. When you bring your pup or new dog home, use his name often so he gets used to the sound of it. He won't know what it means in the beginning, but it won't take him long to realise you're talking to him.

8. DON'T use his name when reprimanding, warning or punishing. He should trust that when he hears his name, good things happen. He should always respond to his name with enthusiasm, never hesitancy or fear. Use words such as "No," "Ack!" or "Bad Boy/Girl" in a stern (not shouted) voice instead. Some parents prefer not to use "No" with their dog, as they use it often around their kids and it can confuse the pup! When a puppy is corrected by his mother, e.g. – if he bites her – she growls at him to warn him not to do it again. Using a short sharp sound like **"Ack!"** can work surprisingly well; it does for us.

9. Don't give your dog lots of attention (even negative attention) when he misbehaves. Dogs like attention. If yours gets lots when he jumps up on you, his bad behaviour is being reinforced. If he jumps up, push him away, use the command "No" or "Down" and then ignore him.

10. Timing is critical to successful training. When your puppy does something right, praise him immediately. If you wait a while he will have no idea what he has done right. Similarly, when he does something wrong, correct him straight away. For example, if he eliminates in the house, don't shout and certainly don't rub his nose in it; this will only make things worse. If you catch him in the act, use your "No" or "Ack" sound and immediately carry him out of the house. Then use the toilet command (whichever word you have chosen) and praise your pup or give him a treat when he performs. If your pup is constantly eliminating indoors, you are not keeping a close enough eye on him.

11. Give your dog attention when YOU want to – not when he wants it. When you are training, give your puppy lots of positive attention when he is good. But if he starts jumping up, nudging you constantly or barking to demand your attention, ignore him. Don't give in to his demands. Wait a while and pat him when you want and after he has stopped demanding your attention.

12. Start as you mean to go on. In other words, in terms of rules and training, treat your cute little pup as though he were a fully-grown Labrador; introduce the rules you want him to live by as an adult. If you don't want your dog to take over your couch or bed or jump up at people when he is an adult, train him not to do it when he is small. You can't have one set of rules for a pup and one set for a fully-grown dog, he won't understand. Also make sure that everybody in the household sticks to the same set of rules. Your dog will never learn if one person lets him jump on the couch and another person doesn't.

Remember this simple phrase: **TREATS, NOT THREATS.**

Teaching Basic Commands

Sit - Teaching the Sit command to your Labrador is relatively easy. Teaching a young pup to sit still for a few seconds is a bit more difficult! In the beginning you may want to put your protégé on a lead to hold his attention.

Stand facing each other and hold a treat between your thumb and fingers just an inch or so above his head. Don't let your fingers and the treat get much further away or you might have trouble getting him to move his body into a sitting position. In fact, if your dog jumps up when you try to guide him into the Sit, you're probably holding your hand too far away from his nose. If your dog backs up, you can practise with a wall behind him.

As he reaches up to sniff it, move the treat upwards and back over the dog towards his tail at the same time as saying "Sit." Most dogs will track the treat with their eyes and follow it with their noses, causing their snouts to point straight up.

As his head moves up toward the treat, his rear end should automatically go down towards the floor. TaDa! (drum roll!)

As soon as he sits, say "Yes!", give him the treat and tell your dog (s)he's a good boy or girl. Stroke and praise him for as long as he stays in the sitting position. If he jumps up on his back legs and paws you while you are moving the treat, be patient and start all over again. Another method is to put one hand on his chest and with your other hand, gently push down on his rear end until he is sitting, while saying "Sit." Give him a treat and praise, even though you have made him do it, he will eventually associate the position with the word 'sit'.

Once your dog catches on, leave the treat in your pocket (or have it in your other hand). Repeat the sequence, but this time your dog will just follow your empty hand. Say "Sit" and bring your empty hand in front of your dog's nose, holding your fingers as if you had a treat. Move your hand exactly as you did when you held the treat.

When your dog sits, say "Yes!" and then give him a treat from your other hand or your pocket.

Gradually lessen the amount of movement with your hand. First, say "Sit" then hold your hand eight to 10 inches above your dog's face and wait a moment. Most likely, he will sit. If he doesn't, help him by moving your hand back over his head, like you did before, but make a smaller movement this time. Then try again. Your goal is to eventually just say "Sit" without having to move or extend your hand at all.

Once your dog reliably sits on cue, you can ask him to sit whenever you meet and talk to people (admittedly, it may not work straight away, but it might calm him down a bit). The key is anticipation. Give your Labrador the cue before he gets too excited to hear you and before he starts jumping up on the person just arrived. Generously reward your dog the instant he sits. Say "Yes" and give him treats every few seconds while he holds the Sit.

Whenever possible, ask the person you're greeting to help you out by walking away if your dog gets up from the sit and lunges or jumps towards him or her. With many consistent repetitions of this exercise, your dog will learn that lunging or jumping makes people go away, and polite sitting makes them stay and give him attention.

You can practise training your bouncy Labrador not to jump up by arranging for a friend to come round, then for him or her to come in and out of the house several times. Each time, show the treat, give the Sit command (initially, don't ask your dog to hold the sit for any length of time), and then allow him to greet your friend. Ask your friend to reach down to pat your dog, rather than standing straight and encouraging the dog to jump up for a greeting.

If your dog is still jumping up, you can use a harness and lead inside the house to physically prevent him from jumping up at people, while still training him to Sit when someone arrives. Treats are the key; if there's one thing the Labrador loves more than visitors, it's a treat! (You can also use the "Off" command - and reward with a treat for success - when you want your dog NOT to jump up at a person, or not to jump up on furniture).

'Sit' is a useful command and can be used in a number of different situations. For example, when you are putting his lead on, while you are preparing his meal, when he returned the ball you have just thrown, when he is jumping up, demanding attention or getting over-excited.

···

Come - This is another basic command that you can teach right from the beginning. Teaching your dog to come to you when you call (also known as 'the recall') is an important lesson. A dog who responds quickly and consistently can enjoy freedoms that other dogs cannot. Although you might spend more time teaching this command to your Labrador than any other, the benefits make it well worth the investment. By the way, "Come" or a similar word is better than "Here" if you intend using the "Heel" command, as these words sound too similar.

Whether you're teaching a young puppy or an older Labrador, the first step is always to establish that coming to you is the best thing he can do. Any time your dog comes to you whether you've called him or not, acknowledge that you appreciate it. You can do this with smiles, praise, affection, play or the magic bullet – treats! This consistent reinforcement ensures that your dog will continue to "check in" with you frequently.

1. Say your dog's name followed by the command "Come!" in an enthusiastic voice. You'll usually be more successful if you walk or run away from him while you call. Dogs find it hard to resist chasing after a running person, especially their owner.

2. He should run towards you. NOTE: Dogs tend to tune us out if we talk to them all the time. Whether you're training or out for an off-lead walk, refrain from constantly chattering to your dog - no matter how much of a brilliant conversationalist you are! If you're quiet much of the time, he is more likely to pay attention when you call him. When he does, praise him and give him a treat.

3. Often, especially outdoors, a dog will start off running towards you but then get distracted and head off in another direction. Pre-empt this situation by praising your puppy and cheering him on when he starts to come to you and **before** he has a chance to get distracted.

Your praise will keep him focused so that he'll be more likely to come all the way to you. If he stops or turns away, you can give him feedback by saying "Uh-uh!" or "Hey!" in a different tone of voice (displeased or unpleasantly surprised). When he looks at you again, smile, call him and praise him as he approaches you.

Progress your dog's training in baby steps. If he's learned to come when called in your kitchen, you can't expect him to be able to do it straight away at the park or on the beach when he's surrounded by distractions. When you first try this outdoors, make sure there's no one around to distract your dog. It's a good idea to consider using a long training lead - or to do the training within a safe, fenced area. Only when your dog has mastered the recall in a number of locations and in the face of various distractions can you expect him to come to you regularly.

Down - There are a number of different ways to teach this command, which here means for the dog to lie down. (If you are teaching this command, then use the "Off" command to teach your dog not to jump up). This does not come naturally to a young pup, so it may take a little while for him to master the Down command. Don't make it a battle of wills and, although you may gently push him down, don't physically force him down against his will. This will be seen as you asserting dominance in an aggressive manner and your Labrador will not like it.

1. Give the 'Sit' command.

2. When your dog sits, don't give him the treat immediately, but keep it in your closed hand. Slowly move your hand straight down toward the floor, between his front legs. As your dog's nose follows the treat, just like a magnet, his head will bend all the way down to the floor.

3. When the treat is on the floor between your dog's paws, start to move it away from him, like you're drawing a line along the floor. (The entire luring motion forms an L-shape).

4. At the same time say "Down" in a firm manner.

5. To continue to follow the treat, your dog will probably ease himself into the Down position. The instant his elbows touch the floor, say "Yes!" and immediately let him eat the treat. If your dog doesn't automatically stand up after eating the treat, just move a step or two away to encourage him to move out of the Down position. Then repeat the sequence above several times. Aim for two short sessions of five minutes or so per day.

If your dog's back end pops up when you try to lure him into a Down, quickly snatch the treat away. Then immediately ask your dog to sit and try again. It may help to let your dog nibble on the treat as you move it toward the floor. If you've tried to lure your dog into a Down, but he still seems confused or reluctant, try this trick:

1. Sit down on the floor with your legs straight out in front of you. Your dog should be at your side. Keeping your legs together and your feet on the floor, bend your knees to make a 'tent' shape

2. Hold a treat right in front of your dog's nose. As he licks and sniffs the treat, slowly move it down to the floor and then underneath your legs. Continue to lure him until he has to crouch down to keep following the treat

3. The instant his belly touches the floor, say "Yes!" and let him eat the treat. If your dog seems nervous about following the treat under your legs, make a trail of treats for him to eat along the way

Some dogs find it easier to follow a treat into the Down from a standing position.

* Hold the treat right in front of your dog's nose, and then slowly move it straight down to the floor, right between his front paws. His nose will follow the treat

* If you let him lick the treat as you continue to hold it still on the floor, your dog will probably plop into the Down position

* The moment he does, say "Yes!" and let him eat the treat

(Some dogs are reluctant to lie on a cold, hard surface. It may be easier to teach yours to lie down on a carpet). The next step is to introduce a hand signal. You'll still reward him with treats, though, so keep them nearby or hidden behind your back.

1. Start with your dog in a Sit

2. Say "Down"

3. Without a treat in your fingers, use the same hand motion you did before

4. As soon as your dog's elbows touch the floor, say "Yes!" and immediately get a treat to give him. Important: Even though you're not using a treat to lure your dog into position, you must still give him a reward when he lies down. You want your dog to learn that he doesn't have to see a treat to get one.

5. Clap your hands or take a few steps away to encourage him to stand up. Then repeat the sequence from the beginning several times for a week or two. When your dog readily lies down as soon as you say the cue and then use your new hand signal, you're ready for the next step. You probably don't want to keep bending all the way down to the floor to make your Labrador lie down. To make things more convenient, you can gradually shrink the signal so that it becomes a smaller movement. To make sure your dog continues to understand what you want him to do, you'll need to progress slowly.

6. Repeat the hand signal, but instead of guiding your dog into the Down by moving your hand all the way to the floor, move it almost all the way down. Stop moving your hand when it's an inch or two above the floor. Practise the Down exercise for a day or two, using this slightly smaller hand signal. Then you can make your movement an inch or two smaller, stopping your hand three or four inches above the floor.

7. After practising for another couple of days, you can shrink the signal again. As you continue to gradually stop your hand signal farther and farther from the floor, you'll bend over less and less. Eventually, you won't have to bend over at all. You'll be able to stand up straight, say "Down," and then just point to the floor.

Your next job is a bit harder - it's to practise your dog's new skill in many different situations and locations so that he can lie down whenever and wherever you ask him to. Slowly increase the level of distraction; for example, first practise in calm places, like different rooms in your house or in your garden, when there's no one else around. Then increase the distractions; practise at home when family members are moving around, on walks and then at friends' houses, too.

....

Stay - This is a very useful command, but it's not so easy to teach a lively and distracted young Labrador pup to stay still for any length of time. Here is a simple method to get your dog to stay; if you are training a young dog, don't ask him to stay for more than a few seconds at the beginning.

 This requires some concentration from your dog, so pick a time when he's relaxed and well exercised, or just after a game or mealtimes - but not exhausted when he is too tired to concentrate.

1. Command your dog to sit or lie down, but instead of giving a treat as soon as he hits the floor, hold off for one second. Then say "Yes!" in an enthusiastic voice and give him a treat. If your dog bounces up again instantly, have two treats ready. Feed one right away, before he has time to move; then say "Yes!" and feed the second treat.

2. You need a release word or phrase. It might be "Free!" or "Here!" or a word that you only use to release your dog from this command. Once you've given the treat, immediately give your release cue and encourage your dog to get up. Then repeat the exercise, perhaps up to a dozen times in one training session, gradually wait a tiny bit longer before releasing the treat. (You can delay the first treat for a moment if your dog bounces up).

3. A common mistake is to hold the treat high and then give the reward slowly. As your dog doesn't know the command yet, he sees the treat coming and gets up to meet the food. Instead, bring the treat toward your dog quickly - the best place to deliver it is right between his front paws. If you're working on a Sit-Stay, give the treat at chest height.

4. When your dog can stay for several seconds, start to add a little distance. At first, you'll walk backwards, because your Labrador is more likely to get up to follow you if you turn away from him. Take one single step away, then step back towards your dog and say "Yes!" and give the treat. Give him the signal to get up immediately, even if five seconds haven't passed. The stay gets harder for your dog depending on how long it is, how far away you are, and what else is going on around him.

5. Trainer shorthand is "distance, duration, distraction." For best success in teaching a Stay, work on one factor at a time. Whenever you make one factor more difficult, such as distance, ease up on the others at first, then build them back up. So, when you take that first step back from your dog, adding distance, you should cut the duration of the stay.

6. Now your dog has mastered the Stay with you alone, move the training on so that he learns to do the same with distractions. Have someone walk into the room, or squeak a toy or bounce a ball once. A rock-solid stay is mostly a matter of working slowly and patiently to start with. Don't go too fast - the ideal scenario is that your Labrador never breaks out of the Stay position until you release him.

If he does get up, take a breather and then give him a short refresher, starting at a point easier than whatever you were working on when he cracked. If you think he's tired or had enough, leave it for the day and come back later – just finish off on a positive note by giving one very easy command you know he will obey, followed by a treat reward.

Don't use the Stay command in situations where it is unpleasant for your Labrador. For instance, avoid telling him to stay as you close the door behind you on your way to work. Finally, don't use Stay to keep a dog in a scary situation.

....

Dealing with Puppy Biting

All Labrador puppies spend a great deal of time chewing, playing, and investigating objects. It's natural for them to use their mouths and their needle-sharp teeth to explore and investigate the world. And we shouldn't be surprised that Labradors and other retrievers often bite more than other breeds when they are young; after all, they were bred to carry things in their mouths.

When puppies play with people, they often bite, chew and mouthe on people's hands, limbs and clothing. Play biting is normal for puppies; they do it all the time with their littermates. They also bite moving targets with their sharp teeth; it's a great game.

But when they arrive in your home, they have to be taught that human skin is sensitive and body parts are not suitable biting material. Biting is not acceptable, not even from a puppy, and can be a real problem initially if you have children. When your puppy bites you or the kids, he is playing and investigating; he is NOT being aggressive. Even though Labradors are gentle dogs, puppy biting can develop into more aggressive rough play if not checked.

Make sure every time you have a play session, you have a soft toy nearby and when he starts to chew your hand or feet, clench your fingers (or toes!) to make it more difficult and distract him with a soft toy in your other hand. Keep the game interesting by moving the toy around or rolling it around in front of him. (He may be too young to fetch it back if you throw it). He may continue to chew you, but will eventually realise that the toy is far more interesting and lively than your boring hand.

If he becomes over-excited and too aggressive with the toy, if he growls a lot, stop playing with him and walk away. When you walk away, don't say anything or make eye or physical contact with your puppy. Simply ignore him, this is extremely effective and often works within a few days. If your pup is more persistent and tries to bite your legs as you walk away, thinking this is another fantastic game, stand still and ignore him. If he still persists, tell him "No!" in a very stern voice, then praise him when he lets go. If you have to physically remove him from your trouser leg or shoe, leave him alone in the room for a while and ignore his demands for attention if he starts barking.

Although you might find it quite cute and funny if your puppy bites your fingers or toes, it should be discouraged at all costs. You don't want your Labrador doing this as an adolescent or adult, when he can inadvertently cause real injury.

You may be surprised to learn that on several lists of dog bites on humans, including one compiled from various resources by the AVMA (American Veterinary Medical Association), Labradors are fairly high on the list: http://bit.ly/1jrLz5n. Jacque Lynn Schultz, CPTD, author and Companion Animal Programs Adviser, National Outreach, Petfinder, says: "Every year in the United States, 800,000 dog bites are severe enough to need medical treatment... Fifty per cent of all American children are bitten by a dog before the age of 13. Literally every dog has the potential to bite. Luckily for us, most don't."

However, she adds: "Some dogs believe the only way to protect their valuables is through an act of aggression. A dog's list of valuables may include food, toys, territory (a house or a car) or even their human family members. Dogs have been known to "protect" one family member from another, driving crying children away from their mothers or chasing amorous husbands out of bedrooms.

"The protection of territory is most often seen in males of guarding/herding breeds, such as German shepherds and rottweilers, while certain cocker spaniels and Labrador retrievers – females more often than males – put on ferocious displays over toys and chewies, resulting in punishing bites to hands and faces. Again, early training and/or lifelong management are the only solutions."

Here are some tips to deal with puppy biting:

- Puppies growl and bite more when they are excited. Don't allow things to escalate, so remove your pup from the situation before he gets too excited by putting him in a crate or pen

- Don't put your hand or finger into your pup's mouth to nibble on; this promotes puppy biting

- Limit your children's play time with pup - and always supervise the sessions in the beginning. Teach them to gently play with and stroke your puppy, not to wind him up.

- Don't let the kids (or adults) run round the house with the puppy chasing – this is an open invitation to nip at the ankles

- If your puppy does bite, remove him from the situation and people – never smack him

Tip Many Labradors are very sensitive and another method that can be very successful is to make a sharp cry of "Ouch!" when your pup bites your hand – even when it doesn't hurt. This worked very well for us. Your pup may well jump back in amazement, surprised that he has hurt you. Divert your attention from your puppy to your hand. He will probably try to get your attention or lick you as a way of saying sorry. Praise him for stopping biting and continue with the game. If he bites you again, repeat the process. A sensitive dog will soon stop biting you.

You may also think about keeping the toys you use to play with your puppy separate from other toys. That way he will associate certain toys with having fun with you and will work harder to please you.

Labradors love playing and you can use this to your advantage by teaching your dog how to play nicely with you and the toy and then by using play time as a reward for good behaviour.

Clicker Training

Clicker training is a method of training that uses a sound - a click - to tell an animal when he does something right. The clicker is a tiny plastic box held in the palm of your hand, with a metal tongue that you push quickly to make the sound.

The clicker creates an efficient language between a human trainer and a trainee. First, a trainer teaches a dog that every time he hears the clicking sound, he gets a treat. Once the dog understands that clicks are always followed by treats, the click becomes a powerful reward.

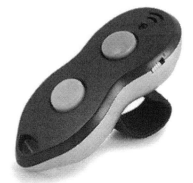

When this happens, the trainer can use the click to mark the instant the animal performs the right behaviour. For example, if a trainer wants to teach a dog to sit, she'll click the instant his rump hits the floor and then deliver a tasty treat. With repetition, the dog learns that sitting earns rewards.

So the 'click' takes on huge meaning. To the animal it means: "What I was doing the moment my trainer clicked, that's what she wants me to do." The clicker in animal training is like the winning buzzer on a game show that tells a contestant he's just won the money! Through the clicker, the trainer communicates precisely with the dog, and that speeds up training.

Although the clicker is ideal because it makes a unique, consistent sound, you do need a spare hand to hold it. For that reason, some trainers prefer to keep both hands free and instead use a one-syllable word like "Yes!" or "Good!" to mark the desired behaviour. In the steps below, you can substitute the word in place of the click to teach your pet what the sound means. It's easy to introduce the clicker to your Labrador. Spend half an hour or so teaching him that the sound of the click means "Treat!" Here's how:

1. Sit and watch TV or read a book with your dog in the room. Have a container of treats within reach.

2. Place one treat in your hand and the clicker in the other. (If your dog smells the treat and tries to get it by pawing, sniffing, mouthing or barking at you, just close your hand around the treat and wait until he gives up and leaves you alone).

3. Click once and immediately open your hand to give your dog the treat. Put another treat in your closed hand and resume watching TV or reading. Ignore your dog.

4. Several minutes later, click again and offer another treat.

5. Continue to repeat the click-and-treat combination at varying intervals, sometimes after one minute, sometimes after five minutes. Make sure you vary the time so that your dog doesn't know exactly when the next click is coming. Eventually, he'll start to turn toward you and look expectantly when he hears the click—which means he understands that the sound of the clicker means a treat is coming his way.

If your dog runs away when he hears the click, you can make the sound softer by putting it in your pocket or wrapping a towel around your hand that's holding the clicker. You can also try using a different sound, like the click of a retractable pen or the word "Yes."

Clicker Training Basics

Once your dog seems to understand the connection between the click and the treat, you're ready to get started.

1. Click just once, right when your pet does what you want him to do. Think of it like pressing the shutter of a camera to take a picture of the behaviour.

2. Remember to follow every click with a treat. After you click, deliver the treat to your pet's mouth as quickly as possible.

3. It's fine to switch between practising two or three behaviours within a session, but work on one command at a time. For example, say you're teaching your Labrador to sit, lie down and raise his paw. You can do 10 repetitions of sit and take a quick play break. Then do 10 repetitions of down, and take another quick break. Then do 10 repetitions of stay, and so on. Keep training sessions short and stop before you or your dog gets tired of the game.

4. End training sessions on a good note, when your dog has succeeded with what you're working on. If necessary, ask him to do something you know he can do well at the end of a session.

Collar and Lead Training

You have to train your dog to get used to a collar - or harness - and lead (leash), and then he has to learn to walk nicely on the lead. Teaching these manners can be challenging because many young Labradors are very lively and don't necessarily want to walk at the same pace as you. All dogs will pull on a lead initially. This isn't because they want to show you who's boss, it's simply that they are excited to be outdoors and are forging ahead.

If you are worried about pulling on your young Labrador's collar, you might prefer to use a body harness instead. Harnesses work well with some dogs, they take the pressure away from a dog's sensitive neck area and distribute it more evenly around the body. Harnesses with a chest ring for the lead can be effective for training. When your dog pulls, the harness turns him around.

Another option is to start your dog on a padded collar and then change to a harness once he has learned some lead etiquette – although padded collars can be quite heavy. Some dogs don't mind collars; some will try to fight them, while others will slump to the floor like you have hung a two-ton weight around their necks! You need to be patient and calm and proceed at a pace comfortable to him; don't fight your dog and don't force the collar on.

1. The secret to getting a collar is to buy one that fits your puppy now - not one he is going to grow into - so choose a small lightweight one that he will hardly notice. A big collar may be too heavy and frightening. You can buy one with clips to start with, just put it on and clip it together, rather than fiddling with buckles, which can be scary when he's wearing a collar for the first time. Stick to the principle of positive reward-based training and give a treat once the collar is on, not after you have taken it off. Then gradually increase the length of time you leave the collar on. IMPORTANT: If you leave your dog in a crate, or leave him alone in the house, take off the collar. He is not used to it and it may get caught on something, causing panic or injury to your dog.

2. Put the collar on when there are other things that will occupy him, like when he is going outside to be with you, or in the home when you are interacting with him. Or put it on at mealtimes or when you are doing some basic training. Don't put the collar on too tight, you

want him to forget it's there. Some pups may react as if you've hung a 10-ton weight around their necks, while others will be more compliant. If yours scratches the collar, get his attention by encouraging him to follow you or play with a toy to forget the irritation. (This photo of mother and daughter in different-sized collars courtesy of Christine Eynon, Baileylane Labradors, Herefordshire).

3. Once your puppy is happy wearing the collar, introduce the lead. An extending or retractable one is not really suitable for starting off with, as they are not very strong and no good for training him to walk close. Buy a fixed-length lead. Start off in the house or garden; don't try to go out and about straight away. Think of the lead as a safety device to stop him running off, not something to drag him around with. You want a dog that doesn't pull, so don't start by pulling him around; you don't want to get into a tug-of-war contest.

4. Attach the lead to the collar and give him a treat while you put it on. The minute it is attached, use the treats (instead of pulling on the lead) to lure him beside you, so that he gets used to walking with the collar and lead. As well as using treats you can also make good use of toys to do exactly the same thing - especially if your dog has a favourite. Walk around the house with the lead on and lure him forwards with the toy.

It might feel a bit odd but it's a good way for your pup to develop a positive relationship with the collar and lead with the minimum of fuss. Act as though it's the most natural thing in the world for you to walk around the house with your dog on a lead – and just hope that the neighbours aren't watching! Some dogs react the moment you attach the lead and they feel some tension on it – a bit like when a horse is being broken in for the first time. Drop the lead and allow him to run round the house or yard, dragging it after him, but be careful he doesn't get tangled and hurt himself. Try to make him forget about it by playing or starting a short fun training routine with treats. Treats are a huge distraction for most young Labradors. While he is concentrating on the new task, occasionally pick up the lead and call him to you. Do it gently and in an encouraging tone.

5. The most important thing is not to yank on the lead. If it is gets tight, just lure him back beside you with a treat or a toy while walking. All you're doing is getting him to move around beside you. Remember to keep your hand down (the one holding the treat or toy) so your dog doesn't get the habit of jumping up at you. If you feel he is getting stressed when walking outside on a lead, try putting treats along the route you'll be taking to turn this into a rewarding game: good times are ahead... That way he learns to focus on what's ahead of him with curiosity and not fear.

Take collar and lead training slowly, give your pup time to process all this new information about what the lead is and does. Let him gain confidence in you, and then in the lead and himself. Some dogs can sit and decide not to move. If this happens, walk a few steps away, go down on one knee and encourage him to come to you using a treat, then walk off again. For some pups, the collar and lead can be restricting and they will react with resistance. Some dogs are perfectly happy to walk alongside you off-lead, but behave differently when they have one on. Proceed in tiny steps if that is what your puppy is happy with, don't over face him, but stick at it if you are met with resistance. With training, your puppy will learn to walk nicely on a lead; it is a question of when, not if.

Walking on a Lead

There are different methods, but we have found the following one to be successful for quick results. Initially, the lead should be kept fairly loose. Have a treat in your hand as you walk, it will encourage your dog to sniff the treat as he walks alongside. He will not pull ahead as he will want to remain near the treat.

Give him the command Walk or Heel and then proceed with the treat in your hand, keep giving him a treat every few steps initially, then gradually extend the time between treats. Eventually, you should be able to walk with your hand comfortably at your side, periodically (every minute or so) reaching into your pocket to grab a treat to reward your dog.

If your dog starts pulling ahead, first give him a warning, by saying 'No' or 'Steady', or a similar command. If he slows down, give him a treat. But if he continues to pull ahead so that your arm becomes fully extended, stop walking and ignore your dog. Wait for him to stop pulling and to look up at you. At this point reward him for good behaviour before carrying on your walk. Be sure to quickly reward him with treats and praise any time he doesn't pull and walks with you with the lead slack. If you have a lively young pup who is dashing all over the place on the lead, try starting training when he is already a little tired - after a play or exercise session – (but not exhausted).

Another way is what dog trainer Victoria Stillwell describes as the Reverse Direction Technique. When your dog pulls, say "Let's Go!" in an encouraging manner, then turn away from him and walk off in the other direction, without jerking on the lead. When he is following you and the lead is slack, turn back and continue on your original way. It may take a few repetitions, but your words and body language will make it clear that pulling will not get your dog anywhere, whereas walking calmly by your side - or even slightly in front of you - on a loose lead will get him where he wants to go. There is an excellent video (in front of her beautiful house!) which shows Victoria demonstrating this technique and highlights just how easy it is with a dog that's easy to please. It only lasts three minutes and is well worth watching: https://positively.com/dog-behavior/basic-cues/loose-leash-walking.

Breeders on Training

All of the breeders involved in this book say that Labradors are easy to train, compared with most other breeds. Here are some of their comments:

"I personally find Labradors very easy to train. I use clicker training. Labradors are very food driven and easy to teach; it is important, however, to phase out food rewards gradually throughout the training process." "They're not that difficult; food's a great motivator. Keep training simple and be patient."

"They are very easy to train and extremely loyal. My pup was extremely obedient at four to five months old. She is now nine months old and pushing boundaries with loads of confidence, which I wish to preserve. I have gone back to basics to reaffirm boundaries. I reward her with treats if she does well."

"Training is easy, providing the correct techniques are used - and these need to be adapted for each individual dog. Training is not a one-size-fits-all approach." "Labs are very easy to train; they just want to please."

"Labradors are very biddable. Training sessions should be short and varied, and all good behaviour should be rewarded with an edible treat." "Labradors are very easy to train - although some can be very strong-willed. They have a desire to please and intelligence." "Very easy, if using lure and reward with consistent body language."

"Labradors are extremely easy to train, provided you put the time in. They are a breed that is eager to learn and so want to please. They do not come pre-programmed, however, so please do not get a puppy if you are not prepared to take it to a training class. I train by association; it is surprising how easy they pick something up once you have shown them what you want of them."

"Labradors are so easy to train – they love food and will do pretty much anything for it. They also love a run and ball chase too as a reward." "Labradors are easy to obedience train - you do get the occasional stubborn one - but usually, with love and time and not overdoing it, they train easily."

"Labs are usually very keen to please, and I've usually found them very trainable. Seek out a good training or socialisation class for lead training, recall, etc. and take advice from an experienced and qualified trainer. Lab pups are naturally greedy, so I make use of this characteristic to help in training, i.e. bribery! But plenty of praise when they get it right also goes a long way."

"Labradors are easy to train if you adopt the right technique. Quite often it's the owners that need to be trained, and it is therefore a great idea to go to classes or have a one-to-one with a trainer who can help and explain the use of recall, especially with a whistle." Another amusing comment came from a UK breeder whose dogs regularly pick up on shoots: "Labradors are born half-trained and Spaniels die half-trained!"

"They are very easy to train. Labradors are highly food-motivated, and as long as 'training' is fun in the early months, then they will be easily conditioned. In fact, I prefer to call this early work 'conditioning', rather than training." "You just need to be consistent in your messages, and firm in voice and hand signals. At 12 weeks, they should know their name, come when called, sit, wait, stop, know NO, and you should be able to take toys and food away without grief."

"Labradors generally want to please, so compared to other breeds they are less defiant and easier to train – particularly as they think with their bellies, and food reward works extremely well. However, they all have their individual personalities and we have had highly biddable Labradors who automatically walk to heal off the lead to much naughtier ones, where it has taken much more effort to rein in a highly independent personality!"

"Having had several breeds in my lifetime, I think the Labradors are the easiest to train. They are very forgiving of human error."

Julie McDonough, Rangemaster Working Gundogs, Powys, Wales: "If the new owner is looking for training for agility or the shooting field, I would suggest purchasing a puppy from a working background as they seem to thrive on training. Labradors are known for their ability to learn simple tasks very quickly. As long as you are consistent with your commands, you can be surprised how quickly they learn."

Lynn Aungier, Alatariel Labradors, Surrey: "I find them very easy to train. They are food-orientated, which helps immensely in the early stages. They pick up things like clicker training very quickly and they also want to make you happy.

"Of our three Labradors, Pip is food-orientated, but she also wants to please; Raven is food obsessed - if he knows you have biscuits or a bit of carrot, he will be very attentive. Luna likes a biscuit, but she equally likes to be told she is a good girl. Of the three, Luna (despite being a fizzy, bouncy dog) is probably the easiest to train, but she lacks some of the focus that the concentration on the biscuit gives to the other two dogs!"

Teresa Gordy-Brown, Ashland Labradors, Tennessee, USA: "One thing to remember about Labradors - and I stress this all the time: they are like little four-legged, fur-covered five-year-old brats with ADD (Attention Deficit Disorder) for the first two, sometimes three, years! Then one day they grow-up mentally (closer to age three, I believe) and you find you have the greatest dog in the world.

"Yes, they are brats and yes, they can be a handful, but once they mature, they are a unique breed like no other. So, if you invest the time into training and socializing them when they are young, you will be rewarded one day soon with the greatest companion you could ever ask for."

GENERAL NOTE: If your puppy is in a hyperactive mood or extremely tired, he is not likely to be very receptive to training.

CREDIT: With thanks to the American Society for the Prevention of Cruelty to Animals for assistance with parts of this chapter. The ASPCA has a great deal of good advice and training tips on its website at: www.aspca.org

11. Labrador Health

It is becoming increasingly evident that genetics can have a huge influence on a person's health and life expectancy – which is why so much time and money is currently being devoted to genetic research. A human is more likely to suffer from a hereditary illness if the gene - or genes - for that disorder is passed on from parents or grandparents. That person is said to have a 'predisposition' to the ailment if the gene(s) is in the family's bloodline.

Well, the same is true of dogs.

There is not a single breed without the potential for some genetic weakness. For example, German Shepherd Dogs are more prone to hip problems than many other breeds, and 30% of Dalmatians have problems with their hearing. If you get a German Shepherd or a Dalmatian, your dog will not automatically suffer from these issues, but if he or she comes from unscreened parents, your dog will statistically be more likely to have them than a breed with no history of the complaint. In other words, 'bad' genes can be inherited along with good ones.

You might have chosen your breeder based on the look of her dogs, their ability to retrieve, or simply their colour, but have you thought about the health of the puppy's parents and ancestors? Could they have passed on unhealthy mutated genes to the puppy along with the good genes for all those features you are attracted to? **The way to reduce this risk is to health test.**

With Labradors, hip, elbow and eye problems are some of the most common hereditary ailments, so genetic testing and 'hip scoring' and 'elbow scoring' are now an everyday part of producing Labrador puppies among responsible breeders. If you see a 'cheap' Labrador or litter of puppies advertised, it is often because little or no screening has taken place. It's an indisputable fact; health tests cost money.

There is no 100% guarantee of perfect health for any dog - or human - but the chances of your dog suffering from an ailment the parents have successfully been screened for will be greatly reduced. That is true of hip and elbow dysplasia, which are caused by a combination of genes. And the good news is that there is zero chance of your Lab puppy going blind from the inherited eye disease prcd-PRA if one parent has a CLEAR result from the OptiGen DNA test – see Eye Diseases later in this chapter for more detail.

So the best way of getting off to a good start is by choosing a puppy from health-tested parents. Of course, this may not be possible if you are taking on a dog from someone else or a rescue centre. If that is the case, try and get as much background health information as you can.

And be aware that just because the puppy and parents are registered with the Kennel Club (or AKC in the USA) and have pedigree certificates, it does not necessarily mean that they have passed any health tests. All a pedigree certificate guarantees is that the puppy's parents can be traced back several generations and the ancestors were all purebred Labradors. Many pedigree (purebred) dogs have indeed passed health tests, but prospective buyers should always find out **exactly** what health screening the sire and dam (mother and father) have undergone - ask to see original certificates - and what, if any, health guarantees the breeder is offering with the puppy.

NOTE: This chapter is intended to be used as a medical encyclopaedia to help you to identify any potential issues and act on them promptly in the best interests of your dog. Your Labrador will NOT get all of these ailments! Read each section to see which ones are the most common health issues to affect Labradors, and which are relevant to the dog population in general.

Health Certificates

In the UK, The Kennel Club's requirements and recommendations for **Assured Breeders** states: "Make health of breeding stock and puppies produced a particular priority and make use of health screening schemes relevant to their breed." In the USA, The AKC has **Breeders of Merit** and those in the H.E.A.R.T. programme, who all meet specific health testing standards.

According to the breeders involved in this book, as well as asking to see the pup or adult dog's pedigree certificate, the following certificates should be available as a **minimum** for both parents - and ask to see the originals. (A 'hip/elbow score' is the name given to BVA (British Veterinary Association) or OFA (Orthopedic Foundation for Animals) test on each hip/elbow):

- Hip evaluation or 'hip score'
- Elbow evaluation or 'elbow score'
- OptiGen prcd-PRA CLEAR (eyes)
- Current (less than 12 months old) annual eye certificates to show that the dog is free of cataracts and other eye diseases at the time of testing; the more recent, the better as a dog can develop an issue the day after the test was carried out

The UK Kennel Club also advises breeders to consider testing for these other diseases: CNM - Centronuclear Myopathy (similar to Muscular Dystrophy), HNPK - Hereditary Nasal Parakeratosis, an inherited skin disorder, and SD2 - Skeletal Dysplasia 2, which leads to dogs being born shorter than normal. (It is more likely to affect working Labs than show ones). The Labrador Breed Council also lists EIC (Exercise Induced Collapse as an inheritable disease, which in the UK is more likely to affect show Labs. The list is similar for the USA, with the AKC requiring hip, elbow, eye and EIC tests for all breeding Labradors.

Once you have your dog, much of the rest is up to you. Taking good care of him or her by feeding a quality food, **monitoring the dog's weight**, giving plenty exercise, socialisation and stimulation, as well as a weekly groom and check-over will all help to keep your Lab happy and healthy.

Labrador Insurance

Insurance is another point to consider for a new puppy or adult dog. The best time to get pet insurance is BEFORE you bring your Labrador home and before any health issues develop. Don't wait until you need to seek veterinary help - bite the bullet and take out annual insurance. If you can afford it, take out life cover. This may be more expensive, but will cover your dog throughout his or her lifetime - including for chronic (recurring and/or long term) ailments, such as eye and joint problems or ear infections.

Insuring a healthy puppy or adult dog is the only sure-fire way to ensure vets' bills are covered before anything unforeseen happens - and you'd be a rare owner if you didn't use your policy at least once during your dog's life. Due to the breed's reputation for being relatively healthy, the Lab is not overly expensive to insure. Cover varies based on a number of factors, including where you live. According to Consumer Intelligence data from more than 200 dog insurance quotes, cover for a Labrador typically varies from £32 per month if you live in Yorkshire, to £60 for Londoners (2017).

In the UK, Bought By Many offers policies from insurers More Than at https://boughtbymany.com/offers/labrador-pet-insurance/ Cover starts at around £10 a month for a Labrador, rising to nearly £30, depending on the level of cover you opt for. Bought By Many gets groups of single breed owners together, so you have to join the Labrador Group, but it claims you'll get a 10% saving on normal Lab insurance. We are not on commission - just trying to save you some money – there are numerous companies out there offering pet insurance. Read the small print and the amount of excess; a cheap policy may not always be the best long-term decision.

Of course if you make a claim, your monthly premium will increase, but if you have a decent insurance policy BEFORE a recurring health problem starts, your dog should continue to be covered if the ailment returns. You'll have to decide whether the insurance is worth the money. On the plus side, you'll have peace of mind if your devoted Labrador falls ill and you'll know just how much to fork out every month.

In the US, policies cost around $25-$37 a month for Labs, depending on where you live and how much excess you're willing to pay. Consumers' Advocate has named the top pet insurance companies, taking into account claims and service (2017): 1. Healthy Paws, 2. Embrace, 3. PetPlan, 4. Pets Best, 5. Nationwide, 6. PetFirst.

With advances in veterinary science, there is so much more vets can do to help an ailing dog - but at a cost. Surgical procedures can rack up bills of thousands of pounds or dollars. These are some of the USA's Embrace Insurance's estimates for diagnosis and treatment for Labradors: Hip Dysplasia $1,500-$6,000, Osteochondrosis of the Ankle/Knee $2,000-$4,000, Osteochondrosis of the Elbow $2,000-$4,000, Cataracts $1,500-$5,000, Patellar Luxation $1,500-$3,000, Exercise Induced Collapse $500-$1,000,and the list goes on.

Another point to consider is that dogs are at increasing risk of theft by criminals, including organised gangs. With the purchase price of puppies rising, dognapping more than quadrupled in the UK between 2010 and 2015, with around 50 dogs a day being stolen. Some 49% of dogs are snatched from owners' gardens and 13% from people's homes. If you take out a policy, check that theft is included. Although nothing can ever replace your beloved Lab, a good insurance policy will ensure that you are not out of pocket.

The information in this chapter is not written to frighten new owners, but to help you to recognise symptoms of the main conditions affecting Labradors and enable you to take prompt action, should the need arise. There are also a number of measures you can take to prevent or reduce the chances of certain physical and behavioural problems developing, including regular daily exercise and socialisation and that perennial challenge with Labradors – keeping their weight in check.

Three Golden Tips

1. **Buy a well-bred puppy** - A responsible breeder selects their stock based on:

   ❖ Temperament

   ❖ General health and DNA testing of the parents

❖ Conformation (physical structure)

❖ The ability to do a job (with working Labs in particular)

Although well-bred puppies are not cheap, believe it or not, committed Labrador breeders are not in it for the money, often incurring high bills for health screening, veterinary fees, specialised food, etc. The main concern of a good breeder is to produce healthy puppies with good temperaments and instincts that are 'fit for function.'

Better to spend time beforehand choosing a well-bred puppy than to spend a great deal of time and money later when your wonderful pet bought from an online advert or pet shop develops health problems due to poor breeding, not to mention the heartache that causes. **Chapter 4. Choosing a Labrador Puppy** has detailed information on how to find him or her and the questions to ask.

❖ Don't buy from a pet shop - no reputable breeder allows her pups to end up in pet shops

❖ Don't buy a puppy from a small ad on a general website

❖ Don't buy a pup or adult dog unseen with a credit card - you are storing up trouble and expense for yourself

2: Get pet insurance as soon as you get your dog - Don't wait until your dog has a health issue and needs to see a vet. Most insurers will exclude all pre-existing conditions on their policies. When choosing insurance, check the small print to make sure that any condition that might occur is covered and that if the problem is recurring, it will continue to be covered year after year. When you are working out costs, factor in the annual or monthly cost of good pet insurance and trips to a vet for check-ups, annual vaccinations, etc.

3: Find a good vet - Ask around your pet-owning friends, rather than just going to the first one you find. A vet that knows your dog from his or her vaccinations as a puppy and then right through their life is more likely to understand your dog and diagnose quickly and correctly when something is wrong. If you visit a big veterinary practice, ask for the same vet by name when you make an appointment.

We all want our dogs to be healthy - so how can you tell if yours is? Well, here are some positive things to look for in a healthy Labrador:

11 Signs of a Healthy Labrador

1. **Eyes** - A healthy black or yellow Labrador's eyes are brown and shiny, while a chocolate has brown or hazel eyes. (Silver Labs' eyes are often grey, which is not an acceptable colour to the Kennel Clubs). Paleness around the eyeball (conjunctiva) could be a sign of underlying problems. A red swelling in the corner of one or both eyes could be cherry eye. Sometimes the dog's third eyelid (the nictating membrane) is visible at the eye's inside corner - this is normal. There should be no thick, green or yellow discharge from the eyes. A cloudy eye could be a sign of cataracts.

2. **Ears** – If you are choosing a puppy, gently clap your hands behind the pup (not so loud as to frighten him) to see if he reacts. If not, this may be a sign of deafness. Also, ear infections can be a problem with some Labradors and other breeds with floppy ears. A pricked-up ear allows air to circulate, while a folded ear flap creates a warm, moist haven for mini horrors such as bacteria and mites. The ear flap can also trap dirt and dust and should be inspected during your weekly grooming routine. An unpleasant smell, redness or inflammation are all signs of infection. Some wax inside the ear – usually brown or yellowy - is normal; lots of wax or crusty wax is not. Tell-tale signs of an infection are scratching the ears, rubbing them on the floor or furniture, or shaking the head a lot, often accompanied by an unpleasant smell around the ears.

3. **Coat and skin** – These are easy-to-monitor indicators of a healthy dog. A Labrador has a dense double coat, and the outer waterproof layer of coat should be glossy, if somewhat coarse to the touch. Dandruff, bald spots, a dull lifeless coat, a discoloured or oily coat, or one that loses excessive hair, can all be signs that something is amiss. Skin should be smooth without redness. (Normal Lab skin pigment can vary from pale pink to brown, black or mottled, depending on coat colour). If a puppy or adult dog is scratching, licking or biting himself a lot, he may have a condition that needs addressing before he makes it worse. Open sores, scales, scabs, red patches or growths can be a sign of a problem. Signs of fleas, ticks and other external parasites should be treated immediately. Check there are no small black specks, which may be fleas, on the coat or bedding.

4. **Weight** – It is a constant challenge for many owners to keep their food-obsessed Labradors trim! A general rule of thumb is that your dog's stomach should be slightly above the bottom of his rib cage when standing, and you should be able to feel his ribs beneath his coat without too much effort. Although show Labs tend to be chunkier than field Labs, the rule still applies. If the stomach hangs below, the dog is overweight - or may have a pot belly, which can also be a symptom of other conditions. (Note the lovely 'otter tail' of the Labrador in this photo).

5. **Nose** – A dog's nose is an indicator of health symptoms. Regardless of colour, it should normally be moist and cold to the touch as well as free from clear, watery secretions. Any yellow, green or foul smelling discharge is not normal - in younger dogs this can be a sign of canine distemper. The nose

can be black, brown or pink - a pink nose is often called a 'winter nose' as the pigment often returns during summer. (A 'Dudley' Labrador is one where the nose, the area around the eyes and the feet lack any pigment from birth to old age and appear pink). Some Labradors' noses turn pinkish with ageing, this is because their bodies are producing less pigment. It is not a cause for concern.

6. **Mouth** – Gums should be a healthy pink or black colour, or a mixture. A change in colour can be an indicator of a health issue. Paleness or whiteness can be a sign of anaemia or lack of oxygen due to heart or breathing problems (this is hard to tell with black gums). Blue gums or tongue are a sign that your Lab is not breathing properly. Red, inflamed gums can be a sign of gingivitis or other tooth disease. Again, your dog's breath should smell OK. Young dogs will have sparkling white teeth, whereas older dogs will have darker teeth, but they should not have any hard white, yellow, green or brown bits.

7. **Temperature** – The normal temperature of a dog is 101°F to 102.5°F. (A human's is 98.6°F). Excited or exercising dogs may run a slightly higher temperature. Anything above 103°F or below 100°F should be checked out. The exceptions are female dogs about to give birth that will often have a temperature of 99°F. If you take your dog's temperature, make sure he or she is relaxed and *always* use a purpose-made canine thermometer, like the one pictured here for rectal use.

8. **Stools** –Poo, poop, business, faeces - call it what you will - it's the stuff that comes out of the less appealing end of your Lab on a daily basis! It should be firm and brown, not runny, with no signs of worms or parasites. Watery stools or a dog not eliminating regularly are both signs of an upset stomach or other ailments. If it continues for a couple of days, consult your vet. If puppies have diarrhoea they need checking out much quicker as they can quickly dehydrate.

9. **Energy** –Labradors have medium to high energy levels. Your dog should have good amounts of energy with fluid and pain-free movements. Lack of energy or lethargy – if it is not the dog's normal character – could be a sign of an underlying problem.

10. **Smell** – There's no getting away from the fact that your Labrador almost certainly gives off a doggie odour (eau de dog!) This is perfectly normal - your Lab should smell like a dog. However, if there is a musty, 'off' or generally unpleasant smell coming from his body, it could be a sign of a yeast infection. There can be a number of reasons for this; often the ears require attention or it can sometimes be an allergy to a certain food. Another reason for an unpleasant smell can be that one of the anal glands has become blocked and needs expressing, or squeezing (a job best left to the vet unless you know what you are doing!) Whatever the cause, you need to get to the root of the problem as soon as possible before it develops into something more serious.

11. **Attitude** –A generally positive attitude is a sign of good health. Labradors are engaged, enthusiastic and willing dogs, so symptoms of illness may include one or all of the following: not eating food (often a sure sign that something is amiss with a Lab), a general lack of interest in his or her surroundings, tail not wagging, lethargy and sleeping a lot (more than normal). The important thing is to look out for any behaviour that is out of the ordinary for your individual dog.

So now you know some of the signs of a healthy dog – what are the signs of an unhealthy one? There are many different symptoms that can indicate your canine companion isn't feeling great. If you don't yet know your dog, his habits, temperament and behaviour patterns, then spend some time getting acquainted with him.

What are his normal character and temperament? Lively or calm, playful or serious, a joker or an introvert, bold or nervous, happy to be left alone or loves to be with people, a keen appetite or a fussy eater? How often does he empty his bowels, does he ever vomit? (Dogs will often eat grass to make themselves sick, this is perfectly normal and a natural way of cleansing the digestive system).

You may think your Lab can't talk, **but he can!** If you really know your dog, his character and habits, then he CAN tell you when he's not well. He does this by changing his patterns.

Some symptoms are physical, some emotional and others are behavioural. It's important for you to be able to recognise these changes as soon as possible. Early treatment can be the key to keeping a simple problem from snowballing into a serious illness. If you think your Labrador is unwell, it is useful to keep an accurate and detailed account of his symptoms to give to the vet, perhaps even take a video of him on your mobile phone. This will help the vet to correctly diagnose and effectively treat your dog.

Four Vital Signs of Illness

1. **Temperature** - A new-born puppy will have a temperature of 94-97ºF. This will reach the normal adult body temperature of 101ºF at about four weeks old. As stated, anything between 100ºF and 103ºF is regarded as normal for an adult dog. The temperature is normally taken via the rectum. If you do this, be very careful. It's easier if you get someone to hold your dog while you do this. Digital thermometers are a good choice, but **only use one specifically made for rectal use,** as normal glass thermometers can easily break off in the rectum.

    Ear thermometers are now available (pictured) making the task much easier, although they can be expensive and don't suit all dogs' ears - Walmart has started stocking them. Remember that exercise or excitement can cause the temperature to rise by 2ºF to 3ºF when your dog is actually in good health, so wait until he is relaxed before taking his temperature. If it is above or below the norms, give your vet a call.

    Ear Thermometer

    2. **Respiratory Rate** - Another symptom of canine illness is a change in breathing patterns. This varies a lot depending on the size and weight of the dog. An adult dog will have a respiratory rate of 15-25 breaths per minute when resting. You can easily check this by counting your dog's breaths for a minute with a stopwatch handy. Don't do this if he is panting; it doesn't count.

    3. **Heart Rate** - You can feel your Labrador's heartbeat by placing your hand on his lower ribcage – just behind the elbow. Don't be alarmed if the heartbeat seems

irregular compared to a human; it IS irregular in some dogs. Your dog will probably love the attention, so it should be quite easy to check his heartbeat. Just lay him on his side and bend his left front leg at the elbow, bring the elbow in to his chest and place your fingers on this area and count the beats.

- Toy dogs have a heartbeat of up to 160 or 180 beats per minute
- Small dogs have a normal rate of 90 to 140 beats per minute
- Dogs weighing more than 30lbs have a heart rate of 60 to 120 beats per minute; the larger the dog, the slower the normal heart rate
- A young puppy has a heartbeat of around 220 beats per minute
- An older dog has a slower heartbeat

4. **Behaviour Changes** - Classic symptoms of illness are any inexplicable behaviour changes. If there has NOT been a change in the household atmosphere, such as another new pet, a new baby, moving home, the absence of a family member or the loss of another dog, then the following symptoms may well be a sign that all is not well:

- Depression
- Anxiety and/or trembling
- Falling or stumbling
- Loss of appetite
- Walking in circles
- Being more vocal - grunting, whining and/or whimpering
- Aggression – Labradors are normally extremely friendly
- Tiredness - sleeping more than normal and/or not wanting to exercise
- Abnormal posture

Your dog may normally show some of these signs, but if any of them appear for the first time or worse than usual, you need to keep him under close watch for a few hours or even days. Quite often he will return to normal of his own accord. Like humans, dogs have off-days too.

If he is showing any of the above symptoms, then don't over-exercise him, and avoid stressful situations and hot or cold places. Make sure he has access to clean water. There are many other signals of ill health, but these are four of the most important. Keep a record for your vet, if your dog does need professional medical attention, most vets will want to know:

WHEN the symptoms first appeared in your dog

WHETHER they are getting better or worse, and

HOW FREQUENT the symptoms are. Are they intermittent, continuous or increasing?

We have highlighted some of the indicators of good and poor health to help you monitor your dog's wellbeing. Getting to know his or her character, habits and temperament will go a long way towards spotting the early signs of ill health.

What the Breeders Say

Health is clearly an important and topical issue. We asked Labrador breeders what the biggest issues are, and many also added that people breeding from non-health tested stock were compromising the future health of the breed. Here is what several had to say:

Christopher Clarke, of Reedfen Labradors, Leverington, Cambridgeshire: "Historically we have been concerned with hips, eyes and elbows, but we now have available several DNA health tests for conditions such as prcd-PRA, CNM, EIC, SD2 and HNPK. These can all be very serious issues for an individual dog and owner, and I am firmly of the belief that all possible testing should be carried out before a mating takes place. We as breeders also have tools available such as the KC's Mate Select service which has proved very helpful to me, and I would not consider a mating before using such an asset."

(In the UK, the Kennel Club's **Mate Select** online service helps breeders choose a healthy dog to breed theirs with. It takes into account results of health tests and the COI - Coefficient of Inbreeding - for a) individual dogs and b) the proposed breeding pair together. COI determines how closely-related a dog's ancestors were; the lower the number the better. Mating closely-related dogs can lead to health issues. It's at: www.thekennelclub.org.uk/services/public/mateselect/)

Nadine Lapskas, of Trencrom Kennels, Bournemouth, adds: "Ensuring the mating is within a good coefficient ensures no or less inbreeding. I believe it is this that causes health issues and it was key to me finding the right mate for Fern, our bitch. In my research for a mate, I found that the weaker hip and shoulder scores tend to come from a high coefficient."

Stephen and Jane Armstrong, of Carnamaddy Labradors, County Antrim, Northern Ireland: "The breed's main health issues are probably skeletal, i.e. hip and elbow dysplasia. The biggest threat to the future of the breed is puppy farms producing pups from stock that hasn't been health tested." And Colin Hinkley, of Sanglier Labradors, East Sussex agrees: "People not doing their health checks on their stud dogs and brood bitches is the biggest threat."

Amanda Deane, of Tanronens Labradors, Lincoln, has been breeding Labradors since 1985, and also shows and judges. She said: "The breed's main health issue is still having hip dysplasia, but the future health issue is how fat the Labrador is becoming. And another thing to be aware of is their length of leg. New owners should look for these certificates: Up-to-date certificate of eye examination (Mandatory), hip (Mandatory), Elbow, EIC, CNM, and HNPK." Pictured is Amanda's two-and-a-half-year-old Mattand Classic Edition of Tanronens (Sophie). Photo by Sharon Rogers.

Guy Bunce, of Dizzywaltz Labradors, Berkshire: "I think the biggest threat is unscrupulous breeders not carrying out the correct medical tests prior to breeding and therefore perpetuating the potential medical problems. Prospective owners should look for hips, eyes, knees certificates; new owners should also check for certificates of vaccinations (at least the first vaccination should be carried out prior to the dog going home).

Christine Eynon, of Baileylane Labradors, Ross on Wye, Herefordshire: "One of the main health threats is Labradors running to fat as owners often overfeed. A Lab will eat for England if given the chance."

Andrew Baker, of Saffronlyn Gundogs, Barnsley, South Yorkshire, said that a whole raft of tests were now available for Labradors, and added: "The main issue for me is that they have clear eyes and good hip and elbow scores. My dogs are all tested or are hereditary clear of CNM and PRA. However, the more testing that is done, eventually you may come across something that your dog is a carrier for or is affected by. Prospective puppy buyers should look for, as a minimum, that the parents have a current clear eye certificate and good hip and elbow scores."

Jenny Dobson, of Lakemeadow Labradors, Doncaster, South Yorkshire, has bred Labradors since 1968 and has seen some changes in the health of the breed over the last five decades: "I think Hip Dysplasia is probably less of an issue nowadays than it was about 10 years ago, but I think the situation regarding elbows has deteriorated over this period, and one seems increasingly to hear more about labs suffering from elbow problems, (ED and OCD). There are also problems with cancers (in various forms) in the breed, though I imagine this is true of many breeds. In Labradors, I feel confident that, in time, a hereditary link will be established to some cancers, as there do appear to be certain breeding lines that have increased susceptibility.

"The surge of popularity of the 'dilutes' is a worry to the health of the breed, as breeders of these 'designer' pups are motivated by making money and not by the welfare of the breed, so they will be less inclined to health test their breeding stock, and have little or no knowledge of the lines from which they are breeding."

(There is much controversy over the dilute (d) gene in Labradors, which produces lighter than normal colours; in particular silver, but also champagne and charcoal. None of these colours are accepted by the Kennel Clubs - although this does not stop the KC or AKC registering these pups if they have parents with pedigrees. Many established Labrador breeders feel that the gene, which is also present in Weimaraners, does not occur naturally in the Labrador and that unscrupulous breeders are cashing in on the craze for these non-conformist colours by focusing on the dilute colour with scant regard for the health of the dogs).

USA breeder Teresa Gordy-Brown, of Ashland Labradors, Tennessee, added: "I really would say that breeding for all the wrong reasons has had the most horrific impact on the Labrador breed as a whole, in both health and temperament. We now have people breeding purely to market 'off-colours' - silver, charcoal, champagne, white, tri-colour, black and tan and such! This is so

devastating to our wonderful breed. In order to get most of those off-colours, other breeds or mixes of breeds have had to be introduced. What a can of worms opens when they decide to change something. We all lose.

"As with all breeds, Labradors suffer from a few health problems. One is no more or no less important than the other. For me in particular, I would say that Progressive Retinal Atrophy (PRA) and Tricuspid Valve Dysplasia (TVD) are two of the most feared Labrador diseases. TVD probably will be our biggest problem in the future, as I see very few doing cardiac exams on their breeding dogs."

UK breeder Caroline Smith, of Flyenpygs Labradors, Lancaster said: "The main issues are still hip and elbow dysplasia. Then there are the DNA tests we can use to our advantage and obliterate the diseases. Obesity is a major problem in that people think Labradors being fat is par for the course and almost amusing. I also think a major problem is the fad of 'rare' colours diluting this fabulous breed and introducing a whole other host of problems." (Pictured is Caroline with Rhodenash Doughnut the Flyenpyg's, where she got a qualifying score at her first competition. For more info on the sport visit http://www.rallynews.co.uk).

"As for health certificates, a bare minimum would be hip scores under 14 (combined and preferably even), only 0:0 elbows should be accepted, clear eye certificate and PRA-prcd DNA clear. I would really want at least one parent to be clear for EIC, HNPK and CNM."

Some breeders feel that a lack of knowledge on the part of new owners can sometimes lead to health issues developing. Julie McDonough, of Rangemaster Working Gundogs, Welshpool, Powys, Wales, said: "Hip and elbow dysplasia are the main issues, although this can be down to environmental issues, i.e. poor quality diet and over-exercising a puppy. Nobody would think of taking their young child on a marathon, yet some new owners walk their pups for hours up and down hard concrete or tarmac roads. Over-walking and over-exercising is hard wearing on the puppy's joints."

Liz Vivash, of Wightfyre Labradors, Isle of Wight, agrees: "Hip and elbow issues are the main problem – mainly the joints not forming correctly, probably coming from people over-exercising the dog; they do not need much for the first two years. Also, eye issues; cataracts etc. The biggest threat to the breed is unscrupulous people over-breeding dogs with poor hip and elbow scores, and people buying dogs from puppy farms because they feel sorry for the puppy when they see it. As far as health certificates go, new owners should ask for ALL the KC expected ones; so the lowest and even hip score, a 0 elbow score, clear PRA etc. eye scores."

Anne Johnson of Teazledown Labradors and Canine Therapies, Preston, Lancashire, thinks that elbows are currently the main problem in the UK and adds: "The biggest threat is from over-zealous breeders who look at one or two particular aspects, rather than the whole dog - and cancer."

Kate Smith, of Ardenbrook Labradors, Warwick, has bred Labs since 1999 and at the time of writing (2017) is a committee member of both The Labrador Retriever Club and The Yellow Labrador Club in the UK. She said: "In my opinion, the biggest threat to the future health of the breed is puppy farmers and mills, who breed in volume with no interest in the future of the breed, or breeding healthy dogs. The main health issues that I would be guiding prospective owners to research can be found on the Labrador Breed Council's website health page at: http://www.labradorbreedcouncil.co.uk/web%20pages/Health_Tests.html Also, and not listed, are cancers. However, my personal view on this is that generally we are filling our dogs with too many chemicals – and this is a whole different topic!

"As far as health certificates go, **at the very least breeding pairs should be** hip scored (score preferably below 15, but there should be some breeder discretion in this area); elbow scored – and

these should be 0/0. **Current** unaffected eye certificate - i.e. examination must have been conducted with the last 12 months. Also, DNA tests as listed on the Breed Council list, with at least one parent being clear of each condition."

The issues are similar in the USA. Robin Anderson, of Grampian Labradors, New England, has been involved with Labradors since 1984 and breeding since 1994. (Photo of this healthy trio courtesy of Robin). She said: "As with any larger breed dog, joint problems persist. Until there is DNA testing to help breeders make even wiser choices than X-rays in the breeding stock, we will continue to have joint problems crop up."

She added: "We have many other health issues that we are always working around. TVD (a heart disease) keeps cropping up, as does Ectopic Ureter and Epilepsy. What I've learned in all my years in the breed is that once you conquer one problem, another one presents itself. Thankfully there are a number of great research laboratories working on finding the genes and creating DNA tests to help us become better at what we do when planning for the next litter of puppies."

"The biggest threat to the breed, in my opinion, is what we commonly call 'back yard breeders' who want to breed to make a few dollars, but have no interest in learning the pedigrees and hidden issues that can and will crop up. Only through doing lots of reading, lots of networking with other breeders, and sharing knowledge will we keep our breed healthy for future fanciers and pet owners alike. The basic health tests recommended by the LRC (Labrador Retriever Club) include: yearly eye exams, hip and elbow certificates indicating passing grades, HNPK, EIC, Dilute-Free, Cardiac Normal."

California breeder of 30 years' standing, Sandra Underhill, of Labs to Love, agrees: "If responsible breeders health test then there won't be any big health issues in the breed. It is irresponsible breeders out there that don't health test that perpetuate the issues that we continue to see in any dog breed. Currently we test for hips, elbows, PRA-prcd, eyes that are normal/clear, cardiac testing, EIC, HU, CY, Degenerative Myelopathy, Dilute Coat, CNM. We AKC DNA profile, full dentition, correct scissors bite, epilepsy, Nasal Parakenisis, and by next year I'm sure there will be more tests available to do."

Hip Dysplasia

Hip Dysplasia (HD) - or Canine Hip Dysplasia (CHD) as it is sometimes called - is the most common cause of hind leg lameness in dogs. Dysplasia means 'abnormal development,' and dogs with this condition develop painful degenerative arthritis of the hip joints. The hips are the uppermost joints on the rear legs of a dog, either side of the tail.

HD is also the most common inherited orthopaedic problem seen in dogs. It can affect virtually all breeds, but is more common in large breeds, and one of these is the Labrador, where the disease is well documented. The Labrador is the most popular breed in both the USA and UK, and more Labs have been tested for HD than any other breed; with America's OFA (Orthopedic Foundation for Animals) having tested more than 250,000 since 1974, and the BVA (British Veterinary Association) more than 75,000 in the UK. Of nearly 20,000 US Labradors born between 2011 and 2015 and tested by OFA, 8.3% - or one in 12 - was found to be 'dysplastic.' This is proof of the success of hip scoring, as it shows a big improvement on the statistics from 1974 to 2015, which show that 12.1% of US Labradors had abnormal hips. (I have been unable to find comparative figures for the UK).

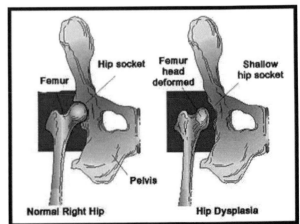

The hip is a ball and socket joint. Hip dysplasia is caused when the head of the femur (thigh bone) fits loosely into a shallow and poorly developed socket in the pelvis. Most dogs with dysplasia are born with normal hips, but due to their genetic make-up, and sometimes caused by or worsened by other factors such as over-exercising young dogs, diet or obesity, the soft tissues that surround the joint develop abnormally.

The joint carrying the weight of the dog becomes loose and unstable, muscle growth lags behind normal growth and is often followed by degenerative joint disease, or osteoarthritis, which is the body's attempt to stabilise the loose hip joint. A dog with canine hip dysplasia often starts to show signs between five and 18 months old.

Occasionally an affected dog will display no symptoms at all, while others may experience anything from mild discomfort to extreme pain. Early diagnosis gives a vet the best chance to tackle the problem as soon as possible, minimising the chance of arthritis developing. If your dog shows any of the following symptoms, it's time to get him to a vet:

- Lameness in the hind legs, particularly after exercise
- Difficulty or stiffness when getting up or climbing uphill
- A 'bunny hop' gait
- Dragging the rear end when getting up
- Waddling rear leg gait
- A painful reaction to stretching the hind legs, resulting in a short stride
- A side-to-side sway of the croup (area above the tail) with a tendency to tilt the hips down if you push down on the croup
- A reluctance to jump, exercise or climb stairs
- Wastage of the thigh muscle(s)

Prevention and Treatment

The best way to avoid having to deal with hip dysplasia is by getting a dog from a dam and sire that have been 'hip scored' with low results. However, you can also play an important part in reducing your dog's chances of showing signs of CHD.

Hip scoring is the name of the test carried out by the OFA in the USA and BVA/Kennel Club in the UK and, as can be seen by the previous statistics, it is playing a vital role in reducing the number of affected dogs in the breeding pool. It is a measure of hip dysplasia (abnormal development) carried out by a vet who X-rays the dog, who is anaesthetised or sedated. These plates are then submitted to the BVA Hip/Elbow scoring panel for scoring. In the UK, the score is a number - two actually - one for each hip. The two numbers are added together to get an overall hip score for a dog. Scores range from 0 to 106; the lower the better, with zero being perfect.

The certificate will have a number written as 4:5 or 4/5, giving a total of 9 and indicating the score for each hip. It is also far better if the dog has evenly matched hips, rather than a low score for one and a high score for the other. The Kennel Clubs advise breeders to only breed from dogs that score below the breed average. In the USA, dogs are given a rating – the equivalent BVA score is in brackets:

Excellent (0-4, with no hip higher than 3)

Good (5-10, with no hip higher than 6)

Fair (11-18)

Borderline (19-25)

Mild (26-35)

Moderate (36-50)

Severe (51-106)

Pictured is an original UK BVA hip score certificate, (the original is green), reproduced courtesy of Kate Smith. It shows that her bitch Ardenbrook Kallisto has a hip score of 4/6, giving a total of 10, which is Good.

 ALWAYS ask to see certificates for both dam and sire, whichever country you live in. If you are getting a puppy, you should ideally be looking for parents with below average hip scores. The BMS (Breed Mean Score) for UK Labradors is 12. Avoid buying a puppy from parents with high scores.

There is no 100% guarantee that a puppy from low scoring parents will not develop hip dysplasia, as the condition is caused by a combination of genes, rather than just a single gene. However, the chances of it happening are significantly reduced. As with most conditions, early detection leads to a better outcome. Treatment is geared towards preventing the hip joint getting worse as well as decreasing pain, and various medical and surgical treatments are now available to ease the dog's discomfort and restore some mobility. Treatment depends upon several factors, such as age, how bad the problem is and, sadly, how much money you can afford for treatment – another reason for taking out insurance early.

Management of the condition usually consists of restricting exercise, keeping body weight down and then managing pain with analgesics and anti-inflammatory drugs. As with humans, cortisone injections may sometimes be used to reduce inflammation and swelling. Cortisone can be injected directly into the affected hip to provide almost immediate relief for a tender, swollen joint. And in severe cases, surgery may be an option.

Causes and Triggers

While hip dysplasia is usually inherited, other factors can trigger or worsen the condition, including:

- Too much exercise, especially while the dog is still growing
- Extended periods without exercise
- Overfeeding, especially on a diet high in protein and calories
- Excess calcium, also usually due to overfeeding

- ❧ Obesity, which places excess stress on joints
- ❧ As with humans, damp or cold weather can worsen arthritic symptoms

Diet can play a role in the development of hip dysplasia. Feeding a high-calorie diet to growing dogs can trigger a predisposition to HD, as the rapid weight gain places increased stress on the hips. During their first year or so of life, it is particularly important that Labrador puppies are fed a diet that contains the right amount of calories, minerals and protein, thereby reducing the risk of hip dysplasia. Ask your breeder or vet for advice on feeding a young Labrador.

Exercise may be another risk factor. Dogs that have a predisposition to the disease may have an increased chance of getting it if they are over-exercised at a young age. Young Labradors are very lively and it's tempting to give them lots of exercise to help them burn off steam, but caution must be exercised. Too much walking on hard surfaces, such as tarmac or concrete, as well as allowing a puppy to run up and down stairs frequently, can also trigger the condition in young dogs. See **Chapter 9. Exercise** for more information.

The key is moderate, low impact exercise for fast-growing young dogs. Activities that strengthen the gluteus muscles, such as running (preferably on grass) and swimming, are probably a good idea. Whereas high impact activities that apply a lot of force to the joint - such and jumping and catching Frisbees, is not recommended with young Labs – however energetic they are. For more information, visit www.bva.co.uk/Canine-Health-Schemes/Hip-Scheme

Elbow Dysplasia

Elbow Dysplasia (ED) is abnormal development of the elbow; it affects many breeds and is thought to be on the increase in the canine population. It is more commonly seen in medium to large fast-growing breeds, and the Labrador is one of these. According to the UFAW (Universities Federation for Animal Welfare) it affects anything from 13% to 21% Labs – or one in every five to eight. (A dog's elbows are at the top of his or her front legs).

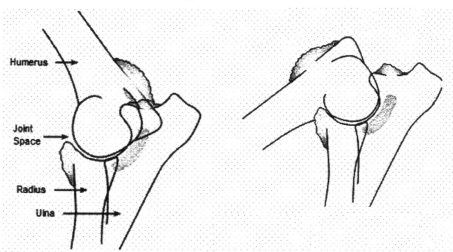

The shaded areas on the left (extended elbow) and right (flexed elbow) show the changes to bone and cartilage as a result of elbow dysplasia. Image courtesy of the BVA.

ED starts in puppyhood, often at four to 10 months, although it can be later. It causes arthritis, which is painful, affects the dog for the rest of his life and is difficult to treat. There are a number of causes, but the biggest one is thought to be genetic, (45% to 71% of the chance of the disease occurring - Guthrie and Pidduck 1990). Dogs who show no symptoms can still be carriers of the disease. Other factors such as rate of growth, diet and level of exercise may influence the severity of the disease in an individual dog, but they cannot prevent it or reduce the potential of the dog to pass it on to offspring.

Many bones in a new-born puppy are not a single piece of bone, but several different pieces with cartilage in between. This is especially true of long limb bones. As the puppy grows, the cartilage changes into bone and several pieces of bone fuse together forming one entire bone (as in the diagram). For instance the ulna, a bone in the forearm, starts out as four pieces that eventually fuse into one bone. Some parts of the joint may have abnormal development, resulting in an uneven joint surface, inflammation, lameness and arthritis. It eventually causes elbow arthritis associated with joint stiffness (reduced range of motion) and lameness.

The most notable symptom is a limp. Your Lab may hold his leg out away from his body while walking, or even lift a front leg completely, putting no weight on it. Signs may be noted as early as four months old and many dogs will go through a period between six months and a year old when symptoms will be at their worst. After this, some may show less severe symptoms. As yet there is no DNA test for Elbow Dysplasia. Vets can often diagnose the condition in young dogs well before they are old enough to be elbow scored; most dogs with diagnosed ED are never scored. 'Elbow Score' is the name given to one-off X-ray tests on dogs aged one year or older. The results are graded from zero to three. Prospective owners should look for a 0/0 Elbow Score from a puppy's parents.

Again there is no 100% guarantee because, as yet, there is no DNA test. This also means there is no way to identify breeding dogs that carry the genes for the ED, but who display no signs of it themselves. It is, however, a very good start to buy a puppy from zero-rated parents. For more info, visit www.bva.co.uk/canine-health-schemes/elbow-scheme

 Visit the Kennel Club's **MyKC** online at www.thekennelclub.org.uk/our-resources/mykc where you can see the health results of your puppies' parents, and whether any pups have been affected by ED or any other hereditary disease.

Treatment

Treatment varies depending on the exact cause of the condition. A young dog is usually placed on a regular, low-impact exercise programme - swimming can be good. Owners must carefully manage their dog's diet and weight. Oral or injected medication such as non-steroid anti-inflammatory drugs (NSAIDS) may be necessary to make him more comfortable; they are prescribed to reduce pain and inflammation.

After the age of 12 to 18 months, sometimes a dog's lameness becomes less severe and some individuals function very well. In most cases, degenerative joint disease (arthritis) occurs as the dog gets older, regardless of the type of treatment. In some severe cases, a dog can be effectively helped with surgery.

Eye Conditions

PRA (Progressive Retinal Atrophy)

PRA is the name for several progressive diseases that lead to blindness. First recognised at the beginning of the 20th century in Gordon Setters, this inherited condition has been documented in over 100 breeds. Labrador Retrievers, Cocker Spaniels and Poodles are all recognised as being among the breeds that can be affected by the disease.

The specific genetic disorder that can affect Labradors is prcd-PRA (progressive rod-cone degeneration PRA). It is sometimes called GPRA - General Progressive Retinal Atrophy. Labradors born with normal eyesight can develop PRA any time from as early as one year old to middle age.

It causes cells in the retina at the back of the eye to degenerate and die, even though the cells seem to develop normally early in life. A dog's rod cells operate in low light levels and are the first to lose normal function, and so the first sign of PRA is night blindness. Then the cone cells gradually lose their normal function in full light situations. Most affected dogs will eventually go blind. (Not all retinal disease is PRA and not all PRA is the prcd form of PRA).

If your dog has PRA, you may first notice that he lacks confidence in low light; he is perhaps reluctant to go down stairs or along a dark hallway. If you look closely into his eyes, you may see the pupils dilating (becoming bigger) and/or the reflection of greenish light from the back of his eyes. As the condition worsens, he might then start bumping into things, first at night and then in the daytime too. The condition is not painful and the eyes often appear normal - without redness, tearing or squinting. The lenses may become opaque or cloudy in some dogs.

It's been proven that all breeds tested for prcd-PRA have the same mutated gene, even though the disease may develop at different ages or severities from one breed to another. There is a DNA test that identifies this gene, and all good Labrador breeders screen for it, so always ask to see certificates for both parents of your chosen puppy – a CARRIER will not show signs of PRA but could pass it on and, if bred, should only be mated with a CLEAR dog. Tested dogs get one of three results.

CLEAR - free from disease

CARRIER - has the gene, is unaffected by it, but could pass the disease on to offspring

AFFECTED - has inherited the disease and could develop PRA

Ideally, only dogs tested **CLEAR** should be used for breeding. However, if bred, a carrier should only ever be mated with a **CLEAR** dog or bitch. The gene is 'Autosomal Recessive;' here are the possible outcomes – and these are the same for all the other conditions caused by **autosomal recessive** traits:

Parent clear + parent clear = pups clear

Parent clear + parent carrier = 50% will carry the disease, 50% will be clear

Parent clear + parent affected = 100% will be carriers

Parent carrier + parent clear = 50% will carry disease, 50% will be clear

Parent carrier + parent carrier = 25% clear, 25% affected and 50% carry disease

Parent carrier + parent affected = 50% affected and 50% carry disease

Parent affected + parent clear = 100% will carry disease

Parent affected + parent carrier = 50% affected and 50% carry disease

Parent affected + parent affected = 100% affected

Sadly, there is no cure, but DNA testing all breeding dogs can avoid PRA in future generations. While eyesight is extremely important to dogs, their other senses are more highly developed than in humans and they do not rely as much as we do on our eyes. PRA develops slowly, giving the dog time to adjust to his changing situation. Many blind dogs live happy lives with a little extra help from their owners. If your Labrador is affected, it may be helpful to read other owners' experiences of living with blind dogs at www.blinddogs.com.

Cataracts

Cataracts occur when the lens of one or both eyes becomes cloudy, which prevents light passing through on to the retina at the back of the eye. This results in poor vision and, as the cataract covers more of the lens, can eventually lead to blindness in one or both eyes.

Cataracts occur in many breeds, including the Labrador. The type that most commonly affects the Lab is HC (hereditary non-congenital cataracts), where the defective gene is passed down from one or other parent, but the cataracts are not present from birth. They can develop when the dog is a puppy, right through to old age. Cataracts that develop due to old age and degeneration in dogs aged six or older are known as senile (late onset) cataracts, which are much less common in elderly dogs than in elderly humans. Other causes of cataracts are diabetes mellitus, trauma/injury, infection or toxins.

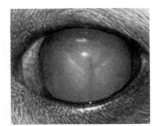 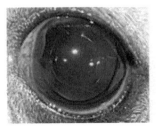

Left: eye with cataracts. Right: same eye with artificial lens

Cataracts can affect the entire lens or a localised area. They may develop rapidly over weeks or slowly over years and can occur in one eye before the other.

If you are buying a puppy, you should ask to see the parents' current annual eye test certificates, which show that the dog was clear on the day he or she was tested – although they do not guarantee that the dog will not develop cataracts in the future.

Hereditary cataracts are usually first diagnosed when the owner sees their dog bumping into furniture, or notices that the eyes are cloudy or the pupils have changed colour. The vet or an ophthalmic specialist will carry out an eye examination, which is a painless and simple process. Drops are put into the eyes and after a few minutes the dog is taken into a dark room for examination and diagnosis.

Corrective surgery is possible, but it is expensive – it can cost thousands of pounds or dollars - and the dog must be suitable. If you think your Lab may have cataracts, it is important to get him to a vet as soon as possible. Early removal of cataracts can restore vision and provide a dramatic improvement in the quality of your dog's life. The only treatment for canine cataracts is surgery (unless the cataracts are caused by another condition like canine diabetes). Despite what you may have heard, laser surgery does not exist for canine cataracts.

However, a word of warning: there is scientific evidence that removal of cataracts can lead to glaucoma in some Labradors. According to one study, one third of all Labradors who had surgery for cataracts contracted glaucoma later, compared with 18% of other breeds - and older Labs were more susceptible than young ones to post-operative problems. You can read the study here: http://onlinelibrary.wiley.com/doi/10.1111/j.1463-5224.2011.00896.x/abstract

Discuss the pros and cons thoroughly with your vet or ophthalmologist before making a decision. If you do opt for surgery, the good news is that it almost always successfully removes cataracts, although it can leave the dog with cloudy vision. The dog has to have a general anaesthetic and the operation is similar to small incision cataract surgery in people, where an artificial lens is implanted in the eye to replace the cataract lens. Dogs can see without an artificial lens, but the image will not be in focus. And once the cataract is removed, it does not recur. However, before your dog can undergo this procedure, he has to be fit and healthy and a suitable candidate for surgery.

After the operation, the dog will probably have to stay at the surgery overnight so that the professionals can keep an eye on him. Once back home, he will have to wear a protective Elizabethan collar, or E collar, for one to two weeks while the eye is healing and you have to keep him quiet and calm – quite a challenge with a lively Lab! He will also require eye drops, perhaps four times a day for the first week and then less frequently after that. The success of cataract surgery also depends to some extent on the owner doing all the right things afterwards.

Retinal Dysplasia (RD)

The retina is the delicate transparent membrane at the back of the eye that is made up of several layers. For dogs (or humans) to see, light passes through the lens on to the retina – similar to light passing through a lens and on to the film at the back of a pre-digital camera. This is processed as an image when it is 'developed' – i.e. relayed to the central nervous system via the optic nerve.

Retinal dysplasia is a disorder in which the cells and layers of retinal tissue do not develop properly. Layers start to separate from the underlying membrane, causing bumps, sometimes called 'rosettes' or 'folds'. It normally develops in puppies at six to eight weeks of age (unless the puppy is born blind) and one or both eyes can be affected.

Some dogs have no symptoms, while more severely affected dogs may display generally poor eyesight, a reluctance to walk into dark areas, bumping into things or a sudden loss of vision.

RD can be diagnosed by a vet using an ophthalmoscope when a puppy is six weeks old or even younger, when the retina will look like layers of folded tissue, rather than one flat layer. There are three types of the disorder:

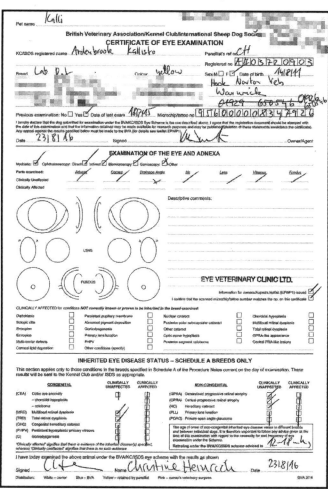

- Focal or multi-focal retinal dysplasia, where small folds occur within the retinal tissue. These may become less pronounced as the dog approaches maturity, but can cause blindness

- Geographic retinal dysplasia has horseshoe or irregular-shaped scars which, unlike focal or multi-focal RD, do not lessen as the dog ages. This can result in a loss of some vision or even blindness

- The most severe type is complete retinal dysplasia, accompanied by detachment of the retina. This causes blindness and can be accompanied by secondary eye problems, such as cataracts or glaucoma

- Pictured is a BVA eye certificate (which is white), courtesy of Kate Smith, which shows that Ardenbrook Kallisto has all ticks – i.e. a clean bill of health, for eyes.

Retinal dysplasia is usually an inherited disorder present from birth, although it can also sometimes be caused by environmental conditions, such as infection. There are two distinct types that affect Labradors. The first type, found predominantly in dogs of European descent, affects only the eyes and is caused by an autosomal recessive gene, which means that a dog must inherit two copies of the faulty recessive gene – one from each parent – to be affected.

The second type is caused by an 'incompletely dominant trait with recessive effects on the skeleton' and is linked to skeletal problems; namely short-limbed dwarfism. It has been associated with certain bloodlines of American field trial Labradors. Dogs that inherit two recessive genes for this defect will develop retinal detachment, resulting in blindness. Dogs inheriting only one recessive gene from one parent (the gene from the second parent is normal), will develop non-progressive retinal folds and may have normal to slightly impaired vision.

Sadly, as yet, there is no treatment for the condition.

If you are buying a puppy, ask to see **current eye certificates** for the parents and ask the breeder if there is any history of retinal dysplasia in her bloodlines. If you want more in-depth information about the eye conditions affecting Labradors and tests available, you can read the BVA leaflet here: www.bva.co.uk/uploadedFiles/Content/Canine_Health_Schemes/Eye_Leaflet(1).pdf

....

Entropion

This is a condition in which the edge of the lower eyelid rolls inward, causing the dog's eyelashes and fur to rub the surface of the eyeball, or cornea. In rare cases the upper lid can also be affected, and one or both eyes may be involved. This painful condition is thought to be hereditary and is more commonly found in dog breeds with wrinkled faces -such as the Bulldog - although other affected breeds include the Labrador and Poodle.

The affected dog will scratch at his painful eye with his paws and this can lead to further injury. If your dog is to suffer from entropion, he will usually show signs at or before his first birthday. You will notice that his eyes are red and inflamed and they will produce tears. He will probably squint.

The tears typically start off clear and can progress to a thick yellow or green mucus. If the entropion causes corneal ulcers, you might also notice a milky-white colour develop. This is caused by increased fluid that affects the clarity of the cornea. For your poor dog, the irritation is constant. Imagine how painful and uncomfortable it would be if you had permanent hairs touching your eyes. It makes my eyes water just thinking about it.

It's important to get your dog to the vet as soon as you suspect entropion before he scratches his cornea and worsens the problem. The condition can cause scarring around the eyes or other issues that can affect a dog's vision if left untreated. A vet will make the diagnosis after a painless and relatively simple inspection of your dog's eyes. But before he or she can diagnose entropion, they will have to rule out other issues, such as allergies, which might also be making your dog's eyes red and itchy.

In young dogs, some vets may delay surgery and treat the condition with medication until the dog's face is fully formed to avoid having to repeat the procedure at a later date. In mild cases, the vet may successfully prescribe eye drops, ointment or other medication. However, the most common treatment for more severe cases is a fairly straightforward surgical procedure – a 'nip and tuck' - to pin back the lower eyelid. Discuss the severity of the condition and all the options before proceeding to surgery.

For anyone with a dog suffering from entropion, there is an interesting post-surgery diary with photos of a Bulldog with the condition, which gives an insight into the condition and recovery at: www.bulldogsworld.com/health-and-medical/post-operative-pictures-and-daily-recovery-log-entropion-surgery

Ectropion

Ectropion is sometimes called 'droopy eyelid'. The lower lids are loose and actually turn outwards, causing a drooping of the eyelid's margins, and one or both eyes may be involved. It does not usually occur in Labradors - but it can - and is included here as it is the opposite of entropion. It normally affects breeds with loose facial folds, such as Bloodhounds,

As the lower lid sags downward, the underlying conjunctiva (the mucous membrane that covers the front of the eye and lines the inside of the eyelids) is exposed. This forms a pouch or pocket, allowing pollens, grasses, dust and all sorts of unwanted debris to accumulate and rub against the sensitive conjunctiva. This constantly irritates the dog and leads to increased redness and watering of the eye.

Many dogs live normal lives with ectropion, but some develop repeated eye infections due to the dirt, dust, etc. constantly getting into the eye. Some dogs require no treatment; however, if eye irritations or infections develop, you should consult a vet. Mild cases can be treated with eye drops or ointment to alleviate irritations and/or infections when they occur. Severe cases may require surgery to remove excess tissue, which tightens the lids and removes the abnormal pocket.

Eyelash Disorders

Distichiasis, trichiasis, and ectopic cilia are canine eyelash disorders that can affect any breed, although some are more susceptible than others. Distichiasis is an eyelash that grows from an abnormal spot on the eyelid, trichiasis is ingrowing eyelashes and ectopic cilia are single or multiple hairs that grow through the inside of the eyelid (cilia means eyelashes).

With distichiasis, small eyelashes abnormally grow on the inner surface or the very edge of the eyelid, and both upper and lower eyelids may be affected. The affected eye becomes red, inflamed, and may develop a discharge. The dog will typically squint or blink a lot, just like a human with a hair or other foreign matter in the eye.

The dog will often rub his eye against furniture, other objects or the carpet. In severe cases, the cornea can become ulcerated and it looks blue. If left, the condition usually worsens and severe ulcerations and infections develop, which can lead to blindness. The dog can make the condition worse by scratching or rubbing his eyes.

Treatment usually involves electro- or cryo-epilation where a needle is inserted into the hair follicle emitting an ultra-fast electric current which produces heat to destroy the stem cells responsible for hair growth. This procedure may need to be repeated after several months because all of the abnormal hairs may not have developed at the time of the first treatment -although this is not common with dogs older than three years.

Sometimes surgery may be required and here the lid is split to remove the areas where the abnormal hairs grow. Both treatments require anaesthesia and usually result in a full recovery. After surgery, the eyelids are swollen for several days and the eyelid margins turn pink. Usually they return to their normal colour within four months. Antibiotic eye drops are often used following surgery to prevent infections.

All three conditions are straightforward to diagnose.

....

Cherry Eye

Humans have two eyelids, but dogs have a third eyelid, called a nictating membrane. This third eyelid is a thin, opaque tissue with a tear gland that rests in the inner corner of the eye. Its purpose is to provide additional protection for the eye and to spread tears over the eyeball.

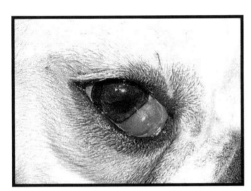

Any dog can suffer from cherry eye, although the 'Bully' breeds, such as Bulldog, French Bulldogs, Boston Terriers and Boxers - as well as Cocker Spaniels - can be more prone to it than other breeds, suggesting that genetics may be a factor.

Usually the third eyelid is retracted and therefore you can't see it, although you may notice it when your dog is relaxed and falling asleep. When the third eyelid becomes visible it may be a sign of illness or a painful eye. Cherry Eye is a medical condition, officially known as 'nictitans gland prolapse', or prolapse of the gland of the third eyelid.

The exact cause of cherry eye is not known, but it is thought to be due to a weakness of the fibrous tissue that attaches the gland to the surrounding eye. This allows the gland to fall down, or prolapse. Once this has happened and the gland is exposed to the dry air and irritants, it can become infected and/or begin to swell. There is sometimes a mucous discharge and if the dog rubs or scratches it, he can further damage the gland and even possibly create an ulcer on the surface of the eye.

The main visible symptom is a red, often swollen, mass in the corner of one or both eyes, which is often first seen in young dogs up to the age of two years. It can occur in one or both eyes and may be accompanied by swelling and/or irritation. Although it may look sore, it is not a painful condition for your dog.

At one time, it was popular to surgically remove the gland to correct this condition. While this was often effective, it could create problems later on. The gland of the third eyelid is very important for producing tears, without which dogs could suffer from 'dry eye', also known as keratoconjunctivitis sicca (KCS). These days, removing the gland is not considered a good idea.

A better and straightforward option is to surgically reposition the gland by tacking it back into place with a single stitch that attaches the gland to the deeper structures of the eye socket. There is also another type of operation where the wedge of tissue is removed from directly over the gland. Tiny dissolving stitches are used to close the gap so that the gland is pushed back into place. After surgery the dog may be placed on antibiotic ointment for a few days. Mostly, surgery is performed quickly and for most dogs that's the end of the matter. However, a few dogs do have a recurrence of cherry eye. The eye should return to normal after about seven days, during which time there may be some redness or swelling.

If the affected eye suddenly seems uncomfortable or painful for your dog, or you can see protruding stitches, then take him back to the vet to get checked out. Other options include anti-inflammatory eye drops to reduce the swelling and manually manipulating the gland back into place.

Sometimes a dog will develop cherry eye in one eye and then the condition will also appear some time later in the other eye. If you have a young dog diagnosed with cherry eye, discuss with your vet whether to delay surgery a few weeks or months to see if the second eye is affected. This will save the dog being anesthetised twice and will also save you money.

Dry Eye (Keratoconjunctivitis sicca)

KCS is the technical term for a condition known as 'dry eye' caused by not enough tears being produced. With insufficient tears, a dog's eyes can become irritated and the conjunctiva appears to be red. It's estimated that as many as one in five dogs can suffer from dry eye at one time or another in their lives.

The eyes typically develop a thick, yellowy discharge. Infections are common as tears also have anti-bacterial and cleansing properties, and inadequate lubrication allows dust, pollen and other debris to accumulate. The nerves of these glands may also become damaged.

In many cases the reason for dry eye is not known, other times it may be caused by injuries to the tear glands, eye infections, reactions to drugs, an immune reaction or even the gland of the third eyelid being surgically removed by mistake. Left untreated, the dog will suffer painful and chronic eye infections, and repeated irritation of the cornea results in severe scarring, and ulcers may develop which can lead to blindness.

Treatment usually involves drugs; cyclosporine, ophthalmic ointment or drops are the most common. In some cases, another eye preparation – Tacrolimus - is also used and may be effective when cyclosporine is not. Sometimes artificial tear solutions are also prescribed. In very severe cases, an operation can be performed to transplant a salivary duct into the upper eyelid, causing saliva to drain into and lubricate the eye. This procedure is rarely used, but is an option.

Centronuclear Myopathy (CNM)

This is a disease of the muscle tissue which results in weakened muscles and an intolerance to exercise which has found its way into the Labrador gene pool. It is also known as hereditary myopathy of the Labrador Retriever (HMLR) and has previously been known by many other names, including muscular myopathy and muscular dystrophy.

According to The Animal Health Trust: "The mutation, or change to the structure of the gene, probably occurred spontaneously in a single dog but, once in the population, has been inherited from generation to generation like any other gene.

"The disorder shows an autosomal recessive mode of inheritance: two copies of the defective gene (one inherited from each parent) have to be present for a dog to be affected by the disease. Individuals with one copy of the defective gene and one copy of the normal gene - called carriers - show no symptoms but can pass the defective gene onto their offspring. When two apparently healthy carriers are crossed, 25% (on average) of the offspring will be affected by the disease, 25% will be clear and the remaining 50% will themselves be carriers."

There is now a DNA test available for CNM which can identify not only affected dogs, but those which are carriers as well. As the gene is recessive, if one of the parents is tested CLEAR, then a puppy cannot display signs of CNM, even if the other parent is a CARRIER (although the pup could also be a carrier for the disease).

Pups with CNM may appear normal when they are born, but will show signs of weight loss, compared with the littermates, by the time they are two weeks old. CNM is a disabling disease and in severe cases an owner or breeder may have to take the terrible decision to have the dog put down. Usually, puppies show signs of disability between two to three and five months of age.

Symptoms

These vary according to the severity of the condition, but here are some things to look out for:

- Slow growth
- Lack of muscle mass
- 'Laziness,' i.e. an unwillingness to exercise
- A 'bunny hop' gait
- Walking awkwardly
- Stumbling
- Difficulty swallowing
- Choking on food
- Possible breathing problems
- In severe cases, unable to hold up their head, or the head turned towards the belly

Sadly, there is no known cure or medication for the condition and affected dogs require lifelong care. Some dedicated owners are prepared to give this, with the oldest Labrador with CNM recorded as 13 years old, according to the CNM DNA Project. The disease is 100% preventable by NOT breeding from dogs which are affected by or carry the CNM gene. The best way to avoid the disorder is to get a Labrador bred from parents that have passed the DNA test for CNM.

There is an excellent video on YouTube by owner Lisa Simpson about living with her mildly affected CNM Labrador, Chico: https://www.youtube.com/watch?v=NceEeiuNJCQ

Exercise Induced Collapse (EIC)

This inherited disease is found in Labradors as well as other breeds (often retrievers), including Curly-Coated and Chesapeake Bay Retrievers, Boykin Spaniels, Bouvier des Flanders, German Wirehaired Pointers, Old English Sheepdogs, Cocker Spaniels and Pembroke Welsh Corgis.

Severely affected dogs typically become weak in the hind legs and can collapse after five to 20 minutes of high intensity exercise, such as field trials or upland game hunting, and in some cases simple fetch and retrieve.

According to research professor Dr Susan M. Taylor, DVM, of Western College of Veterinary Medicine, University of Saskatchewan, Canada, this syndrome is increasingly seen in young adult Labradors and most - but not all - have field trial backgrounds in North America. (The situation is different in the UK where EIC is more commonly found in show lines). Black, yellow and chocolate Labradors of both sexes can be affected.

Signs become apparent in young dogs when they start strenuous activity - usually between seven months and two years of age (the average is 14 months). In field trial dogs this usually coincides with the age at which they enter intensive training. Littermates and other related dogs are commonly affected but, depending on their temperament and lifestyle, they may or may not show symptoms. Affected dogs are usually described as being extremely fit, muscular, and prime athletic specimens of their breed with an excitable temperament and lots of drive.

Affected dogs can tolerate mild to moderate exercise, but five to 20 minutes of strenuous exercise can bring on weakness and then collapse. Severely affected dogs may collapse whenever they are exercised to this extent - other dogs only collapse sporadically and, as yet, scientists are not sure why this is the case.

The first thing you notice about the dog is usually a rocking or forced gait, the rear legs then become weak and unable to support the dog's weight. Many affected dogs continue to run while dragging their back legs. In some dogs this progresses to front leg weakness and occasionally to a total inability to move. Some dogs appear to be uncoordinated and have a loss of balance, particularly as they recover. Most collapsed dogs are totally conscious and alert and still trying to retrieve - there is no denying that the Labrador is a dog with massive heart. Others will appear stunned or disorientated during the collapse.

It's common for the symptoms to worsen for three to five minutes, even after the dog has stopped exercising. In a handful of extreme cases, a dog has died while resting after an episode of EIC, so you should ALWAYS stop the dog from exercising at the first signs of something amiss - which is usually wobbliness. The good news is that most dogs recover quickly and are usually back to normal five to 25 minutes later with no lasting weakness or stiffness.

According to the research report, which can be seen here: http://vetneuromuscular.ucsd.edu/cases/2002/may02.html dogs that experience EIC are most likely to have intense, excitable personalities, and it seems that their level of excitement plays a role in causing the collapse. There are some severely affected dogs who, if they are very excited, do not require much exercise to induce the collapse.

Routine exercise like jogging, hiking, most waterfowl hunting and even agility or flyball training are not very likely to induce an episode in dogs with EIC. It is activities with continuous intense exercise - particularly if accompanied by a high level of excitement or anxiety – which most commonly cause collapse. Dogs with EIC are most likely to collapse when involved in activities they find very exciting or stressful. These activities include upland hunting, repetitive 'happy retrieves', retrieving drills, and repetition of difficult marks or blinds where the dog is being corrected or anticipating correction. Owners of affected dogs should exercise caution with swimming and in hot conditions.

Once again, there is a DNA test for the condition, which is recommended by the UK Kennel Club and mandatory in the USA. If you are buying a puppy from predominantly working lines in North America or show lines in the UK, ask if there is any history of EIC in the bloodlines, and ask to see health certificates for the parents.

Hereditary Nasal Parakeratosis (HNPK)

This is another entirely preventable disease now that DNA testing is available from OptiGen and other laboratories to identify affected dogs. The Kennel Club (UK) is now recording results for this test (along with CNM, EIC and SD2 - when submitted by dogs' owners. HNPK is another autosomal recessive trait, meaning both parents have to have the mutated gene for a puppy to contract the disease.

HNPK is an unpleasant skin disorder causing a crusty, bumpy and deformed nose in Labradors. Symptoms usually appear at six months or so, and there is no cure for the condition. Sometimes the skin may split, which is painful for the dog, causing chronic irritation and inflammation of the skin on the nose. Although the disease is not life-threatening, and Labs appear to be otherwise unaffected, HNPK does not go away.

It requires continuous application of moisturisers and antibiotics on the part of the owner. To date, no other breeds have been affected by HNPK, just the Labrador.

....

Skeletal Dysplasia (SD2)

Also known as Dwarfism, this is a genetic disease in Labradors that causes the dog's limbs to stop growing at a young age. The result is strangely-shaped Labs with normal body sizes and shortened legs.

Again, it is preventable with DNA testing and many responsible breeders of field Labradors now test for this disorder. However, it has become clear that some top Field Trial Champion Labradors who were bred extensively were most probably carriers of SD2. If breeders try to eliminate the gene from the field trial Labrador gene pool too quickly (by not breeding from affected dogs), the gene pool will shrink and that in itself could cause other potentially more serious genetic problems to occur, as inbreeding rates will increase.

If an otherwise healthy breeding dog tests as AFFECTED or CARRIER for SD2, it should either be removed from the breeding pool or only mated with a CLEAR dog or bitch.

According to research carried out by Fischknecht at al. 2013, some 34 affected dogs were studied and in most cases the forelegs were more shortened than the hind legs. The width and length of the body were normal. Affected dogs were all Labradors from working lines.

Males mostly had shoulder heights of less than 55cm (21.65 in) and females mostly had shoulder heights of less than 50cm (19.68 in). This compares to the UK breed standard of dogs 56-57 cm (22-22½in), bitches 55-56 cm (21½-22 in), and the AKC standard for a dog of 22½ to 24½ inches and 21½ to 23½ inches for a bitch. Unlike other types of Dwarfism, which can cause eye, ear, genital, nerve or joint problems, SD2 does not appear to have any negative effects on the dog other than appearance. Still, it is still not a desirable trait in a Labrador.

For a full list of available tests in the UK, visit
www.labradorbreedcouncil.co.uk/web%20pages/Health_Tests.html

Heart Problems

Heart issues are relatively common among the canine population in general. Heart failure, or **congestive heart failure (CHF)**, occurs when the heart is not able to pump blood around the dog's body properly.

The heart is a mechanical pump. It receives blood in one half and forces it through the lungs, then the other half pumps the blood through the entire body. Two of the most common forms of heart failure in dogs are Degenerative Valvular Disease (DVD) and Dilated Cardiomyopathy (DCM), also known as an enlarged heart. One specific disease known to affect Labradors is TVD (Tricuspid Valve Dysplasia). Some dogs can also suffer from Pulmonic Stenosis, which is a congenital narrowing in the region of the pulmonary valve. However, most dogs don't require any medical treatment. Smaller breeds more often suffer from Mitral Valve Disease.

In people, heart disease usually involves the arteries that supply blood to the heart muscle becoming hardened over time, causing the heart muscles to receive less blood than they need. Starved of oxygen, the result is often a heart attack. In dogs, hardening of the arteries (arteriosclerosis) and heart attacks are very rare. However, heart disease is quite common, and in dogs it is often seen as heart failure, which means that the muscles 'give out.' This is usually caused by one chamber or side of the heart being required to do more than it is physically able to do. It may be that excessive force is required to pump the blood through an area and over time the muscles fail.

Unlike a heart attack in humans, heart failure in a dog is a slow insidious process that occurs over months or even years. Once symptoms are noted, they will usually worsen over time until the dog requires treatment.

Symptoms of a Heart Condition

- Tiredness
- Decreased activity levels
- Restlessness, pacing around instead of settling down to sleep
- Intermittent coughing - especially during exertion or excitement. This tends to occur at night, sometimes about two hours after the dog goes to bed or when he wakes up in the morning. This coughing is an attempt to clear the lungs

As the condition worsens, other symptoms may appear:

- Lack of appetite
- Rapid breathing
- Abdominal swelling (due to fluid)
- Noticeable loss of weight
- Fainting (syncope)
- Paleness

Diagnosis and Treatment

If your dog is exhibiting a range of the above symptoms, the vet may suspect congestive heart failure. He will carry out tests to make sure; these may include listening to the heart,

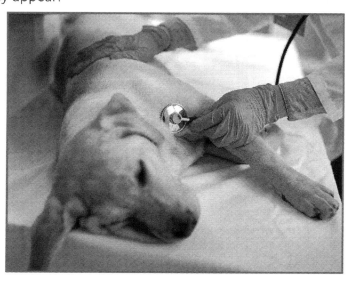

chest X-rays, blood tests, electrocardiogram (a record of your dog's heartbeat) or an echocardiogram.

If the heart problem is due to an enlarged heart (DCM) or valve disease, the condition cannot be reversed. Instead, treatment focuses on managing the symptoms with various medications, which may change over time as the condition worsens. The vet may also prescribe a special low salt diet for your dog, as sodium (found in salt) determines the amount of water in the blood. The amount of exercise will also have to be controlled. There is some evidence that vitamin and other supplements may be beneficial; discuss this with your vet.

The prognosis for dogs with congestive heart failure depends on the cause and severity, as well as their response to treatment. Sadly, CHF is progressive, so your dog can never recover from the condition. But once diagnosed, he can live a longer, more comfortable life with the right medication and regular check-ups.

Heart Murmurs

Heart murmurs are not uncommon in dogs. Our dog was diagnosed with a Grade 2 murmur several years ago and, of course, your heart sinks when the vet gives you the terrible news. But once the shock is over, it's important to realise that there are several different severities of the condition and, at its mildest, it is no great cause for concern.

Our dog is 12 now and fit and active, although he's slowed down a bit. He still has no signs of the heart murmur (except through the vet's stethoscope). However, we are always on alert for a dry, racking cough, which is a sign of Mitral Valve Disease. So far it hasn't happened, touch wood.

Literally, a heart murmur is a specific sound heard through a stethoscope, it results from the blood flowing faster than normal within the heart itself or in one of the two major arteries. Instead of the normal 'lubb dupp' noise, an additional sound can be heard that can vary from a mild 'pshhh' to a loud 'whoosh'. The different grades are:

* ❧ Grade 1 - barely audible

* ❧ Grade 2 - soft, but easily heard with a stethoscope

* ❧ Grade 3 - intermediate loudness; most murmurs which are related to the mechanics of blood circulation are at least grade III

* ❧ Grade 4 - loud murmur that radiates widely, often including opposite side of chest

* ❧ Grades 5 and Grade 6 - very loud, audible with stethoscope barely touching the chest; the vibration is also strong enough to be felt through the animal's chest wall

Murmurs are caused by a number of factors; it may be a problem with the heart valves or could be due to some other condition, such as hyperthyroidism, anaemia or heartworm. In puppies, there are two major types of heart murmurs, and they will probably be detected by your vet at the first or second vaccinations. The most common type is called an innocent 'flow murmur'. This type of murmur is soft - typically Grade 2 or less - and is not caused by underlying heart disease. An innocent flow murmur typically disappears by four to five months of age.

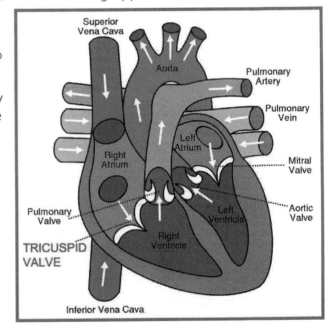

However, if a puppy has a loud murmur - Grade 3 or louder - or if the heart murmur is still easily heard with a stethoscope after four or five months of age, the likelihood of the puppy having an underlying heart problem becomes much higher. The thought of a puppy having congenital heart disease is worrying, but it is important to remember that the disease will not affect all puppies' life expectancy or quality of life.

A heart murmur can also develop suddenly in an adult dog with no prior history of the problem. This is typically due to heart disease that develops with age. In toy and small breeds, a heart murmur may develop in middle-aged to older dogs due to an age-related thickening and degeneration of one of the valves in the heart, the mitral valve. This thickening of the valve prevents it from closing properly and as a result it starts to leak, this is known as mitral valve disease. The more common type of heart disease affecting larger dog breeds in middle age is Dilated Cardiomyopathy (DCM).

Tricuspid Valve Dysplasia (TVD)

This is a heart condition where blood doesn't flow as it should though the heart, either due to the valves not closing enough to stop the blood flow when they are supposed to, or valves becoming too narrow and restricting the flow of blood.

The Labrador is one breed that can be affected. TVD testing is not a mandatory requirement by the Kennel Clubs in the UK or USA, although some USA breeders do test for it.

The heart valves are there to make sure that blood only flows in one direction. Oxygen-depleted blood arrives into the right-hand side of the heart (on the left in the diagram overleaf) through two large veins, the superior and inferior vena cava, which empty oxygen-poor blood from the body into the right atrium.

As the atrium contracts, blood flows down from the right atrium into the right ventricle through the open tricuspid valve. This blood is then pumped into the lungs through the pulmonary artery. The tricuspid valve is made up of two irregular-shaped flaps of tissue, which is connected to the ventricle muscle by tendon-like cords called 'chordae tendineae'.

As the right atrium contracts, blood passes through the tricuspid valve into the right ventricle. When the ventricle contracts, some blood flows backwards, pushing upward against the flaps of the valve, causing them to close. This prevents blood flowing back into the upper chamber (right atrium). It is the chordae tendineae which prevent the flaps from opening.

If the valve and cords do not develop properly while the embryonic puppy is in the mother's womb, the puppy is born with TVD - and a defective tricuspid valve causes the atrium to be dilated and the ventricle to enlarge. Over time, this overload raises pressures on the arteries and causes blood to pool in the body. (If a dog has a **mitral valve disorder**, this causes blood to enter the lungs, rather than the body as is the case with TVD. Valvular stenosis is a narrowing of the valve, causing arteries to dilate and the ventricle on the affected side to shrink).

Although TVD is a heredity congenital disorder - i.e. dogs are born with it - many puppies with the condition do not show any symptoms and often appear healthy for quite some time. The condition might first be discovered by a cardiac murmur at an annual check-up at the vet's, or a dog may suddenly develop one or more of the symptoms associated with congestive heart failure, which are:

- Loud breathing/panting

- 🐾 Exercise intolerance
- 🐾 Fainting
- 🐾 Fluid or swelling in the abdomen
- 🐾 Body extremities cool to the touch

A dog with a mild problem and little blood regurgitation, i.e. backflow, can live a normal lifespan, provided certain precautions are taken, such as not over-exerting the dog and avoiding prolonged exercise and extreme cold conditions. Dogs more severely affected might have a lifespan of just a few months after symptoms of congestive heart failure develop.

An echocardiogram (cardiac ultrasound) is the best way of diagnosing TVD. An X-ray usually reveals an enlarged right side of the heart. A small number of vets perform replacement valve surgery, but it is extremely expensive and not widely practised.

Epilepsy

Epilepsy means repeated seizures (also called fits or convulsions) due to abnormal electrical activity in the brain. It can affect any breed of dog and in fact affects around four or five dogs in every 100. If seizures happen because of a problem somewhere else in the body, such as heart disease (which stops oxygen reaching the brain), this is not epilepsy.

Affected dogs behave normally between seizures. In some cases, the gap between seizures is relatively constant, in others it can be very irregular with several seizures occurring over a short period of time, but with long intervals between 'clusters' of seizures. Some forms of epilepsy are inherited. Another type is Idiopathic Epilepsy (IE) where there is no apparent reason for it, i.e. no detectable injury, disease or abnormality.

Labradors may have a slightly higher incidence than average, compared with some other breeds. A study carried out in Sweden (Heske et al. 2014), based on data from insurance companies on 35 breeds, found that while the Boxer emerged as the breed most likely to be affected by epilepsy, the Labrador was fourth highest of the 35 breeds involved. The results are at: www.instituteofcaninebiology.org/blog/epilepsy-incidence-and-mortality-in-35-dog-breeds.

The characteristics of inherited epilepsy tend to show up between 10 months and three years of age, but dogs as young as six months or as old as five years can show signs. The type more commonly affecting Labradors is **Idiopathic Epilepsy**, for which there is no cure. However, constant medication can help most dogs to manage the disease and stop it from worsening.

Anyone who has witnessed their dog having a seizure knows how frightening it can be. Seizures are not uncommon, and many dogs only ever have one. If your dog has had more than one seizure, it may be that he or she is epileptic. Just as with people, there are medications to control seizures in dogs, allowing them to live more normal lives.

Symptoms

Some dogs seem to know when they are about to have a seizure and may behave in a certain way. You will come to recognise these signs as meaning that an episode is likely. Often dogs just seek out their owner's company and come to sit beside them when a seizure is about to start. Once the seizure starts, the dog is unconscious – he cannot hear or respond to you. Most dogs become stiff, fall onto their side and make running movements with their legs. Sometimes they will cry out and may lose control of their bowels or bladder. While it is distressing to watch, the dog is not in any pain, even if he or she is howling.

Most seizures last between one and three minutes - **it is worth making a note of the time the seizure starts and ends** because it often seems that it goes on for a lot longer than it actually does. If you are not sure whether or not your dog has had a seizure, look on YouTube, where there are many videos of dogs having epileptic seizures.

Afterwards dogs behave in different ways. Some just get up and carry on with what they were doing, while others appear dazed and confused for up to 24 hours afterwards. Most commonly, dogs will be disorientated for only 10 to 15 minutes before returning to their old self. They often have a set pattern of behaviour that they follow - for example going for a drink of water or asking to go outside to the toilet. If your dog has had more than one seizure, you may well start to notice a pattern of behaviour which is typically repeated.

Most seizures occur while the dog is relaxed and resting quietly. It is very rare for one to occur while exercising. They often occur in the evening or at night. In a few dogs, seizures seem to be triggered by particular events or stress. It is common for a pattern to develop and, should your dog suffer from epilepsy, you will gradually recognise this as specific to your dog.

The most important thing is to **stay calm**. Remember that your dog is unconscious during the seizure and is not in pain or distressed. It is likely to be more distressing for you than for him. Make sure that he is not in a position to injure himself, for example by falling down the stairs, but otherwise do not try to interfere with him. Never try to put your hand inside his mouth during a seizure or you are very likely to get bitten.

Seizures can cause damage to the brain and if your dog has repeated occurrences, it is likely that further seizures will occur in the future. The damage caused is cumulative and after a lot of seizures there may be enough brain damage to cause early senility (with loss of learned behaviour and housetraining or behavioural changes).

It is very rare for dogs to injure themselves during a seizure. Occasionally they may bite their tongue and there may appear to be a lot of blood, but's unlikely to be serious; your dog will not swallow his tongue. If it goes on for a very long time (more than 10 minutes), his body temperature will rise, which can cause damage to other organs such as the liver and kidneys and brain.

In very extreme cases, some dogs may be left in a coma after severe seizures. If you can, record your dog's seizure on a mobile phone, as it will be most useful in helping the vet.

When Should I Contact the Vet?

Generally, if your dog has a seizure lasting more than five minutes, or is having more than two or three a day, you should contact your vet. When your dog starts fitting, make a note of the time. If he comes out of it within five minutes, allow him time to recover quietly before contacting your vet. It is far better for him to recover quietly at home rather than be bundled into the car and carted off to the vet right away.

However, if your dog does not come out of the seizure within five minutes, or has repeated seizures close together, contact your vet immediately, as he or she will want to see your dog as soon as possible. If this is his first seizure, your vet may ask you to bring him in for a check-up and some routine blood tests. Always call your vet's practice before setting off to be sure that there is someone there who can help when you arrive.

There are many things other than epilepsy that cause seizures in dogs. When your vet first examines your dog, he or she will not know whether your dog has epilepsy or another illness. It's unlikely that the vet will see your dog during a seizure, so it is **vital** that you're able to describe in some detail just what happens. You might want to make notes or, better still, record it on your mobile phone.

Your vet may need to run a range of tests to ensure that there is no other cause of the seizures. These may include blood tests, possibly X-rays, and maybe even a scan (MRI) of your dog's brain. If no other cause can be found, then a diagnosis of epilepsy may be made. If your Labrador already has epilepsy, remember these key points:

* Don't change or stop any medication without consulting your vet
* See your vet at least once a year for follow-up visits
* Be sceptical of 'magic cure' treatments

Treatment

It is not usually possible to remove the cause of the seizures, so your vet will use medication to control them. Treatment will not cure the disease, but it will manage the signs – even a well-controlled epileptic will have occasional seizures. As yet there is no cure for epilepsy, so don't be tempted with 'instant cures' from the internet.

There are many drugs used in the control of epilepsy in people, but very few of these are suitable for long-term use in a dog. Two of the most common are Phenobarbital and Potassium Bromide (some dogs can have negative results with Phenobarbital). There are also a number of holistic remedies advertised, but we have no experience of them or any idea if any are effective.

Many epileptic dogs require a combination of one or more types of drug to achieve the most effective control of their seizures. Treatment is decided on an individual basis and it may take some time to find the best combination and dose of drugs for your pet. You need patience when managing an epileptic pet. It is important that medication is given at the same time each day.

Once your dog has been on treatment for a while, he will become dependent on the levels of drug in his blood at all times to control seizures. If you miss a dose of treatment, blood levels can drop and this may be enough to trigger a seizure. Each epileptic dog is an individual and a treatment plan will be designed specifically for him. It will be based on the severity and frequency of the seizures and how they respond to different medications.

Keep a record of events in your dog's life, note down dates and times of episodes and record when you have given medication. When you visit your vet, take this diary along with you so he or she can see how your dog has been since his last check-up. If seizures are becoming more frequent, it may be necessary to change the medication. The success or otherwise of treatment may depend on YOU keeping a close eye on your Labrador to see if there are any physical or behavioural changes.

It is rare for epileptic dogs to stop having seizures altogether. However, provided your dog is checked regularly by your vet to make sure that the drugs are not causing any side effects, there is a good chance that he will live a full and happy life. Remember, live *with* epilepsy not *for* epilepsy. With the proper medical treatment, most epileptic dogs have far more good days than bad ones. Enjoy all those good days.

Thanks to **www.canineepilepsy.co.uk** for assistance with this article. If your Labrador has epilepsy, we recommend reading this excellent website to gain a greater understanding of the illness.

Canine Diabetes

Diabetes can affect dogs of all breeds, sizes and both genders, as well as obese dogs. There are two types: *diabetes mellitus* and *diabetes insipidus.*Diabetes mellitus (sugar diabetes) is the most common form and affects one in 500 dogs. Because most Labradors are incredibly greedy, it is often a constant battle to keep them at an ideal weight, but next time your Lab pleads for an extra treat with his beautiful big brown eyes remember that that the threat of diabetes in middle-aged and older overweight Labradors is very real.

Diabetes is now treatable and need not shorten a dog's lifespan or interfere greatly with his quality of life. Due to advances in veterinary science, diabetic dogs undergoing treatment now have the same life expectancy as non-diabetic dogs of the same age and gender.

However, if left untreated, the disease can lead to cataracts, increasing weakness in the legs (neuropathy), other ailments and even death. In dogs, diabetes is typically seen anywhere between the ages of four to 14, with a peak at seven to nine years. Both males and females can develop it; unspayed females have a slightly higher risk. The typical canine diabetes sufferer is middle-aged, female and overweight, but there are also juvenile cases.

Diabetes insipidus is caused by a lack of vasopressin, a hormone that controls the kidneys' absorption of water. *Diabetes mellitus* occurs when the dog's body does not produce enough insulin and cannot successfully process sugars. Dogs, like us, get their energy by converting the food they eat into sugars, mainly glucose. This glucose travels in the dog's bloodstream and individual cells then remove some of that glucose from the blood to use for energy. The substance that allows the cells to take glucose from the blood is a protein called *insulin.*

Insulin is created by beta cells that are located in the pancreas, next to the stomach. Almost all diabetic dogs have Type 1 diabetes; their pancreas does not produce any insulin. Without it, the cells have no way to use the glucose that is in the bloodstream, so the cells 'starve' while the glucose level in the blood rises. Your vet will use blood samples and urine samples to check glucose concentrations in order to diagnose diabetes. Early treatment helps to prevent further complications developing.

Symptoms of Diabetes Mellitus

- ❧ Extreme thirst
- ❧ Excessive urination

- Weight loss
- Increased appetite
- Coat in poor condition
- Lethargy
- Vision problems due to cataracts

Some diabetic dogs go blind. Cataracts may develop due to high blood glucose levels causing water to build up in the eyes' lenses. This leads to swelling, rupture of the lens fibres and the development of cataracts. In many cases, the cataracts can be surgically removed to bring sight back to the dog. However, some dogs may stay blind even after the cataracts are gone, and some cataracts simply cannot be removed. Blind dogs are often able to get around surprisingly well, particularly in a familiar home.

Treatment and Exercise

Treatment starts with the right diet. Your vet will prescribe meals low in fat and sugars and recommend medication. Many cases can be successfully treated with a combination of diet and medication, while more severe cases may require insulin injections. Normally, after a week of treatment, you return to the vet for a series of blood sugar tests over a 12-14 hour period to see when the blood glucose peaks and when it hits its lows. Adjustments are then made to the dosage and timing of the injections. Your vet will explain how to prepare and inject the insulin. You may be asked to collect urine samples using a test strip of paper that indicates the glucose levels in urine.

If your dog is already having insulin injections, beware of a 'miracle cure' offered on some internet sites. It does not exist. There is no diet or vitamin supplement which can reduce your dog's dependence on insulin injections, because vitamins and minerals cannot do what insulin does in the dog's body. If you think that your dog needs a supplement, discuss it with your vet first to make sure that it does not interfere with any other medication.

Managing your dog's diabetes also means managing his activity level. Exercise burns up blood glucose the same way that insulin does. If your dog is on insulin, any active exercise on top of the insulin might cause him to have a severe low blood glucose episode, called 'hypoglycaemia'.

Keep your dog on a reasonably consistent exercise routine. Your usual insulin dose will take that amount of exercise into account. If you plan to take your dog out for some extra demanding exercise, such as running round with other dogs, give him only half of his usual insulin dose.

Tips

- You can usually buy specially formulated diabetes dog food from your vet
- You should feed the same type and amount of food at the same time every day
- Most vets recommend twice-a-day feeding for diabetic pets (it's OK if your dog prefers to eat more often). If you have other pets, they should also be on a twice-a-day feeding schedule, so that the diabetic dog cannot eat from their bowls
- Help your dog to achieve the best possible blood glucose control by not feeding him table scraps or treats between meals

FINE FOODS

Menu

"I DON'T SEE TABLE SCRAPS."

Peter Hesse

- Watch for signs that your dog is starting to drink more water than usual. Call the vet if you see this happening, as it may mean that the insulin dose needs adjusting.

Remember these simple points:

Food raises blood glucose – Insulin and exercise lower blood glucose – Keep them in balance

For more information on canine diabetes visit www.caninediabetes.org

....

Canine Cancer

This is the biggest single killer of dogs of whatever breed and will claim the lives of one in four dogs. It is the cause of nearly half the deaths of all dogs aged 10 years and older, according to the American Veterinary Medical Association. There is anecdotal evidence that some Labrador bloodlines are more prone to cancer than others.

Symptoms

Early detection is critical, and some things to look out for are:

- Swellings anywhere on the body
- Lumps in a dog's armpit or under his jaw
- Sores that don't heal
- Bad breath
- Weight loss
- Poor appetite, difficulty swallowing or excessive drooling
- Changes in exercise or stamina level
- Laboured breathing
- Change in bowel or bladder habits

If your dog has been spayed or neutered, there is some evidence that the risk of certain cancers decreases.* These cancers include uterine and breast/mammary cancer in females, and testicular cancer in males (if the dog was neutered before he was six months old). Along with controlling the pet population, spaying is especially important because mammary cancer in female dogs is fatal in about 50% of all cases.

* Recent studies show that some dogs may have a higher risk of certain cancers after neutering.

Diagnosis and Treatment

Just because your dog has a skin growth doesn't mean that it's cancerous. As with humans, tumours may be benign (harmless) or malignant (harmful). Your vet will probably confirm the tumour using X-rays, blood tests and possibly ultrasounds. He or she will then decide whether it is **benign** (harmless) or **malignant** (harmful) via a biopsy in which a tissue sample is taken and examined under a microscope. If your dog is diagnosed with cancer, there is hope. Advances in veterinary medicine and technology offer various treatment options, including chemotherapy, radiation and surgery. Unlike with humans, a dog's hair will not fall out with chemotherapy. Canine cancer is growing at an ever-increasing rate, and one of the difficulties is that your dog cannot tell you when a cancer is developing. However, if cancers can be detected early enough through a physical or behavioural change, they often respond well to treatment.

Over recent years, we have all become more aware of the risk factors for human cancer. Responding to these by changing our habits is having a significant impact on human health. For example, stopping smoking, protecting ourselves from over-exposure to strong sunlight and eating a healthy, balanced diet all help to reduce cancer rates. We know to keep a close eye on ourselves, go for regular health checks and report any lumps and bumps to our doctors as soon as they appear. Increased cancer awareness is definitely improving human health. The same is true with your dog.

While it is impossible to completely prevent cancer from occurring, a healthy lifestyle with a balanced diet and regular exercise can help to reduce the risk - as can being aware of any new lumps and bumps on your dog's body and any changes in his behaviour. The success of treatment will depend on the type of cancer, the treatment used and how early the tumour is found. The sooner treatment begins, the greater the chances of success.

One of the best things you can do for your dog is to keep a close eye on him for any tell-tale signs. This shouldn't be too difficult and can be done as part of your regular handling and weekly grooming session. If you notice any new bumps, for example, monitor them over a period of days to see if there is a change in their appearance or size. If there is, then make an appointment to see your vet as soon as possible. It might only be a cyst, but better to be safe than sorry.

Research into earlier diagnosis and improved treatments is being conducted at veterinary schools and companies all over the world. Advances in biology are producing a steady flow of new tests and treatments which are now becoming available to improve survival rates and canine cancer care. If your dog is diagnosed with cancer, do not despair, there are many options and new, improved treatments are constantly being introduced.

Our Happy Ending

We know from personal experience that canine cancer can be successfully treated if it is diagnosed early enough. Our dog was diagnosed with T-cell lymphoma when he was four years old. We noticed a black lump on his anus that quickly grew to the size of a small grape and we took him to the vet within the first few days of seeing the lump. After a test, he was diagnosed with the dreaded T-cell lymphoma. This is a particularly nasty and aggressive form of cancer that can spread to the lymph system and is often fatal for dogs.

As soon as the diagnosis was confirmed, our vet Graham operated and removed the lump. He also had to remove one of his anal glands, but as dogs have two this was not a serious worry. Afterwards, we were on tenterhooks, not knowing if another lump would grow or if the cancer had already spread to his lymph system. After a few months, Max had another blood test and was finally given the all-clear. He is now happy, healthy and 12 years old. We were very lucky.

I would strongly advise anyone who suspects that their dog has cancer to get him or her to your local vet as soon as possible.

Disclaimer: The author of this book is not a vet. This chapter is intended to give owners an indication of some of the medical conditions that may affect their dog or dogs and the symptoms to look out for. If you have any concerns regarding the health of your dog, our advice is always the same: consult a veterinarian.

12. Skin and Allergies

Allergies are a growing problem among the canine population in general. Visit any busy vet's surgery these days – especially in spring and summer – and it's likely that one or more of the dogs is there because of some type of sensitivity. Experts are not sure why. It may have something to do with the way we breed or feed our dogs, but as yet there is no scientific evidence to support either theory.

When bred from healthy parents, the Labrador is not considered particularly susceptible to skin problems – although there is some anecdotal evidence that silver Labs can be prone to hair loss and recurring skin issues. However, any dog can potentially develop allergies or intolerances - visit any Labrador forum and you'll see there are plenty of itchy dogs out there.

Skin conditions, allergies and intolerances are on the increase in dogs as well as humans. How many children did you hear of having asthma or a peanut allergy when you were at school? Not too many, I'll bet, yet allergies and adverse reactions are now relatively common – and it's the same with dogs.

This is a complicated topic and a whole book could be written on this subject alone. While many dogs have no problems at all, some suffer from sensitive skin, allergies, yeast infections and/or skin disorders, causing them to scratch, bite or lick themselves excessively on the paws and other areas. Symptoms may vary from mild itchiness to a severe reaction.

The Labrador breeders we asked about this topic were mainly of the opinion that their dog(s) have had little or no problems. However, if you haven't already bought your puppy, it would be one question to ask the breeder. One quite common condition with floppy-eared dogs in general is ear infections – more about these later.

As with humans, the skin is the dog's largest organ. It acts as the protective barrier between your dog's internal organs and the outside world; it also regulates temperature and provides the sense of touch. Surprisingly, a dog's skin is actually thinner than ours, and it is made up of three layers:

1. **Epidermis** or outer layer, the one that bears the brunt of your dog's contact with the outside world

2. **Dermis** is the extremely tough layer mostly made up of collagen, a strong and fibrous protein. This is where blood vessels deliver nutrients and oxygen to the skin, and it also acts as your dog's thermostat by allowing his body to release or retain heat, depending on the outside temperature and your dog's activity level

3. **Subcutis** is a dense layer of fatty tissue that allows your dog's skin to move independently from the muscle layers below it, as well as providing insulation and support for the skin

FACT: In humans, allergies often trigger a reaction within the respiratory system, causing us to wheeze or sneeze; whereas allergies or hypersensitivities in a dog often cause a reaction in his or her **skin**.

Skin can be affected from the **outside** by fleas, parasites, or inhaled or contact allergies triggered by grass, pollen, man-made chemicals, dust, mould etc. These environmental allergies are especially common in some Terriers as well as the Miniature Schnauzer, Bulldog and certain other breeds.

Skin can be affected from the **inside** by things that your dog eats or drinks. Like all dogs, a Labrador can suffer from food allergies or intolerances as well as environmental allergies.

Canine skin disorders are a complex subject. Some dogs can run through fields, digging holes and rolling around in the grass (and far more unpleasant stuff) with no after-effects at all. Others may spend more indoors and have an excellent diet, but still experience severe itching.

Skin problems may be the result of one or more of a wide range of causes - and the list of potential remedies and treatments is even longer. It's by no means possible to cover all of them in detail in this chapter. The aim here is to give a broad outline of some of the ailments most likely to affect Labradors and how to deal with them. We have also included remedies tried with some success by ourselves (we have a dog with skin issues) and other owners of affected dogs, as well as advice from a holistic specialist.

This information is not intended to take the place of professional help. We are not animal health experts and you should always contact your vet as soon as your dog appears physically unwell or uncomfortable. This is particularly true with skin conditions:

If a vet can find the source of the problem early on, there is more chance of successfully treating it before it has chance to develop into a more serious condition with secondary issues.

There is anecdotal evidence from some owners that switching to a raw diet or raw meaty bones diet can significantly help some canines with skin issues. See **Chapter 7. Feeding a Labrador** for more information.

One of the difficulties with this type of ailment is that the exact cause is often difficult to diagnose, as the symptoms may also be common to other issues. If environmental allergies are involved, some specific tests are available costing hundreds of pounds or dollars. You will have to take your vet's advice on this as the tests are not always conclusive and, if the answer is pollen or dust, it is extremely difficult to keep your Labrador away from the triggers while still having a normal life - unless you and your Lab spend all your time in a spotlessly clean city apartment (which is, quite frankly, highly unlikely!) It is often a question of managing a skin condition, rather than curing it.

Skin issues and allergies often develop in adolescence or early adulthood, which may be anything from a few months to two or three years old. Our dog Max was perfectly normal until he reached two when he began scratching, triggered by environmental allergies - most likely pollen. He's now 12 and over the years he's been on various different remedies which have all worked for a time. As Max's allergies are seasonal, he normally does not have any medication between October and March. But come spring and as sure as daffodils are daffodils, he starts scratching again. We now think we have the solution to keep it under control – read more later in this chapter – and Max lives a happy, normal life.

Tip Another issue reported by some owners is food allergy or intolerance (there is a difference) – often to grain. Allergies and their treatment can cause a lot of stress for dogs and owners alike. The number one piece of advice is that if you suspect your Labrador has an allergy or skin problem, try to **deal with it right away** - either via your vet or natural remedies – before the all-too-familiar scenario kicks in and it develops into a chronic (long term) condition.

Whatever the cause, before a vet can diagnose the problem you have to be prepared to tell him or her all about your dog's diet, exercise regime, habits, medical history and local environment. He or she will then carry out a thorough physical examination, possibly followed by further tests, before a course of treatment can be prescribed. You'll have to decide whether these tests are worth the cost, whether they are likely to discover the exact root cause of the problem and whether you are prepared to stick with a course of lengthy hyposensitisation treatment afterwards.

Types of Allergies

'Canine dermatitis' means inflammation of a dog's skin and it can be triggered by numerous things, but the most common by far is allergies. An allergy is an exaggerated response to something in the environment.

In response to these allergens, a dog's immune system overreacts and produces a protein called IgE which triggers the release of compounds called histamines that cause irritation and inflammation. (This is why people and dogs with hay fever and similar allergies may be prescribed **antihistamines**). Vets estimate that one in four dogs in their clinics is there due to some kind of allergy. Typical symptoms are:

- Chewing on paws
- Rubbing the face on the carpet
- Scratching the body
- Scratching or biting the anus
- Itchy ears, head shaking
- Hair loss
- Mutilated skin with sore or discoloured patches or hot spots'

A Labrador who is allergic to something will show it through skin problems and itching; your vet may call this *'pruritus'*. It may seem logical that if a dog is allergic to something he inhales, like certain pollen grains, his nose will run; if he's allergic to something he eats, he may vomit, or if allergic to an insect bite, he may develop a swelling. But in practice this is seldom the case.

The skin is the organ that is often affected by allergies, causing a mild to severe itching sensation over the body and maybe a chronic ear infection. Dogs with allergies often chew their feet until they are sore and red. You may see yours rubbing his face on the carpet or couch or scratching his belly and flanks. Because the ear glands produce too much wax in response to the allergy, ear infections can occur, with bacteria and yeast - which is a fungus - often thriving in the excessive wax and debris.

But your Labrador doesn't have to suffer from allergies to get ear infections, the lack of air flow under the floppy ears make the breed prone to the condition. (By the way, if your dog does develop a yeast infection and you switch to a grain-free diet, avoid those which are potato-based, as these contain high levels of starch).

US holistic vet Dr Jodie Gruenstern highlights the effect that diet can have on allergies: "Grains and other starches have a negative impact on gut health, creating insulin resistance and inflammation.

"It's estimated that up to 80% of the immune system resides within the gastrointestinal system; building a healthy gut supports a more appropriate immune response. The importance of choosing fresh proteins and healthy fats over processed, starchy diets (such as kibble) can't be overemphasized."

An allergic dog may cause skin lesions or 'hot spots' by constant chewing and scratching. Sometimes he will lose hair, which can be patchy, leaving a mottled appearance. The skin itself may be dry and crusty, reddened, swollen or oily, depending on the dog. It is very common to get secondary bacterial skin infections due to these self-inflicted wounds. An allergic dog's body is reacting to molecules called allergens. These may come from:

- Grass, tree or plant pollens
- Foods or food additives, such as specific meats, grains, preservatives or colourings
- Milk products
- Fabrics, such as wool or nylon
- Rubber and/or plastics (e.g. plastic food bowl)
- House dust and/or dust mites
- Mould
- Flea bites
- Chemical products used around the house

These allergens may be **inhaled** as the dog breathes, **ingested** as the dog eats or caused by **contact** with the dog's body when he walks or rolls. However they arrive, they all cause the immune system to produce a protein (IgE), which causes various irritating body chemicals (or hormones), such as histamine, to be released. In dogs these chemical reactions and cell types occur in sizeable amounts only within the skin, hence the scratching.

....

Inhalant Allergies (Atopy)

The most common allergies in dogs are inhalant and seasonal (at least at first; some allergies may develop and worsen). Substances which can cause an allergic reaction in dogs are similar to those causing problems for humans. Dogs of all breeds can suffer from them.

A clue to diagnosing these allergies is to look at the timing of the reaction. Does it happen all year round? If so, this may be mould, dust or some other trigger which is permanently in the environment. If the reaction is seasonal, then pollens may well be the culprit. A diagnosis can be made by one of three methods of **allergy testing.**

The most common is a blood test that checks for antibodies caused by antigens in the dog's blood, and there are two standard tests: a RAST test (radioallergosorbent) and an ELISA test (enzyme-linked immunosorbent assay). According to the Veterinary and Aquatic Services Department of Drs. Foster and Smith, they are very similar, but many vets feel that the ELISA test gives more accurate results.

The other type of testing is intradermal skin testing where a small amount of antigen is injected into the skin of the animal and after a short period of time, the area around the injection site is inspected to see if the dog has had an allergic reaction. This method has been more widely used in the USA than the UK to date. Here is a link to an article written by the owner of a Boxer dog with severe inhalant allergies: www.allergydogcentral.com/2011/06/30/dog-allergy-testing-and-allergy-shots

This photo shows a dog which has undergone intradermal skin testing. In this particular case, the dog has been tested for more than 70 different allergens, which is a lot. In all likelihood, your dog would be tested for less. The injections are in kits. If you consider this option, ask the vet or specialist how many allergens are in the kit.

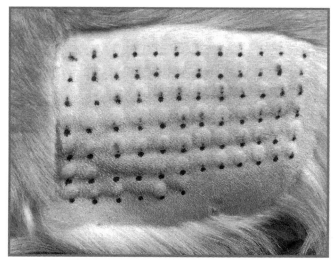

Intradermal skin testing is regarded as 'the gold standard' of allergy testing for atopy. The dog is sedated and an area on his side is shaved down to the skin. A small amount of antigen is injected into the dog's skin on this shaved area. This is done in a specific pattern and order. After a short time the shaved area is examined to detect which antigens, if any, have created a reaction. It may look pretty drastic, but reactions – the visible round bumps -are only temporary and the fur grows back.

Intradermal skin testing works best when done during the season when the allergies are at their worst. The good news is that it is not necessarily much more expensive than blood testing and after a while the dog is none the worse for the ordeal. The procedure is normally carried out by a veterinary dermatologist or a vet with some dermatological experience, and dogs need to be clear of steroids and antihistamines for around six weeks beforehand.

While allergy testing is not particularly expensive, the intradermal method usually requires your dog to be sedated. And there's also no point doing it if you are not going to go along with the recommended method of treatment afterwards - which is immunotherapy, or **'hyposensitisation'**, and this can be an expensive and lengthy process. It consists of a series of injections made specifically for your dog and administered over months (or even years) to make him more tolerant of specific allergens. Vets in the US claim that success rates can be as high as 75%.

But before you get to the stage of considering allergy testing, your vet will have had to rule out other potential causes, such as fleas or mites, fungal, yeast or bacterial infections and hypothyroidism. Due to the time and cost involved in skin testing, most mild cases of allergies are treated with a combination of avoidance, fatty acids, tablets, and sometimes steroid injections for flare-ups. Many owners of dogs with allergies are also looking for natural alternatives as long-term use of steroids, for example, can cause other health issues.

Environmental or Contact Irritations

These are a direct reaction to something the dog physically comes into contact with. It could be as simple as grass, specific plants, dust or other animals. If the trigger is grass or other outdoor materials, the allergies are often seasonal. The dog may require treatment (often tablets, shampoo or localised cortisone spray) for spring and summer, but be perfectly fine with no medication for the other half of the year. This is the case with our dog – although he also has inhalant allergies.

 Let's face it, it is impossible for a Labrador to avoid the Great Outdoors. So, if you suspect yours may have outdoor contact allergies, here's one very good tip: get him to stand in a tray or large bowl of water on your return from a walk – or hose him down underneath. Washing his feet and under his belly will reduce his scratching and biting by reducing the allergens to a tolerable level.

Other possible triggers include dry carpet shampoos, caustic irritants, new carpets, cement dust, washing powders or fabric conditioners. If you wash your dog's bedding or if he sleeps on your bed, use a fragrance-free - if possible, hypoallergenic - laundry detergent and avoid fabric conditioner. The irritation may be restricted to the part of the dog - such as the underneath of the paws or belly - which has touched the offending object. Symptoms are skin irritation - either a general problem or specific hotspots - itching (pruritus) and sometimes hair loss. Readers sometimes report to us that their dog will incessantly lick one part of the body, often the paws, anus, belly or back.

Our dog went through a phase of jumping round like he had been stung like a bee to frantically lick and bite his anus; it made our eyes water just to watch it! A swift trip to the vet resulted in a steroid injection and a cortisone spray which we applied directly to the anus and quickly solved the problem. If he occasionally (every couple of years) has a flare up, we use the spray for a day or so and it clears it up. This type of spray can be very effective if the itchy area is small, but no good for spraying all over a dog's body.

Flea Bite Allergies (FAD, Flea Allergy Dermatitis)

This is an extremely common canine allergy and can affect all breeds. To compound the problem, many dogs with flea allergies also have inhalant allergies. FAD is typically seasonal, worse during summer and autumn – peak time for fleas - and in warmer climates where fleas are prevalent.

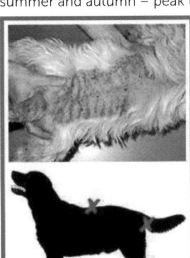

This type of allergy is not to the flea itself, but to proteins in flea saliva, which are deposited under the dog's skin when an adult flea feeds on the dog's blood. Just one bite to an allergic Labrador will cause intense and long-lasting itching. Fleas typically don't stay on the dog except for the minutes to hours when they are feeding, which is why owners often don't see live fleas on their dog, unless there is a severe flea infestation.

The first clues that your Lab may suffer from FAD are itching and hair loss in the area from the middle of the back to the base of the tail and down the rear legs (known to vets as 'the flea triangle'). Intradermal or specialised blood tests can confirm a flea allergy, followed by hyposensitisation treatment. Flea bite allergies can only be totally prevented by keeping all fleas away from the dog. Various flea prevention treatments are available, and it's important to keep up to date with preventative treatments – see the section on **Parasites**. If you suspect your dog may be allergic to fleas, consult your vet for the proper diagnosis and medication.

Diet and Food Allergies

Food is the third most common cause of allergies in dogs. Cheap dog foods bulked up with grains and other ingredients can cause problems. Some owners have reported their dogs having intolerances to wheat and other grains. If you feed your dog a dry commercial dog food, make sure that it's high quality, preferably hypoallergenic, and that the first ingredient listed on the sack is meat or poultry, not grain.

Without the correct food, a dog's whole body - not just his skin and coat - will continuously be under stress and this manifests itself in a number of ways. The symptoms of food allergies are similar to those of most allergies:

- Itchy skin affecting primarily the face, feet, ears, forelegs, armpits and anus
- Excessive scratching
- Chronic or recurring ear infections
- Hair loss
- Hot spots
- Skin infections that clear up with antibiotics, but return after the antibiotics have finished
- Often increased bowel movements, maybe twice as many as normal

The bodily process which occurs when an animal has a reaction to a particular food agent is not very well understood, but the veterinary profession does know how to diagnose and treat food allergies. As many other problems can cause similar symptoms (and also the fact that many sufferers also have other allergies), it is important that any other problems are identified and treated before food allergies are diagnosed.

Atopy, FAD, intestinal parasite hypersensitivities, sarcoptic mange and yeast or bacterial infections can all cause similar symptoms. This can be an anxious time for owners as vets try one thing after another to get to the bottom of the allergy. The normal method for diagnosing a food allergy is elimination. Once all other causes have been ruled out or treated, then a food trial is the next step – and that's no picnic for owners either - see **Chapter 7. Feeding a Labrador** for more information. As with other allergies, dogs may have short-term relief by taking fatty acids, antihistamines and/or steroids, but removing the offending items from the diet is the only permanent solution.

Acute Moist Dermatitis (Hot Spots)

Acute moist dermatitis or 'hot spots' are not uncommon. A hot spot can appear suddenly and is a raw, inflamed and often bleeding area of skin. The area becomes moist and painful and begins spreading due to continual licking and chewing. Hot spots can become large, red, irritated lesions in a short pace of time. The cause is often a local reaction to an insect bite; fleas, ticks, biting flies and even mosquitoes have been known to cause acute moist dermatitis. Other causes include:

- Allergies - inhalant allergies and food allergies
- Mites
- Ear infections
- Poor grooming

- Burs or plant awns
- Anal gland disease
- Hip dysplasia or other types of arthritis and degenerative joint disease

The good news is that, once diagnosed and with the right treatment, hot spots disappear as soon as they appeared. The underlying cause should be identified and treated, if possible. Check with your vet before treating your Labrador for fleas and ticks at the same time as other medical treatment (such as anti-inflammatory medications and/or antibiotics), as he or she will probably advise you to wait. Treatments may come in the form of injections, tablets or creams – or your dog might need a combination of them. Your vet will probably clip and clean the affected area to help the effectiveness of any spray or ointment and your hapless dog might also have to wear an E-collar until the condition subsides, but usually this does not take long.

Interdigital Cysts

If you've ever noticed a fleshy red lump between your dog's toes that looks like an ulcerated sore or a hairless bump, then it was probably an interdigital cyst - or 'interdigital furuncle' to give the condition its correct medical term. These can be very difficult to get rid of, since they are not the primary issue, but often a sign of some other condition.

Several Labrador owners we spoke to have reported having a dog, or knowing of a dog, that has suffered with interdigital cysts. They are often associated with obesity - but even slim Labs can suffer from them.

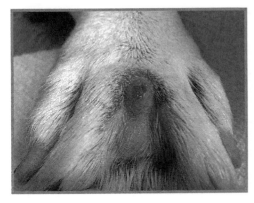

Actually these are not cysts, but the result of *furunculosis*, a condition of the skin which clogs hair follicles and creates chronic infection. They can be caused by a number of factors, including allergies, obesity, poor foot conformation, mites, yeast infections, ingrowing hairs or other foreign bodies, and obesity.

These nasty-looking bumps are painful for your dog, will probably cause him to limp and can be a nightmare to get rid of. Vets might recommend a whole range of treatments to get to the root cause of the problem. It can be extremely expensive if your dog is having a barrage of tests or biopsies and even then you are not guaranteed to find the underlying cause.

The first thing he or she will probably do is put your dog in an E-collar to stop him licking the affected area, which will never recover properly as long as he's constantly licking it. This again is stressful for your dog. Here are some remedies your vet may suggest:

- Antibiotics and/or steroids and/or mite killers
- Soaking his feet in Epsom salts twice daily to unclog the hair follicles
- Testing him for allergies or thyroid problems
- Starting a food trial if food allergies are suspected
- Shampooing his feet
- Cleaning between his toes with medicated (benzoyl peroxide) wipes
- Reducing the dog's weight
- A referral to a veterinary dermatologist
- Surgery

If you suspect your Labrador has an interdigital cyst, take him to the vet for a correct diagnosis and then discuss the various options. A course of antibiotics may be suggested initially, along with switching to a hypoallergenic diet if a food allergy is suspected. If the condition persists, many owners get discouraged, especially when treatment may continue for many weeks.

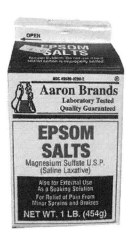

 Before you resort to any drastic action, first try soaking your Labrador's affected paw in Epsom salts for five or 10 minutes twice a day for up to a month until they have completely disappeared. (You will know after a week if they are having any effect). After the soaking, clean the area with medicated wipes, which are antiseptic and control inflammation. In the US these are sold under the brand name Stridex pads in the skin care section of any grocery, or from the pharmacy. If you think the cause may be an environmental allergy, wash your dog's paws and under his belly when you return from a walk, this will help to remove pollen and other allergens.

Some owners have also reported adding human athlete's foot powder to the salts or athlete's foot cream to the dog's paw after bathing.

Surgery can be effective, but it is a drastic option and although it might solve the immediate problem, it will not deal with whatever is triggering the interdigital cysts in the first place. Not only is healing after this surgery a lengthy and difficult process, it also means your dog will never have the same foot as before - future orthopaedic issues and a predisposition to more interdigital cysts are just a couple of problems which can occur afterwards.

All that said, your vet will understand that interdigital cysts aren't so simple to deal with, but they are treatable. Get the right diagnosis as soon as possible, limit all offending factors and give medical treatment a good solid try before embarking on more drastic cures.

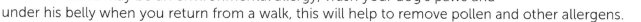

Parasites

Demodectic Mange (Demodex)

Demodectic mange is also known as Demodex, red mange, follicular mange or puppy mange. It is caused by the tiny torpedo-shaped mite Demodex canis — pictured - which can only be seen through a microscope. The mites actually live inside the hair follicles on the bodies of virtually every adult dog, and most humans, without causing any harm or irritation. In humans, the mites are found in the skin, eyelids and the creases of the nose ...try not to think about that!

The Demodex mite spends its entire life on the host dog. Eggs hatch and mature from larvae to nymphs to adults in 20 to 35 days and the mites are transferred directly from the mother to the puppies within the first week of life by direct physical contact. Demodectic mange is not a disease of poorly kept or dirty kennels. It is generally a disease of young dogs with inadequate or poorly developed immune systems (or older dogs suffering from a suppressed immune system).

Vets currently believe that virtually every mother carries and transfers mites to her puppies, and most are immune to the mite's effects, but a few puppies are not and they develop full-blown mange. They may have a few (less than five) isolated lesions and this is known as localised mange — often around the head. This happens in around 90% of cases, but in the other 10% of cases, it develops into generalised mange which covers the entire body or region of the body. This is most likely to develop in puppies with parents that have suffered from mange. Most lesions in either form develop after four months of age. It can also develop around the time when females have their first season, typically around nine months old, and may be due to a slight dip in the bitch's immune system.

Symptoms – Bald patches are usually the first sign, usually accompanied by crusty, red skin which sometimes appears greasy or wet. Usually hair loss begins around the muzzle, eyes and other areas on the head. The lesions may or may not itch. In localised mange, a few circular crusty areas appear, most frequently on the head and front legs of three to six-month-old puppies. Most will self-heal as the puppies become older and develop their own immunity, but a persistent problem needs treatment, as you don't want generalised mange to develop.

With generalised mange there are bald patches over the entire coat, including the head, neck, body, legs, and feet. The skin on the head, side and back is crusty, often inflamed and oozing a clear fluid. The skin itself will often be oily to touch and there is usually a secondary bacterial infection. Some puppies can become quite ill and develop a fever, lose their appetites and become lethargic. If you suspect your puppy has generalised demodectic mange, get him to a vet straight away.

There is also a condition called pododermatitis, when mange affects a puppy's paws. It can cause bacterial infections and be very uncomfortable, even painful. The symptoms of this mange include hair loss on the paws, swelling of the paws (especially around the nail beds) and red/hot/inflamed areas which are often infected. Treatment is always recommended, and it can take several rounds to clear it up.

Diagnosis and Treatment – The vet will normally diagnose demodectic mange after he or she has taken a skin scraping. As these mites are present on every dog, they do not necessarily mean the dog has mange. Only when the mite is coupled with lesions will the vet diagnose mange. Treatment usually involves topical (on the skin) medication and sometimes tablets. In 90% of cases localised demodectic mange resolves itself as the puppy grows.

If the dog has just one or two lesions, these can usually be successfully treated using specific creams and spot treatments. With the more serious generalised demodectic mange, treatment can be lengthy and expensive. The vet might prescribe an anti-parasitic dip every two weeks. Owners should always wear rubber gloves when treating their dog, and it should be applied in an area with adequate ventilation. It should also be noted that **some dogs can react to these dips,** so check with your vet as to whether it will be suitable. Most dogs with a severe case need six to 14 dips every two weeks. After the first three or four dips, your vet will probably take another skin scraping to check the mites have gone. Dips continue for one month after the mites have disappeared, but dogs shouldn't be considered cured until a year after their last treatment.

Other options include the heartworm treatment Ivermectin. This isn't approved by the FDA for treating mange, but is often used to do so. It is usually given orally every one to two days, or by injection, and can be very effective. **Again, some dogs react badly to it.** Another drug is Interceptor (Milbemycin oxime), which can be expensive as it has to be given daily. However, it is effective on up to 80% of the dogs who did not respond to dips – but should be given with caution to pups under 21 weeks of age.

Adult dogs that have the generalised condition may have underlying skin infections, so antibiotics are often given for the first several weeks of treatment. They might also have immune system issues, and because the mite flourishes on dogs with suppressed immune systems, you should try to get to the root cause of the problem, especially if your Labrador is older when he or she develops demodectic mange.

Adult dogs that have recurring or persistent cases of demodectic mange should not be bred.

Sarcoptic Mange (Scabies)

Also known as canine scabies, this is caused by the parasite *Sarcoptes scabiei,* and is often far worse than Demodex. It is also highly contagious.

This microscopic mite can cause a range of skin problems, the most common of which is hair loss and severe itching. The mites can infect other animals such as foxes, cats and even humans, but prefer to live their short lives on dogs. Fortunately, there are several good treatments for this mange and the disease can be easily controlled.

In cool, moist environments, the mites live for up to 22 days. At normal room temperature they live from two to six days, preferring to live on parts of the dog with less hair. These are the areas you may see him scratching, although it can spread throughout the body in severe cases.

Diagnosing canine scabies can be somewhat difficult, and it is often mistaken for inhalant allergies. Symptoms are intense scratching, a skin rash, crusty scabs and hair loss (alopecia). Once diagnosed, there are a number of effective treatments, including selamectin (Revolution), an on-the-skin solution applied once a month which also provides heartworm prevention, flea control and some tick protection. Various Frontline products are also effective – check with your vet for the correct one.

Because your dog does not have to come into direct contact with an infected dog to catch scabies, it is difficult to completely protect him. Groomer's, veterinary clinics, parks and boarding kennels are all places where a dog can catch scabies; symptoms will usually arrive two to six weeks later. Foxes and their environment can also transmit the mite, so you might want to consider keeping your Lab away from areas where you know foxes are active.

....

Fleas

When you see your dog scratching and biting, your first thought is probably: "He's got fleas!" and you may well be right. Fleas don't fly, but they do have very strong back legs and they will take any opportunity to jump from the ground or another animal into your Labrador's lovely warm coat. You can sometimes see the fleas if you part your dog's fur.

And for every flea that you see on your dog, there is the awful prospect of hundreds of eggs and larvae in your home or kennel. So if your dog is unlucky enough to catch fleas, you'll have to treat your environment as well as your dog in order to completely get rid of them.

The best form of cure is prevention. Vets recommend giving dogs a preventative flea treatment every four to eight weeks. This may vary depending on your climate, the season - fleas do not breed as quickly in the cold - and how much time your dog spends outdoors. Once-a-month topical insecticides - like Frontline and Advantix - are the most commonly used flea prevention products on the market. You part the skin and apply drops of the liquid on to a small area on your dog's back, usually near the neck. Some kill fleas and ticks, and others just kill fleas - check the details.

It is worth spending the money on a quality treatment, as cheaper brands may not rid your Labrador completely of fleas, ticks and other parasites. Sprays, dips, shampoos and collars are other options, as are tablets and injections in certain cases, such as before your dog goes into boarding kennels or has surgery. Incidentally, a flea bite is different from a flea bite allergy.

NOTE: There is considerable anecdotal evidence from dog owners of various breeds that the US flea and worm tablet *Trifexis* can cause severe side effects in some dogs. You may wish to read owners' comments at: www.max-the-schnauzer.com/trifexis-side-effects-in-schnauzers.html

Ticks

A tick is not an insect, but a member of the arachnid family, like the spider. There are over 850 types of them, divided into two types: hard shelled and soft shelled. Ticks don't have wings - they can't fly, they crawl. They have a sensor called Haller's organ which detects smell, heat and humidity to help them locate food, which in some cases is a Labrador. Ticks' diets consists of one thing and one thing only – blood! They climb up onto tall grass and, when they sense an animal is close, crawl on.

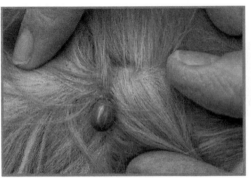

Ticks can pass on a number of diseases to animals and humans, the most well-known of which is **Lyme Disease**, a serious condition which causes lameness and other problems. Dogs which spend a lot of time outdoors in high risk areas, such as woods, can have a vaccination against Lime Disease.

If you do find a tick on your Labrador's coat and are not sure how to get it out, have it removed by a vet or other expert. Inexpertly pulling it out yourself and leaving a bit of the tick behind can be detrimental to your dog's health. Prevention treatment is similar to that for fleas. If your dog has particularly sensitive skin, he might do better with a natural flea or tick remedy.

Heartworm

Heartworm is a serious and potentially fatal disease affecting pets in North America and many other parts of the world but not the UK). Foot-long heartworms live in the heart, lungs and associated blood vessels of affected pets, causing severe lung disease, heart failure and damage to other organs in the body.

The dog is a natural host for heartworms, which means that heartworms living inside the dog mature into adults, mate and produce offspring. If untreated, their numbers can increase; dogs have been known to harbour several hundred worms in their bodies. Heartworm disease causes lasting damage to the heart, lungs and arteries, and can affect the dog's health and quality of life long after the parasites are gone. For this reason, prevention is by far the best option and treatment - when needed - should be administered as early as possible.

The mosquito (pictured) plays an essential role in the heartworm life cycle. When a mosquito bites and takes a blood meal from an infected animal, it picks up baby worms which develop and mature

into 'infective stage' larvae over a period of 10 to 14 days. Then, when the infected mosquito bites another dog, cat or susceptible wild animal, the infective larvae are deposited onto the surface of the animal's skin and enter the new host through the mosquito's bite wound.

Once inside a new host, it takes approximately six months for the larvae to develop into adult heartworms. Once mature, heartworms can live for five to seven years in a dog. In the early stages of the disease, many dogs show few or no symptoms. The longer the infection persists, the more likely symptoms will develop. These include:

- A mild persistent cough
- Reluctance to exercise
- Tiredness after moderate activity
- Decreased appetite
- Weight loss

As the disease progresses, dogs may develop heart failure and a swollen belly due to excess fluid in the abdomen. Dogs with large numbers of heartworms can develop sudden blockages of blood flow within the heart leading to the life-threatening caval syndrome. This is marked by a sudden onset of laboured breathing, pale gums and dark, bloody or coffee-coloured urine. Without prompt surgical removal of the heartworm blockage, few dogs survive.

Although more common in south eastern US, heartworm disease has been diagnosed in all 50 states. Because infected mosquitoes can fly indoors, even dogs which spend much time inside the home are at risk. For that reason, the American Heartworm Society recommends that you get your dog tested every year and give your dog heartworm preventive treatment for 12 months of the year.

Thanks to the American Heartworm Society for assistance with the section.

Ringworm

This is not actually a worm, but a fungus and is most commonly seen in puppies and young dogs. It is highly infectious and often found on the face, ears, paws or tail. The ringworm fungus is most prevalent in hot, humid climates but, surprisingly, most cases occur in autumn and winter. Ringworm infections in dogs are not that common; in one study of dogs with active skin problems, less than 3% had ringworm.

Ringworm is transmitted by spores in the soil and by contact with the infected hair of dogs and cats, which can be typically found on carpets, brushes, combs, toys and furniture. Spores from infected animals can be shed into the environment and live for over 18 months, fortunately most healthy adult dogs have some resistance and never develop symptoms. The fungi live in dead skin, hairs and nails - and the head and legs are the most common areas affected.

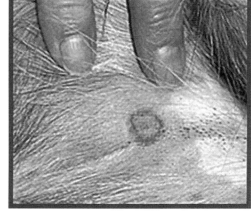

Tell-tale signs are bald patches with a roughly circular shape (pictured). Ringworm is relatively easy to treat with fungicidal shampoos or antibiotics from a vet. Humans can catch ringworm from pets, and vice versa. Children are especially susceptible, as are adults with suppressed immune systems and those undergoing chemotherapy.

Hygiene is extremely important. If your dog has ringworm, wear gloves when handling him and wash your hands well afterwards. And if a member of your family catches ringworm, make sure they use separate towels from everyone else or the fungus may spread. As a teenager I caught ringworm from horses at stables where I worked at weekends - much to my mother's horror - and was treated like a leper by the rest of the family until it had cleared up!

Bacterial infection (Pyoderma)

Pyoderma literally means 'pus in the skin' (yuk!) and fortunately this condition is not contagious. Early signs of this bacterial infection are itchy red spots filled with yellow pus, similar to pimples or spots in humans. They can sometimes develop into red, ulcerated skin with dry and crusty patches.

Pyoderma is caused by several things: a broken skin surface, a skin wound due to chronic exposure to moisture, altered skin bacteria, or impaired blood flow to the skin. Dogs have a higher risk of developing an infection when they have a fungal infection or an endocrine (hormone gland) disease such as hyperthyroidism, or have allergies to fleas, food or parasites.

Pyoderma is often secondary to allergic dermatitis and develops in the sores on the skin which happen as a result of scratching. Puppies often develop 'puppy pyoderma' in thinly-haired areas such as the groin and underarms. Fleas, ticks, yeast or fungal skin infections, thyroid disease, hormonal imbalances, heredity and some medications can increase the risk. If you notice symptoms, get your dog to the vet quickly before the condition develops from *superficial pyoderma* into *severe pyoderma*, which is very unpleasant and takes a lot longer to treat.

Bacterial infection, no matter how bad it may look, usually responds well to medical treatment, which is generally done on an outpatient basis. Superficial pyoderma will usually be treated with a two to six-week course of antibiotic tablets or ointment. Severe or recurring pyoderma looks awful, causes your dog some distress and can take months of treatment to completely cure. Medicated shampoos and regular bathing, as instructed by your vet, are also part of the treatment. It's also important to ensure your dog has clean, dry, padded bedding.

Canine Acne

This is not uncommon and - just as with humans - generally affects teenagers, often between five and eight months of age with dogs. Acne occurs when oil glands become blocked causing bacterial infection, and these glands are most active in teenagers. Acne is not a major health problem as most of it will clear up once the dog becomes an adult, but it can reoccur. Typical signs are pimples, blackheads or whiteheads around the muzzle, chest or groin. If the area is irritated, then there may some bleeding or pus that can be expressed from these blemishes.

Hormonal Imbalances

These occur in dogs of all breeds. They are often difficult to diagnose and occur when a dog is producing either too much (hyper) or too little (hypo) of a particular hormone. One visual sign is often hair loss on both sides of the dog's body. The condition is not usually itchy. Hormone imbalances can be serious as they are often indicators that glands which affect the dog internally are not working properly. However, some types can be diagnosed by special blood tests and treated effectively.

Ear Infections

The Labrador's long, floppy ears mean that the breed can be susceptible to ear infections. Infection of the external ear canal (outer ear infection) is called otitis externa and is one of the most common types seen. However, the fact that your dog has recurring ear infections does not necessarily mean that his ears are the source of the problem – although they might be.

One common reason for them in Labradors is moisture in the ear canal, which in turn allows bacteria to flourish there. But some dogs with chronic or recurring ear infections have inhalant or food allergies or low thyroid function (hypothyroidism). Sometimes the ears are the first sign of allergy. The underlying problem must be treated or the dog will continue to have long term ear infections. Tell-tale signs include your dog shaking his head, scratching or rubbing his ears a lot, or an unpleasant smell coming from the ears.

If you look inside the ears, you may notice a reddy brown or yellow discharge, it may also be red and inflamed with a lot of wax. Sometimes a dog may appear depressed or irritable; ear infections are painful. In chronic cases, the inside of his ears may become crusty or thickened. Dogs can have ear problems for many different reasons, including:

- Allergies, such as environmental or food allergies

- Ear mites or other parasites

- Bacteria or yeast infections

- Injury, often due to excessive scratching

- Hormonal abnormalities, e.g. hypothyroidism

- The ear anatomy and environment, e.g. excess moisture

- Hereditary or immune conditions and tumours

In reality, many Labradors have ear infections due to the structure of the ear. Breeds that have pricked up ears have far few problems because Nature's design allows air to circulate inside the ear, keeping them cool and healthy. However, the Lab's long, floppy ears often prevent sufficient air flow inside the ear. This can lead to bacterial or yeast infections -particularly if there is moisture inside. These warm, damp and dark areas under the ear flaps provide an ideal breeding ground for bacteria.

Treatment depends on the cause and what – if any - other conditions your dog may have. Antibiotics are used for bacterial infections and antifungals for yeast infections. Glucocorticoids, such as dexamethasone, are often included in these medications to reduce the inflammation in the ear. Your vet may also flush out and clean the ear with special drops, something you may have to do daily at home until the infection clears.

A dog's ear canal is L-shaped, which means it can be difficult to get medication into the lower (horizontal) part of the ear. The best method is to hold the dog's ear flap with one hand and put the ointment or drops in with the other, if possible tilting the dog's head away from you so the liquid flows downwards **with gravity**. Make sure you then hold the ear flap down and massage the medication into the horizontal canal before letting go of your dog, as the first thing he will do is shake his head – and if the ointment or drops aren't massaged in, they will fly out.

Nearly all ear infections can be successfully managed if properly diagnosed and treated. But if an underlying problem remains undiscovered, the outcome will be less favourable. Deep ear infections can damage or rupture the eardrum, causing an internal ear infection and even permanent hearing loss. Closing of the ear canal (*hyperplasia* or *stenosis)* is another sign of severe infection. Most extreme cases of hyperplasia will eventually require surgery as a last resort; the most common procedure is called a 'lateral ear resection'. Our dog had a lateral ear resection several years ago following years of recurring ear infections and the growth of scar tissue. It was surgery or deafness, the vet said. We opted for surgery and our dog has been free of ear infections ever since. However, it is an **extremely** painful procedure for the dog and should only be considered as a very last resort.

To avoid or alleviate recurring ear infections, check your dog's ears and clean them regularly. Any excess hair should be regularly plucked from inside your Labrador's ears, and if your Labrador enjoys swimming, care should be taken to ensure the inside of the ear is thoroughly dry afterwards - and after bathing at home if you do occasionally bath your dog. There is more information on how to clean your dog's ears in **Chapter 13. Grooming.**

NOTE: When cleaning your dog's ears, be very careful not to put anything too far down inside. Visit YouTube to see videos of how to correctly clean without damaging them. DO NOT use cotton buds, these are too small and can damage the ear.

If your dog appears to be in pain, has smelly ears, or if his ear canals look inflamed, contact the vet straight away. If you can nip the first infection in the bud, there is a chance it will not return. If your dog has a ruptured or weakened eardrum, ear cleansers and medications could do more harm than good. Early treatment is the best way of preventing a recurrence.

Some Allergy Treatments

Treatments and success rates vary tremendously from dog to dog and from one allergy to another, which is why it is so important to consult a vet at the outset. Earlier diagnosis is more likely to lead to a successful treatment. Some owners whose dogs have recurring skin issues find that a course of antibiotics or steroids works wonders for their dog's sore skin and itching. However, the scratching starts all over again shortly after the treatment stops.

Food allergies require patience, a change of diet and maybe even a food trial, and the specific trigger is notoriously difficult to isolate – unless you are lucky and hit on the culprit straight away. With inhalant and contact allergies, blood and skin tests are available, followed by hyposensitisation treatment. However, this is not inexpensive and in some cases the specific trigger for many dogs remains unknown. So the reality for many owners of Labradors with allergies is that they manage the ailment with various medications and practices, rather than curing it completely.

Our Personal Experience

After corresponding with numerous other dog owners and consulting our vet, Graham, over the last decade, it seems that our experiences with allergies are not uncommon. This is borne out by the many owners who have contacted our website about their pet's allergy or sensitivities. According to Graham, more and more dogs appearing in his waiting room every spring with various types of allergies. The root cause still remains to be seen.

Our dog was perfectly fine until he was about two years old when he began to scratch a lot. He scratched more in spring and summer, which meant that his allergies were almost certainly inhalant or contact-based and related to pollens, grasses or other outdoor triggers. One option was for Max to have a barrage of tests to discover exactly what he was allergic to. We decided not to do this, not because of the cost, but because our vet said it was highly likely that he was allergic to pollens. If we had confirmed an allergy to pollens, we were not going to stop taking him outside for walks, and at that stage time hyposensitisation was not well known, so the vet treated him on the basis of seasonal inhalant or contact allergies, probably related to pollen.

As already mentioned, it's beneficial to have a shallow bath or hose outside and to rinse the dog's paws and underbelly after a walk in the countryside. This is something our vet does with his own dogs and has found that the scratching reduces as a result.

Regarding medications, Max was at first put on to a tiny dose of Piriton (pictured), an antihistamine sold in the millions for hay fever sufferers (human and canine), and for the first few springs and summers, this worked well.

Allergies can often change and the dog can also build up a tolerance to a treatment, which is why they can be so difficult to treat. This has been the case with Max over the years. The symptoms change from season to season, although the main ones remain and they are: general scratching paw biting and ear infections. A couple of years ago Max started nibbling his paws for the first time - a habit he persists with - although not to the extent that they become red and raw. Over the years we have tried a number of treatments, all of which have worked for a while, before he comes off the medication in autumn for six months when plants and grasses mostly stop growing outdoors. He manages perfectly fine the rest of the year without any treatment at all.

If we were starting again from scratch, knowing what we know now, I would certainly investigate a raw diet, if necessary in combination with holistic remedies. Our dog is now 12, we feed him a high quality hypoallergenic dry food. His allergies are manageable, he loves his food, still has plenty energy (although he sleeps a lot more) and is otherwise healthy, and so we are reluctant to make such a big change at this point in his life.

One season Max was put on a short course of steroids. These worked very well for five months, but steroids are not a long-term solution, as prolonged use can cause Cushing's Disease and other problems. Another spring Max was prescribed a non-steroid daily tablet called Atopica, sold in the UK only through vets. The active ingredient is **cyclosporine**, which suppresses the immune system. Some dogs can get side effects, although Max didn't, and holistic practitioners believe that it is harmful to the dog. This treatment was expensive (around £1 or US$1.30 a day), but initially extremely effective – so much so that we thought we had cured the problem completely. However, after a couple of seasons on cyclosporine he developed a tolerance to the drug and started scratching again.

A few years ago he went back on the antihistamine Piriton, a higher dose than when he was two years old, and this worked very well again. One advantage of this drug is that is it manufactured by the million for dogs and is therefore very inexpensive.

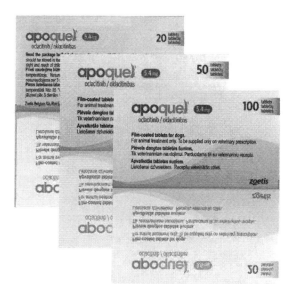

In 2013 the FDA approved **Apoquel** (oclacitinib) to control itching and inflammation in allergic dogs. In some quarters it has been hailed a **'wonder drug'** for canine allergies. In fact it has proved so popular in the UK and North America that in 2014-15 there was a shortage of supply, with the manufacturers not being able to produce it fast enough.

We have tried it with excellent results. There was some tweaking at the beginning to get the daily dose right, but it really has proved effective for us. Like clockwork last spring Max suddenly started scratching like crazy - just as he does every spring. We got him into the vet pretty smartish, where he had a single steroid injection to control the itching until the Apoquel kicked in. He went on a double dose of Apoquel for two weeks and

continued throughout the summer on a normal, single dose. Of course, he still scratches – all dogs do – but I would say it completely controlled that frantic scratching followed by hot spots. For a Labrador weighing 30kg (66lbs) a typical dosage would be one 16mg tablet per day. This currently costs around £2 (US$2.60) per day; you can buy the tablets cheaper online, but you have to produce a prescription from your vet.

Many vets recommend adding fish oils (which contain Omega-3 fatty acids) to a daily feed to keep your dog's skin and coat healthy all year round – whether or not he has problems. We add a liquid supplement called Lintbells' Yumega Itchy Dog, which contains Omegas 3 and 6, to one of Max's two daily feeds all year round and this definitely seems to help his skin. In the past when the scratching got particularly bad, we bathed him in an antiseborrhoeic shampoo (called Malaseb) twice a week for a limited time. This also helped, although this has not been necessary since he started on the Apoquel.

The main point is that most allergies are manageable. They may change throughout the life of the dog and you may have to alter the treatment. Max may have allergies, but he wouldn't miss his walks for anything and, all in all, he is one contented canine. We've compiled some anecdotal evidence from our website from owners of dogs with various allergies. Here are some of their suggestions:

Bathing - bathing your dog using shampoos that break down the oils which plug the hair follicles. These shampoos contain antiseborrhoeic ingredients such as benzoyl peroxide, salicylic acid, sulphur or tar. One example is Sulfoxydex shampoo, which can be followed by a cream rinse such as Episoothe Rinse afterwards to prevent the skin from drying out.

Dabbing – Using an astringent such as witch hazel or alcohop on affected areas. We have heard of zinc oxide cream being used to some effect. In the human world, this is rubbed on to mild skin abrasions and acts as a protective coating. It can help the healing of chapped skin and nappy rash in babies. Zinc oxide works as a mild astringent and has some antiseptic properties and is safe to use on dogs, *as long as you do not allow the dog to lick it off.*

Daily supplements - Vitamin E, vitamin A, zinc and omega oils all help to make a dog's skin healthy. Feed a daily supplement which contains some of these, such as fish oil, which provides omega.

Here are some specific remedies from owners. We are not endorsing them, we're just passing on the information. Check with your vet before trying any new remedies.

A medicated shampoo with natural tea tree oil has been suggested. Some owners have reported that switching to a fish-based diet has helped lessen scratching, while others have suggested home-cooked food is best, if you have the time to prepare the food. Another reader said: "My eight-month-old dog also had a contact dermatitis around his neck and chest. I was surprised how extensive it was. The vet recommended twice-a-week baths with an oatmeal shampoo. I also applied organic coconut oil daily for a few weeks and this completely cured the dermatitis. I put a capsule of fish oil with his food once a day and continue to give him twice-weekly baths. His skin is great now."

Several owners have tried coconut oil with some success. Here is an article on the benefits of coconut oils and fish oils, check with your vet first:
www.cocotherapy.com/fishoilsvsvirginoil_coconutoil.htm

Another reader added a teaspoonful of canola (rapeseed) oil in her dog's food every other day, shampooed the carpets and switched laundry detergent, all of which helped to reduce her dog's scratching.

Breeders on Allergies

The vast majority of the 30 Labrador breeders involved in this book have not had any problems with their dogs and allergies — although a number had heard of dogs with problems.

American breeder Teresa Gordy-Brown, of Ashland Labradors, Tennessee, said: "We have been very fortunate and have avoided allergy issues or food issues. Labradors, however, are prone to ear infections, and yeast and bacterial infections of the skin due to their double coat. They are a water dog, and moisture is the perfect breeding ground for bacteria and yeast. We prefer a vinegar and water rinse in the summer months after swimming."

Photo courtesy of Teresa.

One UK breeder added: "We have experienced ear infections in a chocolate Labrador. Also hyper activity, possibly when a food full of grain is fed. We have had experience of raw feeding and do not believe that grain is a natural food for the canine. Some skin irritations can be caused through poor diet.

"We raw fed our dogs for over five years, initially because one of our chocolate Labradors had consistently infected ears and was hyperactive. The raw diet improved both aspects and all our dogs benefitted; fresh breath, very healthy and good teeth. We now feed a premium dry food which is made from fish. It contains good quality protein and does not contain any grain. Our dogs have a salmon oil supplement, raw bones, raw vegetable, raw eggs and other nutritious scraps when available."

A UK breeder said: "I did one mating where one of the litter turned out to have a grass allergy. Discarding this as just bad luck, a repeat mating occurred two years later and one pup again had a grass allergy. Therefore it was obviously hereditary, so if you can check on previous litters it can be helpful.

"The first owner went through a series of tests and the vets formulated drugs/diet to combat this. When I heard of the second dog, I put the two in contact to shorten the learning curve and they now swap notes and order in bulk. There are no allergies in my other litters, so it must have come from the dog line, possibly."

Robin Anderson, of Grampian Labradors, New England, USA, added: "Dogs, as with people, can experience allergies. While robust, a Labrador can still have allergies on occasion. My advice is to talk to the breeder to see what might be in the lines, and to work with a vet regarding food choices and possible medications that offer allergy relief."

Photo of Mango retrieving a duck courtesy of Robin.

The Holistic Approach

As canine allergies become increasingly common, more and more owners of dogs with allergies and sensitivities are looking towards natural foods and remedies to help deal with the issues. Others are finding that their dog does well for a time with injections or medication, but then the symptoms slowly start to reappear. A holistic practitioner looks at finding the root cause of the problem and treating that, rather than just treating the symptoms.

Dr Sara Skiwski is a holistic vet working in California. She writes here about canine environmental allergies: "Here in California, with our mild weather and no hard freeze in Winter, environmental allergens can build up and cause nearly year-round issues for our beloved pets. Also seasonal allergies, when left unaddressed, can lead to year-round allergies. Unlike humans, whose allergy symptoms seem to affect mostly the respiratory tract, seasonal allergies in dogs often take the form of skin irritation/inflammation.

"Allergic reactions are produced by the immune system. The way the immune system functions is a result of both genetics and the environment: Nature versus Nurture. Let's look at a typical case. A puppy starts showing mild seasonal allergy symptoms, for instance a red tummy and mild itching in Spring. Off to the vet!

"The treatment prescribed is symptomatic to provide relief, such as a topical spray. The next year when the weather warms up, the patient is back again - same symptoms but more severe this time. This time the dog has very itchy skin. Again, the treatment is symptomatic - antibiotics, topical spray (hopefully no steroids), until the symptoms resolve with the season change. Fast forward to another Spring...on the third year, the patient is back again but this time the symptoms last longer, (not just Spring but also through most of Summer and into Fall). By Year Five, all the symptoms are significantly worse and are occurring year round. This is what happens with seasonal environmental allergies. The more your pet is exposed to the allergens they are sensitive to, the more the immune system over-reacts and the more intense and long-lasting the allergic response becomes. What to do?

"In my practice, I like to address the potential root cause at the very first sign of an allergic response, which is normally seen between the ages of six to nine months old. I do this to circumvent the escalating response year after year. Since the allergen load your environmentally-sensitive dog is most susceptible to is much heavier outdoors, I recommend two essential steps in managing the condition. They are vigilance in foot care as well as fur care.

"What does this mean? A wipe down of feet and fur, especially the tummy, to remove any pollens or allergens is key. This can be done with a damp cloth, but my favorite method is to get a spray bottle

filled with Witch Hazel and spray these areas. First, spray the feet then wipe them off with a cloth, and then spray and wipe down the tummy and sides. This is best done right after the pup has been outside playing or walking. This will help keep your pet from tracking the environmental allergens into the home and into their beds. If the feet end up still being itchy, I suggest adding foot soaks in Epsom salts."

Dr Skiwski also stresses the importance of keeping the immune system healthy by avoiding unnecessary vaccinations or drugs: "The vaccine stimulates the immune system, which is the last thing your pet with seasonal environmental allergies needs. I also will move the pet to an anti-inflammatory diet. Foods that create or worsen inflammation are high in carbohydrates. An allergic pet's diet should be very low in carbohydrates, especially grains. Research has shown that 'leaky gut,' or dysbiosis, is a root cause of immune system overreactions in both dog and cats (and some humans). Feed a diet that is not processed, or minimally processed; one that doesn't have grain and takes a little longer to get absorbed and assimilated through the gut. Slowing the assimilation assures that there are not large spikes of nutrients and proteins that come into the body all at once and overtax the pancreas and liver, creating inflammation.

"A lot of commercial diets are too high in grains and carbohydrates. These foods create inflammation which overtaxes the body and leads not just to skin inflammation, but also to other inflammatory conditions, such as colitis, pancreatitis, arthritis, inflammatory bowel disease and ear infections. Also, these diets are too low in protein, which is needed to make blood. This causes a decreased blood reserve in the body and in some of these animals this can leads to the skin not being properly nourished, starting a cycle of chronic skin infections which produce more itching."

After looking at diet, check that your dog is free from fleas and then these are some of Dr Skiwski's suggested supplements:

✓ **Raw (Unpasteurised) Local Honey** - an alkaline-forming food containing natural vitamins, enzymes, powerful antioxidants and other important natural nutrients, which are destroyed during the heating and pasteurisation processes. Raw honey has anti-viral, anti-bacterial and anti-fungal properties. It promotes body and digestive health, is a powerful antioxidant, strengthens the immune system, eliminates allergies, and is an excellent remedy for skin wounds and all types of infections. Bees collect pollen from local plants and their honey often acts as an immune booster for dogs living in the locality.

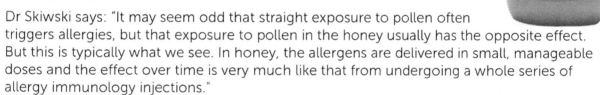

Dr Skiwski says: "It may seem odd that straight exposure to pollen often triggers allergies, but that exposure to pollen in the honey usually has the opposite effect. But this is typically what we see. In honey, the allergens are delivered in small, manageable doses and the effect over time is very much like that from undergoing a whole series of allergy immunology injections."

✓ **Mushrooms** - make sure you choose the non-poisonous ones! Dogs don't like the taste, you so may have to mask it with another food. Medicinal mushrooms are used to treat and prevent a wide array of illnesses through their use as immune stimulants and modulators, and antioxidants. The most well-known and researched are reishi, maitake, cordyceps, blazei, split-gill, turkey tail and shiitake. The mushrooms stabilise mast cells in the body, which have the histamines attached to them. Histamine is what causes much of the inflammation, redness and irritation in allergies. By helping to control histamine production, the mushrooms can moderate the effects of inflammation and even help prevent allergies in the first place.

WARNING! Mushrooms can interact with some over-the-counter and prescription drugs, so do your research as well as checking with your vet first.

✓ **Stinging Nettles** - contain biologically active compounds that reduce inflammation. Nettles have the ability to reduce the amount of histamine the body produces in response to an allergen. Nettle tea or extract can help with itching. Nettles not only help directly to decrease the itch, but also work overtime to desensitise the body to allergens, helping to reprogramme the immune system.

✓ **Quercetin** – is an over-the-counter supplement with anti-inflammatory properties. It is a strong antioxidant and reduces the body's production of histamines.

✓ **Omega-3 Fatty Acids** - these help decrease inflammation throughout the body. Adding them into the diet of all pets - particularly those struggling with seasonal environmental allergies – is very beneficial. If your dog has more itching along the top of their back and on their sides, add in a fish oil supplement. Fish oil helps to decrease the itch and heal skin lesions. The best sources of Omega 3s are krill oil, salmon oil, tuna oil, anchovy oil and other fish body oils, as well as raw organic egg yolks. If using an oil alone, it is important to give a vitamin B complex supplement.

- ✓ Coconut Oil - contains lauric acid, which helps decrease the production of yeast, a common opportunistic infection. Using a fish body oil combined with coconut oil before inflammation flares up can help moderate or even suppress your dog's inflammatory response.

Dr Skiwski adds: "Above are but a few of the over-the-counter remedies I like. In non-responsive cases, Chinese herbs can be used to work with the body to help to decrease the allergy threshold even more than with diet and supplements alone. Most of the animals I work with are on a program of Chinese herbs, diet change and acupuncture. So, the next time Fido is showing symptoms of seasonal allergies, consider rethinking your strategy to treat the root cause instead of the symptom."

With thanks to Dr Sara Skiwski, of the Western Dragon Integrated Veterinary Services, San Jose, California, for her kind permission to use her writings as the basis for this section.

This chapter has only just touched on the complex subject of skin disorders. As you can see, the causes and treatments are many and varied. One thing is true, whatever the condition, if your Labrador has a skin issue, seek a professional diagnosis <u>as soon as possible</u> before attempting to treat it yourself and before the condition becomes entrenched. Early diagnosis and treatment can sometimes nip the problem in the bud.

Some skin conditions cannot be completely cured, but they can be successfully managed, allowing your dog to live a happy, pain-free life. If you haven't got your puppy yet, ask the breeder if there is a history of skin issues or allergies/food intolerances in her bloodlines. Once you have your dog, remember that good quality diet and attention to cleanliness and grooming can go a long way in preventing and managing canine skin problems and ear infections.

13. Grooming

One advantage Labradors have over many other breeds is that, when it comes to grooming, they are fairly low maintenance. When looked after properly, a healthy Lab's coat is sleek and positively shiny, and this is especially visible on black and chocolate dogs.

Easy to look after doesn't mean non-shedding; all Labradors shed. Because of this, they are not suitable for people with dog allergies. Labradors have a double coat that sheds short hair, especially during the moulting seasons when you may find clumps of hair around the house - or your carpets are half an inch thicker! Your dog loses his winter coat in spring and grows a finer, sleeker coat, which in turn will fall out (moult or shed) to make way for the thicker, coarser coat in autumn (fall).

Unfortunately, not all Labradors contain their shedding to a convenient couple of weeks twice a year; some seem to shed hair all year round. How much and how often your dog sheds will depend on a number of factors, including genetics, skin condition, diet, and temperature of the environment (a pet dog kept in a centrally heated house will normally shed for longer than a working dog kept in an outdoor kennel, where the seasons are more evident). There is no evidence that one colour of coat sheds more than another.

The Labrador was bred to retrieve game from land and water and because of this, its coat is particularly dense, compared with many other breeds. It consists of a coarser, waterproof outer layer over a layer of thick, short hair that keeps the dog warm in the coldest of conditions and icy water.

Most breeders agree that, out of the moulting season, a weekly grooming session is usually enough for Labs - unless they have been rolling in or running through something pretty horrible, like the happy Labrador in the picture. (Photo courtesy of Guy Bunce and Chloe Spencer, Dizzywaltz Labradors, Berkshire, England).

However, despite the 'easy maintenance' coat, grooming doesn't just mean giving your Labrador a quick tickle with a brush once a week. There are other facets to grooming that play a part in keeping your dog clean and skin-related issues at bay. Time spent grooming is also time spent bonding with your dog; this physical and emotional inter-reliance brings us closer to our pets. Routine grooming sessions also allow you to examine your Lab's coat, skin, ears, teeth, eyes, paws and nails for signs of problems. Although puppies require fairly minimal brushing, it's important to get yours used to being handled and groomed from an early age; a stubborn adult Lab will not take too kindly to being handled if he is not used to it.

Other benefits of regular brushing are that it removes dead hair and skin, stimulates blood circulation and spreads natural oils throughout the coat, helping to keep it in good condition. If brushed regularly, a Labrador only needs a bath (unless he has a skin condition) when he is covered in mud, fox poo, cow manure or any other unmentionable substances that Labradors enjoy rolling in - and even eating! If you do notice an unpleasant smell - in addition to any normal gassy emissions - and he hasn't been rolling in the aforementioned organic matter, then your dog could have a yeast infection that may require a visit to the vet.

One method of removing dead hair from your Labrador and cutting down on hair shed around the house is to use a grooming tool called a Furminator (pictured, right), which thins out the dense undercoat and removes dead hair. During the moulting season you can use this tool every day or every other day and you will be surprised at the amount of hair which comes out, so make sure you use it outdoors. Normally, the Furminator for short-haired dogs is suitable for Labs. Begin at your dog's head and brush backwards towards the tail; brush strokes should always be in the direction that the hair grows, not against the fur. It's easier to do it when your dog is standing; it's OK if he prefers to sit or lie down, just make sure you cover all areas including his legs and under his belly.

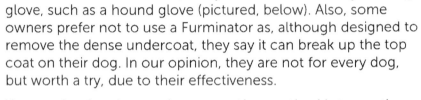

This is a highly effective grooming tool, so don't be too vigorous when you use it. It is not suitable for all Labradors; occasionally, a dog may develop bare patches or simply dislike the Furminator. This may be because he or she has a finer coat or sensitive skin, so try a softer brush or a grooming

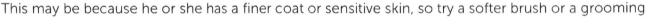

glove, such as a hound glove (pictured, below). Also, some owners prefer not to use a Furminator as, although designed to remove the dense undercoat, they say it can break up the top coat on their dog. In our opinion, they are not for every dog, but worth a try, due to their effectiveness.

You can just brush your dog, or another method is to gently squirt the coat with a fine spray of water to prevent the hairs from breaking. Then rub with a hound glove to remove loose and dead hair, and finally use a bristle brush to remove all the remaining loose hair. Bristle brushes can be expensive, but they last forever.

If your Lab is resisting your grooming efforts, take him out of his 'comfort zone' by placing him on a table or bench - make sure he can't jump off. You'd be surprised what a difference this can make once he is out of his normal environment - i.e. floor level - and at your level, where you can more easily control him. A few things to look out for when grooming are:

Acne - Little red pimples on a dog's face and chin means he has got acne. A dog can get acne at any age, not just as an adolescent. Plastic bowls can also trigger the condition, which is why stainless steel ones are often better. A daily washing followed by an application of an antibiotic cream is usually enough to get rid of the problem; if it persists it will mean a visit to your vet.

Dry skin - A dog's skin can dry out, especially with artificial heat in the winter months. If you spot any dry patches, for example on the inner thighs or armpits, or a cracked nose, massage a little petroleum jelly or baby oil on to the dry patch.

Eyes - These should be clean and clear. Cloudy eyes, particularly in an older dog, could be early signs of cataracts. Red or swollen tissue in the corner of the eye could be a symptom of cherry eye, which can affect dogs of all breeds. Ingrowing eyelashes is another issue which causes red, watery eyes. If your dog has an issue, you can start by gently bathing the eye(s) with warm water and cotton wool - but never use anything sharp; your dog can suddenly jump forwards or backwards, causing injury. If the eye is red or watering for a few days or more, get it checked out by a vet.

Ear Cleaning

It is not uncommon for some Labradors to suffer from ear infections. Breeds with pricked-up ears suffer far fewer ear infections than those with floppy years which hang down, like the Labrador. This is because an upright ear allows air to circulate inside, whereas covered inner ears are generally warm, dark and moist, making them a haven for bacteria and yeast. This can lead to recurring infections and, in severe cases, the dog going deaf or even needing a surgical operation.

Keep an eye out for redness or inflammation of the ear flap or inner ear, or a build-up of dark wax, and if your Lab has particularly hairy ears, the hair inside the ear flap should be regularly plucked to allow air to circulate more freely. Some owners with susceptible dogs bathe the inner ear with cotton wool and warm water or a veterinary ear cleaner as part of their regular grooming routine. Whether or not your dog has issues, it is good practice to check his or her ears and eyes regularly.

Tip Never put anything sharp or narrow - like a cotton bud – inside your dog's ears, as you can cause damage.

Typical signs of an ear infection are: your dog shaking his head a lot, scratching his ears, rubbing his ears on the carpet or ground, and/or an unpleasant smell coming from the ears, which is a sign of a yeast infection. If your dog exhibits any of these signs, consult your vet ASAP, as simple routine cleaning won't solve the problem, and **ear infections are notoriously difficult to get rid of** once your dog's had one. The secret is to keep your dog's ears clean, dry and free from too much hair right from puppyhood and hope that he never gets one.

One method of cleaning your Lab's ears is to get a good quality ear cleaning solution from your vet's or local pet/grooming supply shop. Then squeeze the cleaner into your Lab's ear canal and rub the ear at the base next to the skull. Allow your dog to shake his or her head and use a cotton ball to gently wipe out any dirt and waxy build up inside the ear canal.

Method Two is to use a baby wipe and gently wipe away any dirt and waxy build up. In both cases it is important to only clean as far down the ear canal as you can see to avoid damaging the eardrum. The first method is preferred if you are also bathing your dog, as it will remove any unwanted water that may have got down into the ears during the bath. See **Chapter 12. Skin and Allergies** for more information on ear infections.

Nail Trimming

If your Labrador is regularly exercised on grass or other soft surfaces, his nails may not be getting worn down sufficiently, so they may have to be clipped or filed. Nails should be kept short for the paws to remain healthy. Long nails interfere with the dog's gait, making walking awkward or painful and they can also break easily, usually at the base of the nail where blood vessels and nerves are located. Get your dog used to having his paws inspected from puppyhood; it's also a good opportunity to check for other problems, such as cracked pads or interdigital cysts. (These are swellings between the toes, often due to a bacterial infection). Be prepared: many dogs dislike having their nails trimmed, so it requires patience and persistence on your part.

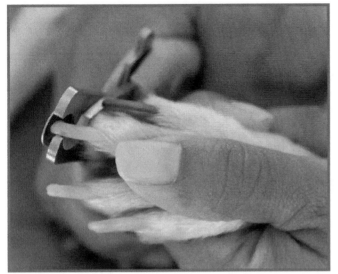

To trim your dog's nails, use a specially designed clipper. Most have safety guards to prevent you cutting the nails too short. Do it before they get too long; if you can hear the nails clicking on the floor, they're too long. You want to trim only the ends, before 'the quick,' which is a blood vessel inside the nail. You can see where the quick ends on a white nail, but not on a dark nail. Clip only the hook-like part of the nail that turns down. Start trimming gently, a nail or two at a time, and your dog will learn that you're not going to hurt him. If you accidentally cut the quick, stop the bleeding with some styptic powder.

Another option is to file your dog's nails with a nail grinder tool. Some dogs may have tough nails that are hard to trim and this may be less stressful for your dog, with less chance of pain or bleeding. The grinder is like an electric nail file and only removes a small amount of nail at a time. Some owners prefer to use one as it is harder to cut the quick, and many dogs prefer them to a clipper. However, you have to introduce your Lab gradually to the grinder - they often don't like the noise or vibration at first. If you find it impossible to clip your dog's nails, or you are at all worried about doing it, take him to a vet or a groomer - and ask him or her to squeeze your dog's anal sacs while he's there!

And while we're discussing the less appealing end of your Labrador, let's dive straight in and talk about anal sacs. Sometimes called scent glands, these are a pair of glands located inside your dog's anus that give off a scent when he has a bowel movement. You won't want to hear this, but problems with impacted anal glands are not uncommon in dogs! When a dog passes firm stools, the glands normally empty themselves, but soft poo(p) or diarrhoea can mean that not enough pressure is exerted to empty the glands, causing discomfort to the dog. If they become infected, this results in swelling and pain. In extreme cases one or both anal glands can be removed.

If your dog drags himself along on his rear end - 'scooting' - or tries to lick or scratch his anus, he could well have impacted anal glands that need squeezing, also called expressing - either by you if you know how to do it, your vet or a groomer. (He might also have worms). Either way, it pays to keep an eye on both ends of your dog!

Bathing Your Labrador

If you groom your Labrador every week, you shouldn't need to bathe him very often – unless, as mentioned, he's been rolling in something smelly. If your dog regularly returns from his daily walks covered in mud, some owners hose the dog down before allowing him back into the house. This is perfectly acceptable; a Labrador's coat is designed to cope with water. But do not regularly use shampoos or other products (unless advised to do so by a vet), as a dog needs to keep his coat naturally oily and shampoos rid the coat of its natural oils.

Never use human shampoos on your Lab as these will only irritate his skin. A dog's skin has a different pH to that of a human. If you do occasionally use a shampoo on your Labrador, use one specially medicated for dogs - such as Malaseb or similar. It is expensive, but lasts a long time. There is also a wide range of shampoos for dogs containing natural organic ingredients.

If a Labrador is left in a dirty condition, this can also cause problems, as it can cause irritation, leading to scratching and excessive shedding. It's all a question of getting the balance right, and this will to some extent depend on how much outdoor exercise your Lab gets, what sort of areas he's running in, how often he swims, whether he is kept indoors or outdoors and what his natural skin condition is like.

 And if you do bathe your dog, or if your dog enjoys swimming, we recommend you carefully dry inside your dog's ears using a towel or large pad of cotton wool every time he gets wet. While your Labrador may love water, the inside of his ears most certainly don't.

Teeth Cleaning

Veterinary studies show that by the age of three, 80% of dogs show signs of gum disease. Symptoms include yellow and brown build-up of tartar along the gum line, red inflamed gums and persistent bad breath.

You can give your dog a daily dental treat, such as Dentastix or Nylabone, or regularly give him a large raw bone (but not chicken, as this splinters) to help with dental hygiene, but you should also brush your Lab's teeth every now and again.

Take things slowly in the beginning and give your dog lots of praise. Labradors love your attention (and food) and many will start looking forward to teeth brushing sessions - especially if they like the flavour of the toothpaste! Use a pet toothpaste, as the human variety can upset a canine's stomach. The real benefit comes from the actual action of the brush on the teeth, and various brushes, sponges and pads are available - the choice depends on factors such as the health of your dog's gums, the size of his mouth and how good you are at teeth cleaning.

Get your dog used to the toothpaste by letting him lick some off your finger when he is young. If he doesn't like the flavour, try a different one. Continue this until he looks forward to licking the paste - it might be instant or take days.

Put a small amount on your finger and gently rub it on one of the big canine teeth at the front of his mouth. Then get him used to the toothbrush or dental sponge - praise him when he licks it - for several days. The next step is to actually start brushing.

Lift his upper lip gently and place the brush at a 45º angle to the gum line. Gently move the brush backwards and forwards. Start just with his front teeth and then gradually do a few more. You don't need to brush the inside of his teeth as his tongue keeps them relatively free of plaque. With a bit of encouragement and patience, it can become an enjoyable, bonding experience for you both.

As you can see, grooming isn't just about brushing your Labrador once a week. Hopefully yours will thrive without too much maintenance, but some Labs do require that little extra bit of care to stay healthy; it's all part of the bargain when you decide to get a dog.

14. The Birds and the Bees

Judging by the number of questions our website receives from owners who ask about the canine reproductive cycle and breeding their dogs, there is a lot of confusion about the doggie

facts of life out there.

Some owners want to know whether they should breed their dog, while others ask if and at what age they should have their dog neutered – this term can refer to both the spaying of females and the castration of males.

Owners of females often ask when she will come on heat, how long this will last and how often it will occur. Sometimes they want to know how you can tell if a female is pregnant or how long a pregnancy lasts. So here, in a nutshell, is a chapter on the facts of life as far as Labradors are concerned.

....

Females and Heat

Just like all other mammal females, including humans, a female Labrador has a menstrual cycle - or to be more accurate, an oestrus cycle. This is the period of time when she is ready (and willing!) for mating and is more commonly called *heat* or being *on heat*, *in heat* or *in season*.

A female Labrador has her first cycle from about six to nine months old. However, there are some bloodlines with longer spans between heat cycles and the female may not have her first heat until she is 10 months to one year old. A UK breeders said that one of her bitches did not have her first season until the age of 18 months.

She will generally come on heat every six to nine months, although some bitches may only have one cycle per year. The timescale also becomes more erratic with old age in unsprayed females. It can also be irregular with young dogs when cycles first begin.

On average, the heat cycle will lasts around 21 days, but can be anything from seven to 10 days up to four weeks. Within this period there will be several days in the middle of the cycle that will be the optimum time for her to get pregnant. This phase is called the *oestrus*. (One breeder added: "I know of one owner whose dog mated accidently on Day 22 – it resulted in a single pup).

The third phase, called *dioestrus*, begins immediately following oestrus. During this time, her body will produce hormones whether or not she is pregnant. Her body thinks and acts like she is pregnant. All the hormones are present; only the puppies are missing. This can sometimes lead to what is known as a 'false pregnancy'.

Responsible Labrador breeders wait until a female is fully health tested, has had one or two heat cycles and is **at least** one year old before mating. Females should not be used for breeding too early; pregnancy draws on their calcium reserves that they need for their own growing bones. And if a female breeds too early, she may break down structurally and have more health issues in later life. Good breeders also limit the number of litters from each female, as breeding can take a lot out of them.

To protect females from overbreeding, the UK's Kennel Club introduced Breeding Restrictions in 2012. Now it will not register a litter from any bitch:

1. That has already had four litters.

2. If she is less than one year old at the time of mating.

3. If she is eight years or older when she whelps (gives birth).

4. If the litter is the result of any mating between father and daughter, mother and son or brother and sister.

5. If she has already had two C-Sections (Caesarean Sections).

Breeders then spend considerable time researching a suitable mate. The Kennel Club's Mate Select programme at www.thekennelclub.org.uk/services/public/mateselect is an excellent tool. It enables breeders to check the health test results of a potential mate, and also gives a figure for the Coefficient of Inbreeding, to ensure that the dog they are thinking of mating theirs with is not too closely related, which can lead to unhealthy puppies.

Heat

While a female dog is on heat, she produces hormones that attract male dogs. Because dogs have a sense of smell thousands of times stronger than ours, your girl on heat is a magnet for all the males in the neighbourhood. It is believed that they can detect the scent of a female on heat up to two miles away!

They may congregate around your house or follow you around the park (if you are foolish enough to venture out there while she is in season), waiting for their chance to prove their manhood – or mutthood in their case. One UK breeder added: "A 15 year old Norfolk Terrier used to turn up on my doorstep every time my bitch was in season. He travelled from 1.2 km away!"

Don't expect your precious Labrador princess to be fussy. Her hormones are raging when she is on heat and, during her most fertile days, she is ready, able and ... VERY willing! As she approaches the optimum time for mating, you may notice her tail bending slightly to one side. She will also start to urinate more frequently. This is her signal to all those virile male dogs out there that she is ready for mating.

The first visual sign of heat that you may notice is that her vulva (external sex organ, or pink bit under her tail) becomes swollen, which she will lick to keep herself clear. She will then bleed; this is sometimes called spotting. It will be a light red or brown at the beginning of the heat cycle, turning more watery later. Some females can bleed quite heavily; this is normal. But if you have any concerns, contact your vet to be on the safe side.

She may also start to 'mate' with your leg, other dogs or objects. These are all normal signs of heat.

Some females naturally want to keep themselves clean by licking; others don't. If your girl is messy and leaves an unwanted trail around the house when she is on heat, cover anything you don't want stained and you might also consider using disposable doggie diapers/nappies or reusable sanitary pants (pictured).

Although breeding requires specialised knowledge on the part of the owner, it does not stop a female on heat from being extremely interested in attention from any old mutt! To avoid an unwanted pregnancy you must keep a close eye on your female and not allow her to freely wander

where she may come into contact with other dogs when she is on heat- and that includes the garden, unless it is 100% dog proof.

It is amazing the lengths some entire (uncastrated) males will go to impregnate a female on heat. Travelling great distances to follow her scent, jumping over barriers, digging under fences, chewing through doors or walls and sneaking through hedges are just some of the tactics employed by randy males on the loose. Some dogs living in the same house as a bitch in season have even been known to mate with her through the bars of a crate. If you do have an entire male, you need to physically keep him in a separate place, perhaps with an understanding friend, outdoor kennel or even boarding kennels. The desire to mate is all-consuming can be accompanied by howling or 'marking' (urinating) indoors from your frustrated male.

There is no canine contraceptive and the only sure fire way of preventing your female from becoming pregnant is spaying. (There is a "morning after pill" – actually a series of oestrogen tablets or an injection - which some vets may administer, but reported side effects are severe, including Pyometra, bone marrow suppression and infertility).

Avoid taking your female out in public places while she is in season, and certainly don't let her off the lead if you are away from home. During this time you can compensate for these restrictions by playing more indoor or garden games to keep her mentally and physically active.

You can buy a spray which masks the natural oestrus scent of your female. Marketed under such attractive names as "Bitch Spray," these will lessen the scent but not eliminate it. They might be useful for reducing the amount of unwanted attention, but are not a complete deterrent.

Unlike women, female dogs do not go through the menopause and can have puppies even when they are quite old. However, a litter for an elderly female (older than seven years) is not advisable as it can result in complications – both for the mother and the pups.

Neutering - Pros and Cons

Once a straightforward subject, this is currently a hot topic in the dog world. My own opinion is that dogs which are kept purely as pets – i.e. not for showing or working – should be spayed or neutered, and that the advantages of doing so far outweigh the disadvantages. That is what we have always done with our dogs and will continue to do so. However, there are those who disagree.

Armed with the facts, it is for each individual owner to decide what is best for their dog.

A major argument for neutering is that there is already too much indiscriminate breeding of dogs in the world. As you will read in the **Chapter 15. Labrador Rescue**, it is estimated that 1,000 dogs are put to sleep **every hour** in the USA alone. It is for this reason that rescue organisations in the UK, North America and Australia neuter all dogs that they rehome. Some areas in the Unites States, e.g. LA, have even adopted a compulsory sterilisation policy: www.avma.org/Advocacy/StateAndLocal/Pages/sr-spay-neuter-laws.aspx aimed at "reducing and eventually eliminating the thousands of euthanizations conducted in Los Angeles' animal shelters every year." The RSPCA, along with most UK vets, also promotes the benefits of neutering: www.rspca.org.uk/adviceandwelfare/pets/general/neutering. In the UK it is estimated that more than half of all dogs are spayed or castrated.

Another point is that you may not have a choice. It is not uncommon for Puppy Contracts from recognised KC and AKC Labrador breeders to stipulate that, except in special circumstances, you agree to neuter the dog as a Condition of Sale. As one UK breeder explained: "When registering my pups I put a breeding restriction on the pedigree, so that any of their future puppies cannot be registered by the Kennel Club without my agreement. I always make it clear to the owners that I will not unreasonably withhold this, but I expect all dogs in a mating to have the same level of health checks that I have gone to the trouble of ensuring my dogs have."

The other side of the coin is that there is recent scientific evidence that neutering – and especially early neutering - can have a detrimental effect on the dog's health, with increased risk of joint disease or cancer. Even if you wait until the dog is older neutering can, in some cases, still have an effect on a dog's health. This has to be weighed against the very real life-threatening risk of Pyometra in unspayed middle- aged females.

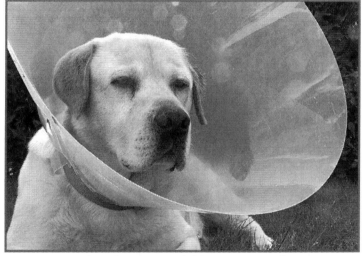

As yet, only a few studies have been done, so nothing is written in stone. It is however fair to say that recent scientific research has highlighted potential issues that people were not previously aware of. Many vets and rescue organisations advise spaying or castrating puppies at just a few months old to reduce unwanted pregnancies. However, in the light of the new evidence, **if you are intending to neuter your dog, it is probably worth waiting until he or she is at least one year old.**

One study often quoted is "Neutering Dogs: Effects on Joint Disorders and Cancers in Golden Retrievers," by Gretel Torres de la Riva, Benjamin L. Hart , Thomas B. Farver, Anita M. Oberbauer, Locksley L. McV. Messam, Neil Willits, Lynette A. Hart, published in 2013. It can be read online at: http://journals.plos.org/plosone/article?id=10.1371/journal.pone.0055937

The study involved 759 Goldens and found that the incidence of Hip Dysplasia doubled and Lymphosarcoma (a blood cancer) trebled in males neutered before one year of age. Late-spayed females were four times more likely to contact Hemangiosarcoma (a blood vessel cancer) than those which were intact or spayed before one year old. The scientists followed this up a year later with another study comparing the effects on Golden Retrievers with those on Labradors and found that the results were not as dramatic for Labs. Labradors neutered before six months old had twice the risk of Hip Dysplasia, while the risk was four to five times higher for Goldens. There was a slight increase in cancers with neutered females, compared with unneutered, while the risk was three to four times higher in Golden Retrievers. (It should be pointed out that Goldens in general have a higher incidence of cancer than Labs, regardless of whether or not the dog is neutered).

In response to a Labrador owner's question following this second study, scientist Benjamin Hart wrote: "Our data, presented in the paper, shows that spaying female Labs before 6 months old, and indeed before 1 year of age, significantly doubles the risk of the dog acquiring at least one joint disorder. Hip dysplasia is the main joint disorder affected. So I suggest your delay the spay until your female is a year of age. You will see in this new paper that mammary cancer is not increased in incidence by delaying spaying until the female is at least a year of age."

Spaying

Spaying is the term traditionally used to describe the sterilisation of a female dog so that she cannot become pregnant. This is normally done by a procedure called an 'ovariohysterectomy' and involves the removal of the ovaries and uterus (womb). Although this is a routine operation, it is major abdominal surgery and she has to be anaesthetised.

One less invasive option offered by some vets is an 'ovariectomy', which removes the ovaries, but leaves the womb intact. It requires only a small incision and can even be carried out by laparoscopy (keyhole surgery). The dog is anaesthetised for a shorter time and there is less risk of infection or excess bleeding during surgery. One major reason often given for not opting for an ovariectomy is that the female still runs the risk of the life-threatening disease Pyometra (infection of the uterus or womb) later in life. However, there is currently little or no scientific evidence of females that have undergone an ovariectomy contracting Pyometra at a later date.

Your vet may encourage you to have your dog spayed while she is still a puppy. As you have just read, there is increasing scientific evidence that early spaying can, in some cases, have a detrimental effect on later health. However, if a female is spayed before her first heat cycle, she will have an almost zero risk of mammary cancer (the equivalent of breast cancer in women). Even after the first heat, spaying reduces the risk of this cancer by 92%. Some vets claim that the risk of mammary cancer in unspayed female dogs can be as high as one in four. Another consideration is Pyometra, infection of the womb or uterus, which is a serious threat for unsprayed middle-aged dogs.

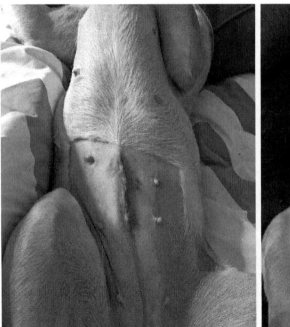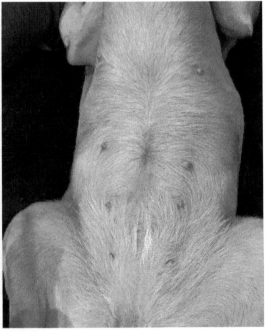

These photographs are reproduced courtesy of Guy Bunce and Chloe Spencer, of Dizzywaltz Labradors, Berkshire, England. The one on the left shows four-year-old Disney shortly after spaying (ovariohysterectomy). The one on the right shows Disney completely healed a few weeks later.

Spaying is a much more serious operation for a female than neutering is for a male. This is because it involves an internal abdominal operation, whereas the neutering procedure is carried out on the male's testicles, which are outside his abdomen. As with any major procedure, there are pros and cons to spaying.

For:

- Spaying prevents infections, cancer and other diseases of the uterus and ovaries
- A spayed bitch will have a greatly reduced risk of mammary cancer
- Spaying eliminates the risk of the potentially fatal disease Pyometra, which results from hormonal changes in the female's reproductive tract and affects many unspayed middle-aged females
- It reduces hormonal changes that can interfere with the treatment of diseases like diabetes or epilepsy
- Spaying can reduce behaviour problems, such as roaming, aggression towards other dogs, anxiety or fear (not all canine experts agree with this)
- You don't have to guard your female against unwanted attention from males as she will no longer have heat cycles
- You no longer have to cope with any potential mess caused by bleeding inside the house during heat cycles
- A University of Georgia study involving 40,000 death records from the Veterinary Medical Database from 1984-2004, found that sterilised dogs lived on average 1.5 years longer: http://journals.plos.org/plosone/article?id=10.1371/journal.pone.0061082
- A spayed dog does not contribute to the pet overpopulation problem

Against:

- There is some scientific evidence that spaying and neutering before 12 months of age can lead to physical or behavioural issues in some dogs. You can read more here: www.dogsnaturallymagazine.com/three-reasons-to-reconsider-spayneuter and at www.akcchf.org/news-events/news/health-implications-in-early.html
- Complications can occur, including an abnormal reaction to the anaesthetic, bleeding, stitches breaking and infections; **these are not common**
- Occasionally there can be long-term effects connected to hormonal changes. These include weight gain or less stamina, which can occur years after spaying
- Older females may suffer some urinary incontinence, but it only affects a few spayed females - discuss it with your vet
- Cost. This can range from £100 to £300 in the UK (approximately $150-$500 at a vet's practice in the USA, or around $50 at a low cost clinic, for those that qualify)

If you talk to a vet or a volunteer at a rescue shelter, they will say that the advantages of spaying far outweigh any disadvantages. If you have a female puppy, when you take her in for her puppy vaccinations, discuss with your vet whether, and at what age, spaying would be a good idea for your Labrador.

Neutering

Neutering male dogs involves castration; the removal of the testicles. This can be a difficult decision for some owners, as it causes a drop in the pet's testosterone levels, which some humans – men in particular! - feel affects the quality of their dog's life.

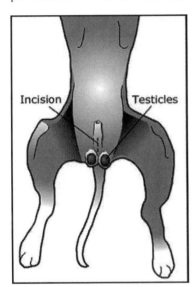

Fortunately, dogs do not think like people and male dogs do not miss their testicles or the loss of sex. Our own experience is that our dog Max is much happier having been neutered. We decided to have him neutered after he went missing three times on walks – he ran off on the scent of a female on heat. Fortunately, he is micro-chipped and has our phone number on a tag on his collar and we were very lucky that he was returned to us on all three occasions.

There are some who say that neutering does not affect a dog's behaviour. Of course, every dog is different. All I can say on a personal level is that after neutering Max stopped running off on walks, although his behaviour remained unchanged in all other respects.

Unless you specifically want to breed, work or show your dog, or he has a special job, neutering is recommended by animal rescue organisations and vets. Even then, Labradors working for Guide Dogs for the Blind, Hearing Dogs for Deaf People and Dogs for the Disabled are routinely neutered and this does not impair their ability to perform their duties.

There are countless unwanted puppies, many of which are destroyed. There is also the problem of a lack of knowledge from the owners of some breeding dogs, resulting in the production of poor puppies with congenital health or temperament problems.

Although technically neutering can be carried out at any age over eight weeks, provided both testicles have descended, recent research is definitely coming down on the side of waiting until the dog is at least one year old.

Surgery is relatively straightforward, and much less of a major operation for a male than spaying is for a female. Complications are less common and less severe than with spaying. Although he will feel tender afterwards, your dog should return to his normal self within a couple of days. Dogs neutered before puberty tend to grow a little larger than dogs done later. This is because testosterone is involved in the process that stops growth, so the bones grow for longer without testosterone.

When he comes out of surgery, his scrotum (the sacs that held the testicles) will be swollen and it may look like nothing has been done. But it is normal for these to slowly shrink in the days following surgery. Here are the main pros and cons:

For:

🐾 Behaviour problems such as aggression and wandering off are reduced (again, some experts disagree with this)

🐾 Unwanted sexual behaviour, such as mounting people or objects, is usually reduced or eliminated

🐾 Testicular problems such as infections, cancer and torsion (painful rotation of the testicle) are eradicated

🐾 Prostate disease, common in older male dogs, is less likely to occur

- A submissive entire (un-neutered) male dog may be targeted by other dogs. After he has been neutered, he will no longer produce testosterone and so will not be regarded as much of a threat by the other males, so he is less likely to be bullied
- A neutered dog is not fathering unwanted puppies

Against:

- As with any surgery, there can be bleeding afterwards, you should keep an eye on him for any blood loss after the operation. Infections can also occur, generally caused by the dog licking the wound, so try and prevent him doing this. If he persists, use an Elizabethan collar (or E-collar, a large plastic collar from the vet). In the **vast majority** of cases, these problems do not occur
- Some dogs' coats may be affected (this also applies to spaying); supplementing the diet with fish oil can compensate for this
- Cost - this starts at around £80 in the UK (in the USA this might cost upwards from $100 at a private veterinary clinic or from $50 at a low cost or Humane Society clinic)

Two other phrases you may hear when discussing are 'tubal ligation' or 'vasectomy'. Many veterinary papers have been written on these topics but as yet, not many vets offer them as options, possibly because they have not been trained to carry out these procedures at vet school. The first is the tying of a female's Fallopian tubes and the second is the clamping shut of the sperm ducts from the male's testicles. In both procedures, the dog continues to produce hormones (unlike with spaying and neutering), but is unable to get pregnant or father puppies.

Myths

Here are some common myths about neutering and spaying:

Neutering or spaying will spoil the dog's character - There is no evidence that any of the positive characteristics of your dog will be altered. He or she will be just as loving, playful and loyal. Neutering may reduce aggression or roaming, especially in male dogs, because they are no longer competing to mate with a female.

A female needs to have at least one litter - There is no proven physical or mental benefit to a female having a litter.

Mating is natural and necessary - We tend to ascribe human emotions to our dogs, but they do not think emotionally about sex or having and raising a family. Unlike humans, their desire to mate or breed is entirely physical, triggered by the chemicals called hormones within their body. Without these hormones – i.e. after neutering or spaying – the desire disappears or is greatly reduced.

Male dogs will behave better if they can mate - This is simply not true; sex does not make a dog behave better. In fact, it can have the opposite effect. Having mated once, a male may show an increased interest in females. He may also consider his status elevated, which may make him harder to control or call back.

Pregnancy

A canine pregnancy will normally last for 58 to 65 days, regardless of the size or breed of the dog. Sometimes pregnancy is referred to as the *'gestation period.'*

It's a good idea to take a female for a pre-natal check-up after mating. The vet should answer any questions you may have about type of food, supplements and extra care needed, as well as informing you about any physical changes likely to occur in your female.

There is a blood test available that measures levels of *relaxin*. This is a hormone produced by the ovary and the developing placenta, and pregnancy can be detected by monitoring relaxin levels as early as three weeks after mating. The levels are high throughout pregnancy and then decline rapidly after the female has given birth.

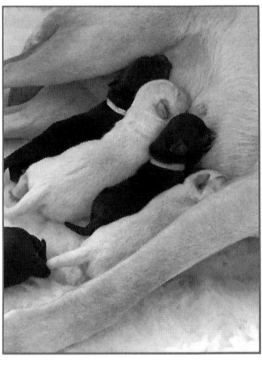

A vet can usually see the puppies using Ultrasound from around the same time. X-rays carried out five or more weeks into the pregnancy give the breeder a good idea of the number of puppies. They can also help to give the vet more information, which is particularly useful if the bitch has had previous whelping problems. (Photo courtesy of Guy Bunce and Chloe Spencer, Dizzywaltz Labradors, Berkshire).

Here are some of the signs of pregnancy:

* After mating, many females become more affectionate. (However, some will become uncharacteristically irritable and maybe even a little aggressive)

* The female may produce a slight clear discharge from her vagina about one month after mating

* Three or four weeks after mating, a few females experience morning sickness – if this is the case, feed little and often. She may seem more tired than usual

* She may seem slightly depressed and/or show a drop in appetite. These signs can also mean there are other problems, so you should consult your vet

* Her teats (nipples) will become more prominent, pink and erect 25 to 30 days into the pregnancy. Later on, you may notice a fluid coming from them

* After about 35 days, or seven weeks, her body weight will noticeably increase

* Her abdomen will become noticeably larger from around day 40, although first-time mums and females carrying few puppies may not show as much

* Many pregnant females' appetite will increase in the second half of pregnancy

* Her nesting instincts will kick in as the delivery date approaches. She may seem restless or scratch her bed or the floor

* During the last week of pregnancy, females often start to look for a safe place for whelping. Some seem to become confused, wanting to be with their owners and at the same time wanting to prepare their nest. Even if the female is having a C-section, she should still be

allowed to nest in a whelping box with layers of newspaper, which she will scratch and dig as the time approaches

If your female becomes pregnant – either by design or accident - your first step should be to consult a vet.

Litter Size

According to the breeders involved in this book, this varies considerably from one Lab to another, but they often have medium to large litters. An average might be seven or eight puppies, but it could range from two to 13.

False Pregnancies

As many as 50% or more of intact (unspayed) females may display signs of a false pregnancy. In the wild it was common for female dogs to have false pregnancies and to lactate (produce milk). This female would then nourish puppies if their own mother died.

False pregnancies occur 60 to 80 days after the female was in heat - about the time she would have given birth – and are generally nothing to worry about for an owner. The exact cause is unknown, however, hormonal imbalances are thought to play an important role. Some dogs have shown symptoms within three to four days of spaying, these include:

- ❖ Making a nest
- ❖ Producing milk (lactating)
- ❖ Mothering or adopting toys and other objects
- ❖ Appetite fluctuations
- ❖ Barking or whining a lot
- ❖ Restlessness, depression or anxiety
- ❖ Swollen abdomen
- ❖ She might even appear to go into labour

Try not to touch your dog's nipples, as touch will stimulate further milk production. If she is licking herself repeatedly, she may need an E-collar to minimise stimulation. To help reduce and eliminate milk production, you can apply cool compresses to the nipples

Under no circumstances should you restrict your Labrador's water supply to try and prevent her from producing milk. This is dangerous as she can become dehydrated.

Some unspayed bitches may have a false pregnancy with each heat cycle. Spaying during a false pregnancy may actually prolong the condition, so better to wait until it is over and then have her spayed to prevent it happening again. False pregnancy is not a disease, but an exaggerated response to normal hormonal changes. Owners should be reassured that even if left untreated, the condition almost always resolves itself.

However, if your Labrador appears physically ill or the behavioural changes are severe enough to worry you, visit your vet, who may prescribe tranquilisers to relieve anxiety, or diuretics to reduce milk production and relieve fluid retention. In rare cases, hormone treatment may be necessary.

Generally, dogs experiencing false pregnancies do not have serious long-term problems, as the behaviour disappears when the hormones return to their normal levels in two to three weeks.

One exception is **Pyometra**, a disease mainly affecting unspayed middle-aged females, caused by a hormonal abnormality. Pyometra follows a heat cycle in which fertilisation did not occur and the dog typically starts showing symptoms within two to four months.

Commonly referred to as 'pyo', there are 'open' and 'closed' forms of the disease. Open pyo is usually easy to identify with a smelly discharge, so prompt treatment is easy. Closed pyo is often harder to identify and you may not even notice anything until your girl becomes feverish and lethargic. When this happens, it is very serious and time is of the essence. Typically, vets will recommend immediately spaying in an effort to save the bitch's life.

Signs of Pyometra are excessive drinking and urination, with the female trying to lick a white discharge from her vagina. She may also have a slight temperature. If the condition becomes severe, her back legs will become weak, possibly to the point where she can no longer get up without help. Pyometra is serious if bacteria take a hold, and in extreme cases it can be fatal. It is also relatively common and needs to be dealt with promptly by a vet, who will give the dog intravenous fluids and antibiotics for several days. In most cases this is followed by spaying.

Should I Breed From My Lab?

The short and simple answer is: Unless you know exactly what you are doing or have expert help, **NO, leave it to the experts.** You need specialist knowledge to successfully breed healthy Labradors with good temperaments that conform to the Breed Standard, but the rising cost of puppies and increasing number of dog owners is tempting more people to consider breeding their dogs.

Prices for Labrador puppies vary from area to area so it's hard to give an exact figure. A straw poll among the 29 breeders involved in this book reveal that you can expect to pay an average of £600 to £900 for a fully health-tested puppy from a Kennel Club Assured Breeder, depending on where you live on the country; Northern Ireland is slightly cheaper. If a pup has show or field trial champion ancestors, expect to pay more. In the USA, prices range a lot from state to state, but a figure of $1,500-$2,500 dollars would not be out of the ordinary for an AKC-registered fully health tested pup.

You can't just put any two dogs together and expect perfect, healthy puppies every time; ethical and successful breeding is much more scientific and time consuming than that. Inexperience can result in poor specimens of the breed or tragic consequences, with the loss of pups - or even the mother. Many approved breeders will insist in their Puppy Contract that you have your pup spayed or neutered to protect the integrity and health of the breed.

Sometimes a C-section (Caesarean section) may be necessary. In the UK, all C-sections have to be registered with the Kennel Club. These are carried out when the mother is unable to birth the pups naturally – and timing is critical. Too early and the pups may be underdeveloped or the mother can bleed to death; too late and the pups can die.

A major study published in 2010 carried out jointly by the BSAVA (British Small Animal Veterinary Association) and the UK's Kennel Club looked at 13,141 bitches from 151 breeds and the incidence of C-Sections over a 10-year period. The resulting report at: http://bit.ly/2cV6MF3. revealed that some 20% or Labradors involved in the study had to have C-Sections. Although anecdotal evidence suggests that the overall percentage is now lower. And since 2012, the UK's Kennel Club will no longer register puppies from a female who has had more than two C-Sections, "except for scientifically proven welfare reasons and in such cases normally provided that the application is made prior to mating."

Anyone who thinks it is easy money should bear in mind that breeding healthy Labs to type is a complex, expensive and time-consuming business when all the fees, DNA and health tests, care, nutrition and medical expenses have been taken into account.

Breeding Costs

Breeder Trudy Williams, of Yaffleswood Labradors, West Sussex, has been kind enough to share details of her bitch Amber's litter in December 2015. The following table not only provides a total breakdown of costs (£1 = approximately US$1.30), but also gives an insight into the stress and trauma that breeding can cause.

BEFORE BREEDING	
Hips & elbows scored, anaesthetic, X-ray & BVA fees	£462.00
Annual eye test	£40.00
PRA genetic test (Not required if your bitch is genetically clear)	£78.00
COMING INTO SEASON	
Bitch came in to season unexpectedly early, so pre-mate tests were done a few times to establish optimum time to breed = 3 x £55	£165.00
Stud fees - generally good to mate twice 2 days apart	£550.00
PREGNANCY	
Ultrasound scan - At about 5 weeks it is possible to have a scan to establish if there are pups and a rough number count	£69.00
Worming = 2 x £39.29	£78.58
Additional Food Natural Instinct, beef mince, eggs, Lactol, puppy food (for bitch)	£185.00
EQUIPMENT	
Whelping box (can use cardboard box for a one-off, but not very hygienic)	£60.00
Vet bed	£50.00
Thermometer, feeding bottles, hibiscrub, etc.	£35.00
Coloured collars for puppies - 2 sets as they wear out during 8 weeks	£17.98
Heat mat	£35.49
Hot water bottle	£8.00
Old towels from charity shop washed, clean	Free
Cardboard box for new-born puppies	Free
(You may also incur costs setting up a secure area/run for when the puppies are mobile)	
LABOUR & BIRTH	
Around midday Amber was restless, panting & digging, but no contractions. Stayed up- all night	
watching her (this was five days earlier than expected)	
Restlessness & digging continued through day, but no contractions, Amber getting distressed & tired	

Vet home visit to check up on her in afternoon	£48.00
Vet home visit + oxytocin to start contractions at 6.30pm	£59.70
Puppies started at 8.30pm but all very slow & contractions poor. Everything stopped at11pm after 6 puppies. (Normally Lab pups weigh c500g. The first boy weighed 175g. Others were 350g-390g	
Had a feeling there were more so went to emergency vets at 1am, - 2nd night with no sleep	
Consultation after 10pm	£130.53
X-rays to check if any puppies were left	£139.00
More oxytocin as X-ray showed 1 puppy	£9.59
Went home & waited for contractions but none started. At this stage mum is great & feeding & cleaning pups. But we have to keep an eye on the tiny little boy & help him to latch on	
Went back to emergency vet at 4.30am – more oxytocin	£9.59
No contractions so left Amber at vet's for a Caesarian Section &prospect of a dead puppy	£1,048.55
Tramadol. 1 puppy found dead & could not be revived, 1 healthy little pup still alive	£4.26
In meantime we are hand-feeding all the puppies continually. We bring mum & pups home pm	
Follow-up check with own vet on Saturday morning	£21.00
More dressings for Caesarean wound	£5.32
By evening Amber was not right, panting heavily & was not producing enough milk to feed the pups - visit to emergency vets again as suspected eclampsia - Consultation charge	£39.60
Blood tests	£60.77
More dressings	£1.10
Amber was fine, but not feeding. Needed better feeding bottles for pups	£31.68
Again I was up all night hand-feeding pups & through day for next 48 hrs when Amber's milk finally came back.	
Home visit by vet to health-check pups	£48.00
Dressings 2 x £5.32	£10.64
Prokolin for Amber's upset tummy	£33.36
Antibiotics to treat Amber's mastitis	£29.16
Again had to top up the pups a bit with hand-feeding as they were not quite able to get enough milk	
THE PUPPIES	
Vet check on Yogi - tiny puppy had large umbilical hernia	£21.00
Vaccinations & microchipping = 7 x £49.65	£347.54
Kennel Club registration = 7 x £16.00	£112.00
1 puppy had cystitis; antibiotics & consultation	£34.80
Operation on Yogi to correct umbilical hernia. I was not prepared to let pup leave with this, so it was operated on & I kept him longer to ensure he recovered well before going to his new home	£244.45
FOOD – POST BIRTH	
Extra food for Amber - Natural Instinct, beef mince, eggs, Lactol, puppy food (for Amber)	£200
Lactol for Amber = 2 x £15.16	£30.32

Puppy Food – Lactol 2 x £15.16	£30.32
Natural Instinct weaning 5 x £3.50	£17.50
Natural instinct puppy = 18 x £3.25	£58.50
James Wellbeloved puppy = 1 x 15kg	£50.00
Bag of food for going home = 6 x £10	£60.00
Various other sundries	£150.00
COST OF BREEDING AND RAISING 7 PUPS	**£4,921.13**
Sale of 6 pups @ £750.00 (kept 1 pup)	£4,500.00
For 8 weeks work!	**-£421.13**

Wow! Who would believe that can cost so much to breed good Labradors? The total expenses were £4,874.58 (US$6,337). Seven puppies were born and Trudy kept one of them. The remaining six were each sold for £750 (US$975), giving a total of £4,500 (US$5,850). You don't have to be Einstein to realise that this works out at a financial loss on the litter.

For eight weeks of hard work, Trudy ended up with a net loss of £374.58 (US$487). Of course, this involved some medical issues with both mother and pups – but don't think that this is rare; it isn't. Trudy added: "We were unlucky that just everything seemed to go wrong for Amber." However, if you are serious about breeding your dog, be prepared to part with considerable hard cash for medical expenses, especially if things go wrong.

In short, breeding healthy Labradors to type is a complex issue. Responsible breeding is backed up by genetic information and screening as well as a thorough knowledge of the desired characteristics of the Lab. Breeding is not just about the look or colour of the dogs; health and temperament are important factors too. Many people do not realise that the single most important factor governing health and certain temperament traits is genetics.

These two beautiful pups are both from Amber's loss-making litter of December 2015. On the left is Mabel and on the right is Talli. Photos courtesy of Trudy Williams.

Ask Yourself This...

1. Did I get my Labrador from a good, ethical breeder? Dogs sold in pet stores and on general sales websites are seldom good specimens and can be unhealthy.

2. Are my dog and his or her close relatives free from health issues? Joint or eye issues are just some of the illnesses Lab pups can inherit. Are you 100% sure your breeding dog is free from them all? Also, an unhealthy female is also more likely to have trouble with pregnancy and whelping.

3. Does my dog have a good temperament? Does he or she socialise well with people and other animals? Dogs with poor temperaments should not be bred, regardless of how good they look.

4. Do I understand COI and its implications? Coefficient of Inbreeding measures the common ancestors of a dam and sire and indicates the probability of how genetically similar they are. Breeding from too closely-related dogs can result in health issues for the offspring.

5. Does my dog conform to the Breed Standard as laid down by the Kennel Club or AKC? Do not breed from a Labrador that is not an excellent specimen, hoping that somehow the puppies will turn out better. They won't. Talk with experienced breeders and ask them for an honest assessment of your dog. (This dam has her paws full with her lively litter, bred by Elizabeth Halsall of Surrey).

6. Is my female at least in her second heat cycle? Breeders often prefer to wait a little longer, until their female is at least two years old and physically mature, when they are able to carry a litter to term and are robust and mature enough to whelp and care for a litter. Also, some health tests cannot be carried out until a dog is 18 months or older. Even then, not all females are suitable. Some are simply poor mothers who don't care for their puppies; others don't produce enough milk - which means you have to do it.

7. Am I financially able to provide good veterinary care for the mother and puppies, particularly if complications occur? If you are not prepared to make a significant financial commitment to a litter, then don't breed your dog. As you have seen, a single litter can easily cost you several thousands of pounds or dollars - and what if you only get a couple of puppies?

8. Have I got the indoor space? Mother and pups will need their own space in your home which will become messy as new-born pups do not come into this world housetrained (potty trained). It should also be warm and draught-free.

9. Can I cope with lots of puppies at once? Some Labs may have large litters of up to 13 pups.

10. Can I devote the time to breeding? Caring for mother and young pups is a 24/7 job in the beginning and involves many sleepless nights. During the day, you cannot simply go off to work or leave the house with the mother and young pups unattended. It is not uncommon for a Lab dam to be unable or unwilling to provide milk for her puppies, particularly when a

C-section is involved as it may take up to 72 hours for the anesthesia to completely wear off. In which case, you have to tube feed the puppies every couple of hours throughout the day and night. Breeding is a huge tie.

11. Am I confident enough in my breeding programme to offer a puppy health warranty?

12. Will I be able to find good homes for all the pups and be prepared to take them back if necessary? Good breeders do not let their precious puppies go to any old home. They often have a waiting list before the litter is born.

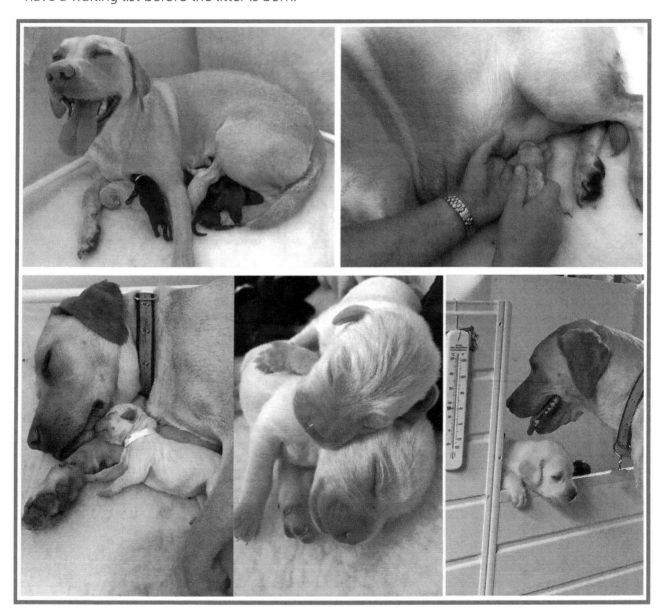

These photos of healthy mother and pups are all courtesy of Guy Bunce and Chloe Spencer, Dizzywaltz Labradors, Berkshire

You may have the most wonderful Labrador in the world, but only enter the world of canine breeding if you have the right knowledge and motivation. Don't do it just for the money or the cute factor – or to show the kids 'The Miracle of Birth!' Breeding poor examples only brings heartache to owners in the long run when health or temperament issues develop.

Having said all of that, good Labrador breeders are made, not born. Like any expert, they do their research and learn their trade over several years. If you're serious, spend time researching the breed and its genetics and make sure you are going into it for the right reasons and not just for the money - ask yourself how you intend to improve the breed.

A great way of learning about breeding Labradors is to find a mentor; someone who somebody who is already successfully breeding Labradors. By 'successful' we mean somebody who is producing healthy puppies with good temperaments, not someone who is making lots of money churning out poor quality puppies.

Talk to the breeder you got your pup from, visit dog shows and make contact with established breeders or look at the Kennel Club or AKC website for details of breeders near you. Contact the Labrador Retriever Club of Great Britain www.thelabradorretrieverclub.com or the Labrador Club (USA) www.thelabradorclub.com and ask them to help find a suitable person who is willing to help you get started.

Committed Labrador breeders aren't in it for the cash. They use their skills and knowledge to produce healthy pups with good temperaments that conform to the Breed Standards and ultimately improve the breed. Our strong advice is: when it comes to Labradors, leave it to the experts. But if you have a fine, health-tested Labrador who conforms to the Breed Standard that you are determined to breed from, here are some tips from established breeders:

....

Advice from the Experts

Trudy Williams, who bred her first litter in 2007: "I would recommend people ask a KC Assured breeder for advice. Anyone who is passionate about dogs will give up their time to talk through it with someone who is interested; I would." Trudy added: "This is the most difficult and stressful part of breeding. I've had people ringing me who live in a flat, have just had a baby and think it's a good time to get a pup. One person was totally unaware that Labradors moulted! One person was quite elderly and I asked them what provisions they had in place should something happen to them, and he said his brother could take the dog to the RSPCA! Another person left home for work at 7.30am in the morning and got home at 8pm and said their mum would pop in for half an hour in the day."

Colin Hinkley, breeder of 30 years' standing, Sanglier Labradors, East Sussex: "Go to the most experienced breeder with the longest history of breeding that you can find, not someone around the corner that has only bred one litter, and get an idea of how much hard work it is and how time consuming it can be."

Hilary and Wayne Hardman, Larwaywest Labradors, Dorset, have been breeding yellow, black and chocolate Labs for seven years: " Breeding should not be undertaken lightly, there are many things to consider; the most important being temperament and health. We would definitely recommend a mentor, someone experienced and knowledgeable."

Pictured is the handsome Larwaywest puppy X-Jay, who is sponsored by Jaguar to train with the charity AbilityDogs4YoungPeople on the Isle of Wight. Photo by Caro Dell of Workingline Images, reproduced courtesy of Hilary and Wayne.

Christopher Clarke, Reedfen Labradors, Leverington, Cambridgeshire, who has bred Labs since 2003: "Go to the Kennel Club website, www.thekennelclub.org.uk, click on every tab available and soak up as much info as you possibly can; it is all on the site! Only consider breeding for the right reasons; you must think of the health of the breed FIRST."

Kirsty Jones, of Serengoch Labradors, Mid Wales, started breeding three years ago: "I would advise anyone to contact the breeder of their dog for advice or, if not, approach the owner of the stud they would be interested in using or attend a show and talk to some of the owners there. Many will be willing to help a newcomer to the breed."

Sharon Jarvis, Paulsharo Labradors, Lincolnshire, has bred Labs for eight years and previously bred German Shepherd Dogs for Lincolnshire Police: "I have had a litter of one pup and the largest litter to date is 12. Regarding a mentor, go to someone who knows what they are doing. I give a lot of advice on Facebook. I am an Administrator on a Fox Red Labrador Group. I am happy to answer questions.

"I do, however, get irritated - as many other breeders do - by people wanting to make a fast buck who can't be bothered to do the intensive research that I have done over the years. They just want it all on a plate. Breeding a good Labrador is hard work. It's expensive if done correctly and looking after the dam (mother) whilst pregnant and then the puppies takes a lot of time. They need love, cleaning, feeding stimulation and new experiences until they go to their new homes."

Sarah Nuttall, Gamblegate Labradors, Lancashire, (17 years' experience) reminds anyone thinking of breeding their dog: "It is likely that the dog will have breeding restrictions on its registration documents, so the breeder would have to agree to lift these."

Guy Bunce and Chloe Spencer confirm this: "We register our pups with the Kennel Club in such a way that there are restrictions on breeding from them. This ensures that if the owner decides to breed a litter, then they need to come back to us first - at which point we would act as mentor. A mentor is essential."

(These two photos are a good example of breeding to type. The mother and daughter are pictured at the same age. Photo courtesy of Guy and Chloe).

Pat Nugent, of Marumrose Labradors, Lincolnshire, has this advice for owners of entire (unneutered) male Labs: "Don't stud your dog unless you are prepared to put up with increased marking (urinating) and interest in every bitch he meets."

New breeder Lynn Aungier, Alatariel Labradors, Surrey, has bred just one litter from her bitch, Pip: "Pip had 10 in her first litter and a friend of mine's had 13 in her first litter. I would recommend going back to the breeder to ask for advice; Pip's breeder was fantastic and was with us all through the whelping via a web chat.

"The vet is a good place to go for advice and getting all the appropriate health testing carried out. The Kennel Club were very helpful for us too, we became Assured Breeders and the Assured

Breeding Scheme staff were really helpful. Our stud dog owner was supportive and helpful all through the pregnancy and whelping, and she really enjoyed being able to come and see the puppies after they were born too."

Another new breeder is Diane Stanford, of Tragenheath Labradors, Warwickshire: "Being a novice breeder, I was recommended 'The Book of the Bitch;' it was my bible for breeding. Also the KC website was good. Not forgetting the stud dog I used, his owner was brilliant and had over 20 years of knowledge to pass on to me – as well as the pitfalls. I read and read lots of books and absorbed as much as I possibly could. With my own dog Freya, things did not go to plan. It was her first litter and she gave birth to one naturally… and then we waited and waited, but no more pups came. A dash down to the vet's ended with a C-section and one more pup. The C-section cost. £1,100 (US$1,430). You only ever hear of Labradors having lots of pups, but never just one or two. I felt lucky that at least Freya had two pups that were fit and healthy - and big, I might add. Hence, we kept one and found a lovely couple in Dudley that had the other."

Nicola Smith, Geowins Labradors, Surrey, has bred working Labs for 18 years: "I would advise that they think very seriously, as a litter of puppies is like having a full-time job and obviously the dog has to have all relevant health checks for the breed. They should speak to their vet and to as many breeders as possible first, too."

Another working dog breeder, Andrew Baker, of Saffronlyn Gundogs, South Yorkshire, says: "If someone is serious about breeding, then talk to an experienced KC Assured Breeder. I always offer lifetime advice and help to anyone who has any of my pups and always offer any advice to anyone who contacts me, whether it is to enquire about a litter, using one of my stud dogs or just Labradors in general."

Julie McDonough, Rangemaster Working Gundogs, Powys, is another who is prepared to share her knowledge and experience: "I personally always mentor the owners of bitches that come to stud my dogs. I keep constantly in touch to see if they require any information; sometimes it is not needed but it is nice to know that somebody is there to talk to if needed. Labradors litters can range from 5 or less to 13 and one needs to be prepared if a large litter is born and the bitch needs help in feeding them."

Caroline Smith, of Flyenpyg Labradors, Lancaster, adds: "Find an Assured Breeder through the Kennel Club – most of us are happy to pass on our knowledge, and don't be afraid to ask questions – we all started somewhere."

Elizabeth Halsall, of Oxted, Surrey, has bred Labs for just three years: "I had a mentor who is a Grade A Kennel Club judge and respected breeder. He was and is the fountain of all knowledge and guided and steered me through the process. It was not something that I undertook lightly – I wanted to do it properly and followed the KC guidelines to the tee and took all of his advice." (This little bundle of joy was bred by Elizabeth).

"I was also audited and visited by the KC regional assessor who came to see the puppies and assess my ability as a breeder in terms of safety, health certificates, cleanliness and my documented records and puppy pack. Breeding any pedigree dog requires investment in terms of tests, memberships, publications, breeding seminars, kennel names etc. It also requires patience and time."

A breeder with 50 years' experience under her belt is Jenny Dobson, of Lakemeadow Labradors, South Yorkshire: "They should go to the breeder of their bitch, without question, even at the point of just thinking about breeding. Most responsible breeders will have endorsed the KC registration (i.e. placed a breeding restriction on it), so their permission would, in any event, need to be obtained prior to breeding. Their breeder should know the lines (including weaknesses) and be able to advise regarding health checks, suitable studs, etc. and also mentor and advise with the whelping and rearing process."

Sarah Edwards, Fernwills Labradors, Essex: "I would always discuss the worst-case scenario with a new breeder. Make sure you can afford to have a Caesarean for your bitch and be prepared for all the pups to die! I became very good friends with our first stud dog's owner, who was a very experienced breeder, so I learnt a lot from her. There are plenty of good quality breeding text books out there to learn general information, and the internet is also a great information source for more breed-specific knowledge. The Kennel Club website is also a good source of health-related information and finding a good mate for your bitch."

US breeder Robin Anderson, of Grampian Labradors, New England, has 23 years' experience with Labradors and added: "Usually a breeder's first mentor is the person they got their dog from. My own mentor is not that person, but the person I got my fifth dog from. Sometimes it takes a while to find the right dog for the purpose and it's the same with a mentor. If a potential breeder really wants to look for a mentor, my best advice is to talk to lots of people at the dog shows, especially the Specialties. When you 'click' with someone, he or she will be a friend and mentor for life."

We'll leave the last word to Teresa Gordy-Brown, of Ashland Labradors, Tennessee, who has bred Labs for more than 30 years: "Labradors generally whelp on average around eight puppies, but there have been 16 in a litter or as little as one puppy born. Timing in breeding and the health of the sire and dam mean everything.

"If you are interested in breeding, please consider starting with the healthiest and best possible example of the breed. Always breed to IMPROVE the breed in health, including longevity, temperament and the breed's purpose (what they were bred for). Never breed to change something you dislike. That is damaging the breed!"

"Don't set out to make dogs that are smaller or larger than the Breed Standard dictates or breed for the lightest shade of yellow. Stay true to the breed and you will be rewarded heavily with many followers in the fancy. Find a respectable breeder to mentor you. That person should have years of experience and have a great reputation, be a member of their breed club and have titled dogs in many venues. Their knowledge is worth its weight in gold." Pictured is Ashland's Don't Rain On My Parade! "Rainy," aged 10 weeks, courtesy of Teresa.

NB: The UK breeders quoted here and elsewhere in this book are all 'Kennel Club Assured Breeders', and the US breeders are among just a handful of American Kennel Club Labrador breeders nationally who have earned the distinction 'AKC Breeders of Merit'.

15. Labrador Rescue

Not everybody who is thinking of getting a Labrador gets one as a puppy from a breeder. Some people prefer to adopt a Labrador from a rescue organisation. What could be kinder and more rewarding than giving a poor, abandoned dog a happy and loving home for the rest of his life?

Not much really; adoption saves lives and gives unfortunate dogs a second chance of happiness. The problem of homeless dogs is truly depressing. It's a big issue in Britain, but even worse in the US, where the sheer numbers in kill shelters is hard to comprehend. Randy Grim states in "Don't Dump The Dog" that 1,000 dogs are being put to sleep every hour in the States.

According to Jo-Anne Cousins, former Executive Director at IDOG, who has spent many years involved in US canine rescue, the situations leading to a dog ending up in rescue can often be summed up in one phrase: 'Unrealistic expectations.'

She said: "In many situations, dog ownership was something that the family went into without fully understanding the time, money and commitment to exercise and training that it takes to raise a dog. While they may have spent hours on the internet pouring over cute puppy photos, they probably didn't read any puppy training books or look into actual costs of regular vet care, training and boarding."

That lack of thought was highlighted in a story that appeared in the Press in my Yorkshire home town. A woman went shopping on Christmas Eve in a local retail centre. She returned home £700 (over $900) poorer with a puppy she had bought on impulse. The pup was in a rescue centre two days later.

Common reasons for a dog being put into rescue include:

- A change in family circumstance, such as divorce or a new baby
- A change in work patterns
- Moving home
- The dog develops health issues

Often, the 'unrealistic expectations' come home to roost and the dog is given up for rescue because:

- He has too much energy, needs too much exercise, knocks the kids over and/or jumps on people (young Labs are boisterous)
- He is growling and/or nipping (all puppies bite, it is their way of exploring the world; they have to be trained not to bite the things, like humans, they are not supposed to bite)
- He chews or eats things he shouldn't (see above)
- He makes a mess in the house (housetraining requires time and patience from the owner)

🐾 He needs a lot more exercise and attention than the owner is able or prepared to give (Labs are not small dogs and, again, time and commitment is required from the owner)

🐾 He costs too much to keep (the costs of feeding a Lab, vets' bills, etc. are not insignificant)

There is, however, a ray of sunshine for some of these dogs. Every year many thousands of people in the UK, North America and countries all around the world adopt a rescue dog and the story often has a happy ending.

The Dog's Point of View...

But if you are serious about adopting a Labrador, then you should do so with the right motives and with your eyes wide open. If you're expecting a perfect dog, you could be in for a shock. Rescue dogs can and do become wonderful companions, but a lot of it depends on you.

Labradors are people-loving dogs. Often those that have ended up in rescue centres are traumatised. Some may have health problems. They don't understand why they have been abandoned, neglected or badly treated by their beloved owners and may arrive at your home with 'baggage' of their own until they adjust to being part of a loving family again. This may take time. Patience is the key to help the dog to adjust to his or her new surroundings and family and to learn to love and trust again.

Ask yourself a few questions before you take the plunge and fill in the adoption forms:

🐾 Are you prepared to accept and deal with any problems - such as bad behaviour, chewing, aggression, timidity, jumping up or eliminating in the house - which a rescue dog may display when initially arriving in your home?

🐾 How much time are you willing to spend with your new dog to help him integrate back into normal family life?

🐾 Can you take time off work to be at home and help the dog settle in at the beginning?

🐾 Are you prepared to take on a new addition to your family that may live for another decade?

🐾 Are you prepared to stick with the dog even if he or she develops health issues later?

Think about the implications before rescuing a dog - try and look at it from the dog's point of view. What could be worse for the unlucky dog than to be abandoned again if things don't work out between you?

Other Considerations

Adopting a rescue dog is a big commitment for all involved. It is not a cheap way of getting a Labrador and shouldn't be viewed as such. It could cost you several hundred pounds - or dollars. You'll have adoption fees to pay and often vaccination and veterinary bills as well as worm and flea medication and spaying or neutering. Make sure you're aware of the full cost before committing.

Although Labradors are known for being faithful and loving companions, some in rescue shelters or foster homes have been badly treated or had difficult lives, and these dogs need plenty of time to rehabilitate. Some may have initial problems with housetraining, others may need socialisation with people and/or other dogs.

And if you are serious about adopting, you may have to wait a while until a suitable dog comes up. One way of finding out if you, your family and home are suitable is to volunteer to become a foster home for one of the rescue centres. Fosters offer temporary homes until a forever home becomes available. It's a shorter-term arrangement, but still requires commitment and patience.

Another point to consider is that it's not just the dogs that are screened - you'll also have to undergo a screening by the rescue organisation. Rescue groups and shelters have to make sure that prospective adopters are suitable and they have thought through everything very carefully before making such a big decision. They also want to match you with the right dog - putting a boisterous young Labrador with an elderly couple might not be the perfect match. It would be a tragedy for the dog if things did not work out.

Most rescue groups will ask a raft of personal questions - some of which may seem intrusive. If you are serious about adopting a Labrador, you will have to answer them. Here are some of the details required on a typical adoption form:

- Name, address, age
- Details, including ages, of all people living in your home
- Size of your garden (if you have one) and height of the fence around it
- Extensive details of any other pets
- Your work hours and amount of time you spend away from the home each day
- Type of property you live in
- Whether you have any previous experience with Labradors
- Your reasons for wanting to adopt a Labrador
- If you have ever previously given up a dog for adoption
- Whether you have any experience dealing with canine behaviour or health issues
- Details of your vet
- If you are prepared for aggression/destructive behaviour/chewing/fear and timidity/soiling inside the house/medical issues
- Whether you agree to insure your dog
- Whether you are prepared for the financial costs of dog ownership
- Whether you are willing to housetrain and obedience train the dog
- Your views on dog training methods classes
- Where your dog will sleep at night
- Whether you are prepared to accept a Labrador cross
- Details of two personal referees

If you work away from the home, it is useful to know that as a general rule of thumb, UK rescue organisations will not place dogs in homes where they will be left alone for more than four or five hours at a stretch.

After you've filled in the adoption form, a chat with a representative from the charity usually follows. There will also be an inspection visit to your home - and your vet may even be vetted! If all goes well, you will be approved to adopt and it's then just a question of waiting for the right match to come along. When he or she does, a meeting will be arranged with the dog for all family members, you pay the adoption fee and become the proud new owner of a Labrador.

It might seem alike a lot of red tape, but the rescue groups have to be as sure as they can that you will provide a loving, forever home for the unfortunate dog. It would be terrible if things didn't work out and the dog had to be placed back in rescue again. If you are not prepared to go through all of this, you may have to reconsider whether rescuing a Labrador is the right path for you.

All rescue organisations will neuter the dog or, if he or she is too young, specify in the adoption contract that the dog must be neutered and may not be used for breeding. Many Labrador rescue organisations have a lifetime rescue back-up policy, which means that if things don't work out, the dog must be returned to them.

Advice from the Experts

Labrador Retriever Rescue Southern England www.labrador-rescue.org.uk/index.html has this advice for anyone thinking of adopting a Labrador:

- Many of the dogs we rehome are from families where they are being left for long periods due to work commitments. When the owner witnesses the dog's distress, they ask us to find their pet a home where someone will be there for him

- WE DO NOT REHOME TO PEOPLE WORKING FULL-TIME. We expect the dog NOT to be left alone for longer than four hours per day. We do not consider a small lunch time visit, neighbours popping in, or a dog walker sufficient.

- When we receive your completed application form, a home check will be arranged to meet all members of your household. Our home checker will sit and talk to you to ascertain what you are able to offer a dog. Once you have had your home check we will then be able to discuss with you any dog/s that we feel might be suitable. We do not discuss details of dogs that we have on our web site until you are registered with us

- Our home checker will take a good look at your garden, to make sure it is a safe environment for a dog. So if you have any fencing that needs repairing or replacing, please have this done before applying for dog. Do remember that Labradors are large dogs and will easily jump a low fence. If you have a back gate, please make sure it has a working lock or bolt

- Please remember no rescue dog is perfect, most dogs will have 'baggage,' which can be anything from training issues to separation anxiety. Normally all that is needed is time, patience and often a good training class to turn your dog around. You will get back tenfold what you put in

- We will not consider rehoming any of our dogs to a home where they will be bred from

- If you are about to move house then we will not rehome a dog with you until you have moved and we have home-checked your new house

- If your rescue dog is not already neutered, we will encourage you to get the operation done, at your own expense, after a period of four months and once your dog has settled in with you

- If you are adopting a puppy, we may insist someone is at home during the day and that you take him to training classes. We will also encourage you to spay or neuter at the appropriate time

- If you have had a home check and have completed our Potential Home Form, you will then be on our waiting list. Rescue dogs will only be offered to homes that are on our waiting list

- From the moment you sign the adoption form when you rehome your dog, all financial costs related to your dog will be your responsibility. We pass on all information from the previous owner, this includes medical conditions. We cannot be held responsible if a problem is not reported prior to rehoming

- We strongly recommend you insure your dog

Rescue Organisations

Rescue organisations are often run by volunteers who give up their time to help dogs in distress. They often have a network of foster homes, where a Labrador is placed until a permanent new home can be found. Foster homes are better than shelters, as Labradors thrive on human contact. Fostering helps to keep the dog socialised, and the people who foster are able to give sufficient attention to the individual dog in their care.

There are also online Labrador forums where people sometimes post information about a dog that needs a new home. Even if you can't or don't want to offer a permanent home to a Lab, there are other ways in which you can help these worthy organisations, such as by short-term fostering or helping to raise money.

UK

There is a range of regional Labrador rescue organisations in the UK:

Labrador Lifeline Trust https://labrador-lifeline.com - Covers Buckinghamshire, Bedfordshire, Northampton, Hampshire, Hertfordshire, and parts of Lincolnshire, Nottinghamshire, Berkshire, Surrey, West Sussex, Middlesex and Cambridge.

Labrador Rescue Trust www.labrador-rescue.com - Covers the South West of England, consisting of Cornwall, Devon, Somerset, Dorset, Wiltshire, Gloucestershire, parts of the Forest of Dean near Chepstow, Herefordshire, Bristol and Bath and adjoining parts of Berkshire, Hampshire, Oxfordshire and Rutland.

Labrador Rescue South East & Central www.loveyourlabrador.co.uk - Covers South and East of England up to the Midlands.

Labrador Retriever Rescue Southern England www.labrador-rescue.org.uk

Labrador Rescue www.labrescuekent.co.uk - Covers Kent and border areas

Labrador Rescue (North West Area) www.homealabrador.net - based in Chorley, Lancashire.

Labrador Rehoming Norfolk – email Mike Hardy at lrnoffice@yahoo.co.uk

Labrador Retriever Rescue Scotland - www.lrrss.co.uk

Labrador Welfare www.labradorwelfare.org - Covers North Derbyshire, South Cheshire, North Nottinghamshire, North Lincolnshire, Yorkshire and the North East.

North West Labrador Retriever Club Rescue –Telephone Mrs B. Brougham, Merseyside, 01942 723847 or Mrs Wendy Manning, Conwy, overmarshlabradors@btopenworld.com

Northumberland and Durham Labrador Retriever Club www.ndlabclub.co.uk/labrador-welfarerescue.html

Labradors in Need http://labradorsinneed.co.uk Covers many areas

Visit the Kennel Club website for contact details of individuals involved in rescue: www.thekennelclub.org.uk/services/public/findarescue/Default.aspx?breed=2048

There's also a number of general adoption websites with Labradors and Labrador crosses for rehoming:

www.oldies.org.uk   www.dogsblog.com/category/labrador-retriever

www.rspca.org.uk/findapet/rehomeapet   www.rainrescue.co.uk/rehoming/dog-rehoming

....

USA

Arizona Labrador & Giant Breed Rescue - www.azlabsandgiants.org

Atlanta Dog Squad http://atlantadogsquad.org

Brookline Labrador Retriever Rescue (New Jersey, Pennsylvania) www.brooklinelabrescue.org

Central California Labrador Retriever Rescue www.cc-labrescue.org

CILRA Lab Rescue & Adoption (IN, IL and surrounding Midwestern states) www.cilra.org

Dallas/Fort Worth Lab Rescue www.dfwlabrescue.org

Desert Labrador Retriever Rescue of Phoenix - DLRR www.dlrrphoenix.org

Fetching Companions Retriever Rescue –FCRR (Southern CA) www.fetchingcompanions.org

For the Love of Labs Rescue (Eastern US, based in CT) www.fortheloveoflabs.com

Fortunate Pooches and Labrador Rescue (IL) www.fortunatelabrescue.org

Golden Gate Labrador Retriever Rescue (Northern CA) www.labrescue.org

Great Lakes Lab Rescue www.greatlakeslabrescue.org

Happy Labs Rescue (IN) http://awos.petfinder.com/shelters/happylabs.html

Heart of Texas Lab Rescue http://hotlabrescue.org/hotlab/index.jsp

Heartland Lab Rescue (OK, KS) www.heartlandlabrescue.com

Illinois Lab Rescue http://lab.rescueme.org/Illinois

Independent Labrador Retriever Rescue of Socal www.indilabrescue.org

Kentucky Lab Rescue www.kylabrescue.com

L.E.A.R.N (Southern WI and northern IL) www.labadoption.org

Lab Rescue of Greater Richmond (Greater Richmond, VA) www.labrescue-richmond.com

Lab Rescue of North Carolina http://labrescuenc.org

Lab Rescue of the LRCP (Labrador Retriever Club of the Potomac) www.imis100us1.com/labs

Lab Rescue OK Inc. (OK) www.labrescue.net

Labrador Friends of the South (South Eastern States) - www.labradorfriends.com

Labrador Rescuers (San Diego) www.labrescuers.org

Labrador Retriever Rescue http://lrr.org (U.S. mid-Atlantic, parts of PA, NJ, DE, MD, DC and VA)

Labrador Retriever Rescue of Cincinnati www.rescuealab.com/blog.asp

Labrador Retriever Rescue of East Tennessee www.labrescuetn.com

Labrador Retriever Rescue of Florida (based Pompano Beach, FL 33060) Phone: +1 877-522-7352

Labradors and Friends Dog Rescue Group (CO and South West) www.labradorsandfriends.org

Labradors, Retrievers and More (Southern CA) www.labsandmore.org

Labs4Rescue (based CT, covers most states) http://labs4rescue.com/index.shtml

Las Vegas Labrador Rescue http://lvlabrescue.com/wedoitforthelabs

Love of Labs (IN) www.lolin.org

Lowcountry Lab Rescue (SC) www.lowcountrylabrescue.org

Lucky Lab Rescue & Adoption (TX and New England) www.luckylabrescue.com

Metro East Lab Rescue (IL) http://metroeastlabrescue.com

Michigan Labrador Retriever Rescue www.angelfire.com/mi/michiganlabrescue/index.html

Midwest Labrador Retriever Rescue www.mlrr.org

Mile High Lab Mission (CO and surrounding states) www.milehighlabmission.com

Monterey Bay Labrador Retriever Rescue www.mbaylabrescue.org

New England Lab Rescue (all New England states) www.newenglandlabrescue.com

NOLA Lab Rescue (Northern LA) www.nolalabrescue.org

North East All Retriever Rescue www.nearr.com

Peak Lab Rescue (NC) www.peaklabrescue.com

Puget Sound Labrador Retriever Association (Washington) http://pslra.org/rescue.html

Retriever Rescue of Colorado http://retrieverrescueofcolorado.com

Retrievers and Friends of South California www.retrieversandfriends.com

Safe Harbor Lab Rescue (CO) www.safeharborlabrescue.org

Save a Lab Rescue (Mississippi-based, Southern and North Eastern states) http://savealabrescue.org

Southeast Texas Labrador Retriever Rescue www.txlabrescue.org/#xl_xr_page_index

Southern California Labrador Retriever Rescue www.sclrr.org/rescue

Southern Skies Rescue and Adoption (AL) www.southernskiesrescue.org

Southwest Pennsylvania Retriever Rescue http://awos.petfinder.com/shelters/sparro.html

And US-wide **Rescue Me** http://lab.rescueme.org Click on the number of dogs rescued in your state on the website map to find local Labradors for rescue.

There are also general websites, such as www.petfinder.com, www.aspca.org/adopt-pet and www.adoptapet.com and Labradors and Labrador mixes US-wide at http://Labradorterrier.rescueme.org/, www.btrescue.org and www.adoptaLabrador.com

This is by no means an exhaustive list, but it does cover some of the main organisations involved. If you do visit these websites, you cannot presume that the descriptions are 100% accurate. They are given in good faith, but ideas of what constitutes a 'lively' dog may vary. Some dogs advertised may have other breeds in their genetic make-up. It does not mean that these are necessarily worse dogs, but if you are attracted to the Labrador for its temperament and other assets, make sure you are looking at a Labrador.

DON'T get a dog from eBay, Craig's List, Gumtree or any of the other general advertising websites that sell golf clubs, jewellery, old cars, washing machines, etc. You might think you are getting a bargain Labrador, but in the long run you will pay the price. If the dog had been well bred and properly cared for, he or she would not be advertised on such websites - or sold in pet shops. Good breeders do not let their dogs end up in these places. You may be storing up a whole load of trouble for yourselves in terms of health and/or behaviour issues, due to poor breeding and environment.

If you haven't been put off with all of the above... Congratulations, you may be just the family or person that poor homeless Labrador is looking for!

If you can't spare the time to adopt - and adoption means forever - you might want to consider fostering. Or you could help by becoming a home inspector or fundraiser to help keep these very worthy rescue groups providing such a wonderful service. However you decide to get involved, Good Luck!

Saving one dog will not change the world,
But it will change the world for one dog

16. Caring for Older Labs

If your Labrador has been well looked after and has suffered no serious diseases, he or she can be expected to live from 10 to 14 or 15 years. A handful may live even longer; one of our breeders had a Labrador that lived to the ripe old age of 18.

US breeder Teresa Gordy-Brown said: "Lifespan is influenced by not only genetics, but also owner philosophies, such as how you feed, care for, exercise and more. Our longest living Labrador made it to 17 and a half years."

At some point before the end, your old dog will start to feel the effects of ageing. After having had to get up at the crack of dawn when your dog was a puppy, you may find that he likes to sleep in longer in the morning now that he is older. Physically, joints may become stiffer and organs - such as heart or liver - may not function as effectively. On the mental side - just as with humans - your dog's memory, ability to learn and awareness will start to dim.

Your faithful companion might become a bit grumpier, stubborn or a little less tolerant of lively dogs and children. You may also notice that he doesn't see or hear as well as he used to. On the other hand, your old friend might not be hard of hearing at all. He might have developed that affliction common to many older dogs - ours included - of 'selective hearing.' Our 12-year-old Max has bionic hearing when it comes to the word "Dinnertime" whispered from 20 yards, yet these days seems strangely unable to hear the commands "Stay" or "Here" when we are right in front of him!

You can help ease your mature dog gracefully into old age by keeping an eye on him or her, noticing the changes and taking action to help him as much as possible. This might involve a visit to the vet for supplements and/or medications, modifying your dog's environment, changing his or her diet and slowly reducing the amount of daily exercise. Much depends on the individual dog. Just as with humans, a Labrador of ideal weight that has been active and stimulated all of his or her life is likely to age slower than an overweight couch potato.

Keeping Labs at that optimum weight is challenging - and important - as they age. Their metabolisms slow down, making it easier to put on the pounds unless their daily calories are reduced. At the same time, extra weight places additional, unwanted stress on joints and organs, making them have to work harder than they should.

We normally talk about dogs being old when they reach the last third of their lives. This varies greatly from dog to dog and bloodline to bloodline. According to the breeders involved in this book, some Labradors may start to show signs of ageing at seven or eight years old, while others may remain fit in mind and body for much longer. Several owners have told us that their dogs are showing few signs of ageing at 10 or even 11 years old. Competitively, a Labrador is classed as a 'Veteran' at seven years old in the show ring and eight years old in Working Tests (although most of them don't act their age!)

Physical and Mental Signs of Ageing

If your Labrador is in or approaching the last third of his life, here are some signs that his body is feeling its age:

🐾 He has generally slowed down and no longer seems as keen to go out on his walks – or if he does want to go, he doesn't want to go as far and is happy pottering and sniffing. Some are less keen to go outside in bad weather

🐾 He gets up from lying down more slowly and he goes up and down stairs more slowly. He can no longer jump on to the couch or bed. These are all signs that his joints are stiffening, often due to arthritis

🐾 He is getting grey hairs, particularly around the muzzle

🐾 He has put on a bit of weight

🐾 He may have the occasional 'accident' (incontinence) inside the house

🐾 He urinates more frequently

🐾 He drinks more water

🐾 He gets constipated

🐾 The foot pads thicken and nails may become more brittle

🐾 He has one or more lumps or fatty deposits on his body. Our dog developed two on top of his head aged 10 and we took him straight to the vet, who performed an operation to remove them. They were benign (harmless), but you should always get them checked out ASAP in case they are an early form of cancer

🐾 He can't regulate his body temperature as he used to and so feels the cold and heat more

🐾 He doesn't hear as well as he used to

🐾 His eyesight may deteriorate – if his eyes appear cloudy he may be developing cataracts and you should see your vet as soon as you notice the signs

🐾 He has bad breath (halitosis), which could be a sign of dental or gum disease. If so, brush his teeth regularly and give him a daily dental stick, such as Dentastix or similar. If the bad breath persists, get him checked out by a vet

🐾 If he's inactive he may develop callouses on the elbows, especially if he lies down on hard surfaces –this is more common with large dogs than small ones

It's not just your dog's body which deteriorates; his mind does too. It's all part of the normal ageing process. Your dog may display some, all or none of these signs of mental deterioration:

🐾 His sleep patterns change; an older dog may be more restless at night and sleepy during the day

🐾 He barks more

🐾 He stares at objects or wanders aimlessly around the house

🐾 He displays increased anxiety, separation anxiety or aggression

- He forgets or ignores commands or habits he once knew well, such as coming when called and sometimes toilet training
- Some dogs may become more clingy and dependent, often resulting in separation anxiety. Others may become less interested in human contact

Understanding the changes happening to your dog and acting on them compassionately and effectively will help ease your dog's passage through his or her senior years. Your dog has given you so much pleasure over the years, now he or she needs you to give that bit of extra care for a happy, healthy old age. You can also help your Labrador to stay mentally active by playing gentle games and getting new toys to stimulate interest.

Feeding

As dogs age they need fewer calories and less protein, so many owners switch to a food specially formulated for older dogs. These are labelled 'Senior,' 'Ageing' or 'Mature.' Check the labelling; some are specifically for dogs aged over eight, others may be for 10 or 12-year-olds. If you are not sure if a senior diet is necessary for your Lab, talk to your vet the next time you are there. Remember, if you do change the brand, switch the food gradually over a week to 10 days. Unlike with humans, a dog's digestive system cannot cope with sudden changes of diet.

Consider feeding your Labrador a supplement, such as Omega-3 fatty acids for the brain and coat, or one to help joints. Our dog gets a squirt of Yumega Omega 3 and half a scoop of Joint Aid in one of his daily feeds. We are also about to splash out on a plastic ramp as he has become hesitant to jump in or out of the car. There are also medications and homeopathic remedies to help relieve anxiety. Again, check with your vet before introducing anything new.

Christine Eynon, of Baileylane Labradors, Herefordshire, says: "I normally stay with my usual feed, and I do not overfeed my dogs. If a dog is overweight or has health issues, then I would then

consult my vet as to the best diet. I have Tammy, a three-legged girl who is 12 (pictured), and it is essential to keep her weight down to keep her mobile. I am therefore prescribed Hills Reduction and I top and tailor amounts with my usual food to keep her weight at 23 kilos. I don't give supplements, but all my dogs have a spoonful of cod liver oil per day; it helps their limbs and coat.

"Working dogs need a richer diet than pet dogs, and I choose a brand with no additional additives. I do feed my dogs vegetables regularly with their food, and two to three times a week they also have fresh cooked meat."

Guy Bunce, of Dizzywaltz Labradors, Berkshire: "It's definitely a good idea to feed a specific diet, i.e. one containing less fat and fewer calories, and perhaps with joint aid supplements included. If degraded teeth are a problem, then moistening dry foods is an option, but the longer a dog can go on eating a dry diet, the better it is for their teeth. I feed Skinners Light and Senior in slightly smaller quantity as mobility decreases, and perhaps giving three smaller feeds instead of two larger ones. I do give a couple of supplements, although it's difficult to know how effective they are - but do no harm so worth continuing: cod liver oil and turmeric with curcumin; both help mobility and the immune system."

Elizabeth Harrington, of Katmistsky Labradors, Suffolk: "We don't necessarily change food, but I do make sure that teeth are checked, and would soak the food as necessary. Less food is needed in old age. Teeth are the most important thing, so I keep giving bones to keep them clean."

Andrew Baker, of Saffronlyn Labradors, South Yorkshire: "I stick to the same diet, but reduce it by a third to take account of the dog naturally slowing down and needing less exercise, so not putting too much pressure on their joints. I do add salmon oil to their diet."

Liz Vivash, of Wightfyre Labradors, Isle of Wight: "We don't change feeds, we still feed our 12½ year old the same as our six-year-old. We give cod liver oil – 500s. It is the same one as I take, and when we first gave them to Jasmine, we noticed a significant difference in her joint mobility within two weeks. We also give her Metacam – 25 ml per day – as she is very stiff now and this does seem to help." The yellow Lab on the left is Jasmine (Kenmilfore Super Trooper) pictured aged 11, courtesy of Liz.

Sarah Edwards, of Fernwills Labradors, Essex, feeds her dogs a raw diet and says: "I don't change to a senior diet – they just need a lot less food as their calorific intake reduces vastly due to moving around less. Labradors have little appetite control themselves, so the owner must restrain themselves from treating too much and spoiling with food. 'Senior diets' are a marketing gimmick – most brands are just reduced fat to reduce calorific load, but fats are good - especially to mobilise joints and give them important vitamins.

"Raw meaty bones are also a good source of the building blocks for bone and cartilage rejuvenation, so the effects I get from giving glucosamine joint supplements, for example, are minimal - however, in highly-processed manufactured diets I would suggest this! I would also consider an Omega 3 supplement – salmon oil for example, but care must be taken again with the calorific content. If not fed a biologically appropriate diet and allowed to chew raw meaty bones, dental care is crucial as, over the years of a kibble-fed diet, tartar will have built up and problems resulting from this can be major...horrendous breath for starters!"

Another raw feeder is Elizabeth Halsall, of Lisouletta Labradors: "Diet would also depend on condition and/or any ailments which have occurred during the dog's life. I think as an owner you have to be entirely responsible for keeping your finest friend fit and well, and that would relate to diet and whether you wished to supplement with some joint aid or cod liver or fish oil later on in life, together with vitamins or essential nutrients which you consider might be lacking. Multi foods have these inbuilt, so I like to add some extra vitamins from time to time. I intend to keep my dogs on a raw diet so long as their digestive systems are up to it. They are not overweight so do not need a weight reduction diet, but obviously as a dog's metabolism slows, then the amount of food needs the necessary adjustment."

Katrina Byrne, of Glenhugo Labradors, South Aberdeenshire: "We would consider our dogs as seniors from the age of seven and would begin changing them onto a Senior version of their food. I would consider a dog to be a true 'Veteran' from the age of 10 and at that point may consider soaking or softening his hard feed. We always feed cod liver oil once our dogs become adults; we also introduce magnetic collars once they start to slow down a little. After that it would be on a dog-by-dog basis."

Exercise - Take the lead from your dog, if he doesn't want to walk as far, then don't. But if your dog doesn't want to go out at all, you will have to coax him out. ALL old dogs need exercise, not only to keep their joints moving, but also to keep their heart, lungs and joints exercised.

Weight - no matter how old your Labrador is, he still needs a waist! Maintaining a healthy weight with a balanced diet and regular, gentler exercise are two of the most important things you can do for your dog.

Environment - Make sure your dog has a nice soft place to rest his old bones, which may mean adding an extra blanket to his bed. This should be in a place which is not too hot or cold, as he may not be able to regulate his body temperature as well as when he was younger. If his eyesight is failing, move obstacles out of his way, reducing the chance of injuries. Jumping on and off furniture or in or out of the car is high impact for his old joints and bones. He will need a helping hand on to and off the couch or your bed, if he's allowed up there, or even a little ramp to get in and out of the car. Make sure he has plenty of time to sleep and is not pestered and/or bullied by younger dogs, other animals or young children.

Consult a Professional - If your dog is showing any of these signs, get him checked out by a vet:

- Increased urination or drinking - this can be a sign of something amiss, such as reduced liver or kidney function, Cushing's disease or diabetes

- Constipation or not urinating regularly could be a sign of something not functioning properly with the digestive system or organs

- Incontinence, which could be a sign of a mental or physical problem

- Cloudy eyes, which could be cataracts

- Decreased appetite – most Labradors love their food and loss of appetite is often a sign of an underlying problem

- Lumps or bumps on the body - which are most often benign, but can occasionally be malignant (cancerous)

- Excessive sleeping or a lack of interest in you and his/her surroundings

- Diarrhoea or vomiting

- A darkening and dryness of skin that never seems to get any better - this can be a sign of hypothyroidism

- Any other out-of-the-ordinary behaviour for your dog. A change in patterns or behaviour is often your dog's way of telling you that all is not well

The Last Lap

Huge advances in veterinary science have meant that there are countless procedures and medications which can prolong the life of your dog, and this is a good thing. But there comes a time when you do have to let go. If your dog is showing all the signs of ageing and has an ongoing medical condition from which he or she cannot recover, or is showing signs of pain, mental anxiety or distress and there is no hope of improvement, then the dreaded time has come to say goodbye. You owe it to him or her. There is no point keeping an old dog alive if all he or she has to look forward to is pain and death. I'm even getting upset as I write this, as I think of parting from my 12-year-old not too many years into the future, as well as the wonderful dogs we have had in the past. But we have their lives in our hands and we can give them the gift of passing away peacefully and humanely at the end when the time is right.

Losing our beloved companion, our best friend, a member of the family, is truly heart-breaking for many owners. But one of the things we realise at the back of our minds when we get that lively little puppy is the pain that comes with it; knowing that we will live longer than him or her and that we will probably have to make this most painful of decisions at some point. It's the worst thing about being a dog owner.

If your Labrador has had a long and happy life, then you could not have done any more. You were a great owner and your dog was lucky to have you. Remember all the good times you had together. And try not to rush out and buy another dog; wait a while to grieve for your Labrador. Assess your current life and lifestyle and, if your situation is right, only then consider getting another dog and all that that entails in terms of time, commitment and expense. A Labrador coming into a happy, stable household will get off to a much better start in life than a dog entering a home full of grief.

Whatever you decide to do, put the dog first.

What the Experts Say

Let's not dwell on the end stages of our dogs' lives, but focus on what life they have left - and what we can do to keep them fit and healthy as the years roll by. Here are some further comments from the eight breeders involved in this chapter:

Guy Bunce: "The two most common signs of old age are decreased mobility and incontinence. The former can be helped by keeping dogs active as they age and maintaining exercise through shorter, more frequent sessions. I've noticed that the longer the old ones lie around sleeping, the harder they find it to get up and about. Continence is also helped by getting them out more often! Other things to look out for are lumps and bumps which if at all worrying should be checked out (although skin tags are quite usual), and signs of diabetes or kidney problems - look out for increased drinking.

"Grooming as Labs get older consists chiefly of managing dead fur and washing any bits that get regularly soiled. By this age I'm not normally bothered about looks, so concentrate on health and cleanliness. Regular baths are not important and can strip too much oil from coat. Our Labs have generally made it to 13 or 14 with a reasonable quality of life. Usually it is some form of cancer which sees them off in the end.

"The most important tip I can give is to know your dog and what is normal for him or her. You probably know your dog better than any vet, but do take advantage of the regular health checks which most practices offer. Quality of life is paramount when looking after an older dog and knowing when the time has come to say goodbye should be vital to the caring owner. After all, it's the dog's life not yours, so don't be selfish."

Elizabeth Halsall: "Walks should accommodate the dog's need - and they will tell you when they just want a walk and not a mad dash around. Care sometimes amounts to common sense and you should not overfeed your dog. Give good food, plenty of exercise and love – bar accidents or ailments, that will navigate you into the senior years. Be guided by the vet and work together to

work out the best plan for your dog and how comfortable you can make him or her. Be patient and understanding, and acknowledge when it is finally time; the hardest and most heart-breaking decision of all."

Katrina Byrne: "Hips and elbows are still a concern for Labradors as they age, but we continue to try and improve this situation by only considering dogs with good hip and elbow scores for breeding. We haven't experienced any changes in behaviour, other than them slowing down. Like humans, the older they become, the less they are able to do. But again, this really needs to be evaluated on a dog-by-dog basis."

Pictured looking very fit is 12-year-old Glenhugo's Kenmilltri Eros (Sonny), courtesy of Katrina.

Andrew Baker: "I have a Labrador coming up to 11 years of age, Murphy. I noticed a change in his obedience behaviour as he approached his senior years. He has always worked and competed, so obedience is a must, but when he got to about eight or nine years old, selective deafness set in and he started to ignore the recall and stay commands if there were other dogs about. However, we compete in Veteran Working Test competitions and he is spot on when he is working. Call it what you like, but he certainly knows the difference when he is competing and when he isn't. His exercise is reduced to half of what the younger dogs receive.

"His coat has become more dense as he as aged. He still gets groomed as regularly as the other dogs. I would advise owners of older Labs to pay more attention to them after exercise and check for lumps and bumps regularly. I also check for any changes to any thickening around their joints, i.e. elbows, shoulders, hocks etc.

"Murphy still competes and picks up on my local shoot (but not on every drive). It is about being sensible with your older dog, but Murphy just loves to work and whilst ever he is enjoying it, he will continue to do it. I always give him a shot of Metacam too after a day's work. I feel this also helps if he may be feeling achy. The only time he has visited the vet is for his boosters - I have been very lucky with him."

Liz Vivash: "We have found toileting issues with the older Labradors – Jasmine cannot hold her wee if she needs to go - and she can be very defiant about going out into the garden - even when the door is open! She loves going for a walk, but about 10 minutes now is all she can manage without becoming very tired. She is quite slow, but can still bounce around like a puppy when she is having a good day. She has difficulty getting in and out of the car and also has to think for a couple of minutes before she gets onto the couch. Other than some greyness and whitening around her muzzle, her coat is exactly the same; shiny and soft. You have to make allowance for everything slowing down and the dog taking longer to make decisions. But love and attention are the same all the way through the dog's life."

Elizabeth Harrington: "As far as health issues go, arthritis seems particularly common, cataracts (which bother them much less than they bother the owner) and deafness. But obesity seems to be a huge issue to be avoided at all costs – it is the biggest killer. Older dogs sleep more! Exercise is so important, as regular walks keep them going so much more easily, and help prevent obesity. The coat can become greasier with harsher hairs, and daily grooming helps give the dog a massage and helps owner spot any sore bits. Behaviour-wise, a dog in pain is, of course, going to be grumpy, and grumpiness is often the first sign of pain. Labradors are such happy-go-lucky dogs, and can mask signs of pain. They rarely say no thanks to any walk or game, even if it hurts. Do look out for indications."

Sarah Edwards: "Older Labradors need much less exercise and are happy just mooching around and snoozing and lounging in front of the fire. They still enjoy the fresh air and a short walk a couple of times a day; it still provides wonderful stimulation and should be well adhered too. Loyalty is still endless as they get older and cuddles a must. Sometimes they can get grumpier and less sociable, and also become happier to be left alone to snooze and while away the day for longer periods.

"Sometimes coats can get drier and shaggier, so I would suggest more brushing. There are various coat types – some are longer and more coarse than others, so it really depends on individuals. Greying around the muzzle and tummy areas can vary widely between individuals – I have a nine-year-old black lab who is hardly sporting any grey hairs, yet I have a four-year-old with a very grey muzzle already! My advice is: Be prepared for rapid increase in vets' bills! Also be aware your Labrador may be in pain if it refuses to go out walking or can't jump in and out of the car any more, and struggles with steps. There may be an increase in 'laziness,' but it could be they are struggling with some joint issues. They can be stoic and not admit to this and try and hide it by moving a lot less."

Christine Eynon: "My longest-lived girl died last January at nearly 15. Ellie was the loveliest, wisest old owl who put my young ones in their place. She remained the Matriarch of the dog family right

to the end, which was lovely. She was deaf and blind and did her own thing. She was nearly white on the underside. Long walks became a thing of the past, but a good mooch around a field (meeting me back at the car) was her thing! Towards the end this had to be monitored, as she would get a scent and take off not knowing where she was heading."

"Senior dogs have a beauty all of their own. They are loyal, wise and have experienced it all. Like humans, they need company, tlc, gentle walks, comfy beds and appropriate food with an owner who knows when it is time to let go. She had a stroke out walking one day and never really recovered, although my vet and I tried. I made the decision to let her go. She had had a wonderful life and it was not fair to keep her for my benefit.

"Being a responsible owner is knowing when to let go. It was right for her, if not me."

Pictured are four generations of Christine's Baileylane chocolate Labradors, left to right: Tammy (12), Willow (8), Ellie (15, R.I.P). and puppy Holly, aged four months.

17. For the Love of the Lab

In this chapter, four experienced breeders share their specialist knowledge of different aspects of the Labrador, passing on a lot of tips along the way.

Starting off on the Right Paw

By Jenny Dobson

Jenny Dobson, of Lakemeadow Labradors, South Yorkshire, knows a thing or two about Labrador puppies. She bred her first litter in 1968 while still living at home with her parents, and over the last half century has bred all three colours. She currently breeds blacks and yellows.

Like all the UK breeders in this book, Jenny is a Kennel Club Assured breeder and strives to produce happy, healthy puppies who will adjust to life quickly in their new homes. Here she gives an insight into the minds of Labrador puppies and shares some tips with new owners on how best to get off to a good start with their new arrivals. (In this article 'she' refers to both male and female puppies).

Getting a Labrador puppy will change your life. If you handle it right, you'll have a wonderful and loving companion as she becomes a member of your family and a firm friend. But getting there will demand a lot of hard work, patience and commitment from you and your family....... Think "new baby", and double it!

Puppies are, of course, totally adorable and Labradors are among the most lovely and lovable of all. But whilst doubly delightful, in reality they are not something from a fairy-tale cartoon, but real-live baby dogs with all the needs and demands that this entails. So be prepared - but definitely not put off - forewarned is forearmed! (Photo of my Labrador, Ruby, with her new-borns).

When people struggle to cope with their new puppy, it is often because their expectations are unrealistic. Remember your puppy is only a baby, and so do not expect too much too soon. She will need you to provide food, water, care, somewhere to sleep, firm guidelines as to what behaviour is acceptable to you, and what is not. She is totally dependent on you to provide a caring and stable environment in which she can grow and develop.

Your loyal family companion does not come ready-made; as with human children, puppies are not born with the social skills required to live with their family - canine or human. Being a family companion is one of the most difficult jobs we ask our dogs to do. It is the breeder's and owner's task to help the puppy through the learning process of acquiring key life skills to ensure that she is happy and confident in her environment and can communicate effectively within her social group.

Early days

By the time you take delivery of your new puppy at around eight weeks of age, she may appear small and vulnerable, but has already undergone huge development since birth. Most Labrador puppies generally weigh about 1lb when they are born; they are blind, deaf and unable even to regulate their own body temperature. Within the first week they will have doubled their birth weight, and by the time they have turned two weeks of age, they will have opened their eyes (though their vision is still very poor) and started to hear what is going on around them as their ear channels gradually become unsealed. At this time, most will be up on their feet and stumbling around, though they are still very helpless.

By the time they reach three weeks, they are able to scramble out of the whelping box, their teeth will have started to come through, and mum's milk is insufficient to keep them contented for more than a couple of hours at a time, so it is time for them to be 'weaned'. Over the next few weeks the breeder will have gradually introduced the litter to a variety of solid foods, and weaned them off their mother's milk completely by about six or seven weeks old. By this stage your pup should weigh around 10 times what she weighed at birth. The pups should have been wormed twice, micro-chipped and health checked, so that all their physical needs have been met ready to leave home.

Furthermore, your pup will by this stage have learned all about how to be a dog from her mother and also her littermates (unless she is a singleton). She should also have had an excellent education from her breeder, who will have tried in these few short weeks to introduce the sort of things she is likely to encounter later in life. From about four weeks of age, puppies start to interact with each other through play fighting; this develops strength, co-ordination, problem-solving abilities and learning to cope with frustration.

From five weeks old until they leave home, their development is driven by curiosity. At this stage they have not yet learned to be fearful of new situations and are consequently into everything! This is the time when they need to meet as many new people and situations as possible, before their natural fear response kicks in at around 12 weeks old.

Socialisation

You will expect your dog to fit into the family, and that could include children, elderly relatives, other dogs and cats, also to behave reasonably towards visitors and to adapt to your existing lifestyle patterns - for example, getting up and going to bed at an acceptable time, a possible work timetable or other commitments. Your new puppy will need to learn to be comfortable with being left alone at times, to cope with loud noises and unpredictable situations and to meet new people

without being either fearful or over-exuberant. The foundations for all this good behaviour are laid down during the first few weeks of a dog's life, through the process of socialisation.

Puppies that have been socialised effectively in these early weeks are far less likely to react negatively to new situations, noises, people, dogs and animals than their counterparts who have not had these important early experiences. A well-socialised puppy is far more likely to integrate easily into your life, therefore making your life together much more enjoyable and rewarding. (Photo of Ruby aged one week, indicated by the arrow).

There are two parts to socialisation and both are equally important. The first is teaching the puppy to be sociable with people and with other dogs, while the other (called habituation) is about teaching all the things you want the puppy to ignore and not be worried about, such as noises, household objects, traffic, etc. - or if you live in the country, possibly livestock or farm machinery.

In the early weeks, the breeder can ensure that your puppy is well-accustomed to being handled, having her nails clipped and mouth and ears inspected. The breeder can also ensure that your puppy has experienced a range of different household noises, surfaces and play items, and has slept and been fed in different locations. She should also have met other dogs, children, possibly cats and been introduced to car travel. It is imperative that you continue this process once your puppy has come home. Although is not possible to take your puppy out and about until she has completed her course of vaccination, socialisation doesn't have to be put on hold. You can carry your pup to introduce her to new situations, invite people to your house or maybe take her to visit a friend. Once your puppy has finished her course of vaccination, she can also attend puppy socialisation classes. These classes not only help your puppy begin to understand basic commands, but also help expose her to other dogs and people. Your vet may have information about puppy classes in your area.

Relationship Building

The first few weeks after bringing the puppy home is a very important time for establishing a relationship and bonding with your puppy. Be aware that, at least initially, this cute and cuddly puppy is going to disrupt your routine totally. She will wee - and probably poo - on your carpet, get you up in the middle of the night and make lots of other demands on you! However, as you start to develop a bond, these demands will feel less onerous and your puppy will start to realise what is expected of her. Get to know your puppy, talk to her, play with her, handle her, and cuddle her. All of these will help you to establish a bond.

Teaching tricks will also help that bond to strengthen. Use these interactions to try to get your puppy to focus on you, by positive reinforcement and rewarding with treats. You need to make yourself more interesting and more important than all other things that might distract her! Be affectionate, but also firm and consistent, and both you and your puppy need to realise that she has to fit around you - not vice versa. (Photo of Ruby at four weeks old).

This forms the absolute basis of all the training you will be giving your puppy over the coming weeks, be it housetraining, lead training, recall or crate training. Many dog books now stress the importance of socialisation, but few seem to mention that this goes hand-in-hand with building a relationship with your puppy. It's great having a well-socialised young Labrador in love with the world and everything in it, until you're out walking and meet a family with a young toddler, or that jogger 50 yards down the path, that your dog simply has to go and greet! Your puppy must learn to focus on YOU, over and above everything else.

Sleepless Nights

Always remember that your puppy is only a baby. She is likely to be very bewildered, and possibly fretful, as not only has she left her mother and littermates, she has been plunged into a world of noise and confusion and a sea of new faces. Even the most outgoing puppy is bound to find this stressful. Be prepared for (at least a few) disturbed nights. If your puppy is unhappy she will let you know...vocally, generally very loudly, and at four in the morning! Do not despair, for however distressing it is listening to a howling puppy, it is very unlikely that your pup is being harmed or in danger, and this normally only lasts for a few days.

If you have decided that your puppy will live in your kitchen overnight, then make her comfortable in her bed, or crate if you are using one, by leaving a toy, comforter, blanket or bedtime treat, with possibly a heat pad, hot water bottle or radio left on low. Tell her "Stay" and leave her. If your puppy persists with howling, check that she is quite safe, or maybe needs to toilet, then re-assure her and leave again. Do not be tempted to cuddle or play with your pup or even interact with her more than absolutely necessary.

Be pro-active in training your puppy to accept isolation and privacy. Accustom your puppy to being left by herself for short periods during the day, even if you are home. This will help prevent separation anxiety and all the problems that accompany it. If she starts whining when you leave, don't rush back to let her out or reassure her, because if you do, the puppy will soon learn that she can control you with her crying. If crying and howling never elicits a response, then the pup will soon learn that this method of communication does not work.

However, there may be reasons why it is simply not possible to allow your puppy to continue whining, e.g. causing a nuisance overnight to neighbours, or your pup becoming so distressed she might harm herself (which, I should add, would be very unusual). Then you may wish to consider allowing her to sleep in her crate in your bedroom. If you do take this step, I would suggest you only do so after several nights with ongoing problems.

If you don't intend your pup to continue sleeping in your bedroom, then once she has settled down and is over the distress (which may take several days) you can start to move the crate to where you really want her to sleep. Start by moving the crate outside the bedroom door, then after a time to the top of the stairs, then the hallway and finally to the place where you want the puppy to be.

Play Biting

Puppies, from about six or seven weeks old until they get their second teeth, can turn into piranhas! Not every pup does, but many do, and this behaviour can be very challenging - particularly to families with small children. Your puppy is not being vicious; she is simply playing, as this is how she has related to her littermates. However, if she gets over-excited, she can bite pretty hard. The key to dealing with this is to try to reduce the level of excitement, by immediately stopping the 'game' with a sharp "No!" indicating that this sort of play is not acceptable. Turn away from the pup, or physically remove the pup from the situation, perhaps offering a toy as a distraction. This is only a temporary phase and puppies have generally grown out of it by about six months of age.

Toilet Training

Consistency and patience are the keys to toilet training your puppy. People often ask how long it takes to toilet train a puppy. I feel it is impossible to generalise, as I have had pups clean within a few days, and others take a couple of months. The most important thing to remember is "don't despair......it will happen." Young puppies **do** need to urinate frequently and it is helpful to be able to anticipate when your puppy is likely to want to relieve herself, e.g. always after waking and after feeding. At such times, get her outside quickly to an area you have designated for such purpose, and when your puppy does perform, use plenty of praise and positive reinforcement.

Crate Training

I always recommend crate training to my puppy purchasers. I only started using a crate myself about 10 years ago, and have found it has made puppy rearing so much less stressful. It is important to make going in the crate a positive experience and NOT a punishment, and puppies do appear to

appreciate having a secure den that they can retire to. Crates can help facilitate housetraining, as pups are generally reluctant to soil the area in which they sleep. Crates can also give peace of mind when the pups are at the 'chewing phase,' which can otherwise be quite destructive. Some puppies never steal items or destroy things, but many do, and having somewhere to safely contain them can be very helpful, especially if you have to go out and leave the puppy unsupervised for a while. (Pictured is Ruby aged 12 weeks. All photos supplied by Jenny).

I would suggest using a crate overnight initially and for short periods during the day, but never for periods of more than a few hours at a time. If you put your puppy in the crate with a Kong or chewy treat, she will very soon come to see being in the crate as a positive experience. Throwing a blanket over the rear part containing the puppy's bed can create a safe den, which many dogs will continue to enjoy using even when the crate door is permanently left open.

And finally...with all these things in place and the bond firmly established between you, your puppy and your family - and bearing in mind not to expect too much too soon - your new arrival should become an absolute joy to you all.

Best of luck and enjoy the journey!

....

A Pleasure of a Toil

By Andrew Baker

Andrew Baker, of Saffronlyn Gundogs, Barnsley, South Yorkshire, got his first Labrador as a child and went on to become a gundog trainer several years ago. He and his dogs have won many awards, and he also judges all gundog breeds at Open, Companion and Limit Shows. Here Andrew writes about his passion for the breed and passes on a few tips to anyone thinking of competing or shooting with their Labrador:

We always had pet dogs at home and I got my first Labrador when I was 15. Deanie was black with working lines from the famous Drakeshead kennels. He was an eight-week-old puppy when we went to collect him and 15 years old when he died.

At that time, I didn't know much about the breed and Deanie taught me a lot about Labradors in terms of temperament, intelligence, working ability and being an all-round family pet. He was a dog in a million and if I knew then what I know now, he would have made a brilliant working and field trialling dog. He was my trusted and faithful companion and went everywhere with me.

I remember taking him to my local park when he was about six months old. Some guys were playing crown green bowls and I sat him on the path surrounding the green and told him 'Stay'. I walked around the path until I was opposite him and gave the recall command. I was taking a chance because if he had run across the bowling green, I would have got into trouble, but I wanted to put into practice what we had been working on.

I put my right arm out and said 'Come Round' - and to my amazement he did! People watching the game commented on what a lovely, intelligent and obedient dog he was. It may sound silly, but anyone who has lost a pet will know what I mean when I say there was a big void in my young life when he died.

It was many years later before I got my second Labrador, as my career in social work took over; I managed a team and also qualified as a Social Work Practice Teacher. I love teaching, imparting my knowledge to others and seeing students progress under my tutelage – it stood me in good stead when I went on to to become a gundog trainer.

My next Labrador was a yellow bitch, Poppy, again just a pet. She proved to be a real handful, very wilful at times, and totally different to Deanie. She was also from working stock, but had much more drive and determination. It was only when various gundog people told me about the dogs in her pedigree that I realised I had a Ferrari, whereas before I'd had a Volvo! Poppy was a great game finder and wouldn't come back until she'd found what she'd been sent for - but used to go 'self-employed' at times, choosing to ignore my commands because she thought she knew best. She was a real character and loved water so much that she would actually dive under the surface looking for shot ducks. I've never had another Labrador do that.

Photo left to right: Saffronlyn Skylark (Dixie), her brother Saffronlyn Swift (Bailey) and their father Swaine Dentanum Of Saffronlyn (Murphy).

My next Labrador was from a litter of black puppies sired by a Drakeshead dog and advertised in the local shooting magazine. Murphy was my type of Labrador, with bone and substance and pleasing to the eye. Choosing a puppy is down to personal preference, but as a rule of thumb, pick one that is outgoing, not shy or retiring. In fact, I find that the puppy quite often chooses you. And when selecting a pup, please, please ensure that the parents have been health tested, with a minimum of a clear eye certificate and good hip scores. There's a number of DNA tests to check for too, and make sure you see the puppies with their mother.

There are many Kennel Club Assured Breeders (of which I am one), all of whom have to undergo regular home visits by the Kennel Club and adhere to a code of conduct to ensure their dogs are fit for purpose. Be aware of puppy farmers, and if you are offered a cheap puppy, it will almost certainly be just that. The old adage: 'You only get what you pay for' is never truer than when looking for a Labrador puppy. If you want a shooting, working or trialling dog, look for FTCH (Field Trial Champion), FTW (Field Trial Winner) or FTAW (Field Trial Award Winner) in the pedigree.

Murphy is nearly 11 years old, he still competes in Working Tests for veterans and picks up with my other dogs on the local shoot. He just loves to work and his enthusiasm for the game is still as strong as ever. I never thought I'd have another dog like Deanie, but Murphy has proved a real star, winning many awards at both Novice and Open level and siring some lovely litters along the way. I have a son and daughter by him, Bailey and Dixie, and recently acquired his granddaughter, Abbey, who is 12 weeks old.

I became involved in gundog training after a friend and fellow trainer I used to help out moved to Scotland and I took over his existing groups; I still have some of the original members. More recently I have become an Instructor for The Gundog Club, a charitable trust that offers graded training for gundogs.

If anyone is thinking of getting a pet gundog, then they should start with a Labrador. I see a lot of different breeds in training, and if Labs are taught from an early age, they are the most willing, loyal and biddable dogs you could wish to own. It's no use waiting until they are 12 months old to start training; they need to begin as soon as they come into your home. I start with food training by sitting them up and placing a bowl of food in front of them and then sending them for their food. It is surprising how quickly they learn.

I give puppies as many positive experiences as possible. I take them to the vets to meet and greet people when I haven't got an appointment, we talk to the receptionist, vets, nurses, and other people with their dogs so the puppy gets used to going to there. I also take them out with my other dogs once they have had their second injection and it is safe to do so. They really pick things up (literally) while watching the older dogs work. (Pictured enjoying himself is Murphy competing in an Open Cold Game Working Test. Photo by Cath Kitching Photography).

I take them in the car from an early age. They come on the shoot with the other dogs at 10 weeks old and are left in the car with another dog while some of the dogs are out working; again it gets them into the routine of a shoot day, listening to gunshot, etc. Obviously, they are not near gunshot, but it is in the background so it isn't a shock when they later go on the shoot. Not one of my dogs is gun shy. They don't formally work on the shoot until 12 to 24 months old. Before this, they will have been on the lead walking round on the drives and sitting at the peg during the drive. Not having any retrieves reinforces steadiness and patience and honouring other dogs working.

If anyone is interested in having a Labrador, whether a pet, shooting companion or to compete in working tests or field trials, the most important advice I can give is to attend training classes. It is vital that a puppy is taught the right way from an early age. If you want a well-rounded, obedient pet, make sure the basics of heel work, sit, stay, recall and the stop whistle are firmly entrenched. I liken it to building a house, you wouldn't start constructing the roof first, you'd start by digging the footings and building the walls. It is the same with gundog training; foundations need to be firmly in place before moving on to retrieving and directions, etc.

There can be many challenges along the way - especially with a young dog - but consistency is the key. Practice as much as time will allow. Ten minutes a day is enough for puppies, you can gradually increase the time spent on various drills as they mature. One of the most common problems I encounter is the dog not respecting the owner, especially if it's a young dog that the owner hasn't done any training with - and suddenly the dog is 12 months old and does as it pleases. I always go back to basics and a programme of obedience. After a few weeks, we start to see progress and the dog starts to see the owner as the pack leader. Some people ask if it's OK to use treats and I say 'of course'. If they achieve the desired effect then use them, gradually reducing the treats as the dog becomes more responsive and obedient.

There are lots of Gundog Clubs registered with the Kennel Club all over the British Isles and some offer training days, Working Tests and Field Trials. The Working Tests are usually held at the weekends and are a good way of measuring where you are with your own dog's training. The morning consists of a set number of tests, either using canvas dummies or cold game depending on the time of year, and involves marked and blind retrieves from land or across a stretch of water, usually a pond. Dogs are marked out of 20 and the top scorers go forward to compete in the afternoon when the tests gradually become more challenging. There is a variety of different competitions, including Novice Dog/Novice Handler, Novice, Intermediate, Open, Veteran and Junior Handler. (Photo of 13.and Murphy).

Field Trials are held throughout the shooting season (August to the end of January, depending on the bird) when live game is shot to test the dogs. The dog is awarded an A or a B for a particular retrieve with a + or -, depending on performance, and again there are a number of different levels. All these events are covered by the Kennel Club's J regulations, applicable to different groups of gundogs, which are Retrievers, Spaniels, Hunt, Point and Retrieve Breeds (HPR) and Pointers and Setters.

The first time I entered a Working Test with Murphy I was extremely nervous, but some of the other competitors put me at ease. I had a good day, we finished in second place - owing more to Murphy's natural ability than my skill as a handler! Seriously though, it is not a race, take your time. Each dog is different and they mature at different rates.

Personally, I prefer a slow-maturing dog who reaches his or her peak at around three to four years old. I've seen many young dogs win but not go on to fulfil their full potential in middle to later years. Murphy was around three when 'the penny dropped' and we had our best season ever with an award at every Working Test we participated in. I was over the moon with him. He is still going strong; his siblings have gone on to achieve lots of success. I am in contact with some of the others who had a pup from that litter and we often reminisce about how good the litter was.

One time I was with Murphy in the Gundog Scurry at the Chatsworth Country Fair, Derbyshire, and I sent him into the river for a canvas dummy retrieve. I couldn't see him after he went over the bank and into the water. A few minutes later – much to everybody's amusement - out he came with a stick in his mouth, and was pleased as punch when he brought it back to me! That is what makes Labradors so special; I absolutely love them, they are everything all rolled into one. They can be deadly serious one minute and the class clown the next.

My aim is to continue imparting my knowledge of gundog training to others and I hope to see some of my students do well with their dogs and maybe one day pass on their knowledge to others. The Labrador is the most popular dog worldwide. I hope that this continues because, in my opinion, it deserves to be so. However, we must be vigilant against puppy farmers and backstreet breeders who have no interest in our lovely breed except to make a profit for themselves and to the detriment of the puppies that they breed.

And finally, competing with your dog should be an enjoyable pastime. It is a partnership between dog and handler, a work in progress, a bond for life and you will certainly get that bond the more time you spend with your dog. It is a mutual respect. When you get in the awards, be grateful and when you don't, be gracious. But above all, enjoy it. You never know...that eight-week-old puppy may one day be a Field Trial Champion!

Showing and Judging in the UK

By Amanda Deane

Amanda Deane was introduced to showing as a child. Her mother showed Chihuahuas and Pekingese under the 'Unicorn' affix, and Amanda first helped get these Toy dogs ready and then went on to show them herself.

She bred her first Labrador more than 30 years ago, and has gone on to have many successes in the show ring, including at Crufts, with her Tanronens Labradors. Amanda's passion for showing led her to become first a steward, then a judge, and latterly a Championship Show judge. Here she gives an insight into the world of showing in the UK and shares some tips for anyone starting out.

It wasn't until I moved to the countryside with my husband and two children in 1983 that we decided to get what we called "a proper dog." After speaking to a few breeders and looking at pedigrees, we found a Labrador puppy that would be our pet and possible show puppy. Her name was Berouch Blue Moon, 'Tanya,' and she was the start of my involvement with Labradors.

Because I was desperate to take part in a show, and also because of my experience with my mother's show dogs, my first show was a Championship Show, which is not the usual route for those new to the hobby. I started to get Tanya ready the day before. Labradors do not need a lot of preparation; you don't need to bath them – unless, of course, they have rolled in the mud, which often happens the day before a show - as too many baths can soften their coats.

So I wiped her down with a cloth, brushed her and checked that her tail didn't have the extra feathering on the end (you just snip the end), made sure that her eyes and ears were clean and got her bag ready with water and a bowl, treats for showing, a bait bag and showing lead, brushes and cloths to wipe her down in case she got dirty before going into the ring. Pictured is Amanda with Mattand Classic Edition at Tanronens (Sophie). Photo by Sharon Rogers

I was up really early as I was so excited; I got to the show early and waited for her class. Fortunately, I didn't have long to wait as she was in the puppy class. When it was our turn in front of the judge, she did everything I asked of her - I think it was me that let her down as I was very nervous! I didn't know anyone and everyone else seemed to know what to do; it was certainly different from showing toy dogs for my Mum. After going over her (looking for the Breed Standard), the judge asked me to run in a triangle and straight up and down and then asked me to stand at the end whilst he went over the other Labradors. I think he realised that I was new to showing.

When the time came, we stood our dogs ready for the judge to look at us all once again and to place the dogs in order. One by one the other Labradors were placed, leaving only me at the side of the ring. I just stood there not knowing what to do - I should have left the ring! The judge saw my predicament and came over and shook my hand, saying that I had a very nice puppy, but unfortunately there were only five placings! But this hadn't deterred me in any way, as I had caught "the showing bug."

In 1985 I decided to breed from Tanya, so after again talking to my friends I chose a stud dog. The mating went well and, with me watching her every move and a vet and friends on the end of the telephone, she had her first litter. Luckily, she was a very good mum, and this litter started my breeding and showing experience.

To this day, I find myself nervous on entering the ring, but try not to let my dog feel it down the lead. Being nervous is okay as it keeps you on your toes. I soon met other Labrador people to chat to and who encouraged me to keep showing; some of those people are still my best friends to this day and we have had great times and a good few laughs. Yes, we have had our ups and downs, but we still continue to go around the country to show.

If you are considering showing, let the breeder know that you would like a potential show puppy and not just a pet. He or she will be able to show you what to look for in a puppy - although there is no guarantee that the pup will be a top winning Labrador or even get placed; this happens to top breeders as well. It is difficult at eight weeks to know what a puppy is going to turn into as an adult; all you can see is the potential.

I look at the head, has it got the correct eye shape, has the muzzle got width, length and depth, are the teeth correct? This last one is difficult as teeth change as the Labrador grows, but don't go for a pup that is undershot (top teeth behind the bottom teeth). Are the ears set right on the head, neither too forward nor too far back, does the puppy have a good length of neck that flows into the body, and is the topline level and the tail set straight from the back? I also look at angulation of the front and back, depth of body and length of leg – and feet, are they nice and tight and not turning out too much? The overall picture of a Labrador needs to be balanced.

You must remember that their bones are tiny and fragile at this stage; they will strengthen as the pup gets older and gets the correct balanced food and exercise. I also look to see how a puppy is behaving with its siblings, you do need one that has the strength and courage to go anywhere, so look for one that is forward and explores his or her area.

When the puppy is nearly six months old, start looking for local shows in the local papers or online. There are fun/companion dog shows which are enjoyable, informal events that all dogs can take part in and are usually held alongside a fete or charity show. If you want to do more serious shows, then these can be found either in 'Our Dogs' or 'Dog World' papers or by going on-line to sites such as Fossedata or Dogbiz.

There are three main types of dog shows in the UK - Limit Shows, Open Shows and Championship Shows, and you usually have to enter around four weeks or more beforehand. Limit shows are 'limited' to members of a particular breed or dog club and also to dogs who have not won the CC.

Over the years I have had numerous successes in the show ring, including Best of Breed and Best Puppy at Open shows and my first major award was a CC (Challenge Certificate), closely followed by a reserve CC a few weeks later at

Championship level. Pictured is Amanda's home-bred Tanronens Theodosius (Theo). Photo by Sharon Rogers Photography.

I will always remember winning my first CC at Peterborough. As the time came to award the CC, the lady next to me said that she thought it was going to be me or her. I had butterflies as the judge walked up to us both... and then he came forward to give it to me! The crowd cheered and clapped and came over to congratulate me; I couldn't believe it; what a day!

I have qualified for Crufts most years. It is the biggest dog show in the world, with more than 22,000 dogs taking part, and the atmosphere and competitiveness is amazing. When you win a class, it is just the most incredible feeling; the large crowds cheer and clap and the photographers come into the ring to take a photo of your dog. It's a tremendous achievement with so much competition as, generally, Labradors have the biggest entry of any breed at Championship Shows across the country as well as at Crufts.

I joined the Midland Counties Labrador Retriever Club, started to go to more shows and after a few years was asked to do some stewarding for the club; becoming one is one of the many criteria required to become a judge.

If you want to become a steward, ask at local dog clubs if you can train alongside a Chief Steward. After each one, ask the judge to fill in a stewarding book, which you can get from the Kennel Club, to keep a record of what you have done. Stewards call the exhibitors' attention to the start of each class, hand out ring numbers and check any absentees. They also hand out place cards and announce the ring numbers of the winners. Anyone new to dog showing will be grateful for the help of a ring steward - mention you are new to this hobby when you first enter the ring and most stewards will keep an eye out for you. The majority of stewards are very helpful and extremely friendly. Although you can talk to the steward, you are not allowed to talk to the judge unless he asks you a question.

The steward is on hand for the judge when he needs his judging book and other paperwork. Although the judge is in charge of the ring, the steward sees that the exhibitors stand where he needs them while judging is progressing. In essence, the steward ensures the smooth and efficient running of the ring. They also ensure that the judge completes his paperwork and signs the Challenge Certificates (CCs) if they are on offer. A steward is not supposed to complete the judge's book but is allowed to advise the judge, particularly if the judge is new to the task. You can obtain a booklet for ring stewards from the Kennel Club.

After a few years of stewarding, I was asked to judge. My first appointment was at Ilkeston and District Canine Society on 25th April, 1998. On the day, I felt really nervous and one of my friends came with me for support, but I needn't have worried. When I started to look around the class, my nerves disappeared and all too soon I had picked out my BOB (Best of Breed) and BP (Best Puppy), and after congratulating them I went to have lunch with the other judges.

The same day or the next day is the time to write your critique while it is still fresh in your mind; normally at an Open Show you only need to write the first placings, but when you get to a breed club and Championship Show you need to write the first two placings, and if you get the honour of judging at Crufts you will be required to write on the first three placings. This can be hard and I don't know anyone that really enjoys doing these - it can be very frustrating to be kind but honest about what you have judged and all judges have their own opinion of the Labrador Breed Standard.

Personally, when I look at a Labrador, I look for a kind head and good eye colour; not too dark and not too light. The muzzle must have the scope to carry game, the teeth must have the correct bite and the ears not too far forward and carried with intelligence; I look for a good front and rear angulation and tail set, nice level topline and good depth and spring of rib, and on the move, I look for the gait to be straight and move with drive from behind.

I also look for good temperament when I go over the Labrador. I have found that over the years Labradors have become shorter in leg, which gives them an overall unbalanced look - and also, they have got fatter. When we judge, we have to remember to look for a Labrador that is "fit for purpose." At Championship Shows, including Crufts, you will see that some Labradors look very lean, these are working dogs that work in the fields and are trained to the gun. Today, more show-type Labradors are becoming Champions in both field and show, and if your interest lies with the show type, you can still train your dog to retrieve and carry game.

After doing my required amount of shows and dogs, I went forward to become a Championship Show judge. At my first show at this level, the committee asked me to judge the dogs and another person to judge the bitches - sometimes you are asked to judge both. The show was held at the most wonderful location – Malvern in Worcestershire. I stayed with a friend the night before as you don't want to get into a panic because you've been caught in a motorway accident.

You have to dress smartly and practically, and I had gone down with a jacket, top and trousers. It was the hottest day of the year and I was judging inside the cattle sheds! There was hardly any breeze coming through the doors and the dogs were panting, so I had to be thorough but quick, as I didn't want the dogs to be standing around too long.

After judging all the classes and awarding the Challenge Certificate, reserve CC and puppy class winner, the other judge and I had a discussion about the BOB and Best Puppy in show. Sometimes you cannot agree, so the referee is called in to make the decision - and it is always nice when the referee chooses what you have put forward! I enjoyed the day immensely with the help of my steward and the next day I got down to writing my critiques and sending these to the dog papers for printing, so that all the winners could see what I had put down about their dog.

It has certainly been an interesting and rewarding 30-odd years. Going forward, I intend to continue breeding Labradors, as well as qualifying - and hopefully winning! - at Crufts. A personal ambition is to be asked to judge abroad. If invited, you can travel to many different countries and judge some outstanding Labradors, the most wonderful of breeds.

....

A Dog for All Seasons

By Robin Anderson

American Kennel Club Breeder of Merit Robin Anderson, of Grampian Labradors Registered, New England, had many different types of dog when she was growing up. Then she got her first Labrador in 1984 - and has never looked back. Rather than breeding specifically for either 'show' or 'shoot', she is a firm believer in the multi-purpose Labrador – and Robin and her dogs have excelled in both disciplines. Along with co-breeder Gerrie Owren, she has bred, trained and handled two dogs to AKC Champion Master Hunter titles; these same dogs have won numerous Best in Breed titles at Conformation Shows. This is her story:

I 'interviewed' many people with dogs and decided the Labrador Retriever was what I wanted as a family pet. We needed a dog with a water-friendly coat who liked playing ball with children, and who could survive if she fell off our sailboat! Ariel, who was black, fitted all our requirements. When she passed away at the age of 11, we immediately looked for our next Labrador.

Alpha came with a pedigree and parents we were able to meet. Although we loved her dearly, she wasn't a good swimmer and didn't like to fetch. So we got another dog who did all of those things. Dory was my first AKC-titled dog and gave us our first litter. Labradors will always be a major part of our family because, unlike most other breeds, they are multi-purpose, easy keepers in many ways - from coat to whelping - and generally have few health problems compared with other breeds.

I was so enamoured with the breed, I decided I would like to breed and train handsome dogs that could perform the job intended; dogs that could hunt in the morning and show in Best of Breed in the afternoon. Since Dory, we've had several of those in our home.

(Pictured is AKC Bronze GrCh/UKC Ch Viking Hil'Die Tanzbarin CD RA MH WCX - 'Hildi'. Photo by Nancy Nosiglia).

Our own Labradors are first and foremost family pets. They are born and live in our house and, when they are ready, get bedroom rights. They love to please, and we give them the opportunity to learn good house manners, while also learning how to look pretty at dog shows. Basic obedience training readies them for AKC and UKC obedience competitions and in good weather we begin Hunt Test training, which the dogs really enjoy. They use their noses and eyes, and they get to run and swim.

Labrador Retrievers, while bred to be gentlemen's hunting companions, suffered a 'split' in the breed which persists today, when we hear the common terms 'American' and 'English' Labs ('show' and 'field' or 'working' in the UK). All Labrador Retrievers are one breed, actually, as described in the Breed Standard, our blueprint.

Most of the breeders who show in Conformation Shows don't test their dogs for ability. Most avid hunters don't care what their dogs conform to - except bringing dinner home! Some of us try and maintain both sides of the Breed Standard by showing in the Conformation Shows and proving our dogs in the field as well. These, in my mind, are the true Labrador Retrievers.

The AKC Hunt Test program was developed to encourage those with 'show dogs' to prove that their dogs still had the instinct to hunt. Originally, I never intended to participate; I was simply interested in a good-looking, obedient dog that could win a few ribbons at dog shows.

My first experience of Hunt Tests was at a Labrador Retriever National Specialty. I sat at the feet of the Master Test judges and was instantly sold on the sport. The participants were friendly, the judges openly explained their tests, and it was obvious that the dogs were having a spectacular time. I never dreamed I could or would ever have such a highly-trained dog, but with my co-breeder, Gerrie, and many wonderful, like-minded people helping us, we achieved the distinction of training two dogs that earned Master Hunter titles and two more dogs that participated and earned 'legs' towards the title. We expect to have two more Master Level dogs soon.

This level of competition doesn't happen overnight. You have to be prepared to start at the bottom and then put a great deal of time in. Just like anyone else, I was a basket of nerves at our first test, and then very proud of our passing score. My advice to any new participant is to be open with others about your new interest in the sport, listen to advice, use what makes sense to you and your dog, and regard any mistakes you make as a learning opportunity. Nobody is perfect and there are no perfect dogs. There is no one correct way to train, because each dog is an individual. No matter what your result at any one test, you will still always go home with your best friend. Give him love and praise generously and wake up in the morning with renewed energy to train some more.

We start off by giving our six-week-old puppies wings to see who seems the most interested. We play fetch games to see which puppy enjoys the chase and returns with the toy for more co-operative play. As the puppy gets older, we expand the variety of retrieving objects to include training dummies and small birds. Patience, kindness, and an upbeat lively attitude on the trainer's part help each puppy achieve their maximum retriever potential. Not every Labrador is a natural retriever, but with patience, most of them can at least meet the basic requirement as outlined in our Parent Club's literature (The Labrador Club, Inc). Puppies are placed in their new homes based on aptitude. If we have a family interested in hunting, this first introduction helps us decide which puppy is the one best suited to their needs. We also actively participate in the sport on many levels ourselves.

All our Labradors try the basic certification in hunting, which is a Working Certificate. Anyone who wants to learn more about this fun introduction to Hunt Tests can find it on The Labrador Club, Inc. website at www.thelabradorclub.com.

Basically, the dogs need to have an interest in game birds, be immune to gunshots, show eagerness to swim twice to retrieve in the water, and be willing to return to the handler with the bird. Tests are offered at the National Specialty every year, as well as by regional dog clubs. Training is minimal because it is a basic instinct test, and I recommend attending a test before trying it out. If your dog is successful, he or she will receive a nice certificate from the Club.

The first AKC title certificate is the Junior Hunter Test, which requires more training because the dog must deliver to hand to pass the test. Two single retrieves on the land and two single retrieves on the water, return to hand, and generally polite attentive attention are the requirements to pass. The retrieving distance is greater and there might be more interesting variations in terrain to train for than the basic Working Certificate test, but it's fun if your dog is ready. Dogs as young as six months old can enter, and they must pass four tests before receiving the JH (Junior Hunter) title.

The next level is Senior Hunter. This requires more training, because to be successful the dog must 'handle'. In other words, he or she must perform a variety of complicated retrieves off-lead, with no collar, be ultimately obedient in heeling and returning, find hidden birds called 'blinds' and respond to verbal and whistle commands. Judges will also offer 'double' retrieves in each test, which is two shot birds from different directions.

The dog needs to watch both birds fall before retrieving them in succession on the command of the handler, and not before the judge gives permission. To receive the SH title, four tests must be passed successfully - but only if the dog is already JH, otherwise, five tests are required. It could take up to a whole season to train for this level of competition, and often, while training for the Junior Hunter title, owners are also working on basic Senior Hunter skills.

Master Hunter is the ultimate title. Once a dog is a reliable Senior Hunter, training continues to include triple retrieves, more blinds, heavier cover, diversion shots and 'poison' birds. These are marks thrown as part of a blind retrieve, either when the dog is still waiting in line or while en route to the blind. It is called 'poison' because if retrieved before the blind, the dog is eliminated.

There are usually three series over a succession of days, depending on the number of dogs. Handlers, as with the Senior tests, must shoulder a gun to demonstrate gun safety, stand very still with the dog in 'honor' while another dog is tested, and, as always, the dog must retrieve to hand without damage to the bird to demonstrate the signature soft mouth. Five more tests must be passed to achieve Master Hunter status. Dogs with the title often attend the Master National Test, which showcases the best Master Hunter dogs in the country every year.

Grampian Labradors currently has two female Master Hunters. Two more of our dogs competed at the level, but missed the title due to old age or illness. It is hard work and rigorous for both handlers and dogs. Senior and Master level dogs must train hard every day, as if they are training for a triathlon, and we are always mindful of health and safety first in training and testing.

Our Master Hunter girls are both AKC breed Champions with multiple Best of Breed wins. They both raised two litters of puppies each, and one of our girls is a multiple Sporting Group winner. Anyone who watches the Westminster Kennel Club Dog Show (or Crufts) will know that the Group Winner moves on to compete for Best in Show.

Our dog competed many times with the other Group winners, and we missed Best in Show by one dog many times. Still, we always bring the 'best' dogs home from every show, because no matter what, we love our dogs.

(Pictured is Ch Grampian Bedizened Viking CD RA MH WCX CGC CC – 'Dazzle'. Photo by Donna Kelliher).

The Labrador Retriever is truly the most versatile of dogs. Our breeding program includes dogs with a variety of AKC and UKC titles in Conformation, Obedience, Rally Obedience and Hunting. We even have a couple of dogs with agility, barn work, and nose work titles. Quite another number are certified therapy dogs that 'read' to children at libraries, visit senior residents in nursing homes, and work the crowds at public events to calm the people who might be stressed.

Because Labradors are so easily trained, love to carry things in their mouths, and are happy-go-lucky ambassadors of goodwill, they can adapt to a variety of 'jobs'. Most of our puppies are placed in families with children, because at heart a Labrador Retriever is always childlike. In addition to being the youngest child in many families, ours are in homes where hunting game birds is a regular occupation during the morning hours and warming stockinged feet is the evening activity.

Labradors are well-known as service dogs for the blind, hearing impaired, and otherwise physically challenged all over the world. One organization we know of gives all their breeding stock the same home life as any pet dog, and when a litter of new candidates is born they move on to training based on each pup's individual strengths, so that children with autism, people with anxiety disorders and our country's Veterans are all offered the opportunity to have a well-trained Labrador assist them in their life's challenges.

Because many Labradors have a high hunting drive and a willingness to please, they also go into explosive detection, cadaver recovery, contraband detection, and human search and rescue work. You can see the VAPOR Wake dogs (trained to detect explosives and the scents of chemicals that make bombs on moving targets) working the crowds at events. Many of our 9/11 heroes were Labrador Retrievers, and many more still go to war with our nation's soldiers. Your town's police K9 might even be a Labrador Retriever.

(Pictured is Robin with Ch Snowden Hill Mango Crazy JH RA WC CGC CC. Photo by Donna Kelliher).

Reputations are built on a foundation of accomplishments and goodwill towards all involved in the sport of dogs. I've been in the sport with my Labradors for over two decades and hope to continue with our new crop of beautiful, willing puppies.

I'm placing some of our best puppies with like-minded people, hoping to share my good fortune with a wider audience as I edge towards retirement. Until then, I continue to breed with an eye towards a handsome dog able to both work in the field and shine in Best of Breed. I willingly share my knowledge with those who care to ask, and am always honored to be asked.

Labradors have enriched my life, opened many doors I never imagined existed, and my sincere hope is that the Labrador Retriever can do the same for generations to come.

Useful Contacts

The Labrador Retriever Club Inc (USA) www.thelabradorclub.com and its list of registered breeders at: www.thelabradorclub.com/subpages/find_breeder.php

American Kennel Club (AKC) www.akc.org/dog-breeds/labrador-retriever

Puppies via AKC marketplace at: http://marketplace.akc.org/puppies/labrador-retriever (NOTE: Only Breeders of Merit have been vetted by the AKC)

The Labrador Retriever Club of Great Britain www.thelabradorretrieverclub.com

The Labrador Breed Council represents all 13 UK breed groups www.labradorbreedcouncil.co.uk

Kennel Club (UK) Assured Breeders of Labrador Retrievers www.thekennelclub.org.uk/services/public/acbr/Default.aspx?breed=Retriever+(Labrador)

Kennel Club Mate Select www.thekennelclub.org.uk/services/public/mateselect

Puppies currently available via Champdogs (UK) – not all are KC members, not all of these breeders health test; check first: www.champdogs.co.uk/breeds/labrador-retriever

Association of Pet Dog Trainers USA www.apdt.com Association of Pet Dog Trainers UK www.apdt.co.uk

Canadian Association of Professional Pet Dog Trainers www.cappdt.ca

Useful information on grain-free and hypoallergenic dog foods www.dogfoodadvisor.com

UK dog food advice www.allaboutdogfood.co.uk

General website with useful information on all aspects of Labradors www.thelabradorsite.com

Helps find lost or stolen dogs in USA, register your dog's microchip www.akcreunite.org

There are also internet forums and Facebook groups that are a good source of information from other owners, including: https://thelabradorforum.com www.labradorforums.co.uk www.justlabradors.com/forum

List of Contributors

(Breeders Alphabetically, by Kennel)

UK

Lynn Aungier, Alatariel Labradors, Coulsdon, Surrey

Kate Smith, Ardenbrook Labradors, Warwick, Warwickshire www.ardenbrook.co.uk

Christine Eynon, Baileylane Labradors, Ross on Wye, Herefordshire

Stephen and Jane Armstrong, Carnamaddy Labradors, County Antrim, Northern Ireland

Guy Bunce and Chloe Spencer, Dizzywaltz Labradors, Berkshire

Sarah Edwards and Guy Stewart, Fernwills Labradors, Colchester, Essex
www.facebook.com/FernwillsLabradors

Caroline Smith, Flyenpyg Labradors, Lancaster, Lancashire
www.leadthedoglancaster.co.uk/?Flyenpyg_Labradors

Sarah Nuttall, Gamblegate Labradors, Lancashire

Nicola Smith, Geowins Labradors, Thorpe, Surrey

Katrina S. Byrne, Glenhugo Labradors, South Aberdeenshire, Scotland
www.facebook.com/Glenhugo-Labradors-936950129752261

Elizabeth Harrington, Katmistsky Labradors, Suffolk

Jenny Dobson, Lakemeadow Labradors, Doncaster, South Yorkshire www.lakemeadow.co.uk

Hilary and Wayne Hardman, Larwaywest Labradors, Dorset www.larwaywestgundogs.co.uk

Elizabeth Halsall, Lisouletta Labradors, Oxted, Surrey

Pat Nugent, Marumrose Labradors, Lincolnshire www.facebook.com/marumrose.labradors

Sharon Jarvis, Paulsharo Labradors, Lincolnshire www.facebook.com/Paulsharolabradors

Avril Bartolomy, Prestonfield Labradors, East Sussex

Julie McDonough, Rangemaster Working Gundogs, Welshpool,Powys
www.rangemasterworkinggundogs.co.uk

Christopher Clarke, Reedfen Labradors, Leverington, Cambridgeshire

Andrew Baker, Saffronlyn Gundogs, Barnsley, South Yorkshire
www.saffronlyngundogs.weebly.com

Colin Hinkley, Sanglier Labradors, East Sussex http://sanglierchocolatelabradors.co.uk

Kirsty Jones, Serengoch Labradors, Mid Wales http://serengochkennels.com

Amanda Deane, Tanronens Labradors, Lincoln, Lincolnshire

Anne Johnson, Teazledown Labradors and Canine Therapies, Preston, Lancashire
www.teazledownlabradors.co.uk

Diane Stanford, Tragenheath Labradors, Leamington Spa, Warwickshire.

Nadine Lapskas, Trencrom Kennels, Bournemouth, Dorset

Liz Vivash, Wightfyre Labradors, Isle of Wight

Trudy Williams, Yaffleswood Labradors, West Sussex

USA

Teresa Gordy-Brown, Ashland Labradors, Tennessee, USA www.ashlandlabradors.com

Robin Anderson and Gerrie Owren, Grampian Labradors, New England, USA
www.grampianlabs.com

Sandra Underhill, Labs To Love, California, USA   www.LabsToLove.com

Other Contributors

Dr Sara Skiwski, The Western Dragon Integrated Veterinary Solutions, San Jose, California, USA
www.thewesterndragon.com

Labrador Retriever Rescue Southern England www.labrador-rescue.org.uk

....

Disclaimer

This book has been written to provide helpful information on Labrador Retrievers. It is not meant to be used, nor should it be used, to diagnose or treat any medical condition. For diagnosis or treatment of any animal medical problem, consult a qualified veterinarian.

The author is not responsible for any specific health or allergy conditions that may require medical supervision and is not liable for any damages or negative consequences from any treatment, action, application or preparation, to any animal or to any person reading or following the information in this book.

The views expressed by contributors to this book are solely personal and do not necessarily represent those of the author. References are provided for informational purposes only and do not constitute endorsement of any websites or other sources.

Author's Notes:

For ease of reading, 'the Labrador Retriever' is generally referred to throughout this book as 'the Labrador', and the masculine pronoun 'he' is often used to represent both male and female dogs.

The Complete Labrador Handbook uses UK English, except where Americans have been quoted, when the original US English has been preserved.

20577190R00161

Printed in Poland
by Amazon Fulfillment
Poland Sp. z o.o., Wrocław